The Lanterne of Liȝt

EDITED FROM MS. HARL. 2324

EARLY ENGLISH TEXT SOCIETY

Original Series, No. 151.

1917 (for 1915).

The Lanterne of Liȝt

EDITED FROM MS. HARL. 2324

BY

LILIAN M. SWINBURN, M.A.

LONDON:
PUBLISHED FOR THE EARLY ENGLISH TEXT SOCIETY
BY KEGAN PAUL, TRENCH, TRÜBNER & CO., Ltd.,
68–74 CARTER LANE, E.C.
AND BY HUMPHREY MILFORD, OXFORD UNIVERSITY PRESS,
AMEN CORNER, E.C.

Great Clarendon Street, Oxford OX2 6DP
United Kingdom

Oxford University Press is a department of the University of Oxford.
It furthers the University's objective of excellence in research, scholarship,
and education by publishing worldwide. Oxford is a registered trade mark of
Oxford University Press in the UK and in certain other countries

© The Early English Text Society 1917

The moral rights of the authors have been asserted

Database right Oxford University Press (maker)

First Edition published in 1917

All rights reserved. No part of this publication may be reproduced,
stored in a retrieval system, or transmitted, in any form or by any means,
without the prior permission in writing of Oxford University Press,
or as expressly permitted by law, or under terms agreed with the appropriate
reprographics rights organization. Enquiries concerning reproduction
outside the scope of the above should be sent to the Rights Department,
Oxford University Press, at the address above

You must not circulate this book in any other form
and you must impose this same condition on any acquirer

Published in the United States of America by Oxford University Press
198 Madison Avenue, New York, NY 10016, United States of America

British Library Cataloguing in Publication Data
Data available

Library of Congress Cataloging in Publication Data
Data available

Original Series, 151

ISBN 978-0-85-991892-3

CONTENTS

	PAGE
INTRODUCTION	vii
Authorship and date of the MS.	vii
Description of the MS.	xvi
Grammar	xvi
TEXT: THE LANTERNE OF LIȜT	1
APPENDIX:	
Sources of the Quotations from the Bible made in the Text	139
NOTES	145
GLOSSARY	153

INTRODUCTION

THE *Lanterne of Liȝt* is a Lollard tract, written in the early fifteenth century, containing an exposition, supported by passages from the Bible and from the writings of the Fathers and mediaeval divines, of the principal tenets of the followers of Wyclif. It is one of a class of books of which there were probably many in circulation during the early years of the fifteenth century, but of which, owing to the rigorous crusade that was carried on against heretical literature, only a few are now extant, such as the *Apology for Lollard Doctrines* and Purvey's *Remonstrance against Romish Corruptions in the Church*.

Authorship and date of the MS.

Like most other religious or theological works of the late fourteenth or early fifteenth centuries with a tendency towards reform, the *Lanterne of Liȝt* has been ascribed to John Wyclif. In the description of the MS. in the catalogue of the Harleian collection, Wanley says:

'The author was a Lollard, as plainly appeareth in fol. 10 and 94 b. He complaineth of the taking away of the Books of Scripture, then translated into English, from the Laity; and for punishing those who did read or quote the same (fol. 17b and 93b). He bitterly inveyeth against the Pope as Anti-Christ; against Bishops and Clergy both regular and secular, and their Offices. As to the author, from the nature of the work itself; the way of handling it; the style; and the authors or books cited by him; I am of opinion that it might be by John Wycliffe : although I have not now Bale at hand to consult; and find that he is omitted (as having been a Heretic, forsooth!) by partial Pitts; and even Mr. Henry Wharton's Account of them is sometimes dubious and (in the main) imperfect.'[1]

The *Lanterne of Liȝt* is also ascribed to Wyclif, though without any evidence in support of the statement, by Archbishop Trench:

---

[1] *Catalogue of Harl. MSS.*, vol. ii, p. 654.

'There were little assemblies or conventicles everywhere; ... men came together by night ... to hear some tract which should expound (the) Word as Wyclif's "Wicket" or his "Lantern of Light"'.[1] On the other hand, the tract is not mentioned in the catalogue of Wyclif's works by Dr. Shirley,[2] although he errs on the side of ascribing too much rather than too little to the reformer,[3] nor do any more recent editors of Wyclif include it in their list of his writings.[4]

The question of authorship is, naturally, closely connected with that of date. Wyclif died in 1384; therefore the possibility of his being the author is precluded if it can be proved that the tract was written after this date.

There is external evidence that the *Lanterne of Liȝt* was written before 1415.[5] On August 17, 1415, John Claydon, currier of London, arrested by the Mayor on suspicion of heresy, was brought up for trial before Henry Chichele, Archbishop of Canterbury. The charge made against him was that he had in his keeping books written in English, which, in the Mayor's opinion, were 'the worst and the most perverse that ever he did read or see',[6] and, chief among these, was a book 'bound in red leather, of parchment, written in a good English hand,'[6] called the *Lanterne of Liȝt*'. Claydon confessed that he had had this book copied at his own expense by 'one called John Grime';[6] that, although he could not read himself, he had heard the fourth part read by 'one John Fuller';[7] and that he thought many things contained in the book were 'profitable, good and healthful to the soul'.[7] His servants were examined, and testified to having heard a book called the *Lanterne of Liȝt* read aloud to Claydon; one of them, David Berde, said that it contained an exposition of the Ten Commandments in English.[8] The tract was examined by Robert Gilbert and William

---

[1] *Mediaeval Church History*, Trench, Lect. XXI, p. 322.

[2] W. W. Shirley, *Catalogue of the Original Works of John Wyclif*, 1865.

[3] *Select English Works of J. Wyclif*, ed. T. Arnold, i, pp. iii-viii. (This edition will be cited as *S. E. W.*)

[4] *S. E. W.*, iii, pp. xvii-xx; Lechler, *J. Wycliffe and his English Precursors*, translated by Prof. Lorimer, pp. 484-96.

[5] Wilkins, *Concilia*, iii, pp. 371-5; Foxe, *Acts and Monuments*, ed. J. Pratt, iii, pp. 531-3.

[6] Foxe, iii, p. 531.

[7] ib., p. 532. [8] *infra*, Chap. XII, pp. 81 ff.

Lyndewode, who drew up a list of fifteen articles contained in it. Foxe gives them as follows:[1]

I. First. Upon the text of the gospel, how the enemy did sow the tares, there is said thus: That wicked Antichrist, the Pope, hath sowed among the laws of Christ his popish & corrupt decrees, which are of no authority, strength or value.[2]

II. That the archbishops and bishops, speaking indifferently, are the seats of the beast Antichrist, when he sitteth in them, and reigneth above other people in the dark caves of errors and heresies.[3]

III. That the bishop's license, for a man to preach the word of God, is the true character of the beast, i.e. Antichrist; and therefore simple and faithful priests may preach when they will, against the prohibition of that Antichrist, & without license.[4]

IV. That the Court of Rome is the chief head of Antichrist, and the bishops be the body; and the new sects (that is, the monks, canons and friars), brought in not by Christ, but damnably by the pope, be the venemous and pestiferous tail of Antichrist.[5]

V. That no reprobate is a member of the church, but only such as be elected & predestined to salvation; seeing the church is no other thing but the congregation of faithful souls, who do, and will keep their faith constantly, as well in deed as in word.[6]

VI. That Christ did never plant private religions in the Church, but, while he lived in this world, he did root them out. By which it appeareth that private religions be unprofitable branches in the church, and to be rooted out.[7]

VII. That the material churches should not be decked with gold, silver, and precious stones sumptuously; but the followers of the humility of Jesus Christ ought to worship their Lord God humbly, in mean and simple houses, and not in great buildings, as the churches be now-a-days.[8]

VIII. That there be two chief causes of the persecution of the Christians; one is, the priests' unlawful keeping of temporal and superfluous goods; the other is, the unsatiable begging of the friars, with their high buildings.[9]

IX. That alms be given neither virtuously nor lawfully, except it be given with these four conditions: first, unless it be given to the honour of God; secondly, unless it be given of goods justly gotten; thirdly, unless it be given to such a person as the giver thereof knoweth to be in charity; and fourthly, unless it be given to such as have need, and do not dissemble.[10]

---

[1] Foxe, iii, pp. 532-3.   [2] infra, pp. 3-4.
[3] infra, p. 15.   [4] infra, p. 14.   [5] infra, p. 16.
[6] infra, pp. 22, 25.   [7] infra, p. 38.   [8] infra, p. 41.
[9] infra, p. 43.   [10] infra, p. 54.

X. That the often singing in the church is not founded on the Scripture, and therefore it is not lawful for priests to occupy themselves with singing in the church, but with the study of the law of Christ, and preaching his word.[1]

XI. That Judas did receive the body of Christ in bread, and his blood in wine;[2] in which it doth plainly appear, that after consecration of bread and wine made, the same bread and wine that was before, doth truly remain on the altar.[3]

XII. That all ecclesiastical suffrages do profit all virtuous and godly persons indifferently.[4]

XIII. That the pope's and the bishop's indulgences be unprofitable, neither can they profit them to whom they be given by any means.[5]

XIV. That the laity is not bound to obey the prelates, whatsoever they command, unless the prelates do watch to give God a just account of the souls of them.[6]

XV. That images are not to be sought to by pilgrimages, neither is it lawful for Christians to bow their knees to them, neither to kiss them, nor to give them any manner of reverence.[7]

There is no doubt that the book, for possessing which Claydon was burnt as a heretic,[8] is the one transcribed here, for the fifteen articles given above can all be closely identified with passages in the text,[9] and other statements, as to the nature and contents of the book, tally with our MS. The *Lanterne of Liȝt* must therefore have been written before 1415.

Internal evidence leads to a still closer approximation of date, but such evidence must be used with care, since it is easy to read more into a reference in the text than is altogether justifiable. For instance, the following passage might be taken as referring to the Statute 'De Heretico Comburendo', passed in 1401, which empowered the Bishops to hand over an obstinate heretic to the secular arm to be burned : ' Whereto make ȝe schrynes to seyntis; & ȝit ȝe drawen hangen & brennen hem þat holden þe weie of Crist & wandren aftir hise holi seyntis & þouȝ þis schewe not in

---

[1] *infra*, p. 58.   [2] *infra*, p. 60.

[3] There is no passage in the text which directly attacks the doctrine of Transubstantiation.

[4] *infra*, p. 75.   [5] *infra*, pp. 75-6.

[6] *infra*, pp. 82-4.   [7] *infra*, pp. 84-5.

[8] Wilkins, iii, p. 375; Walsingham, *Historia Anglicana*, vol. ii, p. 307 (R. S.), where he is called Willelmus Cleydone.

[9] In art. XI (*supra*, p. x) the examiners have added their own conclusions.

ȝoure outwarde dede, ȝe don þis slawȝtir in worde & wille. As pharisees wiþ bischopis in þe þridde oure foriuggid oure Lord wiþ her toungis & aftirward kniȝtis at þe sixte our hangid his bodi upon þe cros, so þise sectis goon biforn to smyte þe peple wiþ her tung & aftir knyȝtis of Herowdis hous ben ful redi to make an ende.'[1] It might seem legitimate to see in the last words a reference to the punishment accorded to an obstinate heretic under the Act, and hence to deduce the fact that the *Lanterne of Liȝt* was written after 1401. But this evidence alone is not conclusive, for references to death by burning as being the penalty for heresy occur in works generally accepted as Wyclif's, as well as in others of more doubtful authenticity, which must have been written before 1384.[2]

Again, in the text there are references to the prohibition of unlicensed preaching.[3] Such preaching was prohibited by the Act 'De Heretico Comburendo' (1401),[4] and again by the Constitutions of Archbishop Arundel, 1409,[5] but unauthorized preaching had been forbidden by the Bishops many years before this. Evidence of this fact is to be found in such passages as 'prelatis letten & forbeden prestis to preche þe gospel in here iurdiccion or bischoperiche, but ȝif þei han leue & letteris of hem'; and, 'þei (i.e. prelates) wollen not suffre trewe men teche frely cristis gospel wiþouten here leue & lettris, þouȝ trewe men ben neuere so mochil charged & stired of god to preche his gospel',[6] which occur in a tract called 'Of Prelates', which, if not by Wyclif himself, must have been written soon after his death.[7]

[1] p. 43.
[2] *S. E. W.*, i, p. 201, 'oure prelatis ... stranglen and killen men, and spoilen hem of her goodis'. ib., p. 205, 'þis word counfortiþ symple men, þat ben clepid eretikes and enemyes to þe Chirche, for þei tellen Goddis lawe; for þei ben somynned and reprovyd many weies, and after put in prison, and brend or kild as worse þan þeves'. ib., p. 211, 'alle þese (popes & bishops, helped by secular lords) bitraien Cristen men to turment, and putten hem to deeþ for hoolding of Cristis lawe'. These three passages occur in sermons which are undoubtedly by Wyclif. Cf. also *English Works of Wyclif*, ed. F. D. Matthew, Early English Text Society, pp. 34, 88, 211, where the references are to works of more doubtful authenticity, but which were probably written by 1384. (This edition will be cited as E.E.T.S.)
[3] pp. 14, 18.
[4] 'None ... shall presume to preach openly or privily without the License of the Diocesan of the same place first required & obtained.' 2 Hen. IV, c. 15.
[5] *infra*, p. xii.   [6] E.E.T.S., pp. 57, 105.   [7] ib., p. 52.

Introduction

However, there is a passage in the *Lanterne of Li3t* which proves conclusively that it must have been written after 1409. In speaking of the five assaults which Antichrist makes upon the servants of God, the author says the first is 'constitution'. He explains the text 'Constitue domine legislatorem super eos' by saying 'Antichrist useþ fals lucratif or wynnyng lawis as ben absoluciouns, indulgence, pardouns, priuelegis, & alle oþir heuenli tresour þat is brou3t in to sale for to spoile þe peple of her worldli goodis, & principali *þise newe constituciouns* bi whos strengþe anticrist enterditiþ chirchis, soumneþ prechours, suspendiþ resceyuours, & priueþ hem her bennefice, cursiþ heerars, & takiþ awey þe goodis of hem þat forþeren þe precheing of a prest, 3he þou3 it were an aungel of heuene, but if þat prest schewe þe mark of þe beast, þe whiche is turned in to a newe name & clepid a special lettir of lisence for þe more blyndyng of þe lewid peple'.[1]

There does not seem to be any doubt that the 'new constitutions' to which the author refers are the Constitutions of Thomas Arundel, Archbishop of Canterbury, which were drawn up at a Council at Oxford in 1408, and published in January, 1409.[2] These constitutions are called 'novellae constitutiones',[3] and the first two are thus given by Foxe:

I. 'We will and command, ordain and decree: that no manner of person, secular or regular, being authorized to preach by the laws now prescribed, or licensed by special privilege, shall take upon him the office of preaching the word of God, or by any means preach unto the clergy or laity, whether within the church or without, in English, except he first present himself, and be examined by the ordinary of the place where he preacheth: and so being found a fit person, as well in manners as knowledge, he shall be sent by the said ordinary to some one church or more, as shall be thought expedient by the said ordinary. . . . Nor any person aforesaid shall presume to preach, except first he give faithful signification, in due form, of his sending and authority; that is, that he that is authorized, do come in form appointed him in that behalf, and that those that affirm they come by special privilege, do show their privilege unto the parson or vicar of the place where they preach. . . . And if any man shall willingly presume to violate this our statute grounded upon the old law, after the publication of the same, he shall incur the sentence of greater excommunication,

---

[1] *infra*, pp. 17-18. [2] Wilkins, *Concilia*, iii, p. 306.
[3] ib., p. 323, 'Pro executione *novellarum constitutionum* citatio'.

"ipso facto".... And that the said person here-upon lawfully convicted (except he recant & abjure after the manner of the church) be pronounced a heretic by the ordinary of the place. And that from thenceforth he be reputed and taken for a heretic and schismatic, and that he incur "ipso facto" the penalties of heresy and schismacy, expressed in the law; and chiefly, that his goods be adjudged confiscate by the law, and apprehended, and kept by them to whom it shall appertain. And that his fautors,[1] receivers, and defenders, being convicted, in all cases be likewise punished, if they cease not off within one month, being lawfully warned thereof by their superiors.'

II. 'Furthermore, no clergyman, or parochians of any parish or place within our province of Canterbury shall admit any man to preach within their churches, church-yards, or other places whatsoever, except first there be manifest knowledge had of his authority, privilege, or sending thither, according to the order aforesaid: otherwise the church, church-yard, or what place soever, in which it was so preached, shall "ipso facto" receive the ecclesiastical interdict, & so shall remain interdicted, until they that so admitted and suffered him to preach, have reformed themselves, and obtained the place so interdicted to be released in due form of law, either from the ordinary of the place, or else his superior.'[2]

The paragraph from the *Lanterne of Liȝt* quoted above refers to these two constitutions, and the correspondence between the passage in the text and the wording of the Constitutions justifies the assumption that the author had the 'new constitutions' vividly in his mind when he wrote the *Lanterne of Liȝt*.[3] It therefore follows that the work must have been written between the years 1409 and 1415. It seems reasonable to assign to it the date 1409–10, a date soon after the publication of the Constitutions, and one which would allow for a period of some four or five years to have elapsed during which it might have been disseminated among the Lollards and have become known to men like John Claydon.

This date is further borne out by the tone of the book. It was evidently written during a time of persecution, when many who

[1] favourers, supporters.
[2] Foxe, iii, pp. 243, 244; cf. also Wilkins, iii, pp. 315, 316.
[3] Compare the wording: 'enterditiþ chirchis, soumneþ prechours, suspendiþ resceyuours, and priueþ hem her bennefice, cursiþ heerars & takiþ awey þe goods of hem þat forþeren þe preching of a prest' with 'the church ... shall receive the ecclesiastical interdict'; 'his goods be adjudged confiscate ... & his fautors, receivers and defenders ... be likewise punished'.

had embraced the new faith drew back from the prospect of a cruel death and recanted: 'For now manye þat semeden to have be stable in vertu fallen from her holi purpose, dredyng losse of worldli goodis and bodili peyne.'[1] A whole chapter is devoted to the encouragement of Christ's servants in a time of persecution.[2] There are several references to the fact that death was the penalty for holding what were considered to be heretical opinions: 'ȝe drawen hangen & brennen hem þat holden þe weie of Crist',[3] 'þe fende settiþ wacche & bisie spie where þat he may fynde ony peple þat wole rede priue or apert Goddis lawe in englische . . . þei sein lyue as þi fadir dide, & þat is ynow for þee, or ellis þou schalt to prisoun as if þou were an heretike & suffre peynes many & strong & ful lickli þe deeþ'.[4]

The general tone of the tract would lead to the conclusion that it was written to encourage a sect in a time of more active persecution than that which marked the last years of Wyclif's life; in such a time, indeed, as the early years of the fifteenth century, during which three Lollards went to the stake for their opinions, and many others were brought before the courts and forced to recant, or else tortured and imprisoned.[5]

It is impossible to say who the author of the *Lanterne of Liȝt* was, for no clue as to his identity is given in the book itself or in the account of the trial of John Claydon. It is evident from the book that he was writing from the Lollard point of view, and the tenets which he held may be briefly summed up as follows:

Holy Scripture is the supreme authority in all matters of faith and conduct; therefore all should be allowed to study the Bible in their mother tongue.

The preaching of God's word is the chief duty of a priest.

Pilgrimage, image-worship, and the costly decoration of churches are unlawful.

The sale of sacraments, absolutions and indulgences, and the traffic in the benefices of the Church are contrary to God's law.

The taking of an oath, or swearing in any form, is forbidden by the teaching of Christ.

---

[1] *infra*, p. 2, ll. 5–7. [2] Chap. XI, 'Of ioie in tribulacioun'.
[3] p. 43. [4] p. 100.
[5] Cf. Foxe, iii, pp. 221 ff., 235 ff., 249 ff., 285, 286. Sawtré was burnt in 1401; John Badby in 1410; John Claydon in 1415.

Introduction

The temporal possessions of the clergy are the cause of most of the evils in the Church.

Holy Church is the company of all faithful souls.

The Pope is Antichrist; therefore obedience should not be rendered to him or to his servants since they command what is contrary to God's law.

The author holds no heretical opinions on the subject of the Seven Sacraments, although the enemies of Lollardy attacked the only passage in which he refers to the Lord's Supper as unorthodox. In this respect he differs from Wyclif, who had discussed the relative value of the Sacraments and had attacked the doctrine of Transubstantiation. There is, however, nothing original in the particular views held by the author; they had all been put forward before by Wyclif either in his English or his Latin works. On the whole, the tone is more moderate and restrained than that of the author's master, for the tract was not written to propound new theories of reform, but to encourage and strengthen an already existing sect in a time of persecution. Besides the fact that the author was a Lollard, we may also deduce that he was a good Latin scholar, since he apparently made his own translation of the passages of Scripture used to illustrate his theme.[1] He seems, moreover, to have been well read in the writings of the Fathers and the mediaeval divines since quotations occur from St. Ambrose, St. Augustine, St. Gregory the Great, St. Hilary, St. Isidore, St. Jerome, St. John Chrysostom, St. Bede, St. Bernard, St. Hugh, Nicholaus de Lyra, Odo of Cheriton, Peter Cantor, Peter Comestor, Peter Lombard, Robert Grosseteste, St. Thomas Aquinas, and William de St. Amour; but investigation has shown that he followed the usual practice of the theological writers of the later Middle Ages, and quoted from works containing excerpts from patristic literature rather than from the originals themselves. His main sources seem to have been the *Decretum* of Gratian, the *Libri Quattuor Sententiarum* of Peter Lombard, and the *Glossa Ordinaria* of Walafrid Strabo.

It is perhaps permissible to assume from these facts that the author was educated at Oxford, where he would come into contact with Wycliffite ways of thinking, but more than this it is impossible to state with any certainty.

[1] See Appendix.

Description of the MS.

The MS. from which the following transcript has been made occurs in the Harleian collection in the British Museum, and is catalogued as No. 2324. It is a small duodecimo volume, the pages measuring 5·6 × 3·8 inches, and contains 128 folios. In addition there are four folios at the beginning and two at the end ruled ready for the scribe, but unused. It is written on vellum, and the handwriting is neat and legible. There are few scribal errors, and the mistakes made have been almost invariably corrected by the scribe himself. The MS. is not illuminated, but the headings of the chapters and the initial letter of the first word of each chapter are written in red. The Latin quotations, which occur frequently, are generally underlined in red. Attention is called to important points in the MS. by marginal notes: nō (nota), nō. bñ. (nota bene), 'be war', or a hand with an outstretched forefinger, are the most usual.

Punctuation, &c. The MS. is punctuated, and the original punctuation has been preserved, except where some alteration seemed advantageous in order to make the meaning clearer. Capital letters are occasionally used for proper names. In the transcript, modern usage has been conformed with in this respect.

Contractions. Many of the shorter words are abbreviated in the MS., and the Latin quotations show the contractions usually employed by the mediaeval scribe. All the contracted words have been expanded in the copy, the letters supplied being printed in italics.

Grammar.

The phonology and grammatical forms of the text are those of the East Midland Dialect, at that time becoming the standard, and do not differ markedly from those of Wycliffe's works or the Wycliffite Bible-translation.[1]

A few Northern features occur, such as the frequent noun plural in -*is*, the occasional substitution of *v* for *w* initially, and the use of the preposition *til* = *to*. The strong past participle regularly

---

[1] Gasner, *Beiträge zum Entwickelungsgang der neuenglischen Schriftsprache auf Grund der mittelenglischen Bibelversionen* . . .

ends in -*n* as in Northern and North Midland, even in such forms as 'bounden', 'soungen', which often lost the -*n* in Midland.¹ On the whole, however, Northern characteristics are less common in the *Lanterne of Liȝt* than in the *Apology for Lollard Doctrines*, another anonymous Lollard tract of about the same date.²

The comparatively late date of the text is indicated by the frequent disregard of the final unaccented -*e*, which was regularly silent in the North before the end of the fourteenth century, and became so in the Midland dialect by the middle of the fifteenth. Thus in the strong plural and the weak declension of the adjective, where final -*e* tended to survive longer than in the noun or verb, forms with and without -*e* occur side by side.

In the strong verbs, levelling of the stem form occurs in the preterite plural where this had a distinctive form in Old English, and several old strong verbs have become weak.

[1] Morsbach, *Über den Ursprung der neuenglischen Schriftsprache*, § 7. 19.
[2] Siebert, *Untersuchungen über 'An Apology for Lollard Doctrines'*, pp. 38-40.

[*This study of the* Lanterne of Liȝt *was presented in an extended form for the degree of M.A. in the University of London.*]

þE LANTERNE OF LIȜT

Take ȝe of oure graciouse God ׃ þis litil tretise þat here is offrid / þe which is clepid a lanterne of liȝt ׃ for ȝe schal se þise þingis þerbi ‖

Cap*itulu*m .I. Of a prolog ‖
5 Cap*itulu*m .II. Of a petici*o*u*n* ‖
Cap*itulu*m .III. What is antic*r*ist in general ׃ wiþ sixe condic*i*ouns ‖
Cap*itulu*m .IV. What is antic*r*ist in special ׃ wi*þ* hise þre parties ‖
10 Cap*itulu*m .V. What is antic*r*ist in special ׃ wi*þ* .V. condic*i*ou*n*s ‖
Cap*itulu*m .VI. What is þe chirche oonli pro*p*rid to God ׃ wi*þ* hir names licknessis & condici*o*u*n*s ‖
Cap*itulu*m .VII. What is þe mat*er*ial chirche ׃ wi*þ* hir ournmentis ‖ •
15 Cap*itulu*m .VIII. Of good & yuel ׃ comyng to þis mat*er*ial chirche ‖
Cap*itulu*m .IX. Of discrescio*u*n to knowe ׃ þe good from þe yuel ‖
Cap*itulu*m .X. How þe good of þe secou*n*de chirche ׃ acorden wi*þ*
20 þe good of þe firste chirche ‖
Cap*itulu*m .XI. Of ioie i*n* tribulaci*o*u*n* ‖
Cap*itulu*m .XII. Of þe fendis cautels. bi whiche he pursueþ in hise me*m*bris ׃ þe kepers of Goddis heestis ‖
Cap*itulu*m | .XIII. What is þe fendis chirche ׃ wi*þ* hir propurtes ‖

PROLOG

Þis is þe prolog. Capitulum .I^m.

The author prays for grace to keep the way of truth in these days of tribulation.
God þat is good in him silf. faire in hise aungelis. merveilouse in hise seintis. and merciful vpon synners ⁘ haue merci on vs now & euer/ and ȝyue vs grace to holde þe weye of truþe ⁘ in þise daies of greet tribulacioun ‖ For now manye þat semeden to haue be 5 stable in vertu ⁘ fallen from her holi purpose. dredyng losse of worldli goodis & bodili peyne as Crist seiþ. Mat. xxiv°. 'Quoniam habundabit iniquitas ⁘ refrigescet caritas multorum'¹/ þat is to seie. þe greet plente and habundaunce of wickidnesse ⁘ schal kele

The unity of Christendom is impaired by Antichrist.
or make coolde. þe charite of many.² For now þe deuel haþ 10 marrid þis world ⁘ bi his leeftenaunt anticrist þat men ben born aboute in diuerse douȝtis ⁘ as wawis of þe see / wrechidli diuidid

Fol. 2 a in wonderful opyniouns ⁘ iche neiȝbore wiþ oþir ‖ But | Seint Poul sett oon acorde ⁘ in al cristendom & seiþ. Eph. iv°. 'Vnus dominus vna fides vnum baptisma' ‖ þat is to seie. þer is but oo 15 lord ⁘ þat alle men schulden drede & loue/ oo feiþ ⁘ þat alle men schulden bileue wiþouten chaungyng/ oo baptem or cristendom ⁘ þat alle men schulden kepe wiþouten defouling ‖ Alas hou is þis oonhed or vnite broken. þat men vnrulid walken aftir her lustis. as beestis in þe corne? certis þe wickid man þat Crist spekiþ of ⁘ 20 haþ done þis dede/ Mat. xiii°. 'Inimicus homo superseminauit zizaunia'³ ‖ Þat is to seie. þe enemy of God haþ sowen taaris ⁘ vpon þe seed of Iesu Crist⁴ ‖ Þis wickid man is anticrist ⁘ þat clowtiþ his lawis as roten raggis. to þe clene cloþ of Cristis gospel/ & wakiþ in malise as Iudas childe ⁘ whilis Symon slepiþ & takiþ 25 noon hede ‖ O þou wickid man. is þer ony oþir þat may saue

---

¹ Vulg. Matt. xxiv. 12.

² W. V. 'And for wickidness schal be plenteous, the charite of manye schal wexe cold.'

³ Vulg. Matt. xiii. 25 'Inimicus eius superseminavit zizania'; but v. 28 'Inimicus homo hoc fecit.'

⁴ W. V. 'His enemy cam and sew above dernel (or cokil) in the midil of whete.' 1388, 'His enemy cam and sewe above taris,' etc.

Capitulum .I.

soulis þan Crist Iesu? God seiþ bi þe mouþe of Moyses. Deut⁰. xxxii⁰. 'percuciam & ego sanabo & non est qui de manu | mea possit eruere'¹ ‖ þat is to seie. I schal smyt & I schal heele ;' & þer is non þat mai skape fro myn hand² ‖ Who haþ þe keies of
5 Dauiþ to opyn heuene ȝatis ;' & þanne noon oþir closiþ to close ;' & þanne noon oþir opyneþ? Seint Jon seiþ, Apoc. iii⁰. 'Sanctus & verus habet clauem dauid qui aperit & nemo claudit. claudit & nemo aperit'³ ‖ Þat is to seie. Holi & trewe Crist Iesu haþ þe keie of Dauiþ þe whiche opineþ & noon oþir closiþ / closiþ ;' &
10 þanne noon oþir opineþ ;' / who dingeþ doun and þanne no man reriþ / who reriþ ;' & þanne no man dingeþ doun. Iob seiþ. xii⁰. 'Si destruxerit nemo est qui edificet ;' si incluserit hominem nullus est qui apariat'⁴ ‖ Þat is to seie. whanne þe Lord God haþ distroied ;' þer may noon oþir bijlde / & whanne þe Lord God stressiþ a man in þe
15 prisoun ;' þer mai noon oþir delyuer him. ne quite him from hise boondis ⁵‖ And þerfore in þe vertu of þis name Iesu ;' stondiþ al mannes saluacioun / as it is writen. Actus iv⁰. 'Nec enim aliud nomen est sub celo datum hominibus vnde oporteat nos saluos fieri'⁶ ‖ Seint Petir seiþ. þer | is noon oþir name vndir heuene ȝyuen to men ;'
20 but þis name Iesu. in þe whiche it bihoueþ vs to be made saaf / for oonli in vertu of þis name ;' comeþ remyssioun of synnes / as it is writen Luc. xxiiii⁰. 'Oportebat predicari in nomine eius penitenciam & remissionem peccatorum in omnes gentes'⁷ ‖ þat is to seie. It bihoued to be prechid among alle folkis ;' penaunce &
25 remissioun of synnes in þe name of Iesu ‖ Art not þou þanne a wickid man. a foultid schepard, a cruel beest. þe sone of perdicioun & anticrist him silf. þat pretendist in þee & in þi membris to bynde & lose. to blesse & curse. biside þis name Iesu? Peple wiþouten noumbre. folowyng þee & þi diuided lawis ;' ben diuidid
30 from Crist Iesu / & gon wiþ þee blyndlingis ;' to helle for euere-

Fol. 2 b

Fol. 3 a

Christ the only means of salvation,

but Antichrist leads men astray by pretending to divine powers;

---

¹ Vulg. Deut. xxxii. 39.

² W. V. 'I schal smyte & I schal heel, & there is not that fro myn hoond may delyuer.' 1388, 'I schale smyte, and I schal make hool; and noon is that may delivere fro myn hond.'

³ Vulg. Apoc. iii. 7 'Haec dicit Sanctus & Verus qui habet,' etc.

⁴ Vulg. Job xii. 14.

⁵ W. V. 'If he destroȝe, no man is that bilde up; if he inclose a man, no man is that opene.' 1388, 'If he destrieth, no man is that bildith, if he schitteth in a man, noon is that openeth.'

⁶ Vulg. Act. iv. 12 'Nec enim aliud nomen est . . . in quo,' etc.

⁷ Vulg. Luc. xxiv. 47.

more ⸝ And þis is greetli to sorow. so ferforþe ⸴ þat Crist makiþ mornyng þervpon & seiþ. Ion v⁰. 'Ego veni in nomine patris mei & non accepistis me ⸴ si alius venerit in nomine eius illum accipietis'¹ ‖ þat is to seie. | I haue comen in þe name of my fadir ⸴ & ȝe haue not taken me ⸝ whanne anoþir comeþ in his 5 owene name ⸴ him ȝe schal take ⸝² And þis is anticrist as seint Ion Crisostum seiþ vpon þis gospel.ᵃ Mat. xi⁰. 'Tu es qui venturus es an alium expectamus'³ ‖ For who þat wole not resceyue Crist ⸴ in peyne of synne he is compellid & constreyned to resceyue anticrist ‖ Þerfore in þis tyme of hidouse derknes 10 somme seeken þe lanterne of liȝt. of þe whiche spekiþ þe prophete. Ps. cxviii. 'Lucerna pedibus meis verbum tuum'⁴ ‖ þat is to seie. Lord þi word is a lanterne to my feet.⁵ ⸝ For as fer as þe liȝt of þis lanterne schineþ ⸴ so fer derkness of synne & cloudis of þe fendis temptaciouns vanischen awey & moun not abide ⸝ And algatis 15 whanne þe lanterne liȝtneþ into þe hert ⸴ it purgeþ & clensiþ from corrupcioun ⸝ it swagiþ & heeliþ goostli soris ⸝ As þe wise man seiþ. Sap. xvi⁰. 'Neque herba neque malagma sanauit illos ⸴ sed | omnipotens sermo tuus domine qui sanat vniuersa'⁶ ‖ þat is to seie. Neiþir herbe ne plaistir haþ helid hem ⸴ but Lord þi 20 miȝti word þat heeliþ alle þingis ⸝⁷ For Lord whanne þou diedist vpon þe cros ⸴ þou puttidist in þi word þe spirit of lijf ⸝ & ȝauest to it power of quickenyng ⸴ bi þin owene preciouse blood. as þou þi silf seist. Ion. vi⁰. 'verba que ego locutus sum vobis spiritus & vita sunt'⁸ ‖ þat is to seie. þe wordis þat I speke to ȝow ⸴ þei 25 ben spirit & lijf ‖

marginalia: Fol. 3 b; therefore true believers seek the Lantern of Light—God's word.; Fol. 4 a

---

¹ Vulg. Joh. v. 43.

² W. V. 'I cam in the name of my fadir, & ȝe token not me. If another schal come in his owne name, ȝe schulen receyve him.'

³ Vulg. Matt. xi. 3.

⁴ Vulg. Ps. cxviii. 105.

⁵ W. V. 'Lanterne to my feet thi woord.' 1388, 'Thi word is a lanterne to my feet.'

⁶ Vulg. Sap. xvi. 12 'Neque herba neque malagma sanavit eos, sed tuus, Domine, sermo qui sanat omnia.'

⁷ W. V. 'Forsothe neither erbe, ne plastre helde them; but thi word, Lord that heleth all thingus.'

⁸ Vulg. Joh. vi. 64.

ᵃ S. Ioan. Chrysostomus, *Homilia XXVII in cap. Matt. xi* (Opera, ed. 1547, tom. ii, col. 913).

Of a peticioun. ‖ Capitulum .IIm. ‖

Dere frendis helpe me wiþ ȝoure preiere ׃ anentis almiȝti God ╱ *The author asks his friends to pray that the Holy Spirit may speak through him in setting forth the Word,*
For seint Iame seiþ ╱ v⁰. 'Multum valet deprecacio iusti assidua.'[1] ‖
Þat is to seie. þe bisi preier of þe riȝtwise ׃ is miche worþe² ‖ þis
5 ȝoure axing & ȝoure desire ׃ is ful chargouse to me ╱ but anentis
God ׃ no þing is vnpossible. as Crist seiþ ╱ Mat. xix⁰. Mar. x⁰.
Luc. xviii⁰³ ╱ And in þis feiþ Isaie seid. xxvi⁰. 'Deus ipse operatur omnia opera nostra in nobis'⁴ ‖ þat is to seie. þe Lord God
him silf worchiþ | alle oure werkis in vs⁵ ‖ Faile we not God *Fol. 4 b*
10 þanne in good lyuyng ׃ & he mai not faile to ȝyue vs suche wisdam
as is nedful to vs ╱ & also to stere yne oure toung. & ȝyue vs trewe
organ of redi eloquens to edifiyng of oure neiȝbour as Crist seiþ
Mat. x⁰. 'Non enim vos estis qui loquimini ׃ sed spiritus patris
vestri qui loquitur in vobis'⁶ ‖ þat is to seie. Forsoþe it arne not
15 ȝe þat speken but þe spirit of ȝoure fadir þat spekiþ in ȝou ╱ For *even as it inspired the unlearned Apostles and Saints,*
þe apostlis of Crist & oþir seintis ׃ weren not graduat men in scolis ╱
but þe Holi Goost sodenli enspirid hem ׃ & maden hem plenteuous
of heuenli loore. & þei þat han traueilid in deedli lettirs ׃ mekid
hem silf as symple ydiotis as seint Ierom seiþ ╱ 'Predicatores
20 illiterati mittuntur ad predicandum vt fides credencium. non *as affirmed by the Fathers.*
virtute humana sed eloquencia & virtute dei fieri putaretur'╱
Hec Ieromus super Mat. li⁰. I⁰ ╱ ᵃ Þat is to seie. prechours
vnlettrid ׃ ben sent for to preche þat þe feiþ of trewe
bileuars ׃ schulde be hopid to be brouȝt in ╱ not bi mannes | vertu ׃ *Fol. 5 a*
25 but bi speche & doctrine of God ╱ And so seiþ seint Austin
writing to Symplician ‖ 'Quid patimur? quid audimus? surgunt
indocti & celum rapiunt ׃ & nos cum doctrinis nostris in infernum
dimergimur ‖ ᵇ Þat is to seie. what suffren we? what heeren we? ╱ *Nota*
vntauȝt men risen & cacchen heuene. & we wiþ oure clergie ben

---

[1] Vulg. Jac. v. 16.

² W. V. 'The contynuel preyer of a just man is miche worth.'

³ Vulg. Matt. xix. 26, Marc. x. 27, Luc. xviii. 27; W. V. 'Anentis God alle þingis ben possible.'

⁴ Vulg. Isaias xxvi. 12 'Domine, dabis pacem nobis: omnia enim opera nostra operatus es nobis.'

⁵ W. V. 'Alle forsothe oure werkis thou wroȝtist in us.'

⁶ Vulg. Matt. x. 20.

ᵃ S. Hieronymus, *Comment. in Evan. Matt.*, Lib. I, cap. iv, v. 19, 20 (Migne, tom. 26, col. 33).

ᵇ Augustinus, *Confessiones*, Lib. VIII, cap. viii (Migne, tom. 32, col. 757).

drowned to helle ‖ And seint Gregor in hise morals ׃ affermeþ þis sentence & seiþ / Sicut incarnata veritas in predicacione sua pauperes symplices & ydiotas elegit ׃ sicut e contra antichristus ad predicandum falsitatem suam astutos & dupplices & huius mundi sapienciam habentes electurus est ᵃ ‖ þat is to seie. riȝt as trouþe incarnat. þat is Crist in manhood chase pore symple & ydiotis to his prechyng / so aȝenwarde anticrist is for to chese ׃ sturdi & duble men / & hauyng þe wisedom of þis world ׃ for to preche his falshede / Haue we þanne ful feiþ ׃ in þis Lord Iesu wiþ perfite lyuyng / & þis Lord þoruȝ | ȝoure preiour ׃ schal lede þis werke aftir his owene plesaunce / & bring it to a perfite ende to his owene worschip ׃ & profite of hise seruauntis ‖

Christ through their prayers shall bring the work to a perfect end.

Fol. 5 b

What is anticrist in general wiþ .VI. condiciouns /
Capitulum .IIIᵐ.

Antichrist in general is every one who lives contrary to Christ.

To speke in general ׃ þat is in moost in comune / anticrist is euery man ׃ þat lyueþ aȝen Crist / as seint Ion seiþ. Ion. iiº. 'Nunc autem sunt multi antichristi'¹ / þat is to seie. forsoþe now ben manye anticristis² / And perfore seiþ seint Austin. who þat lyueþ contrarie to Crist ׃ he is an anticrist / be þou wiþynne be þou wiþoute ׃ & þou lyue contrarie to Crist. þou arte but chaff ᵇ / of þe whiche chaff Crist. Mat. iiiº. 'Paleas autem conburet igni inextinguibli'³ / þat is to seie. Forsoþe þe chaff schal brenne ׃ wiþ fire þat mai not be quenchid⁴ / for it schal brenne & neuer quenche / & þe soule þat is chaff ׃ schal euere suffre & neuer die. as þe prophete seiþ. Isaie. ixº. 'Omnis violenta predacio

Such souls shall be burned as chaff.

Fol. 6 a cum tumultu & omne vestimentum commix-|-tum sanguine erit in combustionem & cibus ignis'⁵ ‖ Þat is to seie. euery proud soule. þat risiþ in swelling aȝens his God / & euery bodi þat is defoulid ׃ in glotenye & in leccherie / schal be in to sweyling ׃ &

---

¹ Vulg. 1 Joh. ii. 18 'Nunc antichristi multi facti sunt.'
² W. V. 'Now many antecristes ben made.'
³ Vulg. Matt. iii. 12.
⁴ W. V. 'But chaffis he schal brenne with fyr unquenchable.' 1388, 'But the chaffe he schal brenne with fier that mai not be quenchid.'
⁵ Vulg. Isaias ix. 5 'Quia omnis violenta praedatio cum tumultu et vestimentum mistum sanguine,' etc.

ᵃ Gregorius Magnus, Moralium Lib. XIII, cap. x. 13 (Migne, tom. 75, col. 1023).
ᵇ Augustinus, Ep. Ioan., Tract. III. 89 (Migne, tom. 35, col. 2001, 2002).

Capitulum .III.

mete of þe fire¹ ⁊ As if he schulde seie. þe bodi & þe soule dampned ⁘ schullen feed and norische þe fire ⁊ þe whiche schal euere brenne hem wiþ moost greuous peyne.

Sixe synnes þer ben ⁘ aȝen þe Holi Goost ⁊ þat turnen þe 5 wrecchid soule ⁘ in to þis chaff ⁊ But þe philosophur seiþ. 'Nullum malum vitatur nisi cognitum' ⁊ þat is to seie. þer is non yuel fled ⁘ but if it be knowen ⁊ & þerfore we schullen name hem ⁘ in þis litil tretise ⁊ for þe more lernyng ⁘ of smale vndirstondars ‖

Nota bene Six sins against the Holy Ghost cause this.

Þe firste of þise synnes is presumpcioun. þat is hiȝe bolnyng 10 of þe spirit ⁘ wiþouten drede of Goddis riȝtwisenesse ⁊ and of þis synne al manere malice & wickidnes cacchiþ roote ⁘ þat regneþ among mankynde in lewid | or in lerned. for þe wise man seiþ Ecc. i. 'Qui non timet non poterit iustificari'² ‖ He þat drediþ not ⁘ he mai not be made riȝtwise³ ⁊ Forsoþe in whom so þat þis 15 synne of presumpcioun haþ noo lordschipe ⁘ in him þe deuel is ouercomen. for it is writen. Ecc. xvº. 'Qui timet deum faciet bona'⁴ ‖ He þat drediþ þe Lord ⁘ schal do good þingis ⁊ & þerfore seiþ þe Holi Goost⁵ Ecc. xxviiº. 'Si non in timore domini tenueris te instanter. cito subuertetur domus tua'⁶ ⁊ ‖ Þat is to seie. but if 20 þou holde þe bisili in þe drede of þe Lord ⁘ þin hous schal soone be turned vpsodoun ⁊ þat is. þi bodi & þi soule schullen be turned from God: into þe fendis seruice ‖

I. Presumption.

Fol. 6 b

Þe secounde synne is desperacioun oþir wanhope. þat is ouere litil triste on þe merci of God ‖ Seint Austin seiþ. 'Amare & timere 25 sunt due ianue vite' ‖ Drede of Goddis riȝtwisenesse. & hope of Goddis merci ⁘ ben twoo ȝatis of lijf ⁊ for bi hem we entren here in to grace ⁘ and aftir in to blisse. as þe prophet seiþ. Ps. cxlvi. 'Bene placitum est Domino super timentes eum ⁘ & in eis qui | sperant super misericordia eius'⁷ ‖ It is wel plesid vnto þe Lord 30 vpon hem þat dreden him: & in hem þat tristen on his mercy⁸ ‖ And aȝenwarde. presumpcioun & disperacioun ⁘ ben twoo ȝatis of

II. Despair.

Fol. 7 a

---

¹ W. V. 'For eche violent reuyng with noise, & clothing mengd with blod shal be in to brennyng, & mete of fyr.'

² Vulg. Ecclesiasticus i. 28 'Nam qui sine timore est, non poterit iustificari.'

³ W. V. 'For who withoute drede is, shal not moun be iustified.' 1388, 'He that is without drede, mai not be iustified.'

⁴ Vulg. Ecclesiasticus xv. 1. ⁵ MS. holgoost.

⁶ Vulg. Ecclesiasticus xxvii. 4. ⁷ Vulg. Ps. cxlvi. 11.

⁸ W. V. 'Wel plesid thing is to the Lord upon men dredende hym; and in hem that hopen on his mercy.' 1388, 'It is wel pleasaunt to the Lord on men that dreden him; and in hem that hopen on his mercy.'

deeþ/ bi þe whiche men entrien ./ in to synne & cumbraunce / & aftir in to þe peyne of helle ./ wiþouten ende / Seint Ion techiþ vs loore aȝen þis synne ./ & seiþ. Ion ii⁰. 'Filioli mei hec scribo vobis vt non peccetis. sed & si quis peccauerit aduocatum habemus apud patrem Iesum Christum iustum & ipse est propiciacio pro peccatis nostris. non pro nostris tantum sed pro tocius mundi'¹ ‖ Mi litil sones. þise þingis I write vnto ȝou ./ þat ȝe synne not in þe synne of dispeire / but if it be so ./ þat ony of vs haue synned / we haue avoket anenst þe fadir ./ Iesu Crist oure iust lord. & he is þe mercy-asker for oure synnes / not oonli for oure synnes ./ but also for þe synnes of al þe world² ‖ Iesu is for to seie. a sauiour in oure tung ./ for he haþ plente of medicyn. to saue all mankynde if þei wolde take þis medicyn ./ & be saaf / for Gregor seiþ / Se ipsum in-|-terimit qui precepta medici obseruare non vult. He sleeþ him silf: þat wole not kepe þe biddingis of his leche ‖

Fol. 7 b

III. Hardness of heart and obstinacy.

Þe þridde synne is obstinacioun or hardnes of herte / þe whiche wole not be contrit. for conpunccioun ./ neiþir be made softe wiþ pite / ne mevid wiþ preiours ne þretingis / & settiþ nouȝt bi betingis / It is vnkynde aȝen good dedis / vnfeiþful to counseils / feeris & wood in doomes / vnschamefast in foule þingis / neiþir feerful in perelis / neiþir manful in manhod / foolhardi aȝens God / forȝetil of tyme þat is passid / necligent in tyme þat is present / not purueiyng for tyme þat is to cum / And schortli for to seie. þis is þat synne ./ þat neiþir drediþ God ne schameþ man ‖ Þus seiþ seint Bernard .V. distinccioun iiii⁰ / A medicyn for þis hard herte ./ techiþ Lincoln where he seiþ. diccio CVI. 'Cor durum debet conteri in mortarialo petrino graui pila. mortarialum sunt vulnera christi. pila ex timore pene peccati' ‖ An harde herte wolde be braied in a morter wiþ an hevi pes-|-tel / þis morter is þe bodi of Crist: hoolid or woundid in his passioun / þis pestel is þe drede of dampnacioun / þat folowiþ aftir þis synne ‖ Þanne þus þou obstinat man. þou endurid man in synne. þou hard hertid wrecche ./ neiȝe þou to þe bodi of Crist / & for drede of dampnacioun ./ conforme þee to Cristis passioun ‖

Fol. 8 a

---

¹ Vulg. 1 Joh. ii. 1.

² W. V. 'My litil sones, I wryte to ȝou these thinges, that ȝe synne not. But and if ony man shal synne, wé han avoket anentis the fadir, Jhesu Crist iust, & he is helpyng for oure synnes; sotheli not onely for oure but also for of al the world.' 1388, 'My litil sones . . . we han an advocat anentis the fadir, Jhesu Crist, and he is the forȝyuenes for oure synnes.'

Capitulum .III.

þe fourþe synne is fynali inrepentaunt ∙ þat is he þat wole IIII. Im-
neuer do verri penaunce / but contynueli lediþ his lijf ∙' aftir þe penitence.
desiris of his fleische / ouercomen wiþ þe fende ∙' & þe fals world ||
For no man doþ verry penaunce to God. but he þat fulli leueþ
5 þat synne ∙' for þe whiche he suffriþ penaunce / þus seiþ seint
Austin ∙' But for þei holden it miche worschipe ∙' to write her
names in þe erþe / þei maken a feyned schrifte to a prest : & taken
part of sacramentis / þei bilden chirches wiþ oþer ournmentis ∙' &
fynden prestis to rede & syng / þei releuen þe pore nedi ∙' & menden
10 placis þat ben perilous / but stille þei lien harde | congelid as Fol. 8 b
froost ∙' in oolde custum of synne || To þise vnrepentaunt men ∙'
spekiþ Gregor moost scharpli in hise pastorals. vpon þis tixte.
Mat. vi⁰. 'Nonne anima plus est quam esca ∙' & corpus plus
quam vestimentum'[1] || wheþir is not þe lijf more þan mete ∙' & þe
15 bodi more þan cloþe ? Vpon þis seiþ þis doctour 'Qui cibum vel
vestem pauperibus largitur & anime vel corporis iniquitate polluitur
quod magis est contulit culpe quod minus est contulit iusticie / sua
dedit deo ∙' se ipsum diabolo'[a] ∙' He þat ȝyueþ mete or cloþe ∙' to
þe pore nedi / & is pollutid or defoulid ∙' in wickidenesse of bodi
20 & of soule / þat þing þat is moost he ȝyueþ to synne / þat þing þat
is leest he ȝyueþ to riȝtwisenesse / hise goodis he ȝyueþ to God ∙'
him silf to þe deuel / for he settiþ more prijs bi worldli richesse ∙'
þan he doþ bi þe bodi or þe soule / & loueþ moost þat God loueþ
leest ∙' wherfore his loue is turned to hate || God haþ ȝouun to
25 man ∙' fyue preciouse | ȝiftis. þe leest of alle is worldli goodis / Fol. 9 a
betir þan þise is mannes bodi ∙' þat God haþ dowid wiþ kyndeli
strengþis / & grauntid in resoun to vse þis world ∙' him silf to
chastise. clooþe & feede / Abouen þise tweyne is mannes soule ∙'
þat beriþ Goddis ymage & his licknes || Lord what profite were it
30 to wynne þis world ∙' & putt peirement to þis soule ? & þe bodi is
a wlatful careyn ∙' whanne þe soule is goo þerfro / But Goddis
grace passiþ þise þre. for where þis failiþ. no wisdam availiþ ||
Loke þise ben not mys dispendid ∙' neiþir worche oony þing biside
þer ordir / but þat þei strecche alle to oo ende ∙' to wynne þe fifþe ∙'
35 þat is þe blisse of heuene for euere || Þou þat chaungist þis ordir

---

[1] Vulg. Matt. vi. 25.

[a] Gregorius Magnus, *Regulae Pastoralis Liber* xliv (Migne, tom. 77, col. 85).

Anticrist wiþ .VI. condiciouns ?

vpsodoun ?' seint Poul axiþ þis questioun of þe. Ro. ii⁰. 'An diuicias bonitatis eius & paciencie & longanimitatis contempnis ? Ignoras quoniam benignitas dei ad penitenciam te adducit / secun-
Fol. 9 b dum autem duriciam tuam & cor impenitens thesaurizas tibi | iram in die ire & reuelacionis iusti iudicii dei qui reddet vnicuique 5 secundum opera eius' ¹ || Wheþir dispisist þou þe richessis of þe goodnes & pacience & longabiding of þi God ? knowist þou not þat þe goodnes of God ?' lediþ oþir dryueþ þee to penaunce ? forsoþe aftir þin hardnes & þin vnrepentaunt herte. þou tresourist to þee wraþþe ?' in þe dai of wraþþe / & schewing of riȝtwise iuge- 10 ment of God. þat schal ȝelde iche man ?' aftir hise werkis ² ||

v .Envy. Þe fifþe synne is envie ?' of þi broþeris grace / as whanne þi neiȝbour is wise. wel gouerned. preisid or born vp. riche. welþi. strong. faire. or vertuouse in greet habundaunce of grace. þanne þis enviouse man. sclaundriþ. vpbreidiþ. reproueþ. dispisiþ. 15 hatiþ. & hyndriþ. scorneþ. & pursueþ. to defoule & waast his broþeris goodis þat ben goostli gracis ?' as miche as he mai ?' as þe wise man seiþ || Prou. xiiii⁰. 'Ambulans recto itinere & timens deum. despicitur ab eo qui infami graditur via' ³ ||
Fol. 10 a A man walking in | þe hiȝe weie & dreding God ?' is dispisid of 20 him þat walkiþ in þe wrong weye / ⁴ whanne Iesu Crist kest out a deuel ?' from a man þat was doumb. as it is writen. Mat. xii⁰. Marc. iii⁰. Luc. xi⁰.⁵ anoon þis man bigan to speke : to As the Scribes and puplische þis miracle among þe peple / Þanne scribis & pharises Pharisees enviouse sectis ?' þat weren a fals priuat religioun / sclaundrid þat 25 slandered Christ for Crist wrouȝt þis miracle ?' in Belsabub þat was prince of deuelis || envy,

¹ Vulg. Rom. ii. 4, 5.

² W. V. 'Wher thou dispisest the richessis of his goodnesse & pacience &' longe abidyng ? Unknowest thou, for the benygnyte (or good wille) of God ledith thee to penaunce ? Forsothe aftir thi hardnesse & unrepentaunt herte, thou tresourist to thee wraþþe in to the day of wraththe & of schewynge of the riȝtful dom of God, that schal ȝelde to ech man up his workis.' 1388, 'Whether dispisist thou the richessis of his goodnesse, and the pacience, and the long abidyng ? Knowist thou not, that the benygnyte of God ledith thee to forthenkyng ? But aftir thin hardnesse and unrepentaunt herte, thou tresorist to thee wraththe in the dai of wraththe and of schewyng of the riȝtful doom of God, that schal ȝelde to ech man aftir his werkis.'

³ Vulg. Prov. xiv. 2.

⁴ W. V. 'The goende in riȝt weie, & dredende God is dispised of hym that goth in the evel losid weie.' 1388, 'A man goynge in riȝtful weie and dredinge God, is dispisid of hym that goith in a weie of yuel fame.'

⁵ Vulg. Matt. xii. 22 ; Marc. iii. 11, 12 ; Luc. xi. 14.

Capitulum .III.

Belsabub is to seie a god of fli3es ; or ellis a god þat makiþ discorde / Lord siþen þise sectis dursten seie ; þus to Crist heed of mannis soule / hou miche werre schullen þey moun dore seie ; to hise hous-meyne ? Þus prelatis & freris in þise daies ; ben traueilid *so prelates and Friars*
5 wiþ þis synne a3en þe Holi Goost / & schamfulli sclaundren her *slander Lollards.* symple briþeren ; þat casten yuel maners from her soule / or prechen þe gospel to Cristis entent ; to turne þe peple to vertuouse lyuyng ‖ Þei seien þis man haþ eten ǀ a fli3e ; þat 3yueþ him lore Fol. 10 *b* of Goddis lawe / þis is more foule to eete a flie ; þan to be a god
10 & chare þise fli3es ; Þus han þey brou3t her malice aboute ; to sclaundir for Lollardis þat speken of God / & dryuen þe peple from þe feiþ ; þat durne not worche ne speke for sclaundir / but certis þey ben not worþi Crist ; þat stonyen for barkyng of þise houndis / for noon is worþi to be wiþ þis Lord ; þat schameþ his
15 seruyse in wel or in woo / & suche men schewen hem traitours to God ; þat wiþ her sclaundris hindren her briþeren / & seyn þe fende mai & wil ; make wise hise membris þat seruen him in synne / but so wole not Crist hise loued seruauntis ; þat lyuen in clennes to serue him in vertu ‖ O I preie 3ou ; who hard euer
20 a fouler blasfemye ? certis þis dispit strecchiþ vnto þe godhed ; to be punyschid in þe dai of iugement / for Goddis lawe techiþ. Prou. iii⁰. 'Noli prohibere benefacere qui potest si vales & ipse benefac'[1] ‖ Forbede him ǀ not þat mai wel do ; but if þou mai do Fol. 11 *a* wel þi silf[2] ‖ Þat a prest schulde not be lettid ; to preche þe *But no priest*
25 trouþe / ne Goddis peple to speke of her bileue ; is opunli tau3t *should be letted from* in þe book of Numeri xi⁰.[3] ‖ Þere it is rad ; þat Heldad & Medad *preaching* prophecied albeit þat þei weren not lisensid bi Moises ‖ Iosue þe *the truth.* mynyster of Moises. and chosen of manye ; grucchiden a3ens þise men. & mad his pleynt to Moises / & Moises seide. whi art þou.
30 enuiouse for me ? who mai werne þat alle þe peple prophecie. & God graunt his spirit to hem ? þis is confermed in þe gospel of oure Lord Iesu Crist ; boþe in Mark ix⁰ & in Luc. ix⁰. 'Magister vidimus quemdam in nomine tuo demonia eicientem qui non sequitur nos & prohibuimus eum / Iesu autem ait / Nolite pro-

---

[1] Prov. iii. 27 'Noli prohibere benefacere eum qui potest,' etc.

[2] W. V. 'Wile thou not forfenden hym that mai wel don, if thou maist, and thiself wel do.' 1388, 'Nil thou forbede to do wel him that mai : if thou maist, and do thou wel.'

[3] Vulg. Num. xi. 24-30.

hibere eum¹'‖ Seint Ion euaungelist seide vnto Crist. Maister we han sen a man casting out deuelis in þi name. þat sweþ not vs ׃ & we han forboden him ׀ forsoþe Iesu seide. Nile ȝe werne him or forbeede him² ‖ Alas howe dorne oure bischopis for schame ׃ offende ǀ aȝens þise boþe Goddis lawes ׀ & docke her prestis on euery side. to ȝyue hem a charge ׃ & priue hem þer office ‖ What is to be sett biforne þe bodi of Crist þat prestis sacren ? And siþen þei treten Cristis bodi. miche raþer seiþ Ierom þei schullen preche & blesse þe peple. Hec dist. 99ª. But here þe enemyes of truþe obiectun & leyn for hem Poul ׃ where he seiþ Ro. xº. 'Quomodo predicabunt nisi mittantur ׃'³ ‖ How schullen þei preche but if þei be sent ? wiþ þis þei blynden mani folk ׃ kutting þe sentence from þe wordis ׀ for Poul meneþ þat prestis schulde preche ׃ for þei ben sent ׀ boþe of God & of þe bischop ׃ for to do þat office ‖ And þe maister of sentence in his fourþe book & þe XXIIII. dist. seiþ ׀ It is þe office of a deken ׃ to preche þe gospel ᵇ ׀ þanne bi more strenger resoun ׃ it perteyneþ to a prest ׀ For seint Ierom & seint Beede acorden togider & seyn ׀ Sicut in forma apostolorum est forma episcoporum ׃ ita in septuaginta duobus discipulis est forma presbiterorum ׀ Riȝt as in þe apostlis is þe forme of bischopis ׃ so in þre score & twelue disciplis. is þe forme ǀ of prestis ׀ But Crist ȝaue charge boþe to þise bischopis & also to þise prestis ׃ & seide ׀ Mat. xº. 'Ecce ego mitto vos '⁴ ׀ & Luc. xº. 'Designauit Iesus alios septuaginta duos & misit illos &c.'⁵ ‖ Loo I sende ȝou as schepe among wolues ‖ And efte Iesu asigned þrescore & twelue ׃ & sent hem to preche ‖ How schal þise bischopis maynten þer constituciouns ׃ aȝens þer God & holi seintis ׀ It schal be more suffurable to Sodom & Gomor ׃ þan to þis peple þat disturblen Goddis ordinaunce ‖

---

¹ Vulg. Marc. ix. 37, 38.

² W. V. 'Maister, we syȝen sum oon for to caste out fendis in thi name, the which sueth not us, and we han forbedun him. Sothli Jhesus seith to him, Nile ȝe forbede him.'

³ Vulg. Rom. x. 15 'Quomodo vero praedicabunt,' etc.

⁴ Vulg. Matt. x. 16.   ⁵ Vulg. Luc. x. 1.

ᵃ Gratian, *Decreti* Pars Prima, dist. xcv, cap. v (Migne, tom. 187, col. 449).

ᵇ Petrus Lombardus, *Sententiarum Libri IV*, Lib. IV, dist. xxiv. 8 (Migne, tom. 191, col. 903).

Capitulum .III.

Þe sixt synne is fiȝting aȝens þe truþe ./ þat a man knowiþ / þat <small>VI. Fighting against the truth.</small>
is. whanne þe truþe is tolde to þe gilti ./ þe whiche disposiþ him
not to be amendid / þanne he makiþ blynde vngroundid resouns.
wiþ sotil argumentis & foltid sophisticacioun / & dampneþ þe
5 truþe aȝens his conscience ./ wiþ a boold forheed þat can not
schame ./ as þe prophet Ieromye seiþ. iii⁰. 'Frons mulieris meretricis facta est tibi ./ & noluisti erubescere ' ¹ ‖ A stroumpetis forhed
is made vnto | þee ./ & þou woldist not be aschamed / But as Poul <small>Fol. 12 b</small>
seiþ. Thimo. iii⁰. 'Quemadmodum Iambres & Mambres resisti- <small>Nota</small>
10 terunt Moisi ./ ita & hij resistent veritati ' ² ‖ Riȝt as Iambres
& Mambres aȝen-stooden Moises in þe siȝt of Pharo ./ so þise aȝenstonden þe truþe corruptid men in þer mynde ‖ And if þou wilt
knowe what þise men ben ./ axe seint Peter & he wole telle þee /
for he clepiþ hem bi þer name in his epistil ./ where seiþ ‖ II. Petir ii⁰.
15 'Magistri mendaces qui introducent sectas perdicionis ' ³ ‖ Seint <small>This introduces false sects.</small>
Petir seiþ. þise ben maistir liears. þat schullen bring in among
þe peple ./ sectis of perdicioun. þat is of losse & deeþ ‖ þouȝ ȝe rise
wiþ Lucifer ./ & make ȝoure nestis among þe sterris / from þens ȝe
schullen be drawen ./ & þrowen to þe grounde ‖ Whanne wole ȝe
20 marke þe wordis of Crist ./ þat cursiþ ȝou for ȝoure apostasie / &
for ȝe pullen as foxis to her hoolis ./ children from fadris. Crist seiþ
to ȝou. Mat. xxiii⁰. 'Ve vobis scribe et pharisei qui cir-|-cuitis terram <small>Fol. 13 a</small>
& mare &c.' ⁴ ‖ Woo to ȝou scribis & pharises ypocritis. þat
cumpassen aboute þe see & þe lond to make ȝou a novise / &
25 whanne ȝe han founden him. ȝe maken him helle broond ./ double þan
ȝoure silf / As þe vnkunnyngnes of Pharoos philosophurs was made
knowen ./ so þe fals impunyng of þe truþe. of þise sotil ypocritis
schal hastli be made open. ‖ Alle men take hede to þise sixe <small>These six sins are the cause of many evils, and at last of the ruin of the soul.</small>
synnes. for þei ben cause of batailes. discenciouns. hounger.
30 pestelence. veniaunce. & of al maner of mischef / & at þe laste
þise synnes ben cause whi soules ben chaff ./ as we seide toforne ‖

What is anticrist in special wiþ hise þre parties.
Capitulum .IIII^m.

But of þe greet cheef anticrist. þat passingli & in special maner <small>Antichrist in particular.</small>
35 bringiþ forþ fals lawes aȝens Iesu Crist & pretendiþ him silf moost

---

¹ Vulg. Jer. iii. 3.   ² Vulg. 2 Tim. iii. 8.
³ Vulg. 2 Pet. ii. 1.
⁴ Vulg. Matt. xxiii. 15 'Vae vobis scribae et pharisaei hypocritae: quia circuitis mare et aridam,' etc.

Anticrist in special?

hooli ? þus techiþ þe Lord God bi þe prophete Isaie ix⁰. 'Longeuus & venerabilis ipse est caput. propheta docens mendacium. ipse est cauda'¹ ‖ A man of greet agee | & worschipful holden to þe world ? he is heed and cheef anticrist / a prophete or a prechour techyng lesing ? he is þe taile of þis anticrist² ‖ Of þis taile spekiþ seint Petir more pleynli & seiþ. II. Pe. ii⁰. 'Fictis verbis in auaricia de vobis negociabuntur'³ ‖ Þat is to seie. Þise ben goostli marchauntis þat schal chaffare wiþ þe peple ? in feyned wordis⁴ / & wiþ her sweet likerouse speche ? þei bigilen þe hertis of innocentis. for Iude seiþ. ii⁰. 'Mirantes personas hominum questus causa'⁵ / Þat is to seie. þei schal worschip þe persoones of men ? bicause of wynnyng ‖ Þis taile of anticrist schal not preche freeli Thomas Alquin seiþ. li⁰. VII⁰. ca. viii⁰ but for 'mammona iniquitatis' / þat is for coueitise. so ferforþe crueli aʒenstonding þe prechours of troupe. þat þei schul be holden in þer daies as cursid of þe peple ‖ And seint Ion euaungelist seiþ. Apoc. xiii⁰. 'Quod nemo emet neque vendet nisi habuerit carecterem bestie'⁶ ‖ þer schal no man in þat | tyme bie ne selle be he boond be he free. but if he haue þe mark of þe beest. eiþer in his forhed or in his riʒt hond or ellis in noumbre /⁷ þat is to seie. þer schal no man preche Goddis word in þoo daies neiþer heere it. but if he haue a special lettir of lisence þat is clepid þe mark of þis beest anticrist / or ellis þat þei maynten bi word or bi dede. or in boþe. þat his lawe & his ordinaunce is good & trewe / & worþi to be holden of þe peple ‖ But it is ferful þat folowiþ aftir. Apoc. xiiii⁰. 'Si quis acceperit carecterem bestie &c.'⁸ ‖ Seynt Ion seiþ. who þat euer worschipiþ þis beest

Marginal notes: Fol. 13 b. False preachers the tail of Antichrist. Fol. 14 a. A Letter of Licence the mark of the beast.

---

[1] Vulg. Isaias ix. 15 'Longaevus & honorabilis ipse est caput,' etc.

[2] W. V. 'The longe lyvende and the w(o)rschepefull, he is the hed, and the profete techende lesyng, he is the tail.' 1388, 'An elde man and onourable, he is the heed, and a profete techynge a leesyng, he is the tail.'

[3] Vulg. 2 Pet. ii. 3.

[4] W. V. 'And thei shulen marchaundise of ʒou in coueitise bi feynyd wordis.' 1388, 'And thei schulen make marchaundie of ʒou in coueytise bi feyned wordis.'

[5] Vulg. Jud. 16 'Mirantes personas questus causa.'

[6] Vulg. Apoc. xiii. 17 'Et ne quis possit emere aut vendere nisi qui habet characterem bestiae.'

[7] W. V. 'No man mai bye, or sille, no but thei that han the caracter, (or lettre) or the name, or the noumbre of his name.' 1388, 'No man may bie, ethir sille, but thei han the caracter, ether the name of the beest, ether the noumbre of his name.'

[8] Vulg. Apoc. xiv. 9.

Cap*itulu*m IIII

anticrist. & takiþ þis forseid mark ∴ he schal drink a drauȝt of þe wyn of Goddis wraþþe / & he schal be turmentid in fire & brymston ∴ in þe siȝt of holi aungelis & in þe siȝt of þe lombe / & þe smoke of her turmentrie. schal stiȝe vp in to þe world of worldis ∴
5 þat is wiþouten ende [1] ||

Of þis anticrist God seiþ to þe prophete Zachare | xi°. 'Sume t*i*bi vasa pastoris stulti' [2] || þat is to seie. take þou to þee. þe vessellis of a foltid schepard / for loo. I schal suffre anticrist to be rerid vp in lond. þe which schal not visite hem þat ben forsaken.
10 neiþ*i*r he schal seke hem þat ben scatrid. neiþ*i*r he schal hele hem þat ben sore [3] || O. þou foltid schepard anticrist. God seiþ þou art an ydole hauyng a bischopis habit. but neiþ*i*r vertu ne spirit. lijf ne dede. þat longiþ to a bischop || for Poul seiþ. Rom. viii°. 'Qui non h*a*bet sp*i*ritu*m* Chri*s*ti nec e*s*t e*ius*' [4] / He þat haþ not þe
15 spirit of Crist ∴ he is not his seruaunt. [5] albeit þat he haue þe outward tookenes / & þerfore seiþ seint Ion. Apoc. xvi°. 'Quintus angel*us* effudit phiolam suam sup*er* sedem bestie &c.' [6] / Þe fifþe aungel pourid his cruet vpon þe seete of þe beest ∴ & his rewme is made derke / & þei eeten her toungis togidir for sorow. & þei
20 blasfemeden God of heuen for her sorowis & her woundis. & þei diden no penaunce of her dedis [7] / Þat is to mene | Archbischopis & bischopis. ben þe seet of þe beest anticrist ∴ for in hem he sittiþ & regneþ ouer oþ*i*r peple. in þe derknes of his heresie & in þis þei deliten hem. magnifiyng wiþ her tungis her fals ordinaunce ∴ þe

Fol. 14 *b*

The false Shepherd Antichrist.

Fol. 15 *a*

---

[1] W. V. 'If ony man shal worschipe the beest, and the image of it, and take the tokne in his forhed, or in his hand, & þis shal drinke of the wijn of Goddis wrath . . . and shal be tourmentid with fijr and brunston, in the siȝt of holy aungelis, and before the siȝt of the lomb. And the smoke of her tourmentis shal stiȝe up in to worldlis of worldlis.'

[2] Vulg. Zach. xi. 15.

[3] W. V. 'ȝit take to thee vessels of a foltishe sheperd; for loo! I shal reyse a sheperd in erthe whiche shal not visite forsaken thingus, . . . and shal not heele the broken togydre.' 1388, 'ȝit take to thee vessels of a fonned scheepherde; for lo! I shal reise a scheepherde in erthe,' etc.

[4] Vulg. Rom. viii. 9 'Si quis autem spiritum Christi non habet, hic non est eius.'

[5] W. V. 'If ony hath not the spirit of Crist, this is not his.'

[6] Vulg. Apoc. xvi. 10.

[7] W. V. 'The fyvethe aungel shedde out his viole on the seete of the beest, and his kingdom is maad derk, and thei eeten togydere her tunges for sorowe, and thei blasfemedem God of heven, for sorowis and her woundis; and thei diden not penaunce of her werkis.'

whiche is sorow to men of trewe vndirstonding / & þus þei putten abak Goddis holi lawe. for prechyng of Cristis gospel ? þe whiche ben sorowis to hem. gendring synnes in her sowlis. þat wounden hem to þe deeþ / And þei þus woundid schullen neuer do medeful penaunce of dedis ? for þe whiche þei schal be dampned || Lyncoln seiþ. I quake I drede & vgli I am aferde ? but I dare not be stille / leste perauenture þat sentence falle on me. þat þe prophete seiþ. Isaie. vi°. 'Ve mihi quia tacui'[1] / wo to me ? for I haue stilled[2] || Þe welle þe bigynnyng & þe cause of al ruyn & myschef. is þe court of Rome [a] || Now bi þe autorite of God. & oone acordaunce of hise holi seintis ? sueþ an open conclucioun. sadli groundid in trewe bileue / þat in þe | court of Rome ? is þe heed of anticrist / And in archebischopis & bischopis ? is þe bodi of anticrist || But in þise cloutid sectis. as mounkis chanouns. & freris ? is þe venymous taile of anticrist || Þise þre parties ben waried of þe apostle seint Iude ? seiyng in þis forme. ca.° 1°. 'Ve qui in via Caym abierunt. & in errore Balaam mercede effuci sunt ? & in contradiccione Chore perierunt'[3] þat is to seie. woo to hem þat walken in þe weye of Caym ? þise ben fals possessioners ? And woo to hem þat ben schadde out for mede in þe errour of Balaam ? þise ben miȝti nedles mendiners || And woo to hem þat han perischide in þe aȝenseiyng of Chore[4] ? þise ben proude sturdi maynteners ||

How þis anticrist schal be destroied. God him silf techiþ bi þe prophete Daniel. & seiþ. ca.° viii°. 'Sine manu conteretur'[5] || þat is to seie. þis anticrist schal be destried wiþouten hand ?[6] þat is wiþouten power of man || For Poul seiþ. II. Thess. ii°. 'Antichristum deus interficiet spiritu oris sui & destruet illustracione

---

[1] Vulg. Isaias vi. 5.

[2] W. V. 'Wo to me, for I heeld my pees.' 1388, 'Wo to me, for I was stille.'

[3] Vulg. Jud. i. 11 'Vae illis quia in via,' etc.

[4] W. V. 'Wo to hem that wenten the weye of Caym; and bi errour of Balaam for meede ben shed out, and perschiden in the aȝen seiynge of Chore.'

[5] Vulg. Dan. viii. 25.

[6] W. V. 'Withouten hond he shal be broken togydre.' 1388, 'Withouten hond he shal be al to-brokun.'

---

[a] 'Sermo Roberti Lincolniensis Episcopi propositus coram Papa & Cardinalibus in Consilio Lugdunensi' (*Fasciculus Rerum expetendarum*, etc., Brown, 1690, vol. ii, p. 252).

Capitulum .IIII.

aduentus sui ' ¹ ‖ Þat is to seie. Crist schal slee anticrist ; wiþ | þe Fol. 16 a
spirit of his mouþe. þat is wiþ þe holi word of his lawe ‖ And þe
lord schal destrie him wiþ schynyng of his comyng.² þat is wiþ
turnyng of mennes hertis bi his grace to his lawe. a litil aforne
5 his doome ‖ But God tauȝt more pleynli þis loore to Ioob ; and
seide / Iob xl. caº. 'Ecce spes eius frustrabitur eum & videntibus
cunctis precipitabitur' ³ ‖ Loo seiþ God þat hope þat anticrist haþ
in richessis & in worldli fauour schal bring him to nouȝt / & alle
men seing ; he schal be þrowen doun heedlingis ⁴ / so þat alle þe
10 peple schal take a weiling vpon him wiþ greet lamentacioun.
wariyng him & dampnyng him. wiþ alle hise fals ordinauncis ‖

What is anticrist in special ; wiþ fyue condiciouns ‖
Capitulum .Vᵐ. ‖

But now at þe last we schullen bring to mynde & to witnesse ; Five 'assaults' of
15 holi Dauiþ þe kyng / þat hadde ȝouun to him ; þe ful spirit of Antichrist wherewith
prophecie / & he seing þe comyng of anticrist ; his lyuyng & his he persecutes the
fal / markiþ fyue hidouse sauȝtis ; þe whiche he schal haunt aȝen | servants of God.
þe seruauntis of God. Ps. foure score & ten /   Fol. 16 b

þe firste sauȝt of anticrist is constitucioun as þe prophete seiþ ‖ I. 'Constitution' or
20 'Constitue domine legis latorem super eos ' ⁵ ‖ Lord suffre þou to Law.
ordeyne a lawemaker vpon þe peple ; ⁶ in peyne of her synne. for
þei wole not consent to þe trouþe ‖ Þat is þus to mene. Anticrist
vseþ fals lucratif or wynnyng lawis as ben absoluciouns. indulgence.
pardouns. priuelegis. & alle oþir heuenli tresour. þat is brouȝt in
25 to sale for to spoile þe peple of her worldli goodis / & principali
þise newe constituciouns. bi whos strengþe anticrist enterditiþ The 'new constitu-
chirchis. soumneþ prechours. suspendiþ resceyuours. & priueþ hem tions.'
þer bennefice. cursiþ heerars. & takiþ awey þe goodis of hem.

---

¹ Vulg. 2 Thess. ii. 8 'Ille iniquus, quem Dominus Iesus interficiet spiritu oris sui & destruet illustratione adventus sui eum.'

² W. V. 'And thanne the ilke wickid man schal be schewid, whom the Lord Jhesu schal sle with the spirit of his mouth, and schal distroye with the illumynyng (or schynyng), of his coming.' 1388, 'And thanne thilke wickid man, etc. . . . and schal distrie with liȝtnyng of his comyng.'

³ Vulg. Job xl. 28; A. V. Job xli. 9.

⁴ W. V. 'Lo! the hope of hym shal maken hym veyn; and alle men seende he shal ben kast doun.' 1388, 'Lo! his hope schal disseyve hym; and in the siȝt of alle men he schal be cast doun.'

⁵ Vulg. Ps. ix. 21 (A. V. Ps. ix. 20).

⁶ W. V. 'Sett, Lord a lawe ȝivere upon hem.' 1388, 'Lord, ordeine thou a lawe makere on hem.'

18   Anticrist wiþ .v. condiciouns ||

þat forþeren þe precheing of a prest ⸴ ȝhe þouȝ it were an aungel of heuene. but if þat prest schewe þe mark of þe beest. þe whiche is turned in to a newe name. & clepid a special lettir of lisence ⸴ for þe more blyndyng of þe lewid peple ||

II. Tribulation.
Fol. 17 a

Þe secounde sauȝt of anticrist ⸴ is tribulacioun as þe prophet 5 seiþ. 'Despicis in oportunitatibus in tribulacione'[1] || | þat is to seie. Anticrist vexiþ þe peple ouer miȝt ⸴ in hunting hem on mawmentrie & doyng of ydolatrie / but euer anticrist makeþ hem to wene ⸴ þat þei gon on pilgrimage / & þerfor he is waried of God. þat seiþ bi þe prophete Isaye. v⁰. 'Ve qui dicitis bonum 10 malum uel malum bonum. ponentes tenebras lucem & lucem tenebras ponentes amarum in dulce & dulce in amarum'[2] || Þat is to seie. woo to ȝou þat seyn ⸴ good is yuel & yuel is good / putting liȝt in to derknes ⸴ & derknes in to liȝt / turnyng sweet in to bittir ⸴ & bittir in to sweet[3] || And þus doþ anticrist whanne he trans- 15 posiþ vertues in to vicis ⸴ & vicis in to vertues / as pilgrimage in to outrage ⸴ & outrage in to pilgrimage / And for þis weywarde entent. God dispisiþ anticrist ⸴ wiþ alle hise blindfelt peple / & wlatiþ alle her mysdispendid goodis ⸴ in her moost tribulaciouns ||

III. Inquisition.
Fol. 17 b

Þe þridde sauȝt of anticrist ⸴ is Inquisiscioun. as þe prophet 20 seiþ 'Secundum multitudinem ire sue non queret'[4] / þat is to seie. Anticrist enqueriþ | sechiþ & herkneþ. where he mai fynde ony man or womman. þat writiþ. rediþ. lerneþ. or studieþ Goddis lawe in her modir tung ⸴ to lede her lijf aftir þe plesing wille of God / and soone he caccheþ hem in hise sensuris ⸴ & aftir smytiþ as he mai 25 moost greuousli hirten hem || But he schal not make þis inquisisioun ⸴ aftir þe multitude or greetnes of his wraþþe / for God schal refreyne & abregge ⸴ þe powere of his malice / so þat he schal no more do ⸴ þan God wole suffre him. þat knowiþ þe mesure of hise dedis / to proue hise seruauntis bi þe furneise of penaunce accep- 30 table ⸴ & anticrist wiþ hise meyne. þus hardid in malice. inexcusable ||

---

[1] Vulg. Ps. x. 1.
[2] Vulg. Isaias v. 20 'Vae qui dicitis malum bonum & bonum malum,' etc.
[3] W. V. 'Wo that seyn euel good, and good euel, puttende derknesses liȝt and liȝt derknesses; puttende bitter into swete and sweete into bittir.' 1388, 'Wo to ȝou that seien yuel good, and good yuel; and putten derknessis liȝt, and liȝt derknessis; and putten bittir thing into swete, and swete thing in to bittir.'
[4] Vulg. Ps. x. 5 (A. V. x. 4).

Capitulum .V.

Þe fourþe sauȝt of anticrist ./ is persecucioun as þe prophet seiþ IV. Persecution.
'Insidiatur ut rapiat pauperem'[1] ‖ Þat is to seie. Anticrist sittiþ
& sottiþ in pees of þis world ./ wiþ riche men in her dennes / but
þe pore meke symple and loweli ./ hem he aspiseþ & pursueþ / hem
5 he ouer-lepiþ & ouer-renneþ. raveisching hem boþe bodili &
goostli / for God seid vnto Iob. xl⁰. | 'Habet fudiciam quod influat Fol. 18 a
Iordanis in os eius'[2] / Anticrist haþ a triste & a trowing ./ þat
Iordan mai flowe in to his mouþe[3] / & þerfor he makiþ his dwelling
place ./ in þe herte of þe see. as God seiþ bi þe prophete Ezechiel.
10 xxviii⁰. 'In cathedra[4] dei sedi in corde maris ./ cum sis homo &
non deus'[5] / Anticrist makiþ his boost & seiþ / I haue sitten in þe
chaier of God ./ in þe herte of þe see / whane þou art but a man ./
& not God / but euer in wlank countre. fat & habunding of worldli
goodis ./ þere anticrist wiþ hise clerkis. bilden her nestis / And if
15 þou loke vttirli aboute þee. þou schalt fynde hem among woodis
& watris. as seint Ion seiþ. Apoc. xvi⁰. 'Vidi de ore draconis
& de ore bestie. & de ore pseudoprophete spiritus tres immundos
exisse in modum ranarum'[6] ‖ I saw seiþ seint Ion. out of þe mouþe
of þe dragoun ./ þat is þe heed of anticrist / & out of þe mouþe of
20 þe beest ./ þat is þe bodi of anticrist / & out of þe mouþe of þe
pseudo-prophete or fals precheour ./ þat is þe taile of anticrist / þre vnclene spiritis to haue passid out ./ in þe maner of froggis ‖ Froggis
sitting | in hoolis bi þe watir-brink ./ purchassen of þe ground. Fol. 18 b
abouen hem. & on eiþer siȝde hem / But þat þat is vndirneþen hem ./ nota
25 þei wole not her þankis. neiþer leesen it ne loosen it ‖ So þise þre
spiritis croking in coueitis. glotenie & leccherie. bitokenen anti- Antichrist known by
crist. in hise þre partise / For þei purchassen of lordis ./ þat ben Covetousness, Gluttony, and Lechery.
abouen hem / miche parte of her good ./ wiþ þe tung of flatering &
feyned ypocrisie / And of þe comunes abouten hem. þei whiȝlen in
30 to her handis ./ miche parte of her catel / But þat þat þei han
wonnen. þei holden fast ./ aȝen þe autorite. of boþe Goddis lawes /
& wiþ þise richessis þei nurischen wilde. sturdi. & laweles hiȝnen.
þat pursuen hem þat wollen ouȝt seie aȝens þis cuisid synne ‖ But
God in þis persecucioun. þoruȝ his prophete counfortiþ hise ser-

---

[1] Vulg. Ps. x. 9.
[2] Vulg. Job xl. 18 (A. V. xl. 23).
[3] W. V. 'He hath trost, that Jordan flowe in to the mouth of hym.'
[4] MS. chathidera.
[5] Vulg. Ezech. xxviii. 2.
[6] Vulg. Apoc. xvi. 13, 'exisse' omitted.

uauntis ? & seiþ Ps. xlv. 'Deus noster refugium & virtus adiutor in tribulacionibus que inuenerunt nos nimis propterea non timebimus dum turbabitur terra ? & transferentur montes in cor maris'[1] || Þat is to seie. Oure God is refute & vertu. oure God is help in tribulaciouns. þe whiche haþ founden vs passingli || | 5
Fol. 19 a Wherefore we schal not drede. whilis þat men lyuyng aftir þis world schullen be troublid. & hillis schullen be born ouer in to þe hert of þe see [2] || þat is. trewe men schal not be abaschid ? þouȝ proud fleischeli men be confedrid to anticrist ? & helpe him in his persecucioun || 10

V. Execution. Þe fifþe sauȝt of anticrist is execucioun. as þe prophet seiþ. 'rapere pauperem dum atrahit eum'[3] || Þat is to seie. whanne anticrist seþ þat he availiþ not in þise forseid turmentis ? þanne he executiþ his malice aȝens Cristis chosen || To þis acordiþ seint Ion in his Apoc. xiii⁰. 'Faciat ut quicunque non adorauerint 15 ymagynem bestie occidantur'[4] || Þat is to seie. þe beest of þe erþe ? schal ȝyue power to þe beest of þe see / for in þis tyme of execucioun. þe viciouse parte of þe laite. fro þe hiȝest vnto þe lowest. schullen consent to execute þe wickidnes of þis viciouse part of þe clergie / þanne schal þis prophecie be fulfillid. Ps. lxxviii. 'Effuderunt 20 sanguinem eorum tanquam aquam & non erat qui sepeliret posue-
Fol. 19 b runt morticina | seruorum tuorum escas volatilibus celi ? carnes sanctorum tuorum bestijs terre'[5] || Þei schal scheed out innocent blood ? & þer schal no man dore birie þer bodies / for þei schal cast þer fleische to foulis of þe heire ? & her careynes to beestis of 25 þe erþe.[6] þanne seiþ þe prophete. 'Cadet cum dominatus fuerit

[1] Vulg. Ps. xlv. 2, 3.

[2] W. V. 'Oure God refut, and vertue: helpere in tribulaciouns, that founden us ful myche. Therefore wee shul not drede, whil the erthe shal be disturbid; and hillis shul be born ouer in to the herte of the se.' 1388, 'Oure God, thou art refuyt, and vertu; helpere in tribulaciouns that han founde us greetly. Therfore we schullen not drede, while the erthe schal be troblid; and the hillis schulen be borun ouer in to the herte of the see.'

[3] Vulg. Ps, x. 9.

[4] Vulg. Apoc. xiii. 15.

[5] Vulg. Ps. lxxviii. 3, 2 'Effuderunt sanguinem eorum tanquam aquam in circuitu Ierusalem,' etc.

[6] W. V. 'Thei shadden out the blod of hem, as water in the envyroun of Jerusalem; and ther was not that shulde birie. Thei putte the smyten to deth of thi servauntis, metis to the foulis of hevene; fleish of thi seintis to the bestis of erthe.' 1388, 'Thei schedden out the blod of hem, as watir in the cumpas of Jerusalem; and noon was that biriede. Thei settiden the slayn

Capitulum .V.

pauperum'¹ ‖ þat is to seie. as seynt Austin declariþ / whanne anticrist weneþ þat he haþ lordschip ׃ ouere alle þe seruauntis of God / rering vpon hem ׃ diuerse gynnes of turmentrie / þanne schal he falle to open reprofe ׃ for euermore ‖

5 Þe ful tyme of anticrist duriþ ׃ þre ȝeer & an half / but þat þe gospel makeþ remyssioun ׃ & elles schulde not alle fleische be saaf ‖ Þis tyme was figurid vnder Helie þe prophete & kyng Acab þat wickid man / þere telliþ þe stori þat reyn was stoppid. III. Reg. xvii⁰. þre ȝeere & sixe moneþes. þat no drope fel on þe erthe /
10 Seint Iame beriþ witnes of þis þing ׃ in his epistil canonysid /² Þe fleeyng of Dauid from kyng Saule ׃ markiþ þis þing. who so takiþ hede. I. Reg. xviii⁰. & rede | þat book to þe last ende / Also þe bisecheing of Ierusalem ׃ makeþ knowen þis tyme as Iosophus telliþ. Daniel tauȝt þis noumbre also ׃ in tyme & tymes & half
15 a tyme. Dan. vii⁰ ³ & þis is þre ȝeere & an half ׃ as seint Ierom declariþ in his book of seyntis ‖ Þe miȝti Machabeies ׃ vndir þis noumbre made clene her temple / wherfore seint Ion in his Apocalyps feele siþis rehersiþ þis noumbre. whanne he spekiþ of anticrist / And Crist kept þis noumbre ׃ for tyme of his precheing / outake
20 þat leest. bi vertu of his passioun ‖ Seint Ion Crisostum vpon Mat. Om. lvii⁰. seiþ þus. 'In tribus annis & sex mensibus. hoc sacrificium christianorum tollendum⁴ est ab antichristo fugientibus christianis per loca deserta / non erit qui aut in ecclesiam intret aut oblacionem offerat deo'ᵃ ‖ Þat is to seie. bi þre ȝeere
25 & sixe moneþis. þe sacrifice of Goddis preising. þat schulde be in mannes mouþe / þe sacrifice of riȝtwisenesse ׃ þat schulde be in mannes werkis / & þe sacrifice of pees ׃ þat | schulde be in treting of Cristis bodi / schal be taken awey from all feiþful ׃ þoruȝ strong woodnes of anticrist / þanne schalle alle trewe cristen ׃ flee þe face
30 of anticrist / so þat noon schullen mowen entre in to þe chirche to do dewe seruyce to her God ‖ Aftir þis. peple schal turne hem ׃ wiþ al her herte / boþe cristen & Iewis. to þe keping of Goddis bodies of thi seruauntis meetis to the volatilis of hevenes; the fleischis of thi seyntis to the beestes of the erthe.'

Antichrist's power shall last but for a time.

Fol. 20 *a*

Fol. 20 *b*

When Antichrist is destroyed, all men will repent and turn to God.

---

[1] Vulg. Ps. x. 10. [2] Vulg. Jac. v. 17, 18.
[3] Vulg. Dan. vii. 25. [4] MS. tellendum.

ᵃ S. Ioan. Chrysostomus, *Homilia XLIX* (*Opera*, ed. 1547, tom. ii, col. 1086).

þe chirche of God ?

lawe. and doing of verry penaunce ? as Poul seiþ. Ro. xi⁰. 'Cecitas ex parte contigit in Israel donec plenitudo gencium intraret ? & sic omnis Israel saluus fieret'[1] ‖ þat is to seie. Blyndnes fel partie in Israel. vntil þe tyme þat plente of heþen men ? schulde entre in to cristendom / & þanne in þe ende of þe world. þat is after þe distruccioun of anticrist. al Israel schulde be mad saaf[2] / No man loke aftir Ennok & Hely in persoone ? for þanne he mai liȝtli be bigilid / but in spirit & in vertu ? now þei ben comen / to make mennes hertis redi ? aforn Cristis doome / to whom be glori now & euere. Amen ‖

What is þe chirche oonli proprid to God ? wiþ hir names licknes-|-sis and condiciouns. ‖ Capitulum .VI^m. ‖

Fol. 21 a
Holy Church.

To speke of holi chirche. firste we taken ground of þe gospel ? where Crist seiþ. Mat. xvi⁰. 'Porte inferi non preualebunt aduersus eam'[3] / ȝatis of helle schullen not mow haue miȝt aȝen holi chirche'[4] / vpon þis tixte seiþ Lire þus 'Ecclesia non consistit in hominibus raticne potestatis vel dignitatis ecclesiastice uel secularis. quia multi principes & summi pontifices inventi sunt apostatasse a fide. propterea quod ecclesia consistit in illis personis in quibus est noticia & vera confessio fidei & veritatis' / [a] Þe chirche is not in men bi weye of powere or dignite spiritual or temperal / for manye princis & hiȝe bischopis & oþir of lowere degree. state or dignite ? are founden to be apostataas. or haue gon abak from þe bileue / wherfore þe chirch stondiþ in þoo persoones ? in whom is knowyng & verri confessioun of feiþ & trouþe ‖ But for þe more cleere declaring of þis mater. and avoiding of obiecciouns þat mai be putt forþe ? we schullen vndirstonde þat þer ben þre chirchis / of þe whiche Goddis lawe ? often makiþ mencioun / | and miche þei diuersen iche from oþir ? to hem þat taken good hede ‖ But witles foolis ben marrid here. þat wil not lerne to knowe iche atwynne /

Three churches
Fol. 21 b
are mentioned in God's word.

I. The first is the Church of God called a little flock.

Þe firste is clepid a litil flok as Crist seiþ in Luc. xii⁰. 'Nolite

---

[1] Vulg. Rom. xi. 25, 26.

[2] W. V. 'Blyndnesse hath felde of party in Israel, til the plente of hethen men entriden, and so all Israel schulde be maad saaf.'

[3] Vulg. Matt. xvi. 18.

[4] W. V. 'ȝatis of helle shulen not han miȝt, (or strengthe) aȝeins it.'

---

[a] Nicolai de Lyra, *Biblia Sacra cum glossis* on St. Matt. xvi. 18.

Capitulum .VI.

timere pusillus grex'¹ ‖ Nile ȝe drede my litil flok ꝑ it plesiþ ȝoure fadir to ȝyue ȝou a kyngdom.

And þis chirche is clepid þe chosun noumbre of hem þat schullen be saued. as it is writen. Ecci. iii⁰. 'Filii sapientie ecclesia
5 iustorum & nacio illorum obediencia & dileccio'² ‖ Þe sones of wisdam ben þe chirche of riȝtwise men. & þe nacioun of hem ꝑ is buxumnesse to God. & loue to her euenecristen³ ‖

II. 'The chosen number of those who shall be saved.'

Þe þridde tyme þis chirche is clepid a clene chaast maiden ꝑ as Poul seiþ. Ephe. v⁰. 'Christus elegit sibi gloriosam ecclesiam
10 non habentem maculam aut rugam aut aliquid huiusmodi ut sit sancta & immaculata'⁴ ‖ Crist haþ chosun him a gloriouse chirche. neiþir hauyng spott ne bleyne. or ony suche oþir þing ꝑ but þat þis chirche mai be holi and vndefoulid⁵ ⁄ To þis acordiþ Lincoln dictio CXXXV. & | seiþ ⁄ 'Ecclesia dei catholica est virgo casta
15 sponsa christi gloriosa sine macula & ruga' ‖ Þe holi chirche of God. is a chaast virgyn Cristis gloriouse spouse. wiþouten spott or bleyne ‖

III. 'A clean, chaste maiden.'

Fol. 22 a

Þe fourþe tyme. þis chirche is clepid Cristis spouse ꝑ & of þis mariage Poul beriþ witnes & seiþ. II Cor. x⁰ ⁄ 'Despondi vos vni viro
20 virginem castam exhibere christo'⁶ ⁄ I haue maried ȝou to oo man ꝑ þis is not to a wowtrere. but to a laweful man Crist Iesu ⁄ þat I mai present ȝou to God. a clene chaast maiden ꝑ at þe daie of doom⁷ ‖ And þus we seyn in þe dedicacioun of þe chirche ‖ 'Qua sponso sponsa iuncta est ecclesia'⁄ þis dai holi chirche a gloriouse spouse ꝑ
25 is maried to Crist her souereyn ‖

IV. 'Christ's spouse.'

Þis chirche is lickned to a womman wiþ childe ꝑ & þus seiþ Crist in þe gospel of Ion xvi⁰. 'mulier cum parit tristiciam habet'⁸ ⁄

V. And likened to 'A woman with child.'

¹ Vulg. Luc. xii. 32.
² Vulg. Ecclesiasticus iii. 1.
³ W. V. 'The sonns of wisdam the chirche of riȝtwis men, and the nacioun of hem obeisaunce and loovyng.' 1388, 'The sones of wisdom ben the chirche of iust men, and the nacioun of hem is obedience and love.'
⁴ Vulg. Eph. v. 25, 27, 'Christus dilexit ecclesiam . . . ut exhiberet ipse sibi gloriosam ecclesiam,' etc.
⁵ W. V. 'Crist louede the chirche . . . that he shulde ȝyue the chirche glorious to himsilf, not havyng wem (or spot) or ryuelyng, or ony such thing, but that it be hooli and undefoulid.'
⁶ Vulg. 2 Cor. xi. 2.
⁷ W. V. 'Sothly I haue bihiȝt, (or become borwe) for to ȝyue ȝou a chast virgyne to a man Crist.' 1388, 'I have spousid ȝou to oon hosebonde, to ȝelde a chast virgyn to Crist.'
⁸ Vulg. Joh. xvi. 21.

Þe chirche of God.'

VI. 'A womman clad in the sun.'
A womman whanne sche traueiliþ ? sche haþ peynes[1] ǁ þis chirche is lickned to a womman ? clad in þe sunne. as seint Ion seiþ in his apocalyps xii⁰. 'mulier amicta sole'[2] / I sauȝ a wounFol. 22 b diiful siȝt ? & þat was a womman cladde in þe ǁ sunne[3]

VII. 'Peter's little boat.'
Þis chirche is lickned to Petris litile boot. þe whiche was in 5 myddis of þe see as it is writen in þe gospel. Mat. xiiii⁰. Mark vi⁰. Luk. viii⁰. 'Nauicula autem in medio mari iactabatur fluctibus'[4] ǁ Forsoþe þe litil boot was cast aboute in middis of þe see ? wiþ þe wawis[5] / þis boot boþe sank & swam ? but drowne myȝt it neuere / so holi chirche suffriþ many periles. & sumtyme bodili deeþ. bi 10 purswet of enemyes ? but it schal neuer be dampned /

VIII. 'Paradise.'
Þis chirche is lickned to paradise ? & þus seiþ þe prophete Ezechiel xxx⁰. 'Cedri non fuerunt altiores eo in paradiso dei'[6] / Cedre-trees weren not hiȝer þan he ? in þe paradise of God / vpon þis seiþ seint Austin. de. ci. dei. li⁰. xiii⁰. 'Paradisus est ecclesia. 15 quattuor flumina quattuor euangelia. ligna fructifera sunt sancti. fructus opera eorum. lignum vite. sanctus sanctorum christus. lignum scientie boni et mali proprium voluntatis arbitrium'[a] ǁ Paradis is holi chirche. þe foure floodis ben þe foure gospeleris / & þise Fol. 23 a weren writen of Mathwe. Mark. Luk. & Ioon / ǁ þe whiche weren 20 figurid in licknesse of foure beestis ? a man. a lioun. a calf. & an egle / for þei prechiden Crist. þe whiche is man. kniȝt. prest. & God / & bi þise foure we ben tauȝt in stori. what is don in allegori ? what we schal bileue / in moral ? what we shall do / in anagogy ? what we schal hope / Þe trees þat beren fruyt ? ben good hooli lyuars 25 here in erþe / Þe fruytis of þise trees ? ben þe werkis of holi seintis. Þe tree of lijf ? is þe seint passing alle seyntis. oure Lord Iesu Crist ǁ Þe tree of knowyng good & yuel ? is þe free choise of mannes wille ǁ Þis is þe holi chirche oonli proprid vnto God ? þat seruen him in vertu nyȝt & dai ǁ   30

---

[1] W. V. 'A womman whanne sche berith child, hath sorowe.' 1388, 'A womman whanne sche berith child, hath heuynesse.'

[2] Vulg. Apoc. xii. 1.

[3] W. V. 'A womman coverid, or clothid, with the sunne.'

[4] Vulg. Matt. xiv. 24, Marc. vi. 47, Luc. viii. 22, 23.

[5] W. V. 'Sothely the boot in the mydil see was throwen with wawis.' 1388, 'And the boot in the myddel of the see was schoggid with wawis.'

[6] Vulg. Ezech. xxxi. 8 'Cedri non fuerunt altiores illo in paradiso dei.'

---

[a] Augustinus, De civitate Dei, Lib. XIII. 21 (Migne, tom. 41, col. 395).

Capitulum .VI.

But how euere we speken in diuerse names. or licknessis of þis holi chirche ꞉ þei techen nouȝt ellis but þis oo name. þat is to seie þe congregacioun or gedering togidir of feiþful soulis ⁄ þat lastingli kepen feiþ & trouþe ꞉ in word & in dede to God & to man ⁄ &
5 reisen her lijf in siker hope of mercy & grace & blisse at her ende ⁄ and ouer-|-coueren or hillen þis bilding in perfite charite. þat schal not faile in wele ne in woo ‖ Of þis spak seint Poul to þe Corinthis ꞉ & in hem to alle oþir seiyng. Cor. iiiº. 'Templum enim dei sanctum est quod estis vos'[1] ‖ Þe temple of God is holi ꞉
10 & þat ben ȝe ⁄ & bi þis we vndirstand. þat þe soule of a riȝtwise man. is þe seet of God ‖ Wel auȝt suche a man to be waker & wise. þat haþ þe greet God Lord of Israel ꞉ dwelling in hise soule. & so seiþ seint Austin. in liº. de doctrina christiana ⁄ 'O anima nota christiana euigila. & si que in te sit virtus caritatis que omnia
15 sustinet ꞉ domini tui imitari vestigia ⁄ Considera quot milia martirum tritam tibi fecerunt viam ⁄ transierunt virgines. transierunt pueri & puelle. & adhuc times ⁄ ducet te qui est via veritas & vita. via non errans. veritas non fallens. vita non deficiens. via in exemplo veritas in promisso. & vita in premio' ‖ O. þou cristen
20 soule awake. & if þer be in þee ony vertu of charite þat susteyneþ alle þingis ꞉ folow þou þe steppis of þis Lord ⁄ take hede how mani þousand of martris. han made a smeþ | pleyne weye to þee ⁄ þer han passid bifore þee virgynes. þer han passid bifore children & ȝong damysellis ꞉ & ȝit þou dredist ⁄ arise þou soule. for he
25 schal lede þee. þat is weye. trouþe. & lijf ⁄ weye. not erring ⁄ trouþe. not bigiling ⁄ & lijf. not failing ‖ weye. in ensaumple ⁄ trouþe in promissioun ⁄ & lijf in mede ⁄ And to þis entent Crist[2] lickned manis soule ꞉ to a womman wiþ childe ⁄ For a womman whanne sche traueiliþ ꞉ sche haþ strong peynes ⁄ but whanne þer
30 is a man born in to þe world ꞉ sche haþ no mynde of hir peyne. for ioye of þis childe ‖ Þus wandriþ holi chirche in erþe ꞉ in preiers. fastingis. & in wakingis ⁄ in abstinence. tribulaciouns. & in angwische ⁄ in persecutiouns. in miche nede. & in prisouns ⁄ in boondis. in coolde. & in greet heuynes ⁄ in þrist. in hounger. &
35 in blamyngis ⁄ in reprouyngis. in sclaundris. & in pacience ⁄ in longabiding. in symplenes. and in weeping ⁄ in forȝuyng. in soburnes. & in chastite ⁄ in spedines. in largenes. and in charite ‖

---

[1] Vulg. 1 Cor. iii. 17.   [2] MS. Cristis.

Fol. 24 b Þise ben groonyngis of mannes | soule ; þat longiþ in loue. aftir Crist hir spouse til sche haue brouȝt hir silf a childe of God ; in to blisse wiþouten ende /   And þanne for greetnesse of Goddis rewarde ; þe more sche suffrid. þe more is hir ioye. for so seiþ seint Poul. Ro. viii⁰. 'Non sunt condigne passiones huius tem- 5 poris ad futuram gloriam que reuelabitur in nobis'¹ ‖ Þe passiouns of þis tyme. þat we suffren in þis deedli lijf. ben as noo passiouns. in comparisoun to þe glorie þat is to come. þat schal be schewid in vs /² for þanne we schal be dowid ; wiþ foure dowers in oure bodi / of þe whiche spekiþ seint Poul. I. Cor. xv⁰. 'Seminatur in 10 corrupcione ; surget in incorrupcione / seminatur in ignobilitate ; surget in gloria / seminatur in infirmitate ; surget in virtute / seminatur corpus animale ; surget corpus spirituale'³ ‖ Þat bodi þat is sowen in corrupcioun ; schal rise wiþouten corrupcioun / in þis chosen chirche ; at þe dai of doome / and þis dowery is clepid 15

and its reward in Heaven.

The heavenly endowments of the body:

Fol. 25 a inmortalite ; or vndeedlines /   Þat bodi þat is sowen vn-|-worþi ; schal rise in glorie / & þis dowery is clepid ; clerte / þat bodi þat is sowen in infirmite or in vnstablenes ; schal rise in vertu / & þis is clepid agilite ; or swiftnes /   Þat bodi þat is sowen beestial ; schal rise spiritual / & þis dowery is clepid sotilte /   But þer ben 20 oþir foure doweris ; of substancial mede / wiþ þe whiche we schal be dowid ; in oure soule ‖   Þe firste doweri is impassibilite / þe secounde dowery is tuicioun ‖   þe þridde perpetual charite / and þe fourþe is fruycioun ‖ or ellis þus in more pleyn speche ‖ Þe firste is knowing ; wiþouten errour ‖ þe secounde mynde ; wiþouten for- 25 ȝeting ‖ þe þridde wille ; wiþouten aȝenseiyng ‖   And þe fourþe fruycioun. or vse of þe godhed ; & loue of God euerlasting ‖ O. a woundirful ioye is þis. where þe soule schal be fedde / wiþ þe siȝt of þe godhed / cladde in þe liȝt of þe godhed /   And euere occupied in þe worschip of þe godhed /   And certis þis is ioye ; 30 wiþouten wrecchidnes / þis is rest ; wiþouten ony chargeouse bisines ‖ þis is mirþe. wiþouten heuynes ‖ þis is swerte endles ;

Immortality,
Glory,
Swiftness,
Subtlety.
Those of the soul:
Impassibility,
Intuition.
Charity,
Fruition.

The joys of Heaven.

Fol. 25 b of al | discorde loþles ‖   Þis is counfort in gladnes ; of ony maner þouȝt or purviaunce carles ‖   Þis witnesiþ þe prophet Isaie. lxiiii⁰.⁴

¹ Vulg. Rom. viii. 18.
² W. V. 'The passions of this tyme ben not euene worthi to the glorie to comynge, that schal be schewid in us.' 1388, 'The passiouns of this time ben not worthi to the glorie to comynge, that schal be schewid in us.'
³ Vulg. 1 Cor. xv. 42-4.
⁴ Vulg. Isaias lxiv. 4 'A saeculo non audierunt, neque auribus per-

Capitulum .VI.

& seint Poul in his epistile. I. Cor. ii⁰. 'Oculus non vidit nec auris audiuit nec in cor hominis ascendit que preparauit deus hijs qui diligunt illum vel diligentibus illum'¹ ‖ Bodili iȝe haþ neuir sen. neiþir eere haþ hard. neiþir it stiȝed in mannes hert. þoo þingis
5 þat God haþ ordeyned to hem þat louen him² ‖ Lord who schulde not remewen hise feble wittis. to þenk on þat amiable quere. þat The choir of Heaven. preisiþ in heuene þe goodnes of þis inserchable godhed ꞉' Fadir & Sone & Holigost ‖ To bigynne at Mary Cristis modir quene of heuene. ladi of erþe. & emparise of helle. nyne ordris of aungelis
10 in gloriouse wise ꞉' Þere dwellen in her heuenli sellis / to do þe plesing wille of God ꞉' in heuene & in erþe as her ordir axeþ / And patriarchis oure elder fadris ꞉' þat streiȝtli kept þe biddingis of God ‖ Þere þei resten of al her traueile ꞉' in lond of lijf wiþ double mede ‖ Þere ben prophetis | þat siȝen in spirit ꞉' þe misterie of Fol. 26 a
15 Cristis incarnacioun / þei tolden þe comyng of þis Lord ꞉' in hope abiding mannes saluacioun ‖ Euaungelistis ben þere hiȝe in blisse ꞉' þat walkiden wiþ Crist & writen hise wordis / Apostlis sent in to al þe world ꞉' & Cristis disciplis to preche þe gospel / turnyng Iewis & heþen men to Cristis lawe ꞉' þere sitten in seetis vpon XII.
20 troones / and schullen iugge wiþ Crist in doome ꞉' þe XII. tribis of Israel. Mat. xix⁰. 'Sedebitis super sedes XII. iudicantes XII. tribus Israel'³ ‖ Þere ben martris þat schedden her blood ꞉' & suffrid peynes to large her ioye / & for þei passid bi fire & watir ꞉' þei han founden refresching to her soulis ‖ Also þere ben con-
25 fessours ꞉' þat opened Cristis lawe in þis world / & noþir for vileny ne for schame ꞉' wolde neuere deneye þat blessid lore ‖ Þere ben virgines in bodi & in soule / þat kepten her clennes from lust of fleische / & to þis blisse ben taken boþe lerid & lewid ꞉' þat done her vttirest wille to holde Goddis heestis ‖ No tung mai telle þe
30 soþe as | it is ꞉' but þus we seyn to mende oure deuocioun þat we Fol. 26 b miȝt haue þis blis in mynde ꞉' & take a parte amonge þise seyntis ‖ But seint Ion whanne he was ledde in spirit ꞉' sawe in heuene

ceperunt: oculus non vidit, Deus, absque te, quae praeparasti expectantibus te.'

[1] Vulg. 1 Cor. ii. 9.

[2] W. V. 'Yȝe syȝ not, ne eere herde, nether it stiȝede in to herte of man, what thingis God made redy bifore to hem that louen him.' 1388, 'Iȝe say not, ne eere herde, nether it stiede in to herte of man, what thingis God arrayede to hem that louen him.'

[3] Vulg. Matt. xix. 28.

28 þe chirche of God?

a wonderful token / & for to chere mankynde in erþe? he left it
writen in his book / Ap. xxii⁰. 'mulier amicta sole & luna sub
pedibus eius & corona in capite eius stellarum XIIcim'¹ / Seint Ion

Holy Church likened to 'a woman clad in the sun': i. e. man's soul. sauȝ a womman cladde in þe sunne. & þe moone vndir hir feet /
& a croune vpon hir heed? of þe XII. sterres ||² Þis womman 5
bitokeneþ mannes soule ? as we took witnesse of Crist aforne / &
certis þis was a blissful siȝt ? to se þe chirche in hir wedding cloþis ||

The sun is man's salvation. Þe sunne þat þis chirche is cladde ynne ? is þat moost worschipful
garment oure saluacioun / þat excellent & moost comendable liuere ?
oure redempcioun / þat hooli & moost preciouse cloþ ? oure cristen- 10
dom & oure religioun / for þis Crist bitook vs. whanne we were
baptised ? as seint Poul seiþ. Gala. iii⁰. 'Quicunque baptizati
estis ? christum induistis'³ || Alle ȝe þat ben baptized ? ȝe ben

Fol. 27 a cladde Crist Iesu ⁴ || Þe sunne beriþ licknes of oure | Baptyme ? for
certeyn propurtees þat it haþ / of þe sunne oþir liȝtis borowen 15
her schynnyng ? boþe moone & sterris. in her due course / & ellis
þei ben ouerledde wiþ derknes ? þat may not counfort to niȝt ne
dai || So alle mennes werke in worde or dede ? borowen her liȝt
at Crist Iesu / for he is þe sunne of riȝtwisenes ? as Mardoche
seide in þe spirit of God. viii⁰. 'lux & sol ortus est & humiles⁵ 20
exaltati sunt'⁶ || Liȝt & sunne is vp spronngen ? & meke loweli
ben vphaunsid.⁷ Dauiþ þe prophet declariþ what þis liȝt meneþ ?
& seiþ. Ps. cxi. 'Exortum est in tenebris lumen rectis misericors
& miserator dominus'⁸ || liȝt is vp spronngen to þe riȝtwise ? þat
wandiriþ in derknes of þis lijf / & þis is oure Lord Iesu Crist ? þat 25
of his owene mercy haþe saued hise peple || And þus we reden of

---

¹ Vulg. Apoc. xii. 1.

² W. V. 'And a greet token apperide in heuene; a womman couerid (or clothid) with the sunne, and the moone undir hir feet, and in the heed of hir a coroun of twelve sterris.'

³ Vulg. Gal. iii. 27 'Quicumque enim in Christo baptizati estis, Christum induistis.'

⁴ W. V. 'Forsothe who euere ȝe ben baptysid in Crist, ȝe han clothid Crist.' 1388, 'For alle ȝe that ben baptisid, ben clothid with Crist.'

⁵ MS. humilis.

⁶ Vulg. Esther xi. 11.

⁷ W. V. 'Liȝt and the sunne is sprungen; and meke men ben enhauncid.' 1388, 'The liȝt and the sunne roos; and meke men weren enhaunsid.'

⁸ Vulg. Ps. cxi. 4 'Exortum est in tenebris lumen rectis: misericors, et miserator, et iustus' but cf. Ps. cx 4 'Memoriam fecit mirabilium suorum, misericors et miserator Dominus.'

Capitulum .VI.

trewe bileue ./ in stori of oure blessid ladi ‖ 'Solem iusticie virgo
paritura supremum'[1] / Mari a virgyn. haþ borne þe souereyn
sunne of riȝtwisenes. þat is Goddis sone of heuene Crist Iesu boþe
God and man ‖ What euere þat ony man doiþ þat failiþ þis liȝt ./
5 it lediþ blyndlingis to þe dungun of helle/ | And whanne þis
sunne schynnyþ in hise werkis ./ he growiþ bi heete of Goddis
grace / & ripeþ in vertu as doþ þe corne ./ to be repid in his tyme
to Goddis berne / O. wiþ how miche diligence schulde þis Lord
be serued for þis lyuerey of þis greet prijs? Certis Moises seid.
10 Deut°. iiii°. 'Non est aliqua nacio tam grandis que habeat deos
appropinquantes sibi sicut adest nobis deus noster'[2] ‖ Þer is no
nacioun vndir heuene þat haþ her goddis neiȝyng to hem ./ as oure
God is til vs'[3] / For Crist seiþ. Mat. xxviii°. 'Ecce ego vobiscum
sum omnibus diebus vsque ad consummacionem seculi.'[4] Loo I am
15 wiþ ȝou alle þe daies of ȝoure lijf ./ in to þe ende of þe world[5] ‖
þe moone vndir þis wommanes feet ./ is þis world putt vndir þe
affecciouns of mannes soule / þe whiche ben foure as seint Austin
seiþ ./ in a book þat he made. de spiritu et anima / 'Gaudium
spes. tristicia & dolor / gaudium de presentibus. spes de futuris.
20 tristicia de presentibus. dolor de futuris'[a] ‖ Ioye & hope ./ drede
& sorowe / Ioye of þingis þat ben present ./ & hope of þingis for
to come / drede of þingis þat ben present ./ | & sorow of þingis for
to come ‖ Þise forsoþe foure affecciouns of þe soule ./ ben þe
bigynnyng of alle vicis & vertues / aftir þei ben rulid þoruȝ
25 mannes powere ./ to good or to yuel. as her eend declareþ ‖ Wherfore. whanne loue & hate ben orderid prudentli. modiratli. strongli.
& iustli ./ þanne þei risen in to vertues / þat is to seie. in to
prudence. riȝtwisenes. temperaunce or mesure. & goostli strengþe ‖

The moon is the world.

---

[1] MS. suppremium.

[2] Vulg. Deut. iv. 7 'Nec est alia natio . . . sicut Deus noster adest.'

[3] W. V. 'Ne there is other nation so greet, that hath goddis neiȝynge to hem, as oure God is nyȝ to alle oure holi preiers.' 1388, 'Noon other nacioun is so greet, that hath goddis neiȝynge to it silf, as oure God is redi to alle oure bisechyngis.'

[4] Vulg. Matt. xxviii. 20.

[5] W. V. 'Lo! I am with ȝou in alle dayes, til the endyng of the world.' 1388, 'Lo! I am with ȝou in alle daies, in to the ende of the world.'

---

[a] Augustinus, *De Spiritu et Anima*, Lib. I, cap. iv (Migne, tom. 40, col. 782).

And if þise affectuousli & vertuousli. be disposid in mannes soule. bi þe hate of þe world & of him silf. he profitiþ in to þe loue of God & of his neiȝbore / And bi þe dispising of temporal & passinge þingis ꝫ he encresiþ & growiþ in to þe desire of euerlasting & heuenli þingis ‖ Þe world is lickned to þe moone ꝫ þat is to seie. vanisching or defauȝt / for in peyne of Adames syne ꝫ in þis world we suffre defauȝt / but þe sunne of Cristis gospel ꝫ turneþ worldis goodis to oure mede / for þe wit of Crist is so clere liȝt ꝫ þat in hise wordis þer may no man erre / he takiþ þe persoone of pore nedi ꝫ & spekiþ in poore men as in him silf. Mat. xxv⁰. 'Venite benedicti patris mei. percipite & pos-|-sidete paratum vobis regnum a constitucione mundi / Esuriui enim & dedistis michi manducare &c.'[1] ‖ Cum ȝe blessid of my fadir. take ye. & haue ȝe in possessioun ꝫ a rewme mad redi to ȝou. fro þe bigynnyng of þe world / Forsoþe I haue hungrid. & ȝe han ȝouun me to eet[2] ‖ Þis is not þe glotun & þe wastur. neiþir þis is not he. þat hiȝdeþ hise owene goodis ꝫ & greedili gadriþ oþir mennes ‖ I haue þristid.

I & ȝe haue ȝouun me to drink / Firste he seiþ. I haue ꝫ to teche
II þat þe pore nedi schulde swe him in lyuyng / Þe secounde tyme he seiþ. I hungrid ꝫ to exclude excesse & drounklewnesse ‖
III I haue ben housles ꝫ & ȝe han herborowid me /[3] þis is not þoo þat haue greete housing of her owene ꝫ wiþ miche wast and
IV costiouse bilding ‖ I haue be nakid ꝫ & ȝe haue clad me[4] / þis is not þos. þat weren wide and siȝde cloþis ꝫ & swymmen
V in cloþis of greete prijs ‖ I was sijk. & ȝe visitid me / þis is
VI not he ꝫ þat haþ no nede to þi visitacioun ‖ I was in prisoun ꝫ & ȝe camen to me / to teche þee þat þe vngilti man ꝫ schulde be holpen out of prisoun / & suffre | þe gilti man wel to be punyschid ꝫ in mending of his trespas ‖ Þus is þis womman treweli tauȝt. bi þe liȝt of Cristis gospel / to wynne hir mede in þis world ꝫ þat is putt vndir hir feet ‖

---

[1] Vulg. Matt. xxv. 34, 35 'Venite, benedicti patris mei, possidete,' etc.

[2] W. V. 'Come ȝee, the blesid of my fadir, welde ȝe (or take ȝee in possessioun) the kyngdam maad redy to ȝou fro the bygynnynge (or makynge) of the world. Forsothe I was hungry, and ȝe ȝaven to me for to ete ' 1388, 'Come ȝe, the blesid of my fadir, take ȝe in possessioun the kyngdoom maad redi to ȝou fro the makyng of the world. For I hungride, and ȝe ȝauen me to ete.'

[3] W. V. 'I was herberlesse, and ȝee gederiden (or herberden) me.' 1388, 'I was herboreles, and ȝe herboriden me.'

[4] W. V. 'I was nakid, and ȝee beliden me.'

Capitulum .VI.

Þe crowne vpon þis wommannes heed is stedfast bileue ꞉ vpon The twelve stars of the crown are the articles of the Creed.
þe principal vertu of mannes soule ‖ Þe .XII. sterres þat schynnen
in þis crowne ꞉ ben .XII. articlis of þe comune crede ‖

   Þe firste article is þis ꞉ I bileue in to God fadir almiȝti maker   I
5 of heuene & of erþe ‖ Þe secounde is þis ꞉ And in to Iesu Crist   II
his oonli son oure Lord ‖ Þe þridde is þis ꞉ whiche was conseyued .III
of þe Holi Goost. born of þe virgyn Mari ‖ Þe fourþe is þis ꞉ he   IV
suffrid vndir Pilat of Pounce. don vpon þe cros. deed & biried ‖
Þe fifþe is þis ꞉ he went doun to hellis ꞉ þe þridde dai he roos fro   V
10 deeþ ‖ Þe sixte is þis ꞉ he stiȝed vnto heuenes he sittiþ on þe riȝt   VI
half of God þe fadir almiȝti ‖ Þe seuenþe is þis ꞉ From þenns he   VII
is to come to deeme þe quik & þe deed ‖ Þe eiȝtiþe is þis ꞉ I bileue   VIII
in to þe Holi Gost ‖ Þe nynþe is þis ꞉ al holi chirche þe comunyng   IX
of seintis ‖ | Þe tenþe is þis ꞉ Forȝyuenesse of synnes ‖ Þe eleuenþe Fol. 29 b
15 is þis ꞉ vprising of fleische ‖ Þe XII. is þis ꞉ and euerlasting[1] lijf   X
amen ‖   XI
  XII

   Þus schal þat soule be araied ꞉ þat is chosen to be Cristis spouse / Holy Church likened to a woman with children begotten in Christ.
& worþili is holi chirche ꞉ lickned to a womman / for sche beriþ
boþe sones & douȝtris ꞉ of hir wombe ꞉ but not wiþouten þe helpe
20 of mannes seed / & so oure modir holi chirch beriþ in hir wombe.
soulis to be born to þe blisse ꞉ but neuere wiþouten þe helpe & þe
grace of oure Lord Iesu Crist. as þe gospel witnessiþ. Ion. xv⁰.
'Sine me nichil potestis facere'[2] / wiþouten me seiþ Crist ꞉ ȝe mai
no þing do / þat is to seie. medfulli or þank-worþi ‖ Here summe The authority of the Word is above that of the Church;
25 obiectun þat þe gospel is not of autorite ꞉ but in as miche as þe
chirche haþ autorised it & cannonisid it / for þei sein þat no man
knowiþ suche wordis to be þe gospel ꞉ but as þe chirche haþ deter-
myned in her determynacioun ‖ Þis conclucioun semeþ to smak
heresie. bi þe witnesse of seint Austin ꞉ seiyng on þis wise /
30 'Heresis | est dogma falsum sacre scripture contrarium pertinaciter Fol. 30 a
defensatum maxime causa honoris & temporalis comodi' ‖ Heresie
is a false teching contrarie to holi writ. fool-hardili defendid ꞉
moost bicause of worschip & worldli wynnyng ꞉ and siþen alle þise
ben founden. in þe forseid obieccioun ꞉ it is ful suspect of heresie /
35 for it is writen fro þe bigynnyng. Ge. ii⁰. þat God ordeyned man ꞉
to heed & lord ouir þe womman / & aȝenward þe womman to be
vndirloute & suget ꞉ vnto þis man ‖ But Poul seiþ. Eph. v⁰.

---

[1] MS. everlast.
[2] Vulg. Joh. xv. 5.

Þe chirche of God?

'Hoc magnum dico sacramentum in christo & in ecclesia'[1] ‖ Þis greet sacrament of kniȝtting togidir a man & his wijf? bitokeneþ þe knitting togidir of Crist & his chirche ‖ Schal not þanne mannes soule vndirloute to Crist in worde & dede in þis spiritual mariage? more perfiȝtlier þan þis womman can or mai in þe sacrament of fleische? Seint Iames distrieþ þise obiecciouns? & seiþ. Iac. i⁰. 'voluntarie enim genuit nos verbo veritatis vt simus inicium aliquod creature eius'[2] ‖ God haþ wilfulli & of his owene free wille gotun us þoruȝ þe worde of | trouþe? þat we mai be summe bigynnyng of his creature[3] / & þis creature is oo passing creature holi chirche? þat was chosen in þe tyme of grace. bi þe watir of clensing. bi Cristis blood of aȝen-biyng? & bi vertu of þe Hooli Goost halowyng ‖ Were it not þanne aȝens resoun & open heresie. to maynten þat þe worde of God. þat haþ gotun þis creature holi chirche? schulde not be of autorite. wiþouten auto-rysing of þis creature holi chirche? ‖ Wherefore þis conclucioun approued. we graunten of bileue. þat þe chirche is vndirloutid to Crist & his gospel? on foure maners ‖ Firste as þe moone to þe sunne? of whom it is liȝtned. Cant. vi⁰. 'Pulcra vt luna'[4] ‖ þat is to seie. þe chirche is faire? as þe moone / Þe secounde tyme as þe erþe to þe firmament? of whom it is mad plenteuouse or watrid. Is. lv⁰. 'Quomodo ymber & nix desendit de celo & illuc vltra non reuertitur. sed inebriat terram &c.'[5] ‖ As dew comeþ doun from þe firmament. & turneþ not þider aȝen. but watriþ þe erþe & makiþ it plen-|-teuouse of fruytis? so þe word of God norischeþ holichirche. & makiþ it to bring forþe good vertues[6] ‖ Þe þridde tyme as þe fleische to þe spirit? of whom it is quickned. Ion. vi⁰.

(marginal notes: since the Church is begotten of the Word; and is subject to it in four manners. I, II, III)

---

[1] Vulg. Eph. v. 32 'Sacramentum hoc magnum est, ego autem dico in Christo et in Ecclesia.' [2] Vulg. Jac. i. 18.

[3] W. V. 'Forsothe wilfully he gendride us with the word of treuthe, that we be sum bigynnyng of the creature of him.' 1388, 'For wilfulli he bigat us bi the word of treuthe, that we be a bigynnyng of his creature.'

[4] Vulg. Cant. vi. 10.   [5] Vulg. Isaias lv. 10.

[6] W. V. 'And what maner cometh doun weder and snoȝ fro heuene, and thider no mor is turned aȝeen, but drunkneth the erthe, and beeldeth in to it and to burioune maketh it, and ȝyueth sed to the sowere, and bred to the etere, so shal be my wrd, that shal gon out of my mouth.' 1388, 'And as reyn and snow cometh doun fro heuene, and turneth no more aȝen thidur, but it fillith the erthe, and bischedith it, and makith it to buriowne, and ȝyueth seed to hym that sowith, and breed to him that etith, so schal be my word, that schal go out of my mouth.'

Capitulum .VI.

'Spiritus est qui viuificat'[1] ‖ It is þe spirit þat quickneþ ‖ þe IV fourþe tyme. as þe bodi is to þe heed of whom it is gouerned. Eph. i⁰. 'Ipsum dedit caput[2] ecclesie'[3] ‖ God þe fadir haþ made his son Crist ꞉ heed cf þe chirche ⸳[4] Coll. i⁰. 'Christus est caput[2]
5 corporis ecclesie'[5] ‖ Crist is heed of þe bodi of þe chirche ‖ And euery chosen man & womman ꞉ is clepid a sone or a douȝtir of þis chirche. but al togidir ben þe ful bodi of þis chirche ⸳ as Poul seiþ. Ro. xii⁰. 'Multi sumus vnum corpus in christo. singuli autem alter alterius membra'[6] ‖ we mani ben oo bodi in Crist ꞉ forsoþe
10 iche of vs ben oþir membris[7] ‖   *All the elect are members of the Church, but differ in function.*

But summe children of þis womman ꞉ ben symple labureris ⸳ & for þat þei parten her trewe traueile ꞉ þerfore þei representen þe good loue of þe Hooli Goost ⸳ And þise dreden þe Lord. & walken in þe weye of hise comaundementis. as þe prophet seiþ. Ps. cxxvii.
15 'Beati omnes | qui timent dominum ꞉ qui ambulant in viis eius ‖ labores manuum[8] tuarum quia manducabis ꞉ beatus es & bene tibi erit.'[9] ‖ Blessed be alle labureris þat dreden þe Lord ꞉ & walken in hise weies ⸳ for þou schalt lyue bi þe labur of þin handis ꞉ þou art blessid & wel schal be to þee ⸳[10] & þis is þe lowest astaat ꞉ þat
20 we clepen comunes ‖   *Some are simple labourers.* Fol. 31 b

Summe of þise womanes children ꞉ taken þe material swerid ⸳ & ben made mynystris ꞉ of Cristis godhed ⸳ hauyng powere & drede ꞉ in to wraþþe & veniaunce of hem þat don yuel ⸳ and preising of hem ꞉ þat don wel ⸳ And so bi þe autorite of seint Ion Baptist in þe   *Some are knights.*

---

[1] Vulg. Joh. vi. 64.

[2] MS. capud.

[3] Vulg. Eph. i. 22 'Ipsum dedit caput supra omnem ecclesiam.'

[4] W. V. '(God) ȝaf him heed upon al the chirche.' 1388, '(God) ȝaf hym to be heed over al the chirche.'

[5] Vulg. Col. i. 18.

[6] Vulg. Rom. xii. 5.

[7] W. V. 'We ben manye oo body in Crist, ech forsothe membris the tother of an other.' 1388, 'We many ben o bodi in Crist, and eche ben membris oon of anothir.'

[8] MS. mauū.

[9] Vulg. Ps. cxxvii. 1, 2.

[10] W. V. 'Blisful alle that dreden the Lord: that gon in his weies. The trauailis of thin hondis for thou shalt ete; blisful thou art, and wel shal be to thee.' 1388, 'Blessid ben alle men that dreden the Lord; that gon in hise weies. For thou schalt ete the travels of thin hondis; thou art blessid, and it schal be wel to thee.'

gospel of Crist. Luc. iii⁰.[1] and of seint Petir I. Pet. ii⁰[2] and of seint Poul. Ro. xiii⁰.[3] and bi þe decre of seint Isodore. XXIII. quest. V. Principes ꞉'[a] it parteyneþ to þe ordir of knyʒthod. to defende Goddis lawe. to maynten[4] good lyuars & to iustifie or soore punysche mysdoars ⸝ And þis is clepid þe secounde astate in hooli chirche ||

<small>Some rise to the high order of priesthood.
Fol. 32 a</small>
But summe children of þis womman. stiʒen in to þe hiʒe ordir of | presthood ꞉' & ben made mynystris of Cristis manhed ⸝ and þise han witt & wisdam. to open to þe peple þe weye of trouþe. & þis astate representiþ. þe secounde persoone in trinite. þat is þe wisdam of þe fadir ꞉' oure Lord Iesu Crist || For þus seiþ seint Austin in de quest. veteris & nove legis. ca⁰. xxxv⁰. & ca⁰. iiii^{xx}xi 'rex est vicarius deitatis. & sacerdos est vicarius christi humanitatis'[b] || knyʒthod representing þe myʒt & þe powere of þe fadir ꞉' is þe viker of þe godhed ⸝ and presthod representing þe wisedam of þe sone ꞉' is þe viker of Cristis manhod || And þise knyʒtis techen til vs ꞉' þe drede of Goddis riʒtwisenes ⸝ þat punyscheþ obstinat synnars ꞉' turnyng from his lawe. in schrewidnes of her hertis ⸝ & prestis techen vs bi weie of office ꞉' þe loue þat God haþ to his peple ꞉' þat forʒyueth hem alle her synnes ꞉' whanne þei comen to him & don verry penaunce ⸝ þanne helpen prestis wiþ sacramentis ꞉' to plese God & wynne his loue ||

<small>The office of priest includes five things.
Fol. 32 b</small>
Poul monestiþ þe prest Thimothie ꞉' & in him alle oþir prestis ⸝ to take good tent to fyue | þingis ꞉' in whiche fulli her office standiþ ⸝ Thimo. iiii⁰. 'Tu vero vigila in omnibus labora ⸝ opus fac euangeliste ⸝ ministerium tuum imple. sobrius esto'[5] ⸝ sicut si diceret vigila orationibus continuis ⸝ labora in omnibus leccioni-

---

[1] Vulg. Luc. iii. 14 'Interrogabant autem eum et milites, dicentes: Quid faciemus et nos? Et ait illis: Neminem concutiatis, neque calumniam faciatis.'

[2] Vulg. 1 Pet. ii. 13, 14 'Subiecti igitur estote omni humanae creaturae propter Deum: sive regi quasi praecellenti: sive ducibus tamquam ab eo missis ad vindictam malefactorum, laudem vero bonorum.'

[3] Vulg. Rom. xiii. 4 'Dei enim minister est: vindex in iram ei qui malum agit.'

[4] MS. maynte.   [5] Vulg. 2 Tim. iv. 5.

---

[a] Gratian, *Decreti* Pars Secunda, causa xxiii, quaest. v, cap. xx (Migne, tom. 187, col. 1223).

[b] Augustinus, *Quaestiones Veteris et Novi Testamenti*, XXXV, XCI (Migne, tom. 35, cols. 2234, 2284).

Capitulum .VI.

bus sacre scripture / opus fac euangeliste. predicando euangelium
vere / ministerium tuum imple. ministrando .VII. sacramentalia
libere. sobrius esto verbo & exemplo' ‖   Awake þou prest in   I
bisi preier ." preiyng for þe peple deuoutli ‖ þe secounde is þis.   II
5 traueile þou prest in þe lessouns of holi writ ." studiyng Goddis
lawe oonli ‖ Þe þridde is þis. do þou þe werk of þe gospel ." III
precheing Goddis word trueli ‖ Þe fourþe is þis. Fulfille þou IV
þi mynysterie ." mynystring þe seuene sacramentis freeli / Þe
fifþe is þis. be þou sobur in worde & dede. doing & suffring   V
10 lastingli ‖

    Vpon þise þre astatis ." standiþ þe chirche þat is apropurid to Holy Church has three states,
God / & bi þe vertu of Cristis incarnacioun ." it growiþ in mede to
cum to blis / as Odo seiþ. þat Crist Iesu tooke fleische & blood ."
in þe maydens wombe / & was borne boþe | God & man ." to anfest Fol. 33 a
15 oure kynde to his godheed / for whanne he took oure manhed ." he
grauntid vs his godhed / & in þis tyme in special manere ." he firste
ʒaue haruest to þis chirche / Aftir þis was Iesu Crist ." baptisid in
watir of Flom Iordan / & temptid þrise of þe fende ." to lerne vs
mekeli suffre temptacioun / & tooke þe deeþ vpon a crose ." bi þe
20 cruel iuggement of þe Iewis / & þanne þe chirche was trouþpliʒt to
Crist ." clepid bi name his faire clene spouse / And as sche hadde
grace bi deuocioun of feiþ ." so haþ sche worþines of þis name ‖ But
whanne þis chirche is brouʒt to heuene ." & restiþ in blisse wiþ
Crist hir spouse / þanne is þis mariage fulli sacrid ." wiþ deyntes of
25 euerlasting delites / Whilis þis lijf duriþ in erþe ." þis chirche is
clepid. militaunt / & whanne it slepiþ in purgatory ." þanne is sche militant, sleeping,
clepid þe chirche slepand / But whanne sche haþ rest of al hir and triumphant.
traueile ." þanne is sche clepid þe chirche triumphaunt | Or ellis Fol. 33 b
þus more pleynli ‖   A trewe soule here in þis lijf ." fiʒtiþ aʒens þe
30 wawis of þe see ‖ to sleke þe suuʒtis of þise feeris enemys ." þe fende.
þe world. & þe wantoune fleische ‖ In purgatori sche clensiþ hir silf ."
from rust and corrupcioun of synne / but in heuene sche holdiþ þe
toure ." & victorie of alle hir enemyes / & haþ wonne þe croune of
lijf ." þat God haþ grauntid to hise louears ‖

What is þe material chirche wiþ hir honourmentis /
36 Capitulum .VIIm.

    The secounde chirche dyuerse from þis ." is comyng togiddir of The second Church is
good & yuel / in a place þat is halowid ." fer from worldi occupa- the Material

Church meeting in any consecrated place. cioun / for þere sacramentis schullen be tretid ./ & Goddis lawe boþe radde & prechid / Of þis chirche spekiþ þe prophet Dauiþ ./ & seiþ. Ps. lxvii. ' In ecclesijs benedicite deo domino '[1] ‖ In chirchis blesse ȝe to þe Lord God[2] ‖ In þis place oure graciouse God ./ heeriþ oure preiers in special manere / & bowiþ his eere to hise seruauntis ./ in 5 forme as he grauntid Salamon. III. Re. ix⁰[3] / II⁰ Paral. vii⁰.

Fol. 34 a ' Oculi quoque mei erunt aperti | & aures mee erecte ad orationem eius qui in loco isto orauerit '[4] / myn iȝen seiþ God schullen be open. & myn eeris schullen be lefte vp ./ to þe preiour of him þat haþ iustli preid in þis place[5] / & þis is clepid a material place ./ for 10 it is made bi mannes crafte / of lyme of tymbre & of stoon ./ wiþ oþir necessarijs þat longen þerto /

This Church is hallowed by man, but does not hallow man. For mannes profite þis place is made ./ but not so man for þe place / as Crist markiþ in his gospel ./ for man schulde not be bigilid. Mat. xii⁰. Mar. ii⁰. Luk. vi⁰. ' sabbatum propter hominem 15 factum est & non homo propter sabbatum '[6] ‖ Þe sabot is made for þe man ./ & not þe man for þe sabot / Man bi vertu of Goddis word halowiþ þis place ./ but þis place mai not halowe man. but if man be firste in cause / as Ierom seiþ. ' locus non sanctificat hominem ./ sed homo locum '[a] ‖ Þe place halowiþ not þe man ./ but þe man halowiþ 20 þe place / Alas what woodnes is þis ./ to boost of hooli placis / & we oure silf to be ./ suche viciouse foolis ‖ Lucifer was in heuene ./ &

Fol. 34 b þat is moost hooli place / but for his synne | he fel to helle ./ þe place myȝt not holde him / Adam was in paradise ./ þe moost miriest place / & for his synne he was dryuen out ./ þe place miȝt 25 not defende him ‖ Þou þat art neiþir in heuene ne in paradise ./ but in þis wrecchid world / where wenest þou to fynde a place to

---

[1] Vulg. Ps. lxvii. 27.

[2] W. V. ' In chirchis blissith to God.' 1388, ' In chirchis blesse ȝe God.'

[3] Vulg. 3 Reg. ix. 3 ' Sanctificavi domum hanc, quam aedificasti, ut ponerem nomen meum ibi in sempiternum, et erunt oculi mei et cor meum ibi cunctis diebus.'

[4] Vulg. 2 Par. vii. 15.

[5] W. V. ' Also myn eeȝen schul ben opened, and my eeris rerid up to the horisoun of hym, that in this place schal preie.' 1388, ' Myn iȝen schulen be openyd, & myn eeren schulen be reisid to the preiere of hym, that preieth in this place.'

[6] Vulg. Matt. xii. 1-8, Marc. ii. 27, Luc. vi. 1-5.

---

[a] S. Ioan. Chrysostomus, *Hom. XLIII*, c. 23.

Capitulum .VII.

halowe þee ·' þat leuest not þi synne? be þou siker as God is in
heuene ·' þat it wole not be / for God is in no place faire serued ·'
but þere as his lawe is faire kept of þe peple ‖ Seint Ambrose seiþ. *Nota*
Adam þat was þe more worþi. was made wiþouten paradise. in þe
5 vnworþier place / Eve þat was lesse worþi ·' was made wiþynne
paradise in þe worþier place ᵃ ‖

Miche peple demen it a medeful werke ·' to iape mennes iȝen wiþ *The curious adornment*
curiouse bilding / & manye veyn staring siȝtis in her chirchis ·' but *of churches forbidden by*
Ierom forbediþ þis þing to be don / & dampneþ it vttirli for greete *the Fathers.*
10 synne ·' now in þis tyme of Cristis gospel. Ieromus xii°. quest. ii°.
' Multi edificant parietes & columpnas ecclesie subtrahunt marmora
nitent auro | splendent laquearia gemmis alteria distinguntur & *Fol. 35 a*
ministrorum christi nulla est eleccio . neque enim michi aliquis
opponat dicens in iudea templum mensas lucernas thuribula¹ patellas
15 ciphos mortariala &c ex auro fabricata tum hec probantur a domino
quum sacerdotes hostias immolabant & sanguis pecudum erat
remissio peccatorum quamquam hec omnia precesserint in figuram
scripta sunt autem propter nos in quos fines seculorum deuenerunt /
nunc vero cum paupertatem domus sue pauper dominus dedicauit /
20 portemus crucem. & diuicias lutum putemus ' ᵇ / Super quo Willumis
de Sancto Amore sic ait ' huiusmodi homines edificia taliter fabri-
cantes / videntur² conuertere panes in lapides . videlicet panes
pauperum in congeries lapidum & ideo videntur diabolo esse crude-
liores. qui petiit lapides in panes conuerti ' ‖ hec ille / Manye bilden *Nota bene*
25 wowis & pilars of þe chirche . þei vndirputten schynyng marbel
stoones. þe beemes glistiren al in gold . þe auters ben dyuerseli
araied wiþ preciouse stoones . but of þe mynystris | of God þer is *Fol. 35 b*
no choise / no riche man leie to me þe temple in Iurie. boordis.
lanterns. sencers. pannes. cuppis. mortars. & suche oþir made of
30 gold / for þanne þise þingis ·' weren proued of þe Lord / whanne
prestis offriden oostis & blood of beestis was remyssioun of synnes ·'
þouȝ alle þise þingis wenten aforne in figure. neþeles þei ben
writen for vs. in to whom þe endis of þe worldis be comen ‖ Now

---

¹ MS. thuriblera. ² MS. videnter.

ᵃ Ambrosius, *Liber de Paradiso*, C. 4; Gratian, *Decreti* Pars Prima, dist. xl, c. ix (Migne, tom. 187, col. 216).
ᵇ S. Hieronymus, *Ad Nepotianum de vita clericorum*; Gratian, *Decreti* Pars Secunda, c. xii, q. 2, c. 71 (Migne, tom. 187, col. 926).

þe chirche material ·/

forsoþe Crist oure pore Lord ·/ haþ halowid þe hous or þe chirche of oure pouerte / Bere we þe cros of Crist ·/ & richesse acounte we as cley. Vpon þis seiþ William de Seint Amor / 'suche men semen to turne ·/ þe breed of pore men in to stoones / & in þis þei ben more cruelar þan þe deuel ·/ þat axid stoones to be turned in to bred ' / 5 To þis acordiþ seint Bernard & seiþ / 'O. vanitas vanitatum & non vanior quam insanior ·/ fulget ecclesia in parietibus & eget in pauperibus. suos lapides. auro induit ·/ & suos filios nudos deserit / *Nota bene* de sumptibus egenorum seruitur oculis diuitum ' / Hec Bernardus *Fol. 36 a* in apolo a / O. vanite | among alle vanites. & no more vanite ·/ 10 þan as miche woden drem / þe chirche schynneþ in wowis ·/ & sche nediþ in þe pore / sche wlappiþ hir stoones in gold ·/ & hir owene sones sche forsakiþ nakid / of þe spensis of nedi is mad a veyn seruise ·/ to riche mennes iȝen ‖

The new orders especially to blame for such adornment. But oure newe feyned sectis ·/ in þis ben moost to blame / þat 15 maken greet bildingis ·/ þere leest nede were. as mounkis. chanouns. & freris / for peple schulde drawe to parische chirchis ·/ & here her seruice þere / as Goddis lawe haþ lymytid ·/ & ellis þei ben to blame / Lord! what meneþ þise waast placis ·/ of þise hidde ypocritis / but to telle men bi her synagogis ·/ where Satanas seet is ? Þere lurken 20 togiddir ·/ manye raueisching wolues / þat spoilen þe peple ·/ wiþ many fals signes ‖ . ‖

Four reasons of holy writ against the excessive adornment of churches. Foure resouns of holi writ ·/ declarid of doctours / schal teche ȝou of þis greet fauȝt ·/ if þat ȝe wil amende / But here me drediþ as Poul seiþ. II° Cor. iiii°.[1] / þat þe god of þis world ·/ þat is clepid 25 *Fol. 36 b* mammon / haþ cast his poudir a-|-fore ȝoure iȝen ·/ & blent ȝoure goostli siȝt / þat ȝe mai not knowe þe gospel ·/ to þe trewe vndirstanding / & þat in peyne of ȝoure greet synne ·/ til þis sentence be fulfillid. Eccⁱ. xiiii°. 'Omne opus corruptible in fine deficiet / & qui fecit illud peribit cum illo '[2] / Iche corruptible werke. or 30 iche werke þat is rotun in þe roote ·/ schal faile in þe ende / & he

---

[1] Vulg. 2 Cor. iv. 4 'In quibus Deus huius saeculi excaecavit mentes infidelium, ut non fulgeat illis illuminatio Evangelii gloriae Christi, qui est imago Dei.'

[2] Vulg. Ecclesiasticus xiv. 20 'Omne opus corruptibile in fine deficiet: et qui operatur illud, ibit cum illo.'

---

[a] St. Bernardus Claravallensis, *Apologia ad Guillelmum S. Theoderici Abbatem*, cap. xii (*Divi Bernardi Opera Omnia*, ed. 1552, p. 1649).

Capitulum .VII.

þat is foundir of suche vngroundid werk ;' schal faile & worþe to
nouȝt þerwiþ. in þe last daies¹ ‖ God plauntid neuere þise newe
sectis ;' in neiþir of hise lawis / neiþir aproued suche manere of
lijf ;' for Crist in his lyuyng / pullid hem vp bi þe rootis ;' þat
5 weren in hise daies / as Essees. Saduceis. & Pharises ;' & dampned
her ordinaunce / & seide whanne þei grewe aȝen ;' in mounkis.
chanouns & freris / þat þei schulde be drawen vp ;' to þis þe
gospel grauntiþ. Mat. xvº. 'Omnis plantacio quam non plantauit
pater meus celestis eradicabitur'² ‖ Iche plaunt / seiþ Crist ;' þe
10 whiche my fadir of heuene haþ not plauntid / schal be rent vp
vttirli ;' þe rootis & al³ ‖ For al synful fyndyng ;' | in man or in Fol. 37 a
place / þat is sett amonge þe peple ;' of whiche God is not autor /
þouȝ it growe fast for a tyme ;' it schal be destried /

þe firste resoun þat we schal make ;' is schewid in þis maner / I. These orders
15 þise sectis ben deed from þis world ;' as þei seyn in word / If þis should be
be soþe ;' þanne schal þei haue pore cootis of mornyng / to telle in dead to the world.
dede þis deeþ is trewe ;' in hem & alle her werkis / & flee þe maner
of þis world ;' in suche staring vanites / as seynt Poul techiþ in his
epistile ;' vnto þe Colosencis / Colosen. iiiº. 'Mortui enim estis &
20 vita uestra abscondita est cum christo in deo. & sequentia. mortificate
ergo membra uestra que sunt super terram. fornicacionem. immun-
diciam. lubidinem. concupicienciam malam & auariciam que est
ydolorum seruitus . propter que venit ira dei in filios incredulitatis'⁴ ‖ ȝe þat ben deed ;' fro maneris of þis world / ȝoure lijf is
25 hidde ;' wiþ Crist in God / & þerfore mortifie or make ȝe deed ;'
ȝoure membris þat ben vpon erþe / þe whiche ben fornicacioun of
ȝoure membris ;' & vnclennes of foule desiris / wiþ corrupt lyking |
of fleischeli lustis ;' & foule coueitises of ȝoure herte / & auarise of Fol. 37 b
gredi gedring ;' þat is foule seruyse þat longiþ to ydols / for of þise
30 comeþ þe wraþþe of God ;' vpon þe sones of mysbileue⁵ ‖ If ȝe

---

¹ W. V. 'Eche corruptible werc in the ende shal faile; and he that
wercheth it, shal go with it.'

² Vulg. Matt. xv. 13.

³ W. V. 'Euery plantynge, the which my fadir of heuen hath not plantid,
shal be drawen up by the roote.'

⁴ Vulg. Col. iii. 3, 5, 6 'Mortui enim estis . . . quae est simulacrorum
servitus, propter quae venit ira Dei super filios incredulitatis.'

⁵ W. V. 'Forsoth ȝe ben deede, and ȝoure lyf is hid with Crist in God.
Therefore sle ȝe ȝoure membris, the whiche ben on the erthe, fornycacioun,
unclennesse, leccherie, yvel couetise, and avarice, the which is seruage of

þe chirche material ⁒

sectis forsaken þis lore ⁒ þe wraþþe of God schal soone asaile ȝou ‖

II. Care for externals leads to neglect of spiritual matters.

þe secounde resoun þat we make ⁒ aȝen suche bildinɡ is seid þus / Bisines aboute suche costious bildinɡ ⁒ wiþ manyfold worldli occupacioun / to reparailen hem whanne þei peyren ⁒ & holde hem 5 vp in þis same forme / bringeþ in necligence of goostli [1] maners ⁒ quenching vertues & good þewis / as Bernard seiþ þat holi mounk ⁒ þat swed þe steppis of Iesu Crist / & wolde not vary from þe

Nota bene gospel ⁒ to blame þise sectis þat gon awey ' Video quod non sine magno dolore debet videri. quosdam post egressam christi militiam 10 rursus terrenis cupiditatibus inmergi. secularibus implicari negociis. cum magna cura erigere muros & necligere mores ' [a] / ' Quid tibi prodest habere templa alta & parietes quasi deauratas. vbi desit

Fol. 38 a spiritus / In eis | enim non delectatur deus. sed vult templa uestra id est animas ornari virtutibus & bonis operibus ' / I see seiþ 15 Bernard þat mai not be seyn ⁒ wiþouten greet sorow / summe aftir þei ben entrid ⁒ in to þe knyȝthod of Crist / þat is to forsake þis world ⁒ & wilfulli suffre peynful lyuyng ‖ eft þei drowenen

Be war. hem in erþeli couetise ⁒ & ben ymplied wiþ worldli nedis ⁒ wiþ greet bisiness þei reren vp wowis ⁒ but þei ben necligent in good 20 þewis / What profite is it to haue hiȝe templis ⁒ & her wowis as gilted wiþ gold. where þat þe spirit of God wantiþ ? Forsoþe God haþ no delite ⁒ in suche wrecchid synful sectis / but God wole þat ȝoure templis ⁒ þe whiche ben ȝoure owene soulis / to be honourid wiþ hooli vertues ⁒ & laste to þe ende in good werkis ‖ 25

III. Men are strangers and pilgrims in this life.

þe þridde resoun is myȝti & stronge ⁒ þat springeþ wiþ oþir in Goddis lawe / þat suche as parten hem bi hem silf ⁒ from comune lijf of oþir men / schulden be algatis in þis weye ⁒ as straungers þat ben fer from home / & pilgrimes in her pilgrimage ⁒ as Poul spekiþ

Fol. 38 b vnto þe Hebrewis. Heb. xiii⁰. | ' Non enim habemus hic manentem 30 ciuitatem ⁒ sed futuram inquirimus ' [2] ‖ we han here no dwelling citee or place ⁒ but we seeken þat is to come [3] ‖ Lord how doren

---

*symylacris : for whiche thingis the wraththe of God cam upon the sones of unbileue.' 1388, *mawmetis.

[1] MS coostli.   [2] Vulg. Heb. xiii. 14.

[3] W. V. ' Sothli we han not here a citee dwellinge, but we seken a citee to comynge.'

---

[a] S. Bernardus, *De Beata Virgine*, Homilia quarta (*Divi Bernardi Opera*, ed. 1552, p. 47).

Capitulum .VII.

þise sectis for schame ." wiþ pore mennes goodis & pilage of lordis /
defende þis foule apostasie ." aȝens her God & holi seintis / & telle
þe peple þat is lewid ." bi wordis of ypocrisie / þat þus þei don to
Goddis worschip / & þis is duble wickidnesse ‖ For Bernard seiþ.
5 'In peregrinacione sumus seculi non edificemus nobis domos ad
inhabitandum ." sed habitacula ad deserendum ut pote cito euocandi
& migraturi in patriam celestem / In castris enim sumus in alieno
militamus. in alieno laboramus' ‖ we þat ben in pilgrimage of þis
world ." as abiect & oute caste / we schulden make no waast housis
10 for to dwelle ynne ." as lordis of þe world / but litil cootis to serue
ynne / as soone to leeue hem & go to blisse / we seruen in a straunge
countre ." we traueilen in a straunge countre ‖ Þus seiþ Bernard ‖

Þe fourþe resoun & þe laste ." is ful cleere seide | & on þis   Fol. 39 a
manere / Goddis lawe chargiþ on alwise ." to loue þi neiȝbor as þi   IV. The orders
15 silf / But þis loue is beest made knowen ." bi good ensaumple in   should set the example
worde & dede ‖ In what þing mowen þise sectis profite ." þat   of humility.
reuersen here Cristis rule / & ȝyuen yuel ensaumple to her neiȝbore ."
in pride & false couetise / & schewen hem richest & moost worldli ."
in mete in clooþe in curiouse bilding / But þis forebediþ þe doctour
20 Bernard ." whom we han often aforn rehersid ‖ 'Humiles enim
domus & pauperes aliis refrenant concupiscentiam & mirari debemus
pocius in aspectu celi ." quam tecti / & pocius mirari opera dei
quam hominum' ‖ Forsoþe loweli housis & pore ." refreynen þe
coueitise of oþir / & we owen raþir to meruaile in þe siȝt of heuene ."
25 þan in þe siȝt of bilding of mannes haudiwerk / & miche more
schulde we meruaile ." þe greet werkis of God / þan þe werkis of
deedli men ." þat duren but a while ‖

Alle holi seyntis ." acorden in þis / þat oure chirche material ."   The Material
þat is ordeyned for parischynes. where þei comen togidir / | schal   Church is Fol. 39 b
30 be made wiþ vertuouse meenes ." & in an honest mesure /   But on   ordained for parishioners.
alwise it must be fled ." þat in þis chirche þer schewe no pride /
neiþir outtrage passingli ." ouer þe boundis of pouert / neiþir in
stoon. tymber or leed ." neiþir in glasse. lyme or plaistir / neiþir
in belle laump or liȝt ." neiþir in chalise booke or vestment / neiþir
35 in stepile seetis or peynting ." or oþir hournementis þat longen to
þis chirche / & diligentli þis must be markid ." þat þei bowe to
pouerte / to eschewe veyn glory of þis world ." & glorifie þe cros
of God / But þis word of Cristis cros ." is foli to hem þat schal be
dampned / þat tenten to signes as comune hooris ." & leesen þe

vertu of her soule ‖ Poul comendiþ þe coming of Crist ׃ & þe lowe meking in his manhed ⁄ II⁰ Cor. viii⁰. 'Scitis enim gratiam domini nostri Iesu Christi quoniam propter vos egenus factus est cum esset diues in omnibus vt illius inopia vos diuites essetis'[1] ‖ Forsoþe ȝe owen for to knowe׃ þe grace of oure Lord Iesu Crist ⁄ for whanne 5 he was riche in alle þingis ׃ he was made pore in man for ȝou ⁄ |

Fol. 40 a þat ȝe schulden be riche in goostli þing ׃ þoruȝ þis vertuouse nede

Ostentation in the Material Church is forbidden by Christ Himself in His condemnation of the Scribes and Pharisees.

in Crist[2] ‖ Crist þat blameþ alle viciouse meenes ׃ in þe seruyce of hise peple ⁄ wil not autorise it to him silf ׃ ne defend it in his owene hous ⁄ as seint Mathew seiþ. þe xxiiii⁰. Mar. xiii⁰. & 10 Luk. xxi⁰ [3] ⁄ 'Egressus Iesu de templo ibat & accesserunt ad eum discipuli eius ut ostenderent ei edificaciones templi. ipse autem respondens dixit eis. videtis hec omnia ⁄ amen dico vobis. non relinquitur hic lapis super lapidem. qui non destruatur' ‖ Mathew Mark & seint Luk. acorden togidir in þis oo sentence ⁄ þat whanne 15 Iesu went out of þe temple ׃ þer neiȝed to him hise disciplis ⁄ for to schewe him þe bildyng þerof ׃ & þe curiouse werk in stoones ⁄ wenyng þus to plese her maistir ׃ in seing of so faire a temple ‖ But Crist þat had an ynward siȝt ׃ how þe dwellars þerynne brooken his lawe ⁄ went awey wiþ doulful chere ׃ & tauȝt hise 20 disciplis of þingis to come ⁄ hou þis temple schulde be destried ׃

Fol. 40 b & bad hem bi war þat no man bigile hem ⁄ And soore Crist | wept vpon þis citee ׃ for mannes bilding stood ful strong ⁄ but bodi & soule þat he made ׃ to be his owene dwelling place ⁄ were fallen from keping of his lawe ׃ in to þe sowel of stinking synne ⁄ But 25 scribis & pharisees weren in cause ׃ of þis greet mischef. as Mathew seiþ ⁄ wherefore Crist waried hem as hise greetest enemyes ׃ & alle her folowars to þe worldis ende ⁄ Mat. xxiii⁰. 'Ve vobis scribe & pharisei qui mundatis quod deforis est ׃ intus autem estis pleni rapina & immunditia'[4] ‖ Crist seiþ. woo to ȝou 30

---

[1] Vulg. 2 Cor. viii. 9 'Scitis enim gratiam domini nostri Iesu Christi quoniam propter vos egenus factus est, cum esset dives, ut illius inopia vos divites essetis.'

[2] W. V. 'Sothli ȝe witen the grace of oure Lorde Jhesu Christ, forwhi he was made nedy for us, whanne he was ryche, that ȝe schulden be maad ryche by his myseste (or nedynesse).'

[3] Matt. xxiv. 1, 2; Marc. xiii. 1, 2; Luc. xxi. 5, 6.

[4] Vulg. Matt. xxiii. 25 'Vae vobis Scribae et Pharisaei hypocritae, quia mundatis quod deforis est calicis et paropsidis: intus autem pleni estis rapina et immunditia.'

Capitulum .VII.

scribis & pharises ./ þat clensen clene. al þat is outward / but
certis wiþynne 3e ben replete ./ wiþ miche raveyn & vnclennes [1] /
3e bilden þe toumbes of holi prophetis. & wondirfulli honouren her
graues / but 3e swen 3oure fadris steppis ./ in purswyng of ri3twise
5 blood / & þise sectis don þe same ./ but wiþ more malice. in worde
& dede / O. 3e eddris venymus welpis ./ hou schullen 3e flee þe
iugement of helle / þus seiþ oure Lord Iesu Crist / Wherto make
3e schry-|-nes to seyntis ./ & 3it 3e drawen. hangen & brennen Fol. 41 a
hem þat holden þe weie of Crist ./ and wandren aftir hise holi
10 seyntis / & þou3 þis schewe not in 3oure outwarde dede ./ 3e don þis
slaw3tir in worde & wille / As pharises wiþ bischopis in þe þridde
oure ./ foriuggid oure Lord wiþ her toungis / & aftirward kni3tis
at þe sixte our ./ hangid his bodi vpon þe cros || So þise sectis goon
biforn ./ to smyte þe peple wiþ her tung / & aftir kny3tis of Herowdis
15 hous ./ ben ful redi to make an ende || But þe cause of þis pursute ./
ben two viciouse extremytees / Oone is temperal possessioun ./ þat
wrongfulli standiþ in prestis handis / þe secounde is synful begry
of mi3ti men ./ wiþ hoge bildyng of many waast placis / and nedis
þei must be mendid ./ for charite of God to saue her soulis || For
20 þoo þat maynten þise twoo outstraies ./ ben ful of many foule disclandris / bi teching of þe deuel of helle ./ leest hise retenwe forsake
him / For þanne | we schal fynde pees in erþe ./ whanne we kepen Fol. 41 b
Cristis ordinaunce / & stynt þou not þou3 þou be sclaundrid ./ so
if þou lyue iust lijf ./ to mende þis mys put to þin hond. & þenk
25 on Cristis rewarde. Mar. viii⁰. 'Qui perdiderit animam suam
propter me & euangelium ./ saluam eam faciet' [2] / þat is to seie.
who þat haþ loost his lijf ./ for me & for þe gospel / he schal make
his soule saaf ./ in to þe blisse of heuene [3] ||

Marginal: So the religious orders make shrines to the saints, yet pursue to the death the faithful.

Of good and yuel comyng to þis material chirche.
30 Capitulum .VIIIᵐ. ||

Aftir þis we schal speke ./ of twoo dyuerse partise / þat comen

---

[1] W. V. 'Woo to 3ou, scribis and Pharisees, ipocritis, that maken clene
that thing of the cuppe and plater, that is without forth; forsothe with ynne
3e ben ful of raueyne and unclennesse.' 1388, 'Woo to 3ou, scribis and
Farisees, ypocritis, that clensen the cuppe and the plater with outforth; but
with ynne 3e ben ful of raueyne and unclennesse.'

[2] Vulg. Marc. viii. 35.

[3] W. V. 'He that schal leese his soule (that is, his lyf) for me, and the
gospel, schal make it saf.'

44 Of good & yuel ?

Good and evil live side by side in the Material Church. togidir to þis chirche ? boþe of good & yuel / Firste we taken for oure grounde ? Cristis holi gospei / where he spekiþ in parable ? to hise owene disciplis. Mat. xiii⁰. 'Simile est regnum celorum sagene misse in mare. & ex omni genere piscium congreganti quam cum impleta esset educentes & secus litus sedentes. elegerunt bonos 5 in vasa sua malos autem foras miserunt'¹ || Þe rewme of heuenes is lijk² to a nett ? þat is sent in to þe see / & gadriþ to-gidre in

Fol. 42 a to his cloos ? of alle þe kynde of diuerse fisches / & | whanne þis nett was ful of fisches ? þe fischers drowen it to þe lond / & þei sitting biside þe see-brynk ? chosen þe good in to her vessellis / þe 10 yuel forsoþe þei sentten oute ? & kesten hem aȝen in to þe see³ ||

The parable of the draw-net typifies this second Church on earth. Þis parable þus to mene ? aftir þe witt of Crist Iesu || Þe secounde chirche here in erþe ? is lijke to a nett sent into þe see / for as þe see ebbiþ & flowiþ ? so þis chirche now riseþ & falliþ / to preise & lake as wawis of þe see ? þat risen feel siþes ouir menes 15

The sea represents the Seven Deadly Sins: I. Pride. miȝt. As þe tempestis of þe see ? ben hidouse & perilouse for þe nett / So pride þat wawiþ in þis world ? is ful noiouse to Cristis chirche / of beaute of fortune of goodis of grace ? al dai men bollen in hiȝenes of herte ||

II. Envy. Þe see watir is al bittir ? & ful sowrische in þe tasting / & þis 20 world is ful of envie ? þat is ful bittir for to taast wiþ haate as bittir as þe soot ? þat noon vnneþ can corde wiþ oþir ||

III. Wrath. On þe see comeþ grevouse stormes ? wiþ pirwittis þat greuen soore / & in þis world riseþ wraþþe ? wiþ hanger of herte þat doiþ miche tene / | 25

Fol. 42 b In þe see no grasse mai growe ? neiþir as fer as it mai flowe / *IV. Sloth.* but it wastiþ al þe grounde ? & makiþ it nakid wiþouten fruyte / And in þis world is viciouse slouþe ? þat stroieþ vertues in bodi & soule / & makiþ man foltid in hise wittis ? in euery parte where euere he strecche || 30

V. Covetousness. Þe see euer purchasiþ wiþ hise wawis ? & wynneþ of ground þat he neiȝeþ / & is not paied of þe termes ? þat God haþ sett if

---

¹ Vulg. Matt. xiii. 47.   ² MS. lijf.

³ W. V. 'The kingdom of heuenes is lic to a nette sent in to the see, and of alle kynd of fishis gedrynge; the whiche whan it was fulfillid, men ledynge out, and sittinge bysidis the brynke, cheesiden the good into her vessels, but thei senten out the yuel.' 1388, 'The kyngdom of heuenes is lijk to a nette cast into the see, and that gaderith to gidere of al kynde of fisschis; which whanne it was ful, thei drowen up, and seten bi the brenke, and chesen the goode in to her vessels, but the yuel thei kesten out.'

Capitulum .VIII

it miȝt scape / And in þis world is couetise ./ of hem þat purchasen wiþ wrong / her neiȝboris ground & her catel ./ wiþ sliȝ cautels of mannes lawe ‖ Þus þei wynnyn more & more ./ & wil not wiseli spende her owene / neiþir þank God in dewe forme ./ til þei be
5 cauȝt[1] in þe fendis snare /

Þe see belchiþ miche filþe ./ & castiþ from him foule corrupcioun ./ & þat is ful abhominable ./ & vgli for man to loke vpon / And in þis world is leccherie ./ þat defouleþ bodi & soule / it turneþ þe preciouse temple of God ./ in to- þe logge of griseli delues / Þe
10 peple þat haunten þis wrecchid synne ./ ben mad as beestis wiþouten lawe / & in þis bestial con-|-dicioun ./ þei fiȝten as beestis wiþouten resoun / and þus þei welken & dwynen awey ./ al wlatsumli to God & man ‖   VI. Lechery.   Fol. 43 a

Þe see feel siþis wiþ hir greet tempestis ./ þat sodenli riseþ to
15 greet harm / drowneþ man & also vessells ./ & leesiþ hem or þei come to lond / And in þis world is glotenye ./ þat drowneþ þe wittis of þe peple / til þat þei be vnresonable & kunnen not knowe whanne þei han wrong ‖ Certis excesse of mete & drink ./ sleeþ many moo þan doiþ þe swerid / for in diuerse metis & drynkis ./
20 greedili taken at a mele / is noo heele þe wiseman seiþ ./ but sijknes boþe to bodi & soule ‖   VII. Gluttony.

We must aspiee to flee þise perellis ./ þat ben in þis greuouse see / & drawe þis nett in watir of wisdam ./ bi vertuouse lyuyng to þe hauen of helþe / wiþ cordis þat ben of verry mekenesse ./ wiþ
25 pacience & wiþ longabiding / seiling wiþ loue & charite ./ in hooli spede & good occupacioun / larging oure handis in dedis of mercy ./ þat pore nedi mai be oure bedemen / leeding oure lijf in discret mesure ./ in what þat we | schal take or leeve / cladde in clennes & chastite ./ & þanne schal Crist be al oure counfort / wheþer   Fol. 43 b
30 euere we be bi lond or watir ./ as he haþ grauntid bi his gospel / Mat. xxviiiº. 'Ego ero vobiscum vsque ad consummacionem seculi'[2] ‖ I schal be wiþ ȝou in wel & woo ./ til þis world be brouȝt to an ende[3] ‖

Þe fisches þat swymmen in þis see ./ ben alle þe peple þat lyuen   The fish are all men on earth.

---

[1] MS. cauȝ

[2] Vulg. Matt. xxviii. 20 'Ego vobiscum sum omnibus diebus, usque ad consummationem saeculi.'

[3] W. V. 'I am with ȝou in alle dayes til the endyng of the world.' 1388, 'I am with ȝou in alle daies, in to the ende of the world.'

Of good & yuel ?

The rich prey on the poor, as large fish on small.

in þis world / boþe good & yuel of euery degree ? of iche staate temperel or spirituel / But as þe greet fisches eeten þe smale ? so miȝti riche men of þis world / deuouren þe pore to her bare boon ? eeting þe moselles þat hem beest likeþ / as þe wise man seiþ. Eccⁱ. xiii^o. 'Venacio leonis onager in heremo ? sic pascua diuitum sunt pauperes'[1] || Þe hounting or þe pray of þe lioun ? is þe feelde-asse in wildirnes / so feding of þe riche men ? ben pore nedi men / And whanne þe sunne schynneþ warme ? & in a mylde wedir / þe greet fisches drawen nyȝ þe eire ? & driuen doune þe smale / and if þer come an aile-storm ? or a coolde cesoun / þise greet fisches falle to þe grounde ? & putt abouen þe smale / So whanne riche men sen a vauntage ? or ony worldis wynnyng / þei risen abouen þe cloudis ? in vauntiug of her richessis / & al tolaken þe symple comvnes ? & seyn 'þei mai not paie / wherof don þei entirmetenen hem ?' þei ben but verry beggers' / But whanne þer comeþ a charge to þe countre ? as taxis. loones. or ony oþir payment / þanne þe riche men fallen doun ? & feynen hem silf nedi / & magnifien þe pore man ? þat wonneþ bisiȝde him / & seiþ he is a pryue man ? & hidiþ miche richesse || And þus seiþ almiȝti God ? bi þe prophete Abacuk. i^o. 'Facies homines quasi pisces maris & quasi reptilia non habentia ducem / Et factum est iudicium & contradictio potencior / propter hoc lacerata est lex ? & non peruenit usque ad finem iudicium / quia impius preualet iustum propterea egreditur iudicium peruersum'[2] || Þe prophet seing in his spirit ? how riche men wasten þe pore nedi / he takiþ his vois of greet moone ? & makiþ his moornyng to his God || Lord schalt þou suffre men[3] to be mad ? as fisches þat swymmen in þe see / & as if þei were creping beestis ? þat han no leeder here in erþe / & iugement is mad | þe cruelar ? & aȝenseiyng þe miȝtiar / wherfor þe lawe is al to-torn ? & iugement comeþ to no perfiȝte ende / for now haþ þe wickid wreche ? miȝt to ouercome þe riȝtwise man / þerfore passiþ forþe among mankynde ? weiward iugment þat stroieþ pees[4] ||

---

[1] Vulg. Ecclesiasticus xiii. 23.

[2] Vulg. Hab. i. 14, 3, 4 'Facies homines quasi pisces maris et quasi reptile non habens principem . . . quia impius praevalet adversus iustum, propterea egreditur iudicium perversum.'

[3] MS. me.

[4] W. V. 'And thou shalt make men as fishis of the se, and as crepyngge

Capitulum .VIII.

But for þat fisches ben riȝt quiuer :// & quik. in plente of þe *The fish also betoken true faith.*
watir / & dreden not þe hidouse wawis :// wheþir þei risen hiȝe or
fallen lowe / In þis place þei schal bitoken :// trewe bileue of mannes
herte / & to þis witt spekiþ Crist :// in þe gospel & stiriþ vs to preie /
5 Luk. xi⁰. 'Quis autem ex vobis patrem petit piscem :// numquid
pro pisce serpentem dabit illi ?'¹ Forsoþe seiþ Crist. whiche of
ȝou axe mi fadir a fishe :// wheþir schal he ȝyue him for þis fische
an addre ?² naye pleynly ‖ Crisostum seiþ vpon þis tixt :// þat þis
fische is mannes seiþ / & aftir þis we schulden preie :// to oure fadir
10 þat is in heuene / þat he wole stable vs in trewe bileue :// & in þe
articlis þat longen þerto / for þanne we schal be wel disposid :// in
þe watir of tribulacioun / to do & suffre as plesiþ God :// lyueli
ioieyng | for þis bileue / & þouȝ þer seeme perel of deeþ :// oure *Fol. 45 a*
conscience schal no þing abasche / for socour is kept for alle seiþ-
15 ful :// in þe tresour of Cristis passioun ‖

Þe fischers þat drawen þis forseid nett :// ben aungelis sent aforn *The fishers are the angels at the Day of Judgment.*
þe doome / þat schal whiȝtli do Goddis message :// and bring alle
folkis in a stounde / beforn þe face of God almiȝti :// in to þe vale
of Iosophat. Ioelis. iii⁰. 'Congregabo omnes gentes & deducam
20 eas in vallem Iosephat & disceptabo ibi cum eis super populo meo
& hereditate mea Israel'³ ‖ Þe Lord God seiþ þat he schal gaddir
togidir alle folkis :// & he schal leede hem in to þe vale of Iosophat /
& þere he schal make wiþ hem :// a riȝtwise reckenyng / vpon hise
peple Israel :// þat is his owene heritage / and þanne schal Crist wiþ
25 hise seintis :// departe þe yuel from þe good / Crist chesiþ þe good
of his chirche :// in to þe vessel of blisse / but þe yuel þei casten
out :// in to þe chymney of fire / þere schal be weeping for bittirnesse
of smook :// and gnasting of teeþ for quaking of coold ‖

---

thingis not hauinge duyk, and dom is maad, and aȝeinsayinge more miȝty.
For this thing law is to-broken, and dom cummeth not vnto the eende : for
vnpitous man hath miȝt aȝeinus the iust, therfore weywerd dom shal go out.'
1388, 'And thou schalt make men as fischis of the see, and as crepynge thingis
not hauynge a ledere ; and doom is maad, and aȝenseiyng is more miȝti. For
this law is to-broken, and doom cometh not til to the ende ; for the unpitouse
man hath miȝt aȝens the iust, therfor weiward doom schal go out.'

¹ Vulg. Luc. xi. 11.
² W. V. 'Who of you axith the fadir fysch, wher he schal ȝyue to him
a serpent for the fysch ?'
³ Vulg. Joel iii. 2.

Discrecioun ||

Fol. 45 b

Of | discrecioun to knowe þe good from þe yuel /
Capitulum IXº /

How to distinguish good and evil in the Second Church.

Noon may discryue þise twoo parties ./ verrili iche from oþir /
wandiryng in þis secounde chirche ./ for licknessis þat þei vsen /
and also þei han in comune mani heuenli þingis || For oure Lord 5
haþ in his chirche ./ laburers aboute his vintre / boþe fastars.
preiars ./ & also wakears || Almisdoars ben in þis chirche ./ wiþ
prechours. & redars of lessouns / & singars traueilen here also ./ wiþ
minastrars of sacramentis / wiþ studiars in Goddis lawe ./ & men
þat maken louedaies || And like seruauntis haþ þe fende ./ in þe 10
pridde chirche / but þei don her seruyse ./ in a straunge manere /
Neþeles þei ben hard to knowe ./ þerfore we schal marke hem / hou
wondirfulli þei varien ./ in þise forseide condiciouns /

Fasters in Christ's church.

Certis Fastars in Cristis chirche ./ abstynen hem from lustis /
for to tempir þe coragenes ./ of þe reble fleishe / & kepe her bodi 15
clene chast ./ & suget to her soule / for seint Austin in his book ./

Fol. 46 a techiþ þis loore || 'Caro tua viuit de anima tua. anima | tua de
tuo deo / vnaquamque eorum secundum vitam suam viuunt / tunc
enim caro tua recte secundum animam tuam viuit ./ si anima viuat
secundum deum || Deus est summe bonum. & anima est magnum 20
bonum viuens inter summum bonum & paruum bonum / quia caro
paruum bonum est ./ quia creatura dei est || Anima enim debetrix
non est carni ut secundum carnem viuat. sed e contra mortificanda
est caro. & illi dum consentis mortificas cum ceperit omnino non
delectari mortificasti / Hec est accio nostra. hec est milicia nostra '/ 25
Hec Augustinus de verbis apostoli sermone iiiˣˣ. xviii.ᵃ Þi bodi lyueþ
of þi soule ./ þe soule haþ hir lyuyng of God / þe bodi lyueþ riȝt lijf
aftir þe soule ./ whanne þe soule lyueþ aftir God / God is oure hiȝe
souereyn good ./ & þe soule a greet good / þat lyueþ bitwixe þe
souereyn good ./ & þe bodi a litil good / for it is Goddis creature ./ 30
þerfore it is clepid a litil good / Forsoþe þe soule is not debitrice ./
to folowe þe lijf aftir þe fleische / but euene on contrari wise ./
þe fleische mut nede be mortified / and whanne þou leeuest

Fol. 46 b foule desiris ./ þanne is þi fleische | mortified / þis is þe dede

Nota þat we schal do ./ þis is þe office of oure knyȝthod / þus seiþ 35
Austin ||

Fasters in the devil's church.

But fastars in þe fendis chirche ./ fasten for vngroundid cause /

ᵃ S. Augustinus, *Sermo CLVI*, cc. vi–ix (Migne, tom. 38. col. 853–855).

Capitulum .IX.

summe fasten for ypocrisie ./ & schewen hem ruful to þe peple /
suche Crist blameþ in his gospel ./ & clepiþ hem sorowful ypocritis.
Mat. vi⁰. 'Cum ieiunatis nolite fieri sicut ypocrite tristes'[1] / for
of þe veyn preising of mannes mouþe ./ þei han resceyued al her
5 mede / Summe wiþdrawen from her wombe ./ boþe mete & drink to
spare her purse / and Gregor seiþ þat þis fasting ./ is for her sachel
& not for God / and þis is a carful fasting ./ to peyne oure fleische
& leese oure mede / as þe wise man seiþ. Eccⁱ. vi⁰. ' Est & aliud
malum quod vidi sub sole & quidem frequens apud homines vir cui
10 deus dedit diuicias substantiam et honorem. & nihil deest anime sue
ex omnibus que desiderat . nec tribuet ei potestatem deus ut
comedat ex eo. sed homo extraneus vorabit illud / sed hoc vanitas
& magna miseria ' ‖[2] Þer is also þe wise man seiþ ./ þat he sauȝ
vndir þe sunne / anoþir yuel þat | is ful rijf ./ & comune amonge þe Fol. 47 *a*
15 peple / a man þat God haþ ȝyuen richesse ./ wiþ catel & miche
worschip / & no þing failiþ to his lijf ./ of al þat he desiriþ / but him
wantiþ grace & powere ./ to eete or take his parte þerof / But a man
þat is a straungere ./ schal deuoure it aftir his dai / but þis a sorowful vanite ./ & a greete wrecchidnes [3] ‖ Summe fasten for a medicyn ./
20 for to gete hem bodili heele / neiþir for God ne for þe soule ./ but
for to clense her beaute / seint Ierom blameþ þis fasting ./ & þat on
a ful blessid maner ‖ 'Tunc preclara est apud deum abstinentia nota
corporis ./ cum animus intus ieiunat a viciis / Quid prodest corpus
tenuare inedia ./ cum animus intus tumescit superbia / Hec
25 Ieromus super Amos ‖ Þat is to seie. þanne abstinence of
bodi is clere to God ./ whanne þe mynde fastiþ from vicis / what
profiteþ it to tere þe bodi wiþ hounger ./ whanne mynde wiþynne
swelliþ wiþ pride ‖ what fasting is þis to wiþdrawe lijflod

[1] Vulg. Matt. vi. 16.

[2] Vulg. Eccles. vi. 1, 2 'Est et aliud malum quod vidi sub sole . . . vir cui dedit deus divitias et substantiam et honorem . . . sed homo extraneus vorabit illud. Hoc vanitas et magna miseria est.'

[3] W. V. 'There is and an other euel, that I saȝ under the sunne: and forsothe ofte anentis men. A man to whom God ȝaf richessis, and substaunce, and worshepe; and no thing lacketh to his soule of alle thingis that he desireth; and God ȝyueth not power to hym, that he ete of it, but a straunge man shal deuouren it. This is vanyte, and gret wrecchidnesse.' 1388, 'Also another yuel is, which Y siȝ undur the sunne; and certis it is oft usid anentis men. A man is, to whom God ȝaf richessis and catel, and onour; and no thing faileth to his soule of alle thingis which he desirith; and God ȝyueth not power to him, that he ete therof, but a straunge man shal deuoure it. This is vanyte, and a greet wretchidnesse.'

E

from þe beli ∶ & to be wood in envie or foule hastite ? God seiþ bi
þe prophete Isaie. lviiio. 'Ecce ad lites | & contenciones ieiunatis
etcetera'[1] idem Zaca. viiio.[2] 'Loo whanne ȝe fasten ȝe maken strijf ∶
& debatis among ȝoure silf'[3] ∕ þis is not þe fasting þat I cheese ∶
seiþ þe Lord God ∕ And siþen þe fende neiþer eetiþ ne drinkiþ ∶ 5
neiþir is wlappid in precious cloþis ∕ ȝit he schal be euir in peyne ∶
for him lackiþ charite ‖ þanne is þis an evidence ∶ þat alle suche
recheles fastars ∕ ben membris in þe fendis chirche ∶ in folowyng
her fadir ‖

II. Men who pray in Christ's church.

Preiers þat ben in Cristis chirche ∶ priien wiþ deuocioun ∕ wiþ 10
al þe strengþe of her herte ∶ & her mouþe acording ∕ knocking wiþ
a perfite dede ∶ aftir belpe of God ∕ of mercy & forȝyuenes ∶ of tymes
mys dispendid ∕ & aftir grace & gouerneaunce ∶ for tyme þat is
present ∕ and for good contynuaunce ∶ for tyme þat is to come ∕
Frecheli bringyng to her mynde ∶ þe kyndenes of God ∕ hou he haþ 15
rulid hem in þis lijf ∶ & kept hem fro mischef ∕ as þouȝ he had noo
moo but oon ∶ so he saueþ alle þat loueþ him ∕ þanne þei þenken on
foule synnes ∶ & feele þat þei haue don ∕ boþe witingli & wilfulli |
aȝens Goddis wille ∕ Þei han ben recheles in his seruice ∶ & þat hem
rwiþ soore ∕ and whanne þei þenken on þis world ∶ how it passiþ 20
sodenli & of þe turmentrie in helle ∶ þat dampned soulis schullen
suffre ∕ & on þe blisse þat God haþ ordeyned ∶ for hise trewe
seruauntis ‖ Anoon þei finden a waschinge welle ∶ þat springiþ fro þe
herte ∕ & renneþ forþe from her iȝen ∶ bi manye warme streemes ‖
as Gregor seiþ. 'Diuisiones aquarum ducimus cum pro singulis 25
peccatis lacrimas fundimus' ‖ þanne we fynden rendels of watris ∶
whanne we wepen for al oure synnes ∕ to wasche clene boþe bodi
& soule ∶ & clense hem of corrupcioun ‖

Men who pray in the devil's church.

But preiars in þe fendis chirche ∶ maken miche noise ∕ mumling
wiþ her lippis ∶ þei reche neuir what ∕ so þat men preise fast. her 30
feyned occupacioun ∕ as Crist seiþ in his gospel. Mat. xvo ‖
'Populus hic labijs me honorat ∶ cor autem eorum longe est a me'[4] ‖
Þis peple worschipiþ me wiþ her lippis ∶ but her herte is feer fro
me[5] ∕ Lord ! whanne þi body is in þe chirche | and þi herte in þe

---

[1] Vulg. Isaias lviii. 4.   [2] Vulg. Zech. vii. 5, 6.

[3] W. V. 'Lo! to ples and to striues ȝee fasten.' 1388, 'Lo! ȝe fasten to chidyngis and stryuyngis.'

[4] Vulg. Matt. xv. 8.

[5] W. V. 'This peple honoureth me with lippis, forsothe her herte is fer fro me.'

Capitulum .IX.

world / or cumbrid wiþ vnclene þouȝtis ." & wiþ veyn fantasies / & þi tounge in minstralsie ." or on lewid iangling / & þi wittis oueresett ." wiþ seculere nedis / art þou not þanne wrechidli diuidid in þi silf¹ ? Seint Iame seiþ. iº. 'Non estimet homo ille quod accipiat aliquid
5 a domino'² / suppose not þis veyn man ." þat he mai take ony þing of þe Lord³ / he mai in nowise be herde in preiour ." þat suffreþ his herte to sleepe in synne ‖ And efte God seiþ bi Isaie ." in general wordis to wickid lyuars. iº. 'Cum multiplicaueritis orationes uestras. ego non exaudiam. quia manus uestre plene sanguinum sunt'⁴ ‖
10 whanne ȝe han multiplied ȝoure preiours ." I schal not heere ȝou graciouseli / & þe cause whi is þis ." for ȝoure handis ben ful of blood⁵ / þat is. ȝoure werkis ben ful of synne ." þat parten ȝou & me atwynne / Þus seiþ þe Lord God ‖ But wite ȝe wel ȝe viciouse preestis ." þat gon from Crist in viciouse lyuyng / and wil not swe
15 hise holi steppis ." but | terren him from dai to dai / þerfore ȝoure preiours ben dispisid ." as Crist seiþ þat mai not lie. Mat. xxiiiº. 've vobis scribe & pharisei ypocrite qui comeditis domos viduarum orationes longas orantes. propter hoc accipietis iudicium amplius'⁶ ‖ Woo to ȝou scribis & pharisees ypocritis / þat eeten þe housis of
20 widowis ." bi ȝoure long preiers / for þis þing ȝe schal take ." þe largear iugement⁵ ‖ vpon þis seiþ Crisostom. om. xliiii. 'Inposturas ypocritarum mulieres non possunt facile cognoscere &c'ª / Þe sleiȝtis or þe whilis of ypocritis ." wommen mai not liȝtli knowe / & bicause of her religioun ." þei wile soone bowe to hem / for þat

Fol. 49 a

---

¹ MS. in þi þi silf.

² Vulg. Jac i. 7.

³ W. V. 'Therfore gesse not the ilke man, that he shal take ony thing of the Lord.'

⁴ Vulg. Isaias i. 15 'Cum multiplicaveritis orationem, non exaudiam: manus enim vestrae sanguine plenae sunt.'

⁵ W. V. 'Whan zee shul multeplien orisoun, I shal not heren; forsothe ȝoure hondis ben ful of blod.' 1388, 'Whanne ȝe multiplien preyer, Y schal not here; for whi ȝoure hondis ben ful of blood.'

⁶ Vulg. Matt. xxiii. 14.

⁷ W. V. 'Woo to ȝou, scribis and Pharisees, ypocritis, that eten the housis of widues, in longe preier preyinge: for this thing ȝe schulen take the more dom.' 1388, 'Wo to ȝou, scribis and Farisees, ipocritis, that eten the housis of widowis, and preien bi longe prier; for this thing ȝe schulen take more doom.'

ª S. Ioan. Chrysostomus, *Homilia XLIV* (*Opera*, ed. 1547, tom. ii, col. 1052).

þei be neische ⁏ & wanen aboute as þe wynde ‖ Þis doctour markiþ

I twoo special causis ⁏ whi þei drawen to widowis housis ⁞ Oone is for wommen þat ben weddid ⁏ & vndir þe power of mannes daunger ⁞ dore not ȝyue þise worldli goodis ⁏ wiþouten counseile of her

II housbond ‖ Anoþir. widowes ben ful of pite. to ȝyue whanne þei ben pitousli axid ⁞ | and han no man to werne þis dede ⁏ for her good is at her wille ⁞ & for þis ende þise flatiryng gloosars ⁏ moost rapest haunten widowis housis ⁞ Crist whischeþ hem woo & warneþ oure prestis ⁏ þat þei forsake þis synful manere ⁞ for it is to cursid a dede ⁏ to hide synne vndir peyntid religioun ⁞ & cloþe wickidnes in ypocrisie ⁏ til it þe trowid for verry pite ⁞ & in þe armour of Iesu Crist ⁏ þei don þe fendis werkis of helle ⁞ whanne þei largen her long preiars ⁏ as nettis þat ben spradde abrood ⁞ & wiþ þis craft þei cacchen awey ⁏ þe goodis of þise celi widowis ⁞ Þise widowis we schullen vndirstonde ⁏ boþe for men & for wymmen ⁞ þat wanten wisdam of Iesu Crist ⁏ þe whiche is spouse of mannes soule ⁞ for Iesu Crist no where delitiþ ⁏ but in hem þat louen his lawe ‖

III. Watchers in Christ's church.

Wakars þat ben in Cristis chirche ⁏ waken in vertu & deuoute preiour ⁞ & avoiden al disynes ⁏ for þei wol not be necligent ⁞ But holden waken her ynward iȝe ⁏ þat feiþfulli seeþ þe werkis of God ⁞ & þanne riseþ vp as seint Poul seiþ ⁏ a newe man | formed aftir God ⁞ & serueþ him in þise þre vertues ⁏ riȝtwisenesse. truþe. & hoolynes ⁞ Þis is wakyng to Goddis worschip ⁏ & her owene saluacioun ⁞ & profitiþ to her euene-cristen ⁏ for þus meneþ Poul in his þre wordis ‖ Þis wecche chasiþ so þe fende ⁏ þat he fleeþ from alle such wakars ⁞ & haþ no myȝt for to noye ⁏ bodi ne soule as þe wise man seiþ ⁞ Ecc[i]. xxxi⁰. ' vigila honestatis tabefaciet carnes & cogitatus illius auferet sompnum ‖ Cogitatus prescientie auertit sensum ⁏ & infirmitas grauis sobriam facit animam '[1] ⁞ Þat is to seie. þe holsum wacche of honeste ⁏ schal make þe flesche[2] to melte fro synne ⁞ & bisy þouȝt in þis faire wacche ⁏ schal dryue awey vnleeful dreemes ⁞ Certis þe þouȝt of þe forknowyng ⁏ turneþ awey þe witt from syne ⁞ & a greet infirmyte ⁏ makiþ a sobre soule[3] ‖

---

[1] Vulg. Ecclesiasticus xxxi. 1, 2.

[2] MS. þe þe flesche.

[3] W. V. 'The waking of honeste shal dwyne the flesh; and the thenking of it shal don awei slep. The thenking of bifor kunnyng turneth awei wit; and heuy infirmyte sobre maketh the soule.' 1388, 'Wakyng of oneste schal make fleischis to faile; and thouȝt therof schal take awei sleep. Thouȝt of

Capitulum .IX. 53

But wakars in þe fendis chirche ∴ vsen a foule flescheli wacche / Watchers for euere þei ben sloumbring ∴ whanne ony good dede is don / in the devil's ouercomen wiþ þe deed sleep ∴ | þat bringeþ hem to mischeef / for church. þe wise man seiþ. Prou. vi⁰. 'vsquequo piger dormis? *Quando* Fol. 50 *b*
5 *consurges e sompno tuo? paululum dormies paululum dormitabis paululum conseres manus vt dormias & veniet tibi quasi viator egestas & pauperies quasi vir armatus*'¹ / Þat is to seie. How long schalt þou sleep þou slouȝ man? whanne schalt þou rise from þi sleep? þou schalt nappe a litil while. þou schalt sloumbre a litil
10 while / þou schalt knytt þi hondis togidir ∴ til þou falle in to þe deed sleep / & þanne schal sodenli com to þee ∴ nede as a weyefering man / & pouert schal steele to þee ∴ as an armyed man ² ||
Napping. sloumbring & deed sleep ∴ ben þe fendis officeris / þanne men nappen whanne men consenten ∴ to do þe fendis stering /
15 & whanne þei worchen opunli ∴ þat þe fende desiriþ / in þe siȝt of þe world ∴ þanne þei ben in sloumbring || But whanne þei mayntynen booldili ∴ what euer þei don amys / þanne þei ben in deed sleep ∴ & waken in her | synnes / chaungyng þe nyȝt in to þe Fol. 51 *a* dai ∴ as hooris & þeues / traueiling fro place to place ∴ to reuel &
20 to rouȝt / assaiyng where þat þei may leeue ∴ tookenes of her synne /

Almysdoars in Cristis chirche ∴ releuen in dwe tyme / wiþ þe IV. Almsplente of her catel ∴ hem þat suffren nede / as seint Poul seiþ. doers in II Cor. viii⁰. '*vestra habundancia illorum inopiam supleat*'³ || Þat church. is to seie. looke þat ȝoure habundaunce ∴ fulfille þe nede of oþir ⁴ ||
25 For ȝe þus doing schullen resceyue ∴ þe blessing of God / as þe prophet seiþ. Ps. xl. '*Beatus qui intelligit super egenum & pauperem*'⁵ || Blessid be he þat takiþ hede ∴ on þe nedi &

---

bifore knowyng turneth awey wit: and greuouse siknesse maketh sobre the soule.'

¹ Vulg. Prov. vi. 9–11.
² W. V. 'Hou longe, thou slowe, shalt thou slepe? whanne shalt thou rise fro thi slep? A litil while thou shalt slepe, a litil while thou shalt nappe; a litil while thou shalt leyn togidere thin hondis, that thou slepe. And ther shal come to thee as a weiegoere, nede; and porenesse, as a man armed.' 1388, 'Hou long schalt thou, slow man, slepe? whanne schalt thou rise fro thi slepe? A litil thou schalt slepe, a litil thou schalt nappe; a litil thou schalt ioyne togidere thin hondis, that thou slepe. And nedynesse, as a weigoere, schal come to thee: and pouert as an armed man.'
³ Vulg. 2 Cor. viii. 14.
⁴ W. V. 'ȝoure haboundaunce fulfille the myseste of hem.'
⁵ Vulg. Ps. xl. 1.

pore[1] / vppon þis seiþ Bernard þus ‖ 'Non super cupidum & elatum ⁚
sed super egenum & pauperem illum inquam pauperem qui inuitus
petit & verecondia accipit & accipiens gratias deo reddit.' Hec
Bernardus ad regem Cecilie[a] / þat is to seie. Not vppon þe
coueitouse man & þe proude ⁚ but vpon þe nedi ⁚ & þe poore / him 5
forsoþe pore nedi ⁚ þat axiþ constreyned wiþ nede / & he taking þis

Fol. 51 b almes wiþ scha-|-me ⁚ doþ þankingis to God / & lyueþ poreli þerbi ‖
In foure þingis Goddis seruauntis ⁚ medfulli don her almes ‖

Firste þei seken Goddis wille ⁚ & done it to his worschip ‖ þe
secounde of trewe gooten good ⁚ cleerli in her conscience / þe þridde 10
þat þei knowe her broþir ⁚ lyue a gracioiuse lijf ‖ Þe fourþe þat he
suffriþ nede ⁚ wiþouten ony feynyng ‖ For if ony of þise faile ⁚ þei
leese boþe good & mede ‖

Almsdoers in the devil's church.
But almysdoars in þe fendis chirche ⁚ feeden many wrecchis / as
strong staff-beggers ⁚ & strikars ouere þe lond / & gronars wiþouten 15
cause ⁚ þat neden not her good ‖ ȝhe to mynstrals to iogullers ⁚ &
oþir veyn iapars / þei delen largeli her good ⁚ & clepen it an almes /
But trewe men seyn al amys ⁚ goodis þus dispendid / For it draweþ
hem toward heuene ⁚ as bocket in to welle / And if þei do ony
þing ⁚ þere as nede is / anoon þei seeken ȝeyne glorie ⁚ & leesen al 20

Fol. 52 a her | mede / for seint Ysodir seiþ. 'Dum causa iactancie pauper
pascitur etiam opus misericordie in peccatum conuertitur' ‖ Þat is
to seie. Whanne þe pore man is fedde ⁚ bi cause of veyn glorie /
þanne is þe werke of mercy ⁚ turned in to synne / And Crist seiþ /
'Si oculus tuus fuerit nequam totum corpus tuum tenebrosum erit'[2] / 25
And þin iȝe be weiward ⁚ al þi bodi schal be derke ‖ Þin iȝe is þin
entent ⁚ þat schulde rule þi conscience / & þis bodi is þi werke ⁚ of
entent þat takiþ his liȝt / þanne is þis þus to mene / whanne þin
entent is not wel rulid ⁚ þou getist no mede what euere þou do ‖

V
Preachers in Christ's church.
Prechars þat ben in Cristis chirche ⁚ comen freeli among þe 30
peple / as Crist cam fro þe toour of heuene ⁚ & ȝaue þis charge to
hise disciplis. Mat. x⁰. 'Gratis accepistis gratis date'[3] ‖ Freeli
ȝe han taken ȝoure wisdam ⁚ freeli ȝyueþ it ȝe aȝen ‖ Poule chase

---

[1] W. V. 'Blisful that understart up on the nedi and pore.' 1388, 'Blessid
is he that undurstondith on a nedi man and pore.'

[2] Vulg. Matt. vi. 23.

[3] Vulg. Matt. x. 8.

[a] S. Bernardus, Ep. CCVII, Ad Rogerium Regem Sicilie (D. Bernardi
Opera Omnia, ed. 1552, p. 1400).

Capitulum .IX.

raþir to be deed ./ þan ony man schulde avoide his glorie / for mede | þat miȝt be ȝouun or taken ./ aȝen þe gospel of Iesu Crist. I. Cor. ixº. Fol. 52 b 'Ego nullo horum vsus sum. bonum est mihi magis mori quam ut gloriam meam quis euacuet'[1] || And þise prechours prechen
5 treweli ./ to edifie þe peple in vertu / as Crist comaundid on hooli þursdai ./ to hise disciplis aforn his stiȝyng || Mar. vltimo || 'Euntes in mundum vniuersum predicate euangelium omni creature'[2] hoc est omni homini qui quodammodo est omnis creatura || Þat is to seie. ȝe goyng forþe in to al þe world ./ preche ȝe þe
10 gospel to iche creature / þat is to iche man ./ þat cheueli is iche creature / and þei lyuen vertuousli ./ hem silf aftir her preching / for to strengþe her hooli wordis ./ wiþ þe spirit of lijf / whanne þei ȝyuen a trewe ensaumple ./ in dede aftir her seiyng / & þis is þe teching of Iesu Crist ./ in þe gospel of seint Mathew. Mat. viº.
15 'Sic luceat lux vestra coram hominibus. vt vidiant opera vestra bona & glorificent patrem vestrum qui in celis est[3] || Þat is to seie. looke ȝoure liȝt schyne so ./ aforn men of þis world / þat þei may se ȝoure good werkis ./ & gloriefie | not ȝou / but ȝoure fadir þat is in Fol. 53 a heuene ./ of whom comeþ al ȝoure grace /[4]
20 But prechours in þe fendis chirche ./ prechen vndir colour for to take ȝiftis ./ but Gregor reproueþ hem / Gregor om. xviii / 'Quisquis ideo predicat. vt hic vel laudis vel muneris mercedem accipiat procul dubio eterna remuneracione se priuat'[a] / Who euere preche Gregor seiþ ./ for goodis of þis world / or to make a gadiryng ./ for suche
25 an heuenli office / wiþouten ony doute ./ þei priuen hem silf / of þe mede þat is to come ./ of euerlasting rewarde / & þei prechen cronyclis ./ wiþ poyses & dremyngis / & manye oþir helples talis ./ þat riȝt nouȝt availen || Þei clouten falsehed to þe trouþe ./ wiþ miche vngroundid mater / tariyng þe peple from trewe bileue ./ þat þei
30 may not knowe it / And þise prechours waveren aboute; in many fleischeli lustis. as Iude seiþ. Iude. iiº. 'Hij sunt macule conuiuantes sine timore semetipsos pascentes mirantes personas hominum questus

nota
Preachers in the devil's church.

---

[1] Vulg. 1 Cor. ix. 15.
[2] Vulg. Marc. xvi. 15.
[3] Vulg. Matt. v. 16.
[4] W. V. 'So shynne ȝoure liȝt before men, that thei see ȝoure good werkis, and glorifie ȝoure fadir that is in heuens.'

---

[a] Gregorius Magnus, *XL Homiliae in Evangelia*, Hom. XVII (Migne, tom. 76, col. 1142).

Fol. 53 b | causa'[1] || þise ben spottis in her metis ./ feestyng & feeding
hem silf wiþouten ony drede / worschiping þe persones of men ./ for
þei wolde haue wynyng [2] ||

VI. Readers in Christ's church. Redars in Cristis chirche ./ reeden hooli lessouns / & tenten to
her reding ./ wiþ myndeful deuociouns / as Ierom seiþ. 'Sic lege 5
sanctam scripturam. vt semper memineris ea esse dei verba / qui
non solum legem suam sciri. sed etiam adimpleri iubet. quid enim
prodest scienda didisce ./ & non facere tamquam speculum vite.
habenda est leccio sacre scripture / ut bona meliorentur & mala
corrigantur / Hec Ieromus || So reede þou hooli writ ./ þat euere 10
þou haue mynde / þat þoo wordis þat þou redist ./ ben Goddis
blessid lawe / þat comaundid it ./ not oonli to be radde / but also
þat þe reedars ./ schulde kepe it in her werkis || what profit is it to
rede þingis to be don ./ & not fulfille hem in dede ? as a clene
mirour of lijf ./ þe lessoun of hooli writ is to be had / þat al þat is 15
Fol. 54 a good ./ mai be mad betir / & þat þat is yeuel ./ | may be amendid /
and þise redars reden diligentli ./ þat þat is tretable & opunli in
scripture / wiþouten interrupcioun ./ or ony fonned intermyssioun /
wiþouten corrupting or ouere-hipping ./ of lettir word or sillable /
& þei schal coorde in charite ./ & do alle þingis in ordre || 20

Readers in the devil's church. But redars in þe fendis chirche ./ ianglen her lessouns / as iaies
chatiren in þe cage ./ & wot not what þei menen / striueyng feel
siþis for nouȝt ./ iche aȝens oþir / for rulis of her ordinal ./ & manye
veyne questiouns /. And if þei vndirstande þe lessoun ./ whanne þat
it is radde / or ony part of Goddis lawe ./ whanne it is declarid / 25
soone þei treden it vndir foot ./ & haaten it in her werkis / as Ierom
seiþ þe prophete ./ in witnessing aȝen alle suche. Iere. viii⁰.
'Quomodo dicitis sapientes sumus & lex dei nobiscum est ? vere
mendacium operatus est stilus mendax scribarum confusi sunt
sapientes perteriti & capti sunt verbum enim domini proiecerunt & 30
sapientia nulla est in eis'[3] / How may ȝe seie. forsoþe we ben

---

[1] Vulg. Jud. ii. 12, 16 (A. V. Jude i. 12, 16) 'Hi sunt in epulis suis
maculae convivantes sine timore semetipsos pascentes: ... mirantes personas
quaestus causa.'

[2] W. V. 'Thes ben in her metys filthes (or defoulinges), feestinge togydere,
with outen dreede fedynge hemsilf; wondringe, (or worschipinge) persones,
bi cause of wynnynge.' 1388, 'These ben in her metis, feestynge togidere to
filthe, with out drede fedinge hemsilf, worschipinge persoones, bi cause of
wynnyng.'

[3] Jer. viii. 8 'Quomodo dicitis: Sapientes nos sumus et lex Domini,' etc.

Capitulum .IX.

wijse ? | and þe lawe of þe Lord is among vs ? Certis þe fals poyntel of þe scribis ." haþ wrouȝt open lesyng / & ȝoure wijse men ben confoundid ." afeerde & cauȝt in her owene snare / þei han þrowen abak þe worde of þe Lord ." þer is no wisdam lefte among hem¹ /
5 And eft God seiþ bi Ieremye ." to þise veyn redars / Iere. xlviiiº. /
'Maleditus qui opus dei agit fraudilenter'²/ Cursid be he ." þat doþ þe werk of God fraudilentli³/ þat is to seie. falseli or disceyuabli / and here seiþ Gregor. / 'Solus in dei opere fraudem non facit qui in studio bone accionis inuigilat nec ad corporalis rei premia nec ad
10 laudis verba nec ad humani iudicii gratiam anhelat⁴' ᵃ/ Oonli in Goddis seruice ." þat man doþ no fraude / þat wakiþ ful bisili ." in studie of good dede / & no þer bowiþ to medis ." of bodili þing / neiþir sekiþ þe worde ." of mannis lewid preisyng / neiþir lookiþ aftir fauour ." of foli iugement ||
15 Syngars ben in Cristis chirche ." þat syngen heuenli songis / | and wiþ her swet melodie ." plesen God at fulle / as Poul seiþ in his pistil ." to þe Colosencis / Colo. iiiº. 'verbum christi habitet in vobis habundanter in omni sapientia docentes & commonentes vosmetipsos in psalmis & ympnis & canticis spiritualibus in gratia cantantes in
20 cordibus vestris deo || Omne quodcumque facitis in verbo aut in opere. in nomine domini nostri iesu christi facite. gratias agentes deo & patri per ipsum'⁵/ þat is to seie. Suffre ȝe þe worde of God ." to dwelle plentiuousli among ȝou / in al manere heuenli wisdam ." encresing ȝou in vertu / teching & monesting ȝoure silf ." in psalmes

Fol. 54 b

Fol. 55 a
VII. Singers in Christ's church.

---

¹ W. V. ' Hou sey ȝee, Wise men wee ben, and the lawe of the Lord is with us ? Verely lesing wroȝte the lyende poyntil of the scribis. confoundid ben the wise men, gast and caȝt thei ben. The wrd forsothe of the Lord thei casten aferr, and no wisdam is in hem.' 1388, ' Hou seien ȝe, We ben wise men and the lawe of the Lord is with us ? Verili the fals writyng of scribis wrouȝte leesyng. Wise men, ben schent, ben maad aferd and taken. For thei castiden awei the word of the Lord, and no wisdam is in hem.'

² Vulg. Jer. xlviii. 10 ' Maledictus qui facit opus Domini fraudulenter.'

³ W. V. ' Cursid that doth the werc of God gilendeli.' 1388, ' He is cursid, that doith the werk of God gilefuli.'

⁴ MS. Anelat.

⁵ Vulg. Col. iii. 16, 17 'Verbum Christi habitet ... commonentes vosmetipsos psalmis ... Omne quodcumque facitis in verbo aut in opere, omnia in nomine Domini Iesu Christi, gratias agentes Deo et Patri per ipsum.'

ᵃ Gregorius Magnus, *Moralium* Liber IX, cap. xxxiv. 53 (Migne, tom. 75, col. 889).

& ympnys & goostli songis ⁄ singyng in grace wiþ feruent deuocioun ⁒ in ȝoure hertis to ȝoure God ⁄ and what euer ȝe schal do ⁒ in word or in werk ⁄ do ȝe þat þing perfiȝtli ⁒ in þe name of oure Lord Iesu Crist ⁄ ȝelding þankingis to þe fadir ⁒ bi þat same Iesu Crist [1] ‖ And siþen he is boþe God & Lord ⁒ & kyng of al þis world ⁄ þe prophete Dauiþ counseiliþ vs ⁒ þat we schulde sing wijseli ⁄ for he þat is | occupied ⁒ in heuenli desiris ⁄ þouȝ his tung be stille ⁒ & make no noyse ⁄ he singe a song seynt Austin seiþ ⁒ þat God likeþ beest ‖ 'Qui desiderat & si lingua taceat corde cantat' ⁄ Hec Augustinus [a] ‖ Ananye & Azarie & Mysael also ⁄ soungen blessing to þe Lord ⁒ in suche manere song ⁄ whanne þei weren in Babiloyne ⁒ in þe brennyng furneise. Dan. iii⁰. [2] ‖

Singers in the devil's church. But syngars in þe fendis chirche ⁒ breken curiouse nootis ⁒ & þat is but a puff of wynde ⁒ as seiþ Seint Bernard wijsli ⁄ to plese þe peple wiþ likerouse voice ⁒ & fylle her eeris wiþ veyn dyn ‖ But se what seint Gregor seiþ. acording wiþ seint Bernard ⁄ 'Dum blanda[3] vox queritur ⁒ perfecta vita deseritur' [b] ‖ Þat is to seie. whanne faging & glosing vois is souȝt ⁒ perfijt lijf is forsaken ⁄ & þe peple is ledde in to synne ⁒ as God seiþ bi his prophet Eze. xxxiii⁰. 'sedent coram te populus meus & audiunt sermones tuos & non faciunt eos ⁒ quia in canticum oris sui vertunt illos & auariciam suam sequitur cor eorum ⁄ & es eis quasi carmen musicum quod suaui dulcique sono canitur | & audiunt verba tua & non faciunt ea' [4] ‖ Þat is to seie. Mi peple sitten bifore þee ⁒ & heeren þi wordis ⁄ but þei don not aftir hem ⁒ whanne her bak is turned ⁄ for þe prestis turnen hem ⁒ in song of her mouþe ⁄ & þe herte of þe peple ⁒ folowiþ her prestis auarice ⁄ & it is to hem ⁒ as a song of musik ⁄ þat is soungen myrili ⁒ wiþ a lusti sounde ⁄ & þei heeren

---

[1] W. V. 'The word of Crist dwelle in ȝou plenteuously, in al wysdam, techinge and monestinge ȝou silf in salmes, and ymnes, and spiritual songis, in grace syngynge in ȝoure hertis to the Lord. Al thing, what euere thing ȝe don, in word or in dede, alle thingis in the name of the Lord Jhesu Crist, doynge thankyngis to God the fadir by hym.'

[2] Vulg. Dan. iii. 24–90 (not in A.V.).

[3] MS. bland.

[4] Vulg. Ezech. xxxiii. 31, 32.

---

[a] Augustinus, *Enarratio in Psalmum LXXXVI* i (Migne, tom. 36, col. 1101).

[b] Gratian, *Decreti* Pars Prima, dist. xcii, ch. ii (Migne, tom. 187, col. 430).

Capitulum .IX.

þi sermouns. but þei kepe hem not seiþ þe Lord God [1] / And efte
God seiþ aȝen ⸴ bi þe prophete Amos. v⁰. 'Aufer a me tumultum
carminum tuorum. & cantica lire tue non audiam' [2] ‖ Þat is to seie.
Do þou awey fro me ⸴ þe pride of þi chauntyng / & I schal not also
5 heere ⸴ þe songis of þin harpe [3] ‖ Lord what may þis bimene ⸴ þat
prestis in þe chirchis / ȝyuen hem þus miche to song ⸴ & so litil to
preching & in fewe placis or ellis in noone ⸴ of þe newe testament /
schullen we grounde þis maner of song ⸴ neiþir among oure doctours ‖
but often þei ben chargid to preche. ȝhe vndir greet peyne / &
10 algatis þat þei haue good wille ⸴ to do þat þei may / þat þe peple
were treweli tauȝt ⸴ to lede a sobre lijf / þerfore Gregor in his
decre ⸴ 92. smyteþ hem wiþ a curse / þat bisien hem in þe courte
of Rome ⸴ aboute suche feyned syngyng / wherþoruȝ schulde be
taried ⸴ þe office of preching [a] ‖

15 Mynystrars of sacramentis ⸴ þat ben in Cristis chirch / biþenken
hem ful wittirli ⸴ of þe greet worþines / hou þise sacramentis comen
of Crist ⸴ & of his holi passioun / taken of his blessid bodi ⸴ for
tresour of his chirche / & þei ben salue & medicyn ⸴ for alle þoo
sijke membris / þat wil schewe her greet sooris ⸴ to Goddis prestis
20 of wise discrecioun / & vse þise sacramentis in her kynde ⸴ as seint
Poul techiþ / I.'Cor. v⁰. / 'Pascha nostrum immolatus est christus.
itaque epulemur . Non in fermento malicie & nequicie ⸴ sed in
azimis sinceritatis & veritatis' [4] / Þat is to seie. Crist is offrid
oure pask ⸴ þat norischeþ vs wiþ hise sacramentis / & þerfore make
25 we vs myry ⸴ in þis goostli food / not in angir & in tene ⸴ of malise
& of wickidnes / But in þe faire pure paast ⸴ of clennes & of
trouþe [5] / Þise twoo vertues techen vs ⸴ to clense bodi & soule /
wheþir þat we schal ȝyue or take ⸴ þise seuene sacramentis / Baptem
confermyng & penaunce ⸴ ordir Cristis bodi matrimonye. & þe last

Fol. 56 b

VIII. Administraters of Sacraments in Christ's church.

The Seven Sacraments avail against the Seven Deadly Sins,

Fol. 57 a

---

[1] W. V. 'Mi peple sitten bifore thee, and heeren thi wordis, and don not hem; for thei turnen hem in to a songe of her mouthe, and the hert of hem sueth her auerise; and it is to hem as a songe of musyke, whiche is sungen by soft and sweet soun.'

[2] Vulg. Amos v. 23.

[3] W. V. 'Do awey from me the noyse of thi songis, (or ditees), and Y shal not heere the songis of thin harpe.'

[4] Vulg. 1 Cor. v. 7, 8.

[5] W. V. 'Crist is offrid oure pask. And so ete we, not in old sourdouȝ, nether in sourdouȝ of malice and weywardnesse, but in therf thingis of clennesse and treuthe.'

[a] Gratian, *Decreti* Pars Prima, dist. cii, cap. ii (Migne, tom. 187, col. 430).

60   Discrecioun!

which are   anoyntyng ‖ Þise helpen vs in þis fiȝting chirche ⸵ aȝen seuene
seven devils.
    I   deedli synnes / þat ben seuen cruel deuelis ⸵ Þe firste is Lucifer /
    II   þat regneþ in his malice ⸵ ouer þe children of pride / Þe secounde
    III   is clepid Belzebub ⸵ þat lordiþ ouer envious / Þe þridde deuel is
    IV   Sathanas ⸵ & wrappe is his lordschip / Þe fourþe is clepid Abadon ⸵ 5
    V   þe slowȝ ben hise retenwe / Þe fifþe deuel is Mammon ⸵ & haþ
               wiþ him þe auarouse / and also oone þat is his feere ⸵ a foule synne
    VI   couetise / Þe sixte is clepid Belphegor ⸵ þat is þe god of glotouns ‖
    VII   Þe seuenþ deuel is Asmodeus ⸵ þat leediþ wiþ him þe leccherouse ‖
               But þe seuene sacramentis ⸵ casten out þise deuelis / from þe 10
               saruauntis of God ⸵ þat resceyuen meedfulli / & stablen hem in
Fol. 57 b   seuene ȝiftis ⸵ þat ben clepid of þe | Hooli Goost /
Administra-   But mynystrars of sacramentis ⸵ þat ben in þe fendis chirche /
ters of
Sacraments   mynystren þise sacramentis ⸵ & treeten hem vnworþili / & alle
in the
devil's   suche boþe lerned & lewid ⸵ ben Iudas goostly children / for he took 15
church.
               þe sacrament ⸵ at Cristis hooli sooper / where Crist dalt his bodi in
               breed ⸵ as oþir apostlis diden / & drank wiþ hem his blood in wyn ⸵
               but wiþ a viciouse conscience / wherfore þe deuel entrid in him ⸵ &
               he bitraied his Lord / Þus it is wiþ þe fendis children ⸵ whanne þei
               resceyue þe sacramentis / þei gon to hem vnworþili ⸵ & so to her 20
               dampnacioun ‖ Summe wiþ polutid handis ⸵ & wiþ a stinking
               careyn / as Parisieus seiþ ⸵ & rehersiþ Austin / 'Nocte amator
               veneris ⸵ cras consecrator filii virginis / Deus auertit[1] aurem suam ⸵
               ab oratione talium' ‖ Þat is to seie. He þat is on þe nyȝt ⸵ þe
               louer of leccherie / & in þe morne a sacrar ⸵ of þe maidens sone / 25
               God turneþ awey hise eeris ⸵ from suche mennes preiours ‖ Manye
               feiþful doctours ⸵ forbeden ful streiȝtli / for to take ony sacramentis ⸵
Fol. 58 a   of suche preestis handis / | But now it is & euer schal be ⸵ vnto þe
               worldis ende / foolis fynden conventiclis ⸵ þat haasten hem to helle /
Traffic in the Summe þer ben as Symoundis eiris ⸵ þat sellen þise sacramentis / 30
Sacraments
is the sin of & summe ben redi wiþ her money ⸵ as chapmen in a feire / to bie
simony.
               of þise marchauntis marchaundise ⸵ merite as þei wenen / but boþe
               þe biggers & þe sellers ⸵ discerueu endeles peyne / Summe seien
               'haue here my moneye ⸵ for cristenyng of my childe' / summe seyn
               'haue here þis money ⸵ & soyle me of my synnes' / summe seyn 35
               'haue here þis money ⸵ & sing for me a messe' ‖ Summe seyn 'haue
               þis money ⸵ & graunt me þi pardon' / summe seyn 'haue þis money ⸵
               for þou hast made þis mariage' / summe seyn 'haue þis money &

[1] MS. avertiþ.

Capitulum .IX.

sacre me to presthod '/ summe seyn 'haue þis money ;' for þou hast
often visitid me '/ summe seyn ' haue here þis money ;' & good sire
preie for me ' ‖ Summe maken lettris ;' for sotiler ypocrisie / to selle
alle her suffragis ;' where euere þei fynden þe chapman / þat wole
5 paie lar-|-geli perfore ;' þanne is þe bargayn made / Lord hou reden Fol. 58 b
þise fendis lymes ;' þe decre saluator ª / or studien Goddis lawe ;'
in Dedis of þe Apostlis / where suche marchaundise is dampned ;'
for þus it is seide of cursid Symound / Actus viiiº. / 'Cum vidisset nota
autem symon quia per imposicionem manus daretur spiritus sanctus ;'
10 optulit eis peccuniam dicens ‖ Date & mihi hanc potestatem vt
cuicumque¹ imposuero manus accipiat spiritum sanctum / Petrus
autem dixit ad eum. Pecunia tua tecum sit in perdicionem ;' quoniam
donum dei existimasti peccunia possideri / Non est tibi pars neque
sors. in sermone isto ' ² / Þat is to seie. Forsoþe whanne Symon
15 magus had seyn ;' þat bi touching of þe apostlis handis / þe Holi
Goost was ȝouun to þe peple ;' he profrid hem money & seide to
hem / ȝyue ȝe to me also þis powere ;' þat whom so euere I touche
wiþ handis / may resceyue þe hooli goost ;' forsoþe þanne Petir seide
to him / þi money be wiþ þee for vs ;' take it þi silf to þi dampna-
20 cioun / for þou trowist | þe ȝift of God ;' to be hadde in sale for Fol. 59 a
moneye / þer is no parte neiþir lott ;' to þee in þis sermon of God ³ ‖
Þanne þise þat we han markid aforn ;' in þis ben verrey Symoundis
eiris / for þei wenen whanne þei han money ;' to graunt þe peple
þise goostli ȝiftis / and Symon is dampned & alle hise folowars ;' hou
25 miche more raþer þise cursid takars / For if seint Petir hadde

---

¹ MS. circumque.

² Vulg. Act. viii. 18-21.

³ W. V. 'Forsoth whanne Symound hadde seyn, for the Hooli Gost was
ȝouun by puttyng on of the hond of apostlis, he offride to hem money, seyinge,
ȝyue ȝe to me and this power, that to whom euere I schal putte on houdis, he
receyue the Hooly Gost. Forsoth Petre seide to him, Thi money be with
thee into perdicioun, for thou gessidist the ȝifte of God for to be had, (or
weeldid), by money. Part is not to thee, nethir sort, in this word.' 1388,
'And whanne Symount hadde seyn, that the Hooly Goost was ȝouun bi
leiyng on of the hoondis of the apostlis, and he proferide to hem money, and
seide, ȝyue ȝe also to me this power, that whom euere Y schal leye on my
hoondis, that he resseyue the Hooli Goost. But Petir seide to hym, Thi
money be with thee into perdicioun, for thou gessidist the ȝifte of God schulde
be had for monei. There is no part, ne sort to thee, in this word.'

ª Gratian, *Decreti* Pars Secunda, causa i, quaest. iii, c. viii (Migne,
tom. 187, col. 549, 550).

taken þis money ./ he hadde ȝouun leue to vse symonye / but Petir forsook it & blamed þis man ./ & ȝaue a rule þat euer schal last / þat cursiþ & dampneþ boþe þe ȝyuars & takars ./ for boþe partijs ben symonyentis / O. Iudas made a couenaunt ./ wiþ þe Iewis for þritti platis / and soold his maistir Iesu Crist ./ bitraiyng his bodi in to 5 her hondis / whanne he cam cheueli for to die ./ & his deeþ is oure redempcioun / þerfore his name is cursid Iudas ./ & worþili for his fals trayne / But hise children don myche warre ./ | in selling þe sacramentis & for lesse prijs / þat ben vndeedli & moun not suffre ./ neiþir ony profite comeþ of suche sale / But veniaunce here & ellis 10 where ./ alas whanne wole þise wrecchis be war ||

Fol. 59 b

IX. Students in Christ's church.

Studiars in Cristis chirche ./ studien dai & nyȝt / in þe lawe of þe Lord ./ as þe prophet seiþ. Ps. i⁰. 'In lege domini fuit voluntas eius ./ & in lege eius meditabitur die ac nocte '/ &c ¹ || Þat is to seie. Blessid be þat man ./ þat haþ his wille in þe lawe of þe Lord / & schal þink 15 in his lawe ./ boþe nyȝt & day / for he schal be as a tree ./ þat is wijsli plauntid / biside þe rendels of watris ./ þat schal ȝyue his fruyte. in his due tyme / and his leef þat is his vertu ./ schal not falle awey / but alle þingis þat he schal do ./ in grace schullen be welþi ² / wel is him þat so may studie ./ to fynde þise preciouse fruytis / to make 20 faire her owne soule ./ wiþ flouris of holi writ / þanne Crist wole take his resting place ./ in þe chaumbre of her conscience / for þe wijs man seiþ. Eccˡⁱ. xxxiiii⁰. 'Flores mei fructus | honoris & honestatis ' ³ / þat is to seie. mi flouris be fruytis ./ of worschip & honeste ⁴ / and þerfore seint Ierom counseiliþ ./ in his prolog vpon 25 þe bible. prologo I⁰. ca. viii⁰. 'Oro te frater karissime inter hec viuere ista meditari nil aliud noscere nichilque aliud querere '/ I preie þee broþir seiþ Ierom ./ þat þou haue þi studie / & þi mynde among þe lessouns ./ þat ben in holi writ / bisie þee no þing ellis to knowe ./

Fol. 60 a

¹ Vulg. Ps. i. 2 'In lege domini voluntas eius,' etc.
² W. V. 'In the lawe of the Lord his wil; and in the lawe of hym he shal sweteli thenke dai and nyȝt. And he shal ben as a tree, that is plauntid biside the doun rennyngis of watris : that his frut shal ȝive in his time. And the lef of hym shal not fade; and alle thingus what euere he shal don shul waxe welsum.' 1388, 'His wille is in the lawe of the Lord; and he schal bithenke in the lawe of hym dai and nyȝt. And he schal be as a tree, which is plauntid bisidis the rennyngis of watris; which tre schal ȝyue his fruyt in his tyme. And his leef schal not falle doun; and alle thingis which euere he schal do schulen haue prosperite.'
³ Vulg. Ecclesiasticus xxiv. 23.
W. V. 'My floures frutes of honour, and of honeste.'

Capitulum .IX.

bisi þee no þing ellis to seeke ‖ Sett þin herte in holi studie ./ & purswe aftir wiþ al þi strengþe / & þou schalt fynde it in schort while ./ more swetter þan þe honycombe / as þe wijs man seiþ. Ecc[i].
vi[o]. 'Cogitatum[1] habe in preceptis dei & in mandatis illius maxime
5 assiduus esto. & ipse dabit tibi cor & concupiscencia[2] sapientie dabitur tibi '[3] ‖ Haue þou þi þouȝt in Goddis heestis ./ & in hise comaundementis be þou moost bisy / & he schal graunt an hert to þee ./ & lust of wisdam schal be ȝouun to þee [4] ‖

But studiars in þe fendis chirche ./ studien in her maddid lawis / *Students in the devil's*
10 al for richesse ¦ and for pride ./ & for her worldli worschip / ȝhe so *Fol. 60 b* ferforþe. þat vnneþ ./ ony man is founden / þat abidiþ wiþ Goddis *church.* lawe ./ cleere wiþouten medlyng / but drawiþ him to mannes lawe ./ *nota* for þat smacchiþ wynnyng / & þere þei studien sadli & soore ./ but at her laste ende / þis schal be her payment ./ as God seiþ bi þe
15 prophete. Iere. xvii[o]. 'Maledictus homo qui confidit in homine et ponit carnem brachium suum & a domino recedit cor eius ' [5] / Cursid mot þat man þe ./ þat settiþ his feiþ in man / & puttiþ his trist & his strengþe ./ in mannes maddid ordinaunce / & suffriþ his herte to wade awey ./ from his Lord God / Certis þis man schal be as a broom ./
20 þat growiþ in wildirnes / & he schal not see in inward siȝt ./ whanne þat good of soule haþ comen / but he schal dwelle in drynes ./ in þe lond of wildirnes [6] / Þus seiþ þe Lord God ‖ Suche men sclaundren Crist ./ þat is boþe God & man / & haþ halowid his boþe lawes ./ wiþ his preciouse deeþ / & putt in hem þe spirit of lijf ./ bi quicknyng
25 of his ¦ blood / to rere soulis from þe deeþ ./ & bring hem aȝen to *Fol. 61 a* lijf / as þe gospel witnessiþ. Ion. xi[o]. 'Qui credit in me etiamsi mortuus fuerit viuet ' [7] / Crist seiþ. who þat euere bileueþ in me ./

---

[1] MS. cagitatum.   [2] MS. concupiscenciā.
[3] Vulg. Ecclesiasticus vi. 37 ' Cogitatum tuum habe,' etc.
[4] W. V. 'Thenking haue thou in the hestes of God, and in the maundemens of hym most bisi be thou ; and he shal ȝyue to thee herte, and coueitise of wisdam schal be ȝouun to thee.'
[5] Vulg. Jer. xvii. 5.
[6] W. V. 'Cursid the man that trostith in man, and putteth flesh his arm, and fro the Lord his herte goth awei. Forsothe it shal ben as iencian trees in desert, and he shal not see, whan shal come good ; but he shal dwelle in droȝte in desert.' 1388, ' Cursid is the man that trestith in man, and settith fleisch his arm, and his herte goith awei fro the Lord. For he schal be as bremes in desert, & he schal not se, whanne good schal come; but he schal dwelle in drynesse in desert.'
[7] Vulg. Joh. xi. 25.

ȝhe þouȝ þat he be deed / neþeles he schal lyue aȝen ? boþe in grace
& glorie'¹ ‖ But þis is not in mannes lawe ? þat may ȝyue þis
powere / Þanne is þis foule sclaundir ? of þise weiward foolis / þat
þus studien in mannes lawe ? as if it were þe betir / & þerfore
suche froward þouȝtis ? departen her soule from God / Of alle þise 5
spekiþ Ieremye ? & seiþ of hem ful scharpli / Iere. viº. 'A minore
quippe vsque ad maiorem omnes auaricie student / A propheta vsque
ad sacerdotem cuncti faciunt dolum / Quamobrem cadent inter
ruentes. in tempore visitacionis corruent dicit dominus'² ‖ From
þe leest vnto þe moost ? alle studien coueitise / þat is vndirstandid ? 10
of hem oonli þat ben in þe fendis chirche / from þe prechour vnto
Fol. 61 b þe prest ? alle wirchen gile / þerfore | þei schal falle ? amonge hem
þat fallen / þei schal falle in tyme of visitacioun ? seiþ þe Lord
God /³ God rehersiþ þis sentence aȝen ? for we schulde take good
hede þerto / but for þei wole not amende her studies ? & turne þe 15
þouȝt to Goddis lawe / þerfore God wischiþ hem woo ? & seiþ þus bi
þe prophete. Miche. iiº. 've qui cogitatis invtile ? & operamini
malum in cubilibus vestris'⁴ ‖ Woo to ȝou þat þenken ? þing þat is
vnprofitable / and wirchen yuel in ȝoure studies ? in þe morowe liȝt ‖

X. Peace-makers in Christ's church.

Pees-makars in Cristis chirche ? moven men to reest / þat 20
Crist bihiȝt to hise disciplis ? whanne he was here amonge hem /
Ion. xiiiiº. 'Pacem meam do vobis pacem meam relinquo vobis'⁵ ‖
Þat is to seie. Mi pees I ȝiue to ȝou ? my pees I bileue to ȝou /
his pees he bilefte wiþ vs ? whanne he went to heuene / his
pees he schal ȝyue to vs ? in þe worldis ende / his pees he bitook 25
to vs ? to helpe vs in þis world / his pees he schal graunt to vs ?
Fol. 62 a to solace vs in blisse ‖ | He haþ lefte vs his pees ? to be oure
tristi cloþing / for if we be cladde þerynne ? we schal ouercome
oure enemyes / He schal graunt vs his pees ? & þanne we schal be

¹ W. V. 'He that bileueth in me, ȝhe, if he schal be deed, schal lyve.'
1388, 'He that bileueth in me, ȝhe, thouȝ he be deed, he schal lyve.'

² Jer. vi. 13, 15.

³ W. V. 'Fro the lasse forsothe unto the more, alle to auarice studien; and
fro the profete unto the prest, alle don treccherie. Wherfore thei shul falle
among the men fallende; in tyme of ther visitacioun thei shul falle togidere,
seith the Lord.' 1388, 'Fro the lesse til to the grettere, alle studien to
auerise; and alle doon gile, fro the profete til to the preest. Wherfor thei
schulen falle doun, among hem that schulen falle doun; thei schulen falle
doun in the tyme of her visitacioun, seith the Lord.'

⁴ Vulg. Mich. ii. 1.

⁵ Vulg. Joh. xiv. 27 'Pacem relinquo vobis, pacem meam do vobis.'

Capitulum .IX.

siker / to regne world wiþouten ende ./ wiþoute ony enemyes / He
haþ leeft vs his pees ./ þat we deme not falsli / of oure neiȝbore
biside vs ./ of þingis þat ben vncerteyne / He schal ȝyue to vs
pees ./ whanne he schal make knowen / þe priuetees of mannes
5 herte ./ & þanne schal be preising / to euery man of his god ./ aftir
he haþ discerued ‖ Crist haþ leeft among vs pees ./ þat we schulde
loue togidir / hatyng synne & louyng vertu ./ for þus he loued vs /
for þer is no charite ./ but if synne be hatid / & rendid vp bi þe
rootis ./ in vs & in alle oþir ‖ Þanne Crist schal ȝyue vs ful pees ./
10 where we may neuere discorde / þus seiþ seynt Austin ./ vppon þis
same gospel / þat is aforne rehersid ./ now grounde we it in oure
mynde ‖

Þise peesmakars for þei wolde haue ./ þis verrey | pees among Fol. 62 b
hem ./ stonden armed at alle peesis ./ for drede of her enemyes / in
15 þe armour of Iesu Crist ./ þat seint Poul techiþ / Ephe. vi⁰ /
'Accipite armaturam dei '¹ ‖ Sixe armours þe apostle rehersiþ ./ The six armours of
þat armyn þe soule / fyue for to defende wiþ ./ þe sixte for to the soul.
assaile /

Þe firste is a girdil of chastite ./ & þerbi mai we knowe / þat I. The girdle of
20 Poule vsiþ þe witt of þe soule ./ & leeueþ bodili armour ‖ Þis girdile chastity.
girdiþ vp her lendis ./ & saueþ² chastite / and pees of bodi from
leccherie ./ in þise þre degrees / In maidens it kepiþ virginite ./ in
weddid trewe matrimonye / & in widowis continence ./ þat is from
al vnclennes / Take vp þis girdile in Goddis name ./ þat ȝe moun
25 stonde perfijte / in þe pees of ȝoure soule ./ aȝen alle fleischeli
steryngis ‖

An haburioune of riȝtwisenesse ./ is þe secounde armour / þat is II. The breastplate
þicli mailid ./ for falsheed schulde not entre / for to greue God or of righteous-
man ./ or sturble þis trewe pees / ness.

30 Þe þridde armour is leggeharnes ./ & schoyng of affecciouns / | Fol. 63 a
in þe gospel of Iesu Crist ./ & þanne þei ben disposid / to make pees III. Leg and feet armour
among men ./ not as þe world axiþ / But þat þei stonde perfiȝtli ./ of the affections.
in al aduersite / wiþ Crist & his gospel ./ to þe deeþ dai ‖

A schilde of feiþ is þe fourþe ./ in whiche þei schal quenche / alle IV. The shield of
35 þe fendis brennyng daitis ./ þat ben hise temptaciouns / Certis þer faith.
may no deedli dynt ./ steele in þat man / þat haþ þe schelde of trewe
bileue ./ hanging on his herte / þerfore he lediþ his lijf in pees &
quart ./ from al goostly sijknes ‖

---

¹ Vulg. Eph. vi. 13. ² MS. saue.

F

Discrecioun?

V. The helmet of salvation.

Þe fifþe armour of þe soule ؛ is an helme of helþe ؍ þat is clepid tristi hope ؛ for it beriþ of strookis ‖ Þe fende þrowiþ at mannes soule ؛ wiþ twoo dispitouse gynnes ؍ þe toone is obstinacioun ؛ or

nota bene hardenes of herte ؍ þe toþir is desperacioun ؛ or ellis wanhope ؍ But who þat haþ þe helme of hope ؛ þouȝ strookis liȝten on him ؍ þei 5 schal on nowise breest þis palet ؛ ne synk vnto þe soule ؍ þerfore he lyueþ peesibly ؛ in hoope of Goddis mercy ‖

Fol. 63 b
VI. The sword of the spirit.

Þe | sixte armour of Goddis knyȝtis ؛ wiþ whiche þei done assaile ؍ is þe swerid of þe spirit ؛ þat is Goddis worde ؍ wiþ þis swerid Iudith þe widowe ؛ smot Holofernes ؍ & kitt his heed from 10 his bodi ؛ in sauyng of hir peple. Iudith. xiii⁰ [1] ؍ And in þis swerid Iesu Crist ؛ assailed þe fende of helle ؍ whanne Crist seide 'goo Satanas' ؛ anoon he fledde awey ؍ Mar. iiii⁰ [2] ؍ For þis swerid is ful scharpe ؛ and bitiþ on boþe sidis ؍ for it departeþ at a strook ؛ þe soule from þe bodi ؍ & it departiþ in þis lijf ؛ vertu fro synne ؍ 15 & it schal departe at domesdai ؛ þe good from þe yuel ‖ In þis swerid kyng Salamon ؛ ȝaue a trewe iugement ؍ & diuidid wiþ þis swerid ؛ truþe from þe falshede ‖ III. Re. iii⁰ [3] ‖ God ȝyue vs grace to take þis swerid ؛ & þenk on kyng Salamon ؍ wiþ Iudith & wiþ Iesu Crist ؛ & þanne is þer no doute ؍ For alle þat taken vp þis 20 swerid ؛ & stonden in þis armour ؍ Crist oure capteyn blessiþ hem ؛ & clepiþ hem his children ؍ Mat. v⁰. 'Beati pacifici ؛ quoniam filii

Fol. 64 a dei vocabuntur' [4] ‖ þat is to seie. Blessid be alle þise pees-|-makars ؛ for þei schal be clepid þe sones of God [5] ؍ And efte Crist seiþ. 'Diligite inimicos vestros. benefacite hijs qui oderunt vos. & orate 25 pro persequentibus & calumpniantibus vos vt sitis filii patris vestri qui in celis est' [6] ‖ Loue ȝe ȝoure enemyes seiþ Crist. do ȝe wel to hem þat haten ȝou ؍ & preie ȝe for ȝoure purswars & ȝoure sclaunderars . þat ȝe mai be þe sones of ȝoure fadir þat is in heuenes [7] ‖

[1] Vulg. Judith xiii. 7-9.
[2] Vulg. Matt. iv. 10.
[3] Vulg. 3 Reg. iii. 16-28.
[4] Vulg. Matt. v. 9.
[5] W. V. 'Blessid be pesible men, for thei shuln be clepid the sonys of God.' 1388, 'Blessid ben pesible men, for thei schulen be clepid Goddis children.'
[6] Vulg. Matt. v. 44, 45.
[7] W. V. 'Loue ȝee ȝoure enmyes, do ȝee wel to hem that haten ȝou, and preye ȝee for men pursuynge, and falsly chalengynge ȝou; that ȝee be the sonys of ȝoure fadir that is in hevenes.' 1388, 'Love ȝe ȝoure enemyes, do ȝe wel to hem that hatiden ȝou, and preye ȝe for hem that pursuen, and sclaundren ȝou; that ȝe be the sones of ȝour fadir that is in heuenes.'

Capitulum .IX.

But pees-makars in þe fendis chirche ? confidren hem togidir in a fals pees / aftir þe maner of þis world ? þat Cristis gospel dampneþ / Mat. x⁰. & Luk. xii⁰. 'Non veni pacem mittere ? sed gladium'[1] ‖ I haue not comen seiþ Crist ? to maynten viciouse
5 pees / but to sende a scharpe sweride[2] ? to smyte synne from mannes soule / & þis þise synful wrechid foolis ? þrowen vndir foot / Feiþ. troupé. & riȝtwisenesse ? þei counten at no prijs / for þei ouereleden þe countre ? aftir her owene lust / perfore þe prophete Dauiþ ? sorowiþ on þis mischef / Ps. lxxii / 'Zelaui super iniquos.
10 pacem peccatorum videns'[3] / I haue sorowid on wickid | men ? seyng þe pees of synnars[4] ‖

<small>Peace-makers in the devil's church.</small>

But prestis & knyȝtis ? of þis synne ben moost to blame / Prestis þat schulden be goostli lechis ? and recounseile þe peple / bi good counseile to her God ? & heele hem wiþ his lawe / what wiþ pride &
15 coueitise ? & many fleischeli lustis / þise prestis ben so blyndid ? þat þei knowe no wisdam / for Iob seiþ. xxviii⁰. 'vbi invenitur sapientia ? non enim in terra suauiter viuencium'[5] / Iob axiþ þis questioun ? where wisdam mai be founden / anoon he answeriþ wiþ þe spirit of God ? not in þe lond of lusti lyuars[6] / And vpon þis
20 seiþ Gregor in hise morals ? þise wordis of greet sorow. to hem þat ben gilti / 'Quisquis presentis vite voluptatibus pascitur procul dubio eterne sapientie intellectu separatur'[a] ‖ Þat is to seie. who þat is fedde ? wiþ lustis of þis present lijf / wiþouten ony doute ? þat man is departid / fro þe vndirstanding ? of euerlasting wisdam ‖
25 And siþen þise prestis ? ben moost ȝouun / to þise fleischeli lustis ? þei failen | goostli siȝt / and wisdam to ransake ? ony goostli sijknes / or to serche al aboute ? þe perel of a wounde / & ȝit þei ben presumptuouse ? to profre fals medicyn / & vndirtake greet curis ?

<small>Priests and knights are most to blame for this evil in the church.</small>

<small>nota bene</small>

<small>The priests follow Fol. 65 a fleshly lusts and lack spiritual wisdom.</small>

---

[1] Vulg. Matt. x. 34; Luc. xii. 51.

[2] W. V. 'I cam not to sende pees in to erthe, but swerd.'

[3] Vulg. Ps. lxxii. 3.

[4] W. V. 'For I enuyde up on wicke men; seande the pes of synners.' 1388, 'For I louede feruentli on wickid men; seynge the pees of synneris.'

[5] Vulg. Job xxviii. 12, 13 'Sapientia vero ubi invenitur? ... nec invenitus in terra suauiter viuentium.'

[6] W. V. 'Wisdam forsothe, wher is it founde? ... ne it is founde in the lond of sweteli lyuende men.'

---

[a] Gregorius Magnus, *Moralium* Lib. XVIII, cap. xli. 66 (Migne, tom. 76, col. 75).

Discrecioun ?

for to make hem hool / But þei hirten myche sorer ? þan þei were aforn / as þe Lord moneþ him ? bi þe prophet Ieremye. Iere. viii⁰. 'Sanabant contricionem populi mei ad ignominiam dicentes. Pax. pax. cum non esset pax / Confusi sunt qui abhominacionem fecerunt / Quinimo confusione¹ non sunt confusi ? & erubescere nescierunt'²‖ 5 Þise prestis³ heliden þe contricioun of my peple ? wiþ schenschip or wiþ schame / þat is wiþ foule symonye ? as we rehersid aforn / and þei seyn pees pes ? whanne þer was no pees / þei ben worþi to be schent ? þat han done abhominacioun / miche raþer in þis confucioun ? þei be not confoundid / for þei can not be aschamed ? of 10 her owene vilenye⁴ / Þus seiþ þe Lord God / and efte he seiþ ca⁰. xxiii⁰. 'A prophetis enim Ierusalem egressa est pollucio super | omnem terram. hec dicit dominus . Nolite audire verba prophetarum qui prophetant vobis & decipiunt vos / visionem cordis sui locuntur ? non de ore domini / Dicunt hijs qui blasfemant me. locutus est 15 dominus pax erit vobis & omni qui ambulant in prauitatem cordis sui dixerunt. non veniat super uos malum'⁵ ‖ From þe prechours of þe chirche ? comeþ defoiling vppon al þe erþe / þise þingis seiþ þe Lord / Nile 3e heere þe wordis of þise precheours ? þat prechen & disceyuen 3ou | þei speken þe visioun of her herte ? but not of þe 20 Lordis mouþe / Þei seyn to þoo þat blasfemen me ? þe Lord spekiþ þat pees schal be to 3ou / & þei han seide to iche a man ? þat walkiþ in schrewidnes of his herte. þer schal non yuel cum vpon 3ou⁶ ‖ And Gregor seiþ. 'Causa ruine populi ? sunt sacerdotes

Fol. 65 b (margin)

nota bene (margin)

---

¹ MS. confucōe.
² Vulg. Jer. viii. 11, 12 'Sanabant contritionem filiae populi,' etc.
³ MS. perstis.
⁴ W. V. '(Thei) heleden the tobrosing of the do3ter of my puple to shenshipe, seiende, Pes, pes, whan ther was not pes. Confoundid thei ben, for abhomynacioun thei diden; but myche more by confusioun thei ben not confoundid, and shamen thei kouthen not.' 1388, 'Thei heeliden the sorowe of the dou3tir of my puȝ le to schenschipe, seiynge, Pees, pees, whanne no pees was. Thei ben schent, for thei diden abhomynacioun; 3he, rather thei weren not schent bi schenschipe, and kouden not be aschamed.'
⁵ Vulg. Jer. xxiii. 15, 16 'A prophetis enim . . . haec dicit dominus exercituum,' etc.
⁶ W. V. 'Fro the profetus forsothe of Jerusalem is gon out defouling upon al erthe. These thingus seith the Lord of ostus, Wileth not heren the wrdus of the profetes, that profecien to 3ou, and desceyven 3ou; the viseoun of ther herte thei speken, not of the mouth of the Lord. They seyn to them that blasfemen me, The Lord spac, Pes shal be to 3ou; and to eche that goth in the shreudnesse of his herte thei seiden, Ther shal not come up on 3ou euel.'

Capitulum .IX.

mali 'ᵃ/ yuel prestis ben cause of ruyn or mischef of þe peple/ and
no wondir. for whanne þat liȝt is quenchid . þat schulde schyne
in | prestis/ þanne is þer miche stink ./ wiþ wickid sauour/ & Fol. 66 a
blyndnes þat combriþ ./ þe leder & þe folowar/ in to þe derckness
5 of helle ./ þe gospel beriþ witnes/ Mat. xvº. Luk. viº. 'Cecus
autem si ceco ducatum prestet ./ nonne ambo in fouiam cadunt ' ¹ ||
Whanne þe blynde lediþ þe blynde. falle þei not þanne boþe in to
þe lake ? ² ȝhis pleynli || Þe former blynde is þe preest/ þat wantiþ
vndirstonding/ for þouȝ he haue lettrure ./ & faile in good lyuyng/
10 þanne he is a blynde prest ./ of whom Crist spekiþ/ as þe comune
gloose seiþ. 'Frustra iactat legis noticiam ./ qui operibus destruit nota
doctrinam '/ Aboute nouȝt he boostiþ ./ þe knowing of Goddis lawe/
þat distrieþ þe loore ./ wiþ his wickid werkis/ Þe toþir blynde is
man & womman ./ þat tristen in suche prestis ./ to lede hem in þe
15 weie of lijf ./ & bringe hem to saluacioun || But Crist haþ iuggid
þise boþe parties ./ to falle in to þe doungun/ Of suche prestis
comeþ debate ./ in al þis brood world/ þat distur-|-bliþ verry pees ./ Fol. 66 b
& crieþ open veniaunce/ And þise prechours ben no prechours ./
but oonli in name/ as a luschborue is clepid a peny ./ þat is riȝt
20 nouȝt worþe ||

    KnyȝTis also ben to blame ./ þat mysvsen her powere/ and wole Knights
not reede in Goddis lawe ./ neiþir lerne her office/ & perfore þe wise misuse their power to
man ./ blameþ hem & seiþ/ Sap. viº. 'Audite reges & intelligite do sin.
& sequentia. quoniam data est a domino potestas & virtus ab
25 altissimo qui interrogabit opera uestra & cogitaciones scrutabitur/
Quoniam cum essetis ministri regni illius. non recte iudicastis neque
custodistis legem iusticie neque secundum dei voluntatem ambu-
lastis ' ³/ Heere ȝe kyngis ./ & vndirstonde ȝe knyȝtis/ for power is
oonli of þe Lord ./ & strengþe comeþ of him þat is hiȝest/ þat schal
30 aske reckenyng ./ of alle ȝoure werkis/ & schal serche fulli ./ þe
inward of ȝoure þouȝtis/ For whanne þat ȝe were mynystris ./ of

---

¹ Vulg. Matt. xv. 14 'Caecus autem si caeco ducatum praestet, ambo in
foveam cadunt.' Luke vi. 39 'Numquid potest caecus caecum ducere, nonne
ambo in foveam cadunt?'

² W. V, 'ȝif a blynd man ȝeue ledynge to a blynd man, bothe fallen doun
in to the diche.'

³ Vulg. Sap. vi. 2, 4, 5 'Audite ergo reges . . . quoniam data est a domino
potestas vobis,' etc.

ᵃ Gregorius Magnus, *Homiliae in Evangelia*, Lib. II, Hom. xxxix. 2 (Migne,
tom. 75, col. 1295).

Discrecioun.

Goddis rewme / neiþir ȝe demed riȝtwiseli ; neiþir ȝe kept his lawe /
Fol. 67 a neiþir ȝe walkid in þe weye ; aftir Goddis wille [1] / but ȝe | straied
al awey ; as if it were wilde syouns / In often takyng of miche
mete ; þat steriþ ȝou to miche drinking || Þanne ȝe liggen longe in
couchis ; þat drawiþ ȝou to leccherie / as sumtyme to spousebreche ; 5
& oþir foule vnclennes / & of þis comeþ stryuyng ; & fiȝtynge euer
anoon / þat bringiþ ȝou to enemyte ; & hate of iche oþir / How
schulde ȝe knyȝtis maynten pees ; whanne ȝe forsake it in ȝoure silf ?
for wiþ ȝoure greuouse tirauntrie ; oppressioun & extorcioun / ȝoure
awe is lawe. who dar seie naye ; but as ȝe wole ȝoure silf / But wite 10
ȝe wel þis is þe vois ; of hem þat schal be dampned / as þe wiseman
seiþ. Sap. ii⁰. / 'Sit fortitudo nostra lex iusticie ' [2] || Oure strengþe
or oure powere ; be it to us þe lawe of riȝtwisenesse [3] / Heere ȝe þerfore ; hou dredfulli it folowiþ / of þe sentence seide aforn ; if þat ȝe
wole amende ȝou / Sap. vi⁰. / 'Horrende & cito apparebit vobis quo- 15
niam iudicium durissimum in hijs qui presunt fiet / exiguo conceditur
Fol. 67 b misericordia potentes potenter tormenta pacientur / | Non enim
personam subtrahet cuiusquam dominus qui est omni dominator. nec
verebitur magnitudinem cuiusquam. quoniam pusillum & magnum
ipse fecit. & equaliter cura est illi de omnibus forcioribus autem forcior 20
instat cruciacio ' [4] || Ferfulli & soone ; it schal schewe to ȝou / þat
moost hardest iugement ; schal be to hem þat lorden / or þat holden
lordschip ; ouer her pore briþeren / mercy is grauntid ; to hem þat
ben lowe in herte / myȝti men myȝtili ; schullen suffre turmentrie /
forsoþe þe Lord schal not wiþdrawe ; þe persoone of ony man / 25

---

[1] W. V. 'Hereth thanne, ȝee kingis, and undirstondith; for ther is ȝouen of the Lord power to ȝou, and vertue of the heiȝeste, that shal aske ȝoure werkis, and thoȝtis serchen. For whan ȝee weren mynestres of his reume, not riȝtli ȝee demeden, ne kepten the lawe of riȝtwisenesse, ne aftir the will of God ȝee wenten.' 1388, 'Therfor, ȝe kingis, here, and understonde; for whi power is ȝouun of the Lord to ȝou, and vertu is ȝouun of the hiȝeste, . . . and schal serche thouȝtis. For whanne ȝe weren mynystris of his rewme, ȝe demeden not riȝtfuli, nether ȝe kepten the lawe of riȝtfulnesse nether ȝe ȝeden bi the wille of God.'

[2] Vulg. Sap. ii. 11.

[3] W. V. 'Be forsothe oure strengthe the lawe of unriȝtwisenesse.' 1388, 'But oure strengthe be the lawe of riȝtfulnesse.'

[4] Vulg. Sap. vi. 6-9 'Horrende et cito apparebit vobis quoniam iudicium durissimum his qui praesunt fiet. Exiguo enim conceditur misericordia; potentes autem potenter . . . Non enim subtrahet personam cuiusquam Deus, nec verebitur . . . cruciatio.'

Capitulum .IX.

neiþir he schal be aschamed ." of ony mannes greetnes ⸝ for he haþ made boþe smale & greet ." & chargiþ neiþir oon ne oþir ⸝ forsoþe to þe strenger ." is ordeyned strenger cruciacioun & peyne [1] ∥ Þise forseide prestis & knyȝtis ." þoruȝ suche vicious dedis ⸝ leden þe
5 comunes on her ryng ." and boolden hem in synne ⸝ þat al þis worlde is sett in rore ." in bataile & in werre ∥ But now ben comen to þe proof ." þe wordis þat God haþ seide ⸝ bi þe prophete Ieremye ." to teche hise chosen seruantis ⸝ Iere. ix⁰. ' Omnes adulteri | sunt & cetus preuaricatorum extenderunt linguam suam quasi arcum
10 mendacii & non veritatis ⸝ confortati sunt in terra quia de malo ad malum egressi sunt. & me non cognouerunt dicit dominus vnusquisque a proximo suo se custodiat. & in omni fratre suo non habeat fiduciam ⸝ quia omnis frater supplantans supplantabit ⸝ & omnis amicus fraudilenter incedet ⸝ & vir fratrem suum deridebit
15 & veritatem non loquetur ' [2] ∥ Alle þise ben avowtreris ." & a cumpany þat breken þe lawe ⸝ þei han strecchid forþe her tung ." as a bent bowe ⸝ to schete lesyng & no trouþe ." iche man at oþir ⸝ þei ben counfortid in þe erþe ." for þei goon from yuel to yuel ⸝ & þei han not knowen me ." seiþ þe Lord God ⸝ Iche man from his neiȝbore ."
20 kepe he him ful wiseli ⸝ & in his owene broþir ." he mai haue no trist ⸝ for iche a broþir in disceyte ." schal bigile oþir ⸝ & iche a frende falseli ." schal goo awei from oþir ⸝ & þe man schal scorne his broþir ." & þei schal not speke trouþe ⸝ forsoþe þei han tauȝt her tung ." for to speke | lesing ." and for þei wolde do wickidli ." þei
25 han soore traueiled ⸝ þei han forsaken in treccherie. to knowe me seiþ þe Lord God ∥ Wherfore þise þingis ." seiþ þe Lord of oostis ⸝ Loo I schal welle hem togidir ." & I schal proue hem ∥ what schal

Fol. 68 a

Fol. 68 b

On such God will take vengeance.

---

[1] W. V. 'Orribleli and soone he shal apere to ȝou; for most hard dom shal ben don in hem, that ben biforn. Forsothe to the litle is grauntid mercy; myȝty men forsothe myȝtili tormentis shul suffre. Forsothe he shal not withdrawe the persone of any man, the Lord, that is lordshipere of alle thingus, and he shal not drede the mykilnesse of any man; for litil and gret he made, and euenli cure is to hym of alle. To the strengere forsothe strengere stant in tormenting.' 1388, 'Hidousli and soone he schal appere to ȝou forwhi hardeste doom schal be maad in hem, that ben souereyns. Forsothe merci is grauntid to a litil man; but miȝti men schulen suffre turmentis miȝtili. For the Lord, which is lord of alle thingis, schal not withdrawe the persoone of ony man, nether he schal drede the greetnesse of ony man; for he made the litil man and the greet man, and charge is to hym evenli of alle men. But strongere turment neiȝeth to strongere men.'

[2] Vulg. Jer. ix. 2-5.

I ellis do ׃ fro þe face of my peple ? an arow wounding is her tunᵹ ׃ for it spekiþ gile ⁄ & he spekiþ wiþ his frende ׃ pees wiþ his mouþe ⁄ but prvieli he leieþ for him ׃ spies to disceyue him. No wheþir schal I not visite vpon þise þingis ׃ seiþ þe Lord God ⁄ or schal not my wille be vengid ׃ vpon suche a folk ? ¹ As if he wolde 5 seie ׃ I schal be vengid ⁄ for as her wille is to go fro me. so my wille is to be vengid vpon hem ׃ whanne I se my tyme ‖ But happeli here summe wole seie. God wole not take veniaunce ׃ vpon hise cristen peple ⁄ God wole not leese þat he deere bouȝt ׃ wiþ his
I   preciouse blood ⁄ To þe firste we answeren ׃ bi þe mouþe of God ⁄ 10 Iere. xvi⁰. 'Deriliquerunt me patres vestri ait dominus & abierunt
Fol. 69 a   post deos alienos & ser-|-uierunt eis & adorauerunt eos & me deriliquerunt & legem meam non custodierunt ⁄ sed & vos peius operati estis quam patres vestri ⁄ Ecce enim ambulat vnusquisque

---

¹ W. V. 'For alle auoutreris thei ben, and cumpanye of lawe brekeres: and thei benten out ther tung as ther bowe of lesyng, and not of treuthe. Thei ben coumfortid in erthe, for fro euel to euel thei wenten out and me thei knewe not, seith the Lord. Eche kepe hymself fro his neȝhebore, and in eche brother of hym have he not trost: for eche brother supplauntende shal supplaunte, and eche frend gilendely shal go. And a man his brother shal scorne and treuthe shal not speke; thei taȝten forsothe ther tunge to speke lesing; that wickely thei schulden don, thei traueileden. Thi dwelling in the myddel of treccherie; in treccherie thei forsoke me to knowen, seith the Lord. Therfore these thingus seith the Lord of ostus. Lo! I shall ȝeete and preve them; what forsothe other thing shal Y do fro the face of the sone of my puple? An arwe woundende the tunge of hem, treccherie it spak; in his mouth pes with his friend he speketh, and priveli he putteth to hym aspies. Whether up on these thingus I shal not visite, seith the Lord, or in to such a maner folc shal not be vengid my soule?'

1388, 'Forwhi alle ben auowteris, and the cumpenyes of trespassouris aȝens the lawe; and thei helden forth her tunge as a bouwe of leesyng, and not of treuthe. Thei ben coumfortid in erthe, for thei ȝeden out fro yuel to yuel, and thei knewen not me, seith the Lord. Ech man kepe hym from his neiȝbore, and haue no trist in ony brother of hym; for whi ech brother disseyvyng schal disseyve, and ech frend schal go gilefuli. And a man schal scorne his brother, and schal not speke treuthe ; for thei tauȝten her tunge to speke leesyng; thei traueliden to do wickidli. Thi dwellyng is in the myddis of gile; in gile thei forsoken to knowe me, seith the Lord, Therfor the Lord of oostis seith these thingis, Lo! Y schal welle togidere; and Y schal preue hem; for whi what other thing schal Y do fro the face of the douȝter of my puple? The tunge of hem is an arowe woundynge and spak gile; in his mouth he spekith pees with his frend, and priueli he settith tresouns to hym. Whether Y schal not visite on these thingis, seith the Lord, ether schal not my soule take veniaunce on siche a folc?'

Capitulum .IX.

post prauitatem cordis sui mali. & me non audiat ‖ Et eiciam vos
de terra hac in terram quam ignoratis vos & patres vestri & seruietis
ibi dijs alienis die ac nocte qui non dabunt vobis requiem'[1] ‖ Þe
Lord seiþ. ȝoure fadris han forsaken me ʹ & gon aftir straunge
5 goddis / for to do hem seruyce ʹ & worschipe hem also / but þei han
forsaken me ʹ & not kept my lawe ‖ But & ȝe do miche werre ʹ þan
euere wrouȝt ȝoure fadris / Loo iche of ȝou walkiþ ʹ aftir þe
schrewidnes of his yuel herte / þat he heere not me ʹ seiþ þe Lord
God / & I schal kast ȝou awey ʹ oute of þis erþe / in to a lond þat
10 is vnknowen ʹ to ȝou & to ȝoure fadris / & þere ȝe schal do seruice ʹ
to alien goddis / þat schullen ȝyue no rest to ȝou ʹ neiþir dai ne
nyȝt[2] / And to þe secounde we answeren ʹ as Crist seiþ in his II
gospel / Mat. xxii°. | 'Amice quomodo huc intrasti non habens Fol. 69 b
vestem nupcialem at ille obmutuit / Tunc rex ait ministris. ligatis
15 manibus eius & pedibus mittite eum in tenebras exteriores. ibi erit
fletus & stridor dencium'[3] ‖ Frende hou entridist þou hidir ʹ not
hauyng þe bridal clooþ ? & he wex doombe / þanne þis kyng Iesu
Crist ʹ seide to hise mynystris / þis wrecche bounden hand & foot ʹ
sende him in to þe vttirar derckenes / þere schal be weping ʹ &
20 gneching of teeþ /[4] vndirstande bi þis frende ʹ boþe man &

---

[1] Vulg. Jer. xvi. 11-13.

[2] W. V. 'For forsoken me ȝoure fadris, seith the Lord, and ȝiden awei aftir
aliene goddis, and serueden to them, and honoureden hem, and me forsoken,
and my lawe kepten not. But and ȝee wers wroȝten than ȝoure fadris; lo!
forsothe eche goth after the shreudenesse of his euel herte, that me he here
not. And Y shal caste ȝou out fro this lond, in to the lond that ȝee and ȝoure
fadris knowe not; and ȝee shul serue there to alien goddis dai and nyȝt, that
shul not ȝiue to ȝou rest.' 1388, 'For ȝoure fadris forsoken me, seith the
Lord, and ȝeden aftir alien goddis, and seruyden hem, and worschipiden hem,
and thei forsoken me, and kepten not my lawe. But also ȝe wrouȝten worse
than ȝoure fadris; for lo! ech man goith aftir the shrewidnesse of his yuel
herte, that he here not me. And Y shal caste ȝou out of this lond, in to the
lond which ȝe and ȝoure fadris knowen not; and ȝe schulen serue there to
alien goddis dai and nyȝt, whiche schulen not ȝive reste to you.'

[3] Vulg. Matt. xxii. 12, 13 'Amice, quomodo . . . Tunc dixit rex ministris,'
etc.

[4] W. V. 'Frend, hou entridist thou hidir, not hauynge brijd clothe? And
he was doumbe. Thanne the kyng seide to the mynystris, His hondis and
feet bounden, sende ȝee hym into uttermore derknessis: there shal be weepyng
and betyng to gidre of teeth.' 1388, 'Freend, hou entridist thou hidir without
bride clothes?. And he was doumbe. Thanne the kyng bad hise mynystris,
Bynde hym bothe hondis and feet, and sende ȝe him in to utmer derknessis:
there schal be wepyng and grentyng of teeth.'

womman / þat haþ taken cristendom ./ & holden þe name / but þci
wanten in her lyuyng ./ werkis of trewe bileue / þerfore Crist
wardiþ hem ./ in to þe peyne of helle ||

How þe good of þe secounde chirche acorden wiþ þe firste chirche. Cap^m .X^m. || 5

The good of the Second Church are united to the first Church by a threefold cord.

Here schullen we telle ./ hou þe good of þe secounde chirche /
acordiþ wiþ þe firste chirche ./ appropurid to God / Feiþ. hope. &
charite ./ as we han seid aforn / knytten God & man togidir ./ in
oonhed of þis | chirche / þis knott is knitt so sikerli ./ þat it schal
neuer more faile / neiþir here ne ellis-where ./ as þe wise man seiþ / 10

nota Eccles. iiii°. 'Triplex funiculus difficile rumpitur' [1] || A þrefolde
corde ./ ful looþe is brostun [2] || For to make þis þrefolde corde ./ we
must haue þre lynkis / & eeke hem forþe perfiȝtli ./ til þis corde be
wrouȝt ./ bi whiche þis chirche schal be drawen ./ vnto þe 'holi
trinite / Þise ben þe firste þre ./ a chaast bodi. a clene soule. & goodis 15
treweli disposid / þanne it schal be eekid. wiþ good worde. holi
þouȝt. & a perfiȝte dede / moreouere we must large forþe ./ schrifte
of mouþe. sorow of herte. & amendis makyng / Aftir þis it axiþ ./
preiour. fasting. & almes dede / Aftir þis we must putt to. noumbre.
weiȝt. & mesure / Also we must eeke þis corde ./ wiþ mynde. wille. 20
& resoun / & helpe forþe to þe eende ./ wiþ feiþ. hope. & charite /
Þanne we schal neiȝ to oure God ./ þoruȝ grace. mercy. & riȝtwisenes /
til we se God in trinite ./ Fadir & Sone & Holi Goost /

Fol. 70 b   Euery membre of | þis chirche ./ helpiþ þat it may / for to
worche a parte of þis corde ./ for þe comune profite / as seint Austin 25
seiþ. 'Ecclesia est quedam forma forma iusticie. id est commune ius
omnium. in communi orat. in communi operatur. sine ecclesie
catholice societate nec baptismus alicui prodesse potest. nec opera
misericordie . nisi forte vt minus torqueatur' || Holi chirche is
a forme ./ of al riȝtwisenes / þat is to seie a comune acorde ./ of alle 30
good þingis / & þis chirche preieþ in comune ./ and worchiþ hir
werkis in comune ./ for wiþouten felaschip ./ of þis general chirche /
baptem may not profiȝte ./ ne þe dedis of mercy / but if it be þat þe
peyne ./ be þe lesse in helle ||

As in the physical body all the members

Alle þe membris of a man ./ traueilen in her ordir / iche for to 35
socour oþir ./ & noon for to hindir / but for to do her comune

---

[1] Vulg. Eccles. iv. 12.

[2] W. V. 'A thre fold corde hard is to-broken.' 1388, 'A threfolde corde is brokun of hard.'

helpe ꞉ to profite of þe bodi ‖ Þus it is of þe membris ꞉ þat ben in
Cristis chirche ⁄ for it is a goostli bodi ꞉ þat growiþ wiþ hir
membris ⁄ þere oone failiþ anoþir helpiþ ꞉ til þis corde be made ‖
Summe haue myche of wisdam ꞉ to knowe holi writ ⁄ summe haue
5 faire eloquence ꞉ to preche it to þe peple ⁄ summe han myche of
goostli strengþe ꞉ to suffre tribulacioun ⁄ summe han pite & releuen ꞉
her pore nedi neiȝboris ⁄ summe tenten vertuouseli to mynystir þe
sacramentis ⁄ summe stiȝen hiȝeli ꞉ to rest in heuenli likyngis ⁄ But
alle suche þingis ben in comune ꞉ to hem þat schal be saued ⁄ as þe
10 prophet seiþ. Ps. cxv. ⁄ 'Particeps ego sum omnium timencium te ꞉
& custodiencium mandata tua'[1] ⁄ Þe prophete spekiþ in þe
persoone ꞉ of þe general chirche ⁄ Lord I am partenere ꞉ of alle
þat dreden þee ⁄ & of alle þat kepen ꞉ þi hooli comaundementis[2] ⁄
Þis techeþ also þe comune crede ꞉ of þe .xii. apostlis ⁄ In an article
15 of oure feiþ ꞉ þat must nede be grauntid ⁄ 'Sanctorum com-
munionem.' comunyng of seintis ⁄ For what þat euer be done in
Rome ꞉ or in ony oþir placis ꞉ if þat þing be couenable ꞉ in þe siȝt
of God ⁄ þanne is it comune to alle þise membris ꞉ þat seruen God
in vertu ⁄ to helpe hem to her endeles ioye ꞉ as we han seide aforn ⁄
20 Herto acordiþ seint Ierom ꞉ vpon þis tixte of Cristis gospel ⁄
Mat. xvi°. 'Tibi dabo claues regni celorum'[3] ⁄ Crist seid to Petir ꞉
& in him to alle his folowars ⁄ to þee and alle | suche as þou art ꞉
I schal ȝyue þe keyes of þe rewme of heuenes[4] ‖ Þise twoo keies.
þe tone is kunnyng of worde ꞉ þe toþir is power of presthood ⁄ Þe
25 rewme of heuenes ꞉ is þe chirche here in erþe ⁄ Ierom seiþ ꞉ & þe
maistir of sentence rehersiþ him ⁄ li°. IIII°. dist. xix. 'Habent
inquit eandem iudiciariam potestatem omnes ecclesie ministri in
episcopis & presbiteris sicut petrus . sed ideo petrus eam specialiter
accepit vt omnes intelligant quod quicumque ab vnitate fidei &
30 societate ecclesie se separauerit. nec a peccatis solui. nec celum
potest ingredi'[a] ‖ Alle þe mynystris of þe chirch ꞉ in bischopis

[1] Vulg. Ps. cxviii. 63.

[2] W. V. 'Parcener I am of all men dredende thee : and of kepende thin
hestis.' 1388, 'I am parcener of alle that dreden thee ; and kepen thin
heestis.'

[3] Vulg. Matt. xvi. 19.

[4] W. V. 'To thee I shal ȝeue the keies of the kyngdam of heuenes.'

[a] Petrus Lombardus, *Sententiarum Libri quatuor*, IV, dist. xix (Migne, tom. 191, col. 890).

& in prestis / han þe same iudiciarij powere ./ as seint Petir
hadde / But þerfore Petir speciali ./ tooke of God þis power /
þat alle men moun vndirstand ./ þat who euer depart him / fro
vnite of stedfast feiþ ./ & felaschip of þis chirche / he mai neiþir
be asoyled ./ from bondis of hise synnes / neiþir he mai entre ./ in to 5
þe blisse of heuene ‖

All spiritual benefits are for the common good of the whole church. Se now þanne boþe lewid & lerned ./ hou preiars ben in comune /
and alle oþir suffragis ./ to þis go-|-ostli chirche ‖ Whennes comeþ
þanne þis outcry ./ þat is sette on broche / saale keene in euery
chirche ./ to selle þise goostli þingis / wiþ suffragis & soilmentis ./ 10
& manye ȝeeris of pardoun / & a plener indulgence ./ 'a pena & a
culpa '/ But miche raþir it schulde be seide ' a gloria & peccunia '/
Certis þei comen fro beneiþe ./ of þe fendis tempting / & ben borne
al aboute ./ of hise cursid membris / to poysen þe peple in
mysbileue ./ as seint Ierom seiþ / & parte hem from Goddis 15
felaschip ./ bi witnesse of seint Austin / & dryue hem to her
eendeles peyne ./ as we han seide aforn ‖

Of Ioye in tribulacioun / Cap^m .XI^m. ‖

The good in the second church are persecuted by the evil. But for þat we reproue þise synnes ./ þis yuel parti grucchiþ / and
pursueþ wiþ strong hand ./ to prisoun & to slee / þerfore must we 20
lerne þe loore ./ of Cristis hooli gospel / Mat. v⁰. ' Beati estis cum
maledixerint vobis homines & persecuti vos fuerint & dixerint
omne malum aduersum vos mencientes propter me &c '[1] ȝe ben
blessid whanne men han cursid ȝou. & han pursued ȝou. & seid al
yuel | aȝens ȝou lying for me ./ Ioye & be myry. for ȝoure mede is 25
miche in heuenes[2] / And also seint Petir seiþ. I. Pe. iii⁰. ' Siquid
patimini propter iusticiam ./ beati '[3] ‖ Whanne þat ȝe suffren ony
þing for riȝtwisenesse ./ blessid mut ȝe be[4] ‖ Seint Poul affermeþ
þis sentence ./ þat Goddis trewe seruauntis / schullen haue peyne in
þis lijf ./ to kepe hem in vertu / II. Thimo. iii⁰. ' Omnes qui pie 30
volunt viuere in christo iesu ./ persecucionem pacientur '[5] ‖ Alle

---

[1] Vulg. Matt. v. 11 ' Beati estis cum maledixerint vobis et persecuti,' etc.

[2] W. V. ' Ȝee shulen be blessid, when men shulen curse ȝou, and shulen pursue ȝou, and shulen say al yuel aȝeins ȝou leeȝing for me. Joye ȝee with yn forth, and glade ȝee with out forth, for ȝoure meede is plenteuouse in heuenes.'

[3] Vulg. 1 Pet. iii. 14.

[4] W. V. ' But if ȝe suffren ony thing for riȝtwisenesse, ȝe ben blessid.'

[5] Vulg. 2 Tim. iii. 12.

Capitulum .XI.

þat euer wole lyue mekeli in Crist Iesu ./ schal suffre persecucioun [1] ||
And seint Luk seiþ of þe wordis of Poul ./ in dedis of þe apostlis.
Actus xiiii⁰. 'Per multas tribulaciones oportet nos intrare in regnum
dei' [2] || Bi manye tribulaciouns . it bihoueþ vs to entre ./ in to þe
5 rewme of God [3] / And þus seiþ þe prophete. Ps. xxxiii. 'Multe tribulaciones iustorum ./ et de omnibus hijs liberabit [4] eos dominus' [5] /
many be þe tribulaciouns ./ þat fallen to þe riȝtwise / and from hem
alle whanne tyme comeþ ./ God schal delyuer hem [6] || Crist bihiȝt þis Tribulation
maner of lijf ./ to hise owene disciplis / and | ȝaue hem in counfort þat leads to joy.
10 þei schal haue ./ a graciouse delyueraunce / for þanne schal blisse be Fol. 73 a
miche þe swetter ./ whanne þei comen þerto / Ion. xvi⁰. / 'Amen amen
dico vobis. quia plorabitis & flebitis vos mundus autem gaudebit
vos autem contristabimini. sed tristicia uestra vertetur in gaudium
& gaudium vestrum. nemo tollet a vobis' [7] || Treweli I seie to ȝou
15 þe trouþe ./ ȝe schal greete & weepe / forsoþe þis world schal ioye ./
& ȝe schal be ful heuy / and aftir þis ȝoure heuynes ./ schal be
turned in to ioie / & ȝoure ioye schal be so siker ./ þat no man
schal take it fro ȝou [8] / And for þis ioie schulde sauour wel ./ to
hem þat ben hise louears / he sendeþ hem tribulacioun ./ as seint
20 Gregor seiþ / 'Deus electis suis iter ostendit asperum ./ ne si nota
delectentur in via obliuiscantur eorum que sunt in patria' [a] / &
iterum / 'tribulaciones que in hoc mundo nos premunt. nos ad
deum ire compellunt' / Iterum. 'Oculos quos culpa claudit ./

---

[1] W. V. 'Alle men that wolen lyue piteuously in Crist Jhesu, schulen suffre persecucioun.' 1388, 'Alle men that wolen lyue feithfull in Crist Jhesu schulen suffre persecucioun.'

[2] Vulg. Acts xiv. 21.

[3] W. V. 'By manye tribulaciouns it behoueth us for to entre into the kingdom of heuenes.'

[4] MS. biberauit.

[5] Vulg. Ps. xxxiii. 19.

[6] W. V. 'Manye tribulaciouns of the riȝtwise ; and of alle these schal delyuere them the Lord.' 1388, 'Many tribulaciouns ben of iust men ; and the Lord schal delyuere hem fro alle these.'

[7] Vulg. John xvi. 20, 22.

[8] W. V. 'Treuli treuli, I seye to ȝou, for ȝe schulen morne and wepe. forsothe the world schal enioye ; forsoþe ȝe schulen be sorwful, but ȝoure sorwe schal turne into ioye, and no man schal take fro ȝou ȝoure ioye.'

---

[a] Gregorius Magnus, Moralium Lib. XXIII, cap. xxiv. 47 (Migne, tom. 76, cols. 279, 280).

Ioye ׃ in tribulacioun ׃

  pena aperit' ᵃ ‖ God schewiþ to hise chosen ׃ scharpnes in þis
iourney ׃ lest bihap | if þei delited hem ׃ in þis deedli weye ׃ þei
my3t for3ete þe þingis ׃ þat ben in heuenli countre ׃ Tribulaciouns
þat brisen vs doun ׃ in þis wrecchid world ׃ þei constreynen vs to
go to God ׃ þat li3tli my3t be dampned ׃ for þoo i3en þat synne 5
closiþ ׃ peyne makiþ hem open ׃ and many a man þat hauntiþ
þeeft ׃ wiþ manye oþir synnes ׃ if þei were lame. blynde. or crokid ׃
of Goddis visitacioun ׃ þei schulden cese & serue her God ׃ & do
penaunce ful treweli ׃ as Crisostom seiþ. om. iii. 'Anima spiritus
est & spirituales penas timet. carnales non timet. verum & sancti 10
penas huius seculi contempnunt & futurum iudicium timent vbi
spiritus cruciantur ‖ Caro autem spirituales penas non timet.
carnales autem timet. ideo mali non cessant peccare nisi eos iudicia
carnalia & terrena conpescant propterea mittet dominus super
seruos suos carnales temptaciones ut conbusta caro non concupiscat 15
malum ' ᵇ ‖ Þe soule is a spirit ׃ & drediþ spiritual peynes ׃ but it
wole not drede ׃ | þe peynes of þe fleische ׃ & þerfore seyntis
dispisiden ׃ peynes of þis world ׃ & dreden þe last iugement ׃ where
spiritis ben turmentid ׃ Forsoþe þe fleische cannot drede ׃ goostli
peynes to cum ׃ but he drediþ in þis lijf ׃ to suffre ony peynes ׃ 20
þerfore þe yuel cessen not ׃ for to do synne ׃ but if iugement of þe
fleische ׃ constreynen hem to be stille ׃ & for þis cause þe Lord schal
sende ׃ vpon hise seruauntis ׃ sore punysching to her fleische ׃ &
oþir tribulaciouns ׃ þat lust of þe fleische mai be sweilid ׃ from
coueiting of yuel. We must nede breke þe nutt ׃ if we wole haue 25
þe kirnel ׃ we must nedis suffre traueile ׃ if we desiren rest ׃ So
must we nede suffre peyne ׃ if we wole cum to blisse ‖

  He is a fals coward kny3t ׃ þat fleeþ & hideþ his heed ׃ whanne
his maistir is in þe feelde ׃ beten among hise enemyes ‖ But oure
Lord Iesu Crist ׃ was beten of þe Iewis ׃ & aftir died in þe felde ׃ 30
on þe mount of Calverie ׃ to paye oure raunsum he tooke his | deeþ ׃
for he no þing giltid ׃ and his bodi whanne it was offrid ׃ made
aseeþ at fulle ׃ in redempcioun of mankynde ׃ þerfore þe wise man
seiþ | Ecc¹. xxix°. 'Gratiam fideiussoris ne obliuiscaris dedit enim
pro te animam suam¹ ' ׃ For3ete þou not þe kyndenes of þi borow ׃ 35

---

[1] Vulg. Ecclesiasticus xxix. 20.

[a] Gregorius Magnus, *Moralium* Lib. XV, cap. li. 58 (Migne, tom. 75, col. 1111).

[b] S. Ioan. Chrysostomus, (*Homilia III, Opera*, ed. 1547, tom. ii, col. 763).

Capitulum .XI.

forsoþe he haþ ʒouun for þee his lijf[1] ‖ Þis borow is oure Lord
God ∴ þat wiþouten mede ⁄ cam from heuene in to þis world ∴ for
to borow hise peple ⁄ and in takyng fleische & blood ∴ of þe virgyn
Mary ⁄ he schewid vs grace & kyndenes ∴ boþe in worde & worchyng ⁄
5 But in ʒyuyng of his lijf ∴ he leide his bodi in plege ⁄ ʒhe to þe
deeþ he wolde not spare ∴ so miche he loued hise peple ‖ If þat
feiþ be trewe in vs ∴ þis mai not be forʒeten ‖

 Summe forsaken synnes ∴ & swen Crist in vertu ⁄ & þis is *Man can show no*
a greet kyndenes ∴ þouʒ þei stiʒe no hiʒer ‖ Summe done wake in *greater love*
10 abstinence ∴ & studien holi lessouns. þis is þanne a gretter kynde- *to God than by giving up*
nes ∴ if þey flee from synne ⁄ summe ben redi whanne þei ben clepid ∴ *his life for his faith.*
of þe Hooli Goost ⁄ to suffre deeþ for Iesu Crist ∴ & witnesse of | his *Fol. 75 a*
lawe ⁄ and whanne þei haue clennes in lyuyng ∴ þis is þe greetest
kyndenes ⁄ as þe gospel schewiþ. Ion. xv⁰. ' Maiorem hac dilec-
15 cionem nemo habet vt animam suam ponat quis pro amicis suis '[2] ⁄
A gretter loue or charite mai no man haue ∴ þan to leie his lijf. in
sauyng of hise frendis soule[3] ‖ we were leef & dere to God ∴ I
whanne we took þe baptem ⁄ but we ben miche derworþier ∴ whanne II
we done þe werkis ⁄ þat God haþ boden in his lawe ∴ wiþouten ony
20 grucchyng ‖ And if we maynten þis bileue ∴ & wole not go þerfro ⁄ III
neiþir bicum renagatis ∴ for peyne þat mai falle ⁄ but þenk on
Cristis passioun ∴ þat swagiþ al heuynes ⁄ Þanne ben we moost
derworþiest ∴ and worþi hiʒest merit ⁄ & þerfore seiþ seint Poul
vnto þe Galatheis ⁄   Gala. vi⁰. ' Michi autem absit gloriari nisi in
25 cruce domini nostri Iesu Christi per quem mihi mundus crucifixus
est & ego mundo '[4] ⁄ Fer be it to me seiþ seint Poul ∴ to make ony
glory ⁄ but in þe cros ∴ þat is þe passioun ∴ | of oure Lord Iesu *Fol. 75 b*
Crist ⁄ bi whom þis world is crucified to me ∴ & I am crucified to
þe world [5] ‖ For þis world dispisid Poul ∴ & he dispised þe world ⁄
30 Summe be not crucified to þe world ∴ but þe world is crucified to

---

[1] W. V. 'The grace of the borʒ ne forgete thou; forsothe he ʒaf for thee
his soule.' 1388, 'Forʒete thou not the grace of the borewe; for he ʒaf his
lijf for thee.'

[2] Vulg. Joh. xv. 13.

[3] W. V. 'No man hath more loue than this, that ony man putte his soul
(that is, lyf), for his frendis.'

[4] Vulg. Gal. vi. 14.

[5] W. V. 'Be it ferr to me to glorie, no but in the cross of oure Lord Jhesu
Christ, by whom the world is crucified to me, and I to the world.' 1388,
'But fer be it fro me to haue glorie, no but in the crosse of oure Lord Jhesu
Crist, bi whom the world is crucified to me, and Y to the world.'

hem / for þei dispisen þis world ; but þis world dispiseþ not hem /
Summ ben crucified to þe world ; but not so þe world to hem / for
þouȝ þe world dispise hem ; þei dispisen it not aȝen ‖ Summe ben
noþir crucified to þe world ; ne þe world to hem / for neiþir þei
dispise þe world ; ne þe world hem / In þe firste degre ; weren þe 5
apostlis / and in þe secounde degre ; ben oþir good lyuars ‖ But in
þe þridde & þe fourþe degree ; ben þoo þat schal be dampned /
And þerfore we schal vndirstande ; þat summe suffren peyne / for
to saue þe peple ; & so dide Iesu Crist / whanne þei myȝt not saue
hem silf ; & schewid his greet kyndenes ‖ Summe suffren peyne ; & 10
largen her mede / as dide Cristis apostles ; & manye oþir martris /
Summe suffren peyne ; to purge hem of her synne / þat þei han
done in tyme bifore ; & crien God of mercy / Summe | suffren
peyne ; to kepe hem from synne / þat þei schulde be acumbrid wiþ ;
if ne peyne were / But summe suffren peyne ; for þei haunten synne / 15
& for þei make non ende þerof ; þe peyne schal laste wiþouten
ende ‖ Ioyne we þanne þe cros of God ; vnto oure bare fleische /
þat oure part mai be founden ; among þise hooli seyntis / þat
wilfulli forsoke hem silf ; & ioyed in tribulacioun / as seint Iames
seiþ. Iaco. iᵒ. 'Omne gaudium existimaste fratres mei cum in 20
temptaciones varias incideritis. scientes quod probacio fidei vestre
operatur pacienciam. paciencia autem opus perfectum habet'[1] ‖
Mi briþeren hope ȝe al ioye ; whanne ȝe han sliden in among
diuerse temptaciouns / witing þat þe prouyng of ȝoure feiþ ;
worchiþ pacience / forsoþe pacience haþ a perfiȝt werk ; þat ȝe 25
moun be perfiȝt in soule / & hool in bodi ; & in no þing failing[2] ‖

Of þe fendis cautels bi whiche he pursueþ in hise membris ; þe kepers of Goddis heestis ‖ Capitulum .XIIᵐ. ‖

The yuel part of þis chirche ; schal neuer cese / wiþ þe malice
þat þei | may ; to purswe good lyuars / But for hise chosen 30
children ; God schal abrege / þe daies of her woodnes ; & þat schal

---

[1] Vulg. Jac. i. 2.

[2] W. V. 'My britheren, gesse ȝe, (or deme), al ioye, whan ȝe shulen falle in to diuerse temptaciouns, (or tribulaciouns), witynge, that the prouyng of ȝoure feith werchith pacience; sotheli pacience hath parfijt werk, that ȝe be parfijt and hool, in no thing faylinge.' 1388, 'My britheren, deme ȝe al joye, whanne ȝe fallen in to diuerse temptaciouns, witynge, that the preuyng of ȝoure feith worchith pacience; and pacience hath a perfit werk, that ȝe be perfit and hole, and faile in no thing.'

Capitulum .XII.

men wel knowe / as seint Ion seiþ to þe chirche ." & ȝyueþ it good to persecute the good.
counfort / Apoc. ii⁰. 'Nichil horum timeas que passurus es /
Ecce missurus est diabolus ex vobis in carcerem & habebitis
tribulacionem diebus decem. esto fidelis vsque ad mortem & dabo
5 tibi coronam vite / qui habet aures audiendi audiat quid spiritus
dicat ecclesijs / qui vicerit a morte secunda non ledetur ' ¹ / Drede
þou not þoo þingis ." þat þou arte for to suffre / Lo þe deuel is for
to sende ." of ȝou into þe prisoun / & ȝe schal haue tribulacioun ."
ten daies bidene / Be þou feiþful to þe deeþ ." & I schal ȝyue to þee
10 a croune of lijf / he þat haþ eeris of heering heere he ." what þe
spirit seiþ to þe chirchis / who þat haþ ouercomen ." schal not be
hirt of þe secounde deeþ ² ‖ vndirstonde þou bi þis deuel ." alle þe
yuel peple / þat schal purswe good lyuars ." vnto þe worldis ende /
sumtyme more sumtyme lesse ." wiþ diuerse peynes of turmentrie ‖
15 And vndirstonde þou | bi þise ten daies ." þe ten comaundementis / Fol. 77 a
for þei ben lyȝt of mannes witt ." in dercknes of þis world / as þe The Ten Commandments are likened to 'ten days' of tribulation, since the devil makes special attack upon each as is here told.
dai passiþ þe nyȝt ." in his cleer schynyng ‖ Of þese ten comaunde-
mentis ." þe fende feyneþ his accioun / to trouble þe good of þe
chirche ." & sende hem to þe prisoun / And here it semeþ spedy ."
20 to telle þe fendis cautells / þat he vsiþ in hise membris ." aȝen
Goddis heestis / & as þe cloude in þe dai ." so marriþ he mannes
wittis ‖ **þe firste heest** |

The firste heeste of God is þis. Ex⁰. xx⁰. Mat. xxii⁰. Mar. xiii⁰ ² / The First Commandment.
'I am þe Lord þi God. þat haue ledde þee out of þe lond of Egipt
25 from þe hous of þraldom / bifore me þou schalt not haue noon alien
goddis. þou schalt make to þee no grauen þing. neiþir ony licknes
of ony þing þat is in heuene aboue. or in erþe bineþ. or of þoo
þingis þat ben in watir vndir-neþe. þou schalt not worschip hem
ne loute hem ‖ I am þe Lord þi God strong loue-gelous. visiting
30 þe wickidnes of fadris vpon sones. in to þe | þridde & þe fourþe Fol. 77 b

---

¹ Vulg. Apoc. ii. 10, 11 'Nihil horum timeas quae passurus es . . . diabolus aliquos ex vobis in carcerem, ut tentemini, et habebitis . . . qui habet
aurem,' etc.

² W. V. 'Drede thou no thing of thes whiche thou art to suffringe. Lo !
the deuel is to sendinge summe of ȝou in to prisoun, that ȝe be temptid ; and
ȝe shulen haue tribulacioun in ten dayes. Be thou feithful unto the deeth,
and I shal ȝiue to thee a coroun of lijf. He that hath eres, here, what the
spirit shal seie to the chirchis. He that shal ouercome, shal not be hirt of
the secounde deeth.'

Vulg. Ex. xx. 2–6 ; Matt. xxii. 37 ; Marc. xii. 29, 30.

Persecucioun.

Against this the fiend lays two snares.

Against this generacioun of hem þat haten me / & I doing mercy in to þousandis to hem þat louen me & kepen myn heestis [1] ||

Aȝen þis comaundement ؛ þe fende haþ leied twoo snaris / & in hem he caccheþ þe peple ؛ þat þei moun not scape / but oþir þey musten graunt his wille ؛ or elles þei schal to prisoun || 5

I. Wrongful Obedience.

Þe firste is clepid obedience ؛ þat þe fende chalengeþ / cheueli to be don to him ؛ or to hise leeftenauntis / as to prelatis or to prestis ؛ þat ben hise officeris / and asken þis obedience ؛ what euer þei comaunde / þat symple men obeye to hem ؛ in hiȝe & in lowe || Al þis world crieþ lowid ؛ aftir þis obedience / & seyn 10 'whateuer þi souereyn biddiþ ؛ þou schalt obeye þerto' || Here we graunten of bileue ؛ þat we owen obedience / to oure souereyns þat techen vs ؛ to knowe God & drede him / ȝhe wheþir þat þei ben mynystris ؛ in þe spiritual part / or officeris in temperalte ؛ we must obeye to hem / in þat þat þei obei to God ؛ & lerne vs 15

Fol. 78 a þis obedi-|-ence / for þus it is writen. I. Re. xv⁰. 'Numquid uult dominus holacausta aut victimas & non pocius vt obediatur voci domini ? melior est enim obediencia quam victime & ascultare magis quam offerre adipem arietum quoniam quasi peccatum ariolandi est repugnare & quasi scelus ydolatrie nolle adquiescere. 20 Pro eo ergo quod abiecisti sermonem domini ؛ abiecit te dominus

Nota ne sis rex' [2] / Samuel seide to kyng Saule. No wheþir wol þe Lord brende offryngis or sacrificis. & not raþer þat it þe obeied to þe vois of þe Lord ? forsoþe obedience is betir þan sacrificis. &

---

[1] W. V. 'Y am the Lord thi God, that hath lad thee out of the loond of Egipte, fro the hows of thraldom. Thow shalt not haue alyen goddis before me. Thow shalt not mak to thee grauen thing, ne eny licknes that is in heuene aboue, and that is in erthe benethe, ne of hem that ben in watrys under erthe; thow shalt not anoure hem, ne herye hem; I forsothe am the Lord thi God, strong gelows, visitynge the wickidnes of fadris in sones into the thridde and the ferthe generacioun of hem that hatiden me, and doynge merci into thousyndes to hem that louen me, and kepen myn heestis.' 1388, 'Y am thi Lord God, that ladde thee out of the lond of Egipt, fro the hous of seruage. Thou schalt not haue alien goddis before me. Thou schalt not make to thee a grauun ymage. nethir ony licnesse of thing which is in heuene aboue, and which is in erthe bynethe, nether of tho thingis, that ben in watris undur erthe : thou schalt not herie tho, nether thou schalt worschipe; for Y am thi Lord God, a stronge gelouse louyere; and Y visite the wickidnesse of fadris into the thridde and fourthe generacioun of hem that haten me, and Y do mercy in to a thousynde, to hem that louen me, and kepen myn heestis.'

[2] Vulg. 1 Reg. xv. 22, 23.

Capitulum .XII.

myche betir it is to take hede to þe lawe ׃ þan to offre þe fattnes / of rames / for it is as þe synne of wichcrafte. to fiȝt aȝen God / & as þe felonye of ydolatrie ׃ not to consent to Goddis word / For þis cause. perfore þat þou hast cast awey þe worde of þe Lord ׃ þe
5 Lord haþ cast þe awey. þat þou be not kyng[1] ‖ and to þis þe wise man acordiþ & seiþ. Eccⁱ. iiii^o. 'Multo enim melior est obediencia quam stultorum victime. qui nesciunt quid faciunt mali'[2] / þat is to seye. ǀ Miche betir is obedience þan sacrifice of foolis ׃ Fol. 78 b for yuel folkis wot not what þei do[3] ‖ And seint Poul techiþ an
10 open rule ׃ of þis maner obedience ׃ wiþ þe cause of souerente ׃ & knittiþ hem boþe togiddir / Heb. vlti^o. 'Obedite prepositis vestris & subiacete eis. ipsi enim peruigilant quasi rationem pro animabus vestris reddituri'[4] / þat is to seie. Obeie ȝe to ȝoure souereyns ׃ & vndirloute ȝe to hem / & cause whi is þis. forsoþe
15 þei walken perfiȝtli. as for to ȝelde a reckenyng for ȝoure soulis[5] ‖ If þis cause be taken awey ׃ obedience cesiþ þere also / as þe philosophur seiþ 'Cessante causa ׃ cessabit officialis' / whanne þe cause cesiþ ׃ þe spede þerof schal cese ‖ But seint Petir techiþ obedience ׃ þat we schal do to lordis / & þat in more larger
20 maner ׃ þan we owen to þe clergie. I. Pe. ii^o. ‖ 'Serui subdite estote in omni timore dominis. non tantum bonis & modestis. sed

---

[1] W. V. 'Whether wole the Lord brent sacrifices or slayn offryngis and not more that it be obeishid to the voice of the Lord? Forsothe betre is obeishaunce than slayn sacrificis, and to take heed more than to offre the fatnes of wetheris; for as synne of denyynge bi deuelis is to repugne and as hidows trespas of mawmetrye to wiln not assent. Forthi thanne that thow hast throwen awey the word of the Lord, the Lord hath throwen awey thee, that thow be not kyng.' 1388, 'Whether the Lord wole brent sacrifices, ethir slayn sacrifices and not more that me obeie to the vois of the Lord? For obedience is betere than sacrifices, and to herkene Goddis word is more than to offre the ynnere fatnesse of rammes; for it is as the synne of mawmetrie to fiȝte aȝens Goddis heest, and it is as the wickidnesse of ydolatrie to nyle ascente to Goddis heest. Therfor for that, that thou castidest awey the word of the Lord, the Lord castide thee awei, that thou be not kyng.'

[2] Vulg. Eccles. iv. 17.

[3] W. V. 'Myche betere is obeisaunce than victori sacrifises of foolis, that wite not what thei don of yuel.' 1388, 'Myche betere is obedience than the sacrifices of foolis, that witen not what yuel thei don.'

[4] Vulg. Heb. xiii. 17.

[5] W. V. 'Obeye ȝe to ȝoure prouostis, (or prelatis), and undirligge to hem; thei perfytly waken, asto ȝeldinge resoun for ȝoure soulis.' 1388, 'Obeie ȝe to ȝoure souereyns, and be ȝe suget to hem; for thei perfitli waken, as to ȝeldinge resoun for ȝoure soulis.'

etiam discolis'[1]/ þat is to seie. Seruauntis be ȝe suget in al
drede to ȝoure temperal lordis / & not oonli to good & to esy lordis.
þat is to seie. in loue. but | also to tyrauntis. þat is to seie. in
pacience / But fendis lymes feynen hem : to be on Cristis siȝde /
& to do correcciouns: aftir Cristis wille / & seyn þei aske obe- 5
dience : to amende soulis / whanne þei do þis þing in dede : þat þei
here speken / þanne we schal obeie to hem : & ellis we schal
answere / as Petir seide to bischopis: & prestis of þe lawe /
Act. v⁰. / 'Obedire oportet deo magis quam hominibus'[2] || It
bihoueþ more to obeie to God : þan to men / Seint Ierom seiþ. 10
If þe prelat or þe lord : bidde ony þink / þat accordiþ to Goddis
wille : obeie þou þanne to hem / If þei bidde þe contrarie : to
God & to his lawe / þanne seie þus. I must raþer obeie to þe lord
of þe soule : þan to þe lord of þe bodi / for Crist seiþ. Mat. x⁰.
Luk xii⁰. 'Nolite timere eos qui occidunt corpus animam autem 15
non possunt occidere sed pocius timete eum qui potest animam &
corpus perdere in gehennam[3] / Ita dico vobis hunc timete'[4] / þat
is to seie. Nile ȝe drede hem þat slen þe bodi : forsoþe þei may
not slee þe soule / but raþer drediþ him. þat mai lese boþe bodi
& soule : in to þe pitt of helle / þus I | seie to ȝou : drede ȝe him / 20
and seint [5] Gregor seiþ. þis forseide rule of obedience : schal be
streiȝtli kept / in children to her parentis: in seruauntis to her
lordis / in clerkis to her maistris: in prestis to her prelatis ||
And if we passe þis rule : in doing of obedience / þanne we ben
vnbuxum to God : & folowars of Lucifer || 25

Þe secounde trappe of þe fende : is clepid pilgrimage / But
miche raþer it schulde be seide : þe outrage of folis / for pilgrimage
in due forme : is euere-more good || Þe peyntour makiþ an ymage :
forgid wiþ diuerse colours / til it seme in foolis iȝen : as a lyueli
creature || Þis is sett in þe chirche : in a solempne place / fast 30
bounden wiþ boondis : for it schulde not falle / Prestis of þe
temple : bigilen þe peple / wiþ þe foule synne of Balaam : in her
open preching || Þei seyn þat Goddis powere : in worching of hise
miraclis / loweþ doun in oo ymage : more þan in anoþir / & þerfore
cum & offre to þis : for here is schewid miche vertu || Lord hou 35
dar þise fendis for drede | þus blasfem her God / & vse þe synne

---

[1] Vulg. 1 Pet. ii. 18. [2] Vulg. Act. v. 29.
[3] Vulg. Matt. x. 28. [4] Vulg. Luc. xii. 5.
[5] MS. sein.

Capitulum .XII.

of Balaam ׃ þat Goddis lawe haþ dampned ⫽ siþen Crist & hise
seyntis ׃ forsoke þis worldis welþe ⫽ & lyueden a pore lijf ׃ as oure
bileue techiþ ⫽ whi gedre ȝe prestis richesses ׃ bi ȝoure peyntid
ymages ⫽ to make ȝoure silf worldli riche ׃ in spoiling of þe peple ?
5 And ȝit ȝe do miche werre ׃ & þat is knowen in parti ⫽ for boþe
ȝe & ȝoure consentours ׃ þus doyng ben verry ydolatreris ⫽ as
seint Poul seiþ. Rom. i⁰. 'Dicentes se esse sapientes stulti facti
sunt & mutauerunt gloriam incorruptibilis dei in similitudinem
ymaginis corruptibilis hominis'[1] ‖ Þat is to seie. Þis peple seiyng
10 hem silf to be wijs ׃ þei ben made foolis ⫽ for þei han chaungid þe
glorie of God ׃ þat mai not be defoulid ⫽ in to þe licknes of mannes
ymage ׃ þat mai be defoilid[2] ⫽ as Poul seiþ. whanne þei knewe
þe riȝtwisenes of God ׃ þei wolde not vndirstande ⫽ þat þei þat
don suche þingis ׃ ben worþi þe deeþ ⫽ Not oonli þe doars ׃ but
15 also þei þat consenten [to þe yuel doars ⫽ For God seiþ. þou
schalt neiþir worschip hem ne loute hem ⫽ for þou schalt
neiþir do sacrifice to ymage ׃ ne offryng ⫽ & þat meneþ God
whanne he seiþ ׃ þou schalt not worschip hem. wiþ ⁊o godli
worschip ⫽ but þat þei be treweli peyntid ׃ as nyȝ as man may ⫽
20 to brynge to mynde as Gregor seiþ ׃ þe passioun of Iesu Crist ⫽ &
martirdam of seyntis ׃ as lewid mennes bookis ‖ But seint Austin
seiþ. vpon al wise þei han discerued to erre ׃ þat seeken God &
hise seyntis ⫽ not in bookis ׃ but in peyntid wowis seiþ seint
Austin ‖ Þou schalt not vowe to þise ymagis ׃ þou schalt not seke
25 þise ymagis ⫽ þou schalt not swere bi hem. neiþir knele to hem.
ne kisse hem ⫽ neiþir putt feiþ hope ne trist in oo ymage ׃ more
þan in anoþir ⫽ and þus meneþ God whanne he seiþ ׃ þou schalt
not loute hem |

But trewe pilgrimage ׃ is don on sixe maneres ‖ Firste we **Six manners of true pilgrimage.**
30 ben pilgrimes ׃ whanne þat we ben born ⫽ as þe comune glose
seiþ ׃ vpon Genesis ‖ 'Omnis ciuis patrie celestis per-|-egrinus Fol. 81 a
est mundi toto tempore vite presentis ⫽' Euery citizen of þe
heuenli countre ׃ is a pilgrime of þis world. for al tyme of þis

---

[1] Vulg. Rom. i. 22, 23.

[2] W. V. 'Sothli thei seynge hem selue for to be wyse men ben maad foolis.
And thei chaungiden the glorie of God uncorruptible, (that may not deie, ne
be peirid) in to the lyknesse of an ymage of coruptible man.' 1388, 'For
thei seiynge that that hem silf weren wise, thei weren maad foo is. And thei
chaungiden the glorie of God uncorruptible in to the licnesse of an ymage of
a deedli man.'

present lijf / And whanne we traueilen sore ./ to kepe Goddis heestis / þanne we done oure pilgrimage ./ as þe prophete seiþ / Ps. cxviii. 'Cantabiles michi erant iustificaciones tue in loco peregrinacionis me'[1] || Lord þi comaundementis weren my songis ./ in tyme of my pilgrimage[2] || 5

II Þe secounde tyme we ben pilgrimes ./ whanne we gon to chirche / as it is writen. Luk. xxiiii°. / 'Tu solus peregrinus es in Ierusalem &c'[3] / whanne we don in þe chirche ./ in forme as God haþ tauȝt vs / þanne we do oure pilgrimage ./ for þus seiþ seint Luk / Lucas. ii°. 'Cum factus esset Iesu annorum. xii. &c.'[4] / 10

III Þe þridde tyme we ben pilgrimes ./ whanne we visiten þe nedi / & whanne we delen almes-dede ./ we don oure pilgrimage / Luk. xiiii°. 'Exi cito in plateas & vicos ciuitatis & pauperes ac debiles cecos & claudos introduc huc'[5] / Go þou forþe anoon ./ in to stretis & weies & bring in to þin hous / þise þre | maner of peple ./ 15 pore feble. pore blynde. & pore crokid[6] ||

IV Þe fourþe tyme prestis ben pilgrimes ./ þat studien holi writ / til þei haue plente in her mynde ./ of þis heuenli wisdam / and þanne þei hiȝen hem fast aboute ./ in al þe brood world / to dele þis goostli tresour ./ among þis witles peple / þat is in poynt to 20 spille for hunger ./ in wanting goostli teching / as it is writen. III. Ion. Karissime fideliter agis quicquid operaris in fratres & hoc in peregrinos'[7] || Dere frende þou doist feiþfulli ./ what euer þou doist to oure briþeren / & namli in to pilgrimes[8] ./ þat prechen þe gospel / & ben apaied where þei cum ./ wiþ pore symple lyu- 25 lood ||

V Þe fifþe tyme þo ben pilgrimes ./ þat wonnen in a toune / where

---

[1] Vulg. Ps. cxviii. 54.

[2] W. V. 'Chauntable weren to me thi iustefiyngus : in the place of my pilgrimaging.' 1388, 'Thi iustifiyngis weren delitable to me to be sungen: in the place of my pilgrimage.'

[3] Vulg. Luc. xxiv. 18. [4] Vulg. Luc. ii. 42.

[5] Vulg. Luc. xiv. 21.

[6] W. V. 'Go out soone in to grete stretis and smale streetis of the citee, and brynge in hidur pore men, and feble, and blynde, and crokid.' 1388, 'Go out swithe in to the grete stretis and smal stretis of the citee, and brynge ynne hidir pore men, and feble, blynde, and crokid.'

[7] Vulg. 3 Joh. i. 5 'Charissime, fideliter facis,' etc.

[8] W. V. 'Moost dere, thou doist feithfully, what euer thou werchist in to britheren, and this thing in to pilgrimys.' 1388, 'Most dere brother, thou doist feithfuli, what euer thou worchist in britheren, and that in to pilgrymys.'

Capitulum .XII.

is noþir prest ne lord ./ to teche hem ne to rule hem / and þanne
þei gon vnto þe place ./ where þei may be tauȝt / & rulid vndir
gouerneaunce ./ þis is her¹ pilgrimage / as it is writen Genesis. xii⁰.
xx⁰. & xxvi⁰.² Þer is non oþir pilgrimage ./ þat mai plese God /
outtake þis þat we haue seide ./ al holi writ beriþ witnes / | For
whanne þe bodi is leide in graue ./ & þe soule forþe passid /
to blisse oþir peyne wheþir þat it be ./ þanne þe sixte is
ended ||

Þe .II. heest ||

Þe secounde comaundement of God is þis. Ex⁰. xx⁰. 'Non
assumes nomen dei tui in uanum. nec enim habebit dominus
insontem eum ./ qui assumpserit nomen dei sui frustra'³ / þat is
to seie. þou schalt not take þe name of þi God in veyn / forsoþe
þe Lord schal not haue him clene ./ þat haþ taken þe name of
God in veyn ⁴ / and Crist seiþ in his gospel. Mat. v⁰. / 'Ego
autem dico uobis non iurare omnino. neque per celum quia
thronus dei est / neque per terram. quia scabellum pedum eius est /
neque per Ierusalem. quia ciuitas est regis magni / neque per
caput⁵ tuum iuraueris. quia non potes vnum capillum album facere
aut nigrum / Sit autem sermo uester. est est. non non'⁶ || For-
soþe I seie to ȝou ./ not swere on ony wise / neiþir bi heuene ./ for
it is þe trone of God / neiþir bi þe erþe ./ for it is þe stool of his
feet / neiþir bi Ierusalem ./ for it is þe cite of a greet kyng /
neiþir bi þi heed ./ for | þou maist not make a heer whiȝt or blak /
forsoþe be ȝoure worde ȝhe ȝhe nay nay ./ wiþ herte & mouþe
acording⁷ ||

The Second Commandment.

Fol. 82 a
VI

Fol. 82 b

---

¹ MS. þis is is her.
² Vulg. Gen. xii. 4–9, xx. 1, xxvi. 17.
³ Vulg. Ex. xx. 7.
⁴ W. V. 'Thou schalt not tak the name of the Lord thi God in veyn, ne forsothe the Lord shal haue innocent hym, that takith the name of the Lord his God in ydel.' 1388, 'Thou schalt not take in veyn the name of thi Lord God, for the Lord schal not have hym giltles, that takith in veyn the name of his Lord God.'
⁵ MS. capud.
⁶ Vulg. Matt. v. 34–6.
⁷ W. V. 'Forsothe Y say to ȝou, to nat swere on al manere: neither by heuene, for it is the trone of God; nether by the erthe, for it is the stole of his feet; neither by Jerusalem, for it is the citee of a greet kyng; neither thou schalt swere by thin heued, for thou maist not make oon heer whyt, or blak; but be ȝoure word ȝea, ȝea; nay, nay.'

The fiend's snares are forced oaths and perjury.

Aȝen þis comaundement ; þe deuel in hise membris / constreynen men for to swere ; & leie her hand on bookis / & þanne he puttiþ hem to open schame ; & if þei leeue his bidding / he seiþ bi lawe þei ben relaps ; & þanne þei schal be brent / And þis is an hidouse cloude ; vpon þis schynful dai / to peyne men for keping of Goddis comaundement / for seynt Austin seiþ vpon þe gospel. 'Christus quod perfectus est docuit. quod infirmitatis est indulsit / quod supersticiosum est resecauit. perfeccionis est non iurare omnino / infirmitatis iurare conpulsi sed supersticionis iurare inaniter' Hec Augustinus om. 6 / þat is to seie. Crist haþ tauȝt þat þing ; þat is more perfiȝt / þat þing þat is of infirmite ; he haþ suffrid / þat þing þat is supersticiouse ; he haþ kitte awey ‖ It is of perfeccioun ; not to swere in ony manere / It is of infirmite ; to swere constreyned / but it is of supersticioun ; to swere veynli /

Fol. 83 a for þe vise man ‖ seiþ ; Sap. xiiii°. 'Non enim iuramentum est virtus sed peccancium pena perambulat semper iniustorum preuaricacionem '[1] / Þat is to seie. Sweryng is no vertu ; but peyne of synnars[2] / eiþir of hem þat wole not ȝyue credence ; but if men swere / or ellis of hem ; þat sweren wiþouten cause / and þerfore seint Ion Crisostom ;[a] blameþ prestis / for þei bringen forþe bookis ; to compelle þe peple for to swere on hem ; & askiþ þis questioun ‖ wheþir is not he þat settiþ an hous on brennyng. gilti of þis brennyng ? wheþir is not he þat bringiþ a swerid. wiþ whiche

The guilt lies with those who impose forced oaths.

manslauȝtir is don ; gilti of þis manslauȝtir ? So þei þat bryngen forþe bookis. on whiche men forsweren hem ; ben gilti of þis forswering / and he seiþ. If þis peple wil seie þe soþe wiþouten ony ooþ ; wherto schulde þei swere / & if þei suppose þei wole seie fals ; whi schulde þei compelle hem to forswere hem ? & so þe greetnesse of synne ; stondiþ cheeuli in suche ordinarijs / eiþir seculere or spirituel ; as þis doctour proueþ / not accepting pur-

Fol. 83 b gacioun ; wiþouten suche ooþis ǀ and of þis sweryng comeþ wickidnes ; and Goddis greuouse veniaunce / as þe wise man seiþ. Eccles. xxiii°. 'Vir multum iurans implebitur iniquitate ; & a domo eius

---

[1] Vulg. Sap. xiv. 31 ' Non enim iuratorum virtus,' etc.
[2] W. V. 'Forsothe of men swerende is not vertue, but the peyne of synneres.' 1388, ' Forwhi an ooth is not vertu, but the peyne of synneris.'

---

[a] S. Ioan. Chrysostomus, *Homilia XII* (*Opera*, ed. 1547, tom. ii, col. 819).

Capitulum .XII.

non discedet plaga'[1]/ þat is to seie. A man miche swering schal
be fillid of wickidnes.' & veniaunce schal not go from his hous ||
ȝit enemyes purswen aȝen þis comaundement/ & seyn þat Crist *nota*
him silf swore.' & hise seintis boþe / swere bi þis book þou
5 obstinat man.' or ellis þou schalt to prisoun / Þou schalt swere in
oure courte.' bicause of þin infirmite/ as seint Austin haþ tauȝt.'
whanne þou art constreyned [a] || To þis we seyn þat Iesu Crist.'
forbediþ on alwise swering / bi ony of þise foure þingis.' þat he Conditions
him silf rehersiþ/ þat is to seie. heuene or erþe.' eiþir bi Ierusalem whereby men may
10 or bi þin owene heed || And whanne þise foure ben outaken.' wiþ swear.
al þat is in hem/ ȝe schal not grounde ȝoure viciouse sweryng.'
til þat heuene be fallen || To þis þat seint Austin seiþ.' þou
schalt swere compellid [a] / we graunten wel aforne a iugge.' if ellis
men wollen not tro-|-we vs || But neiþir on bookis schullen we Fol. 84 a
15 swere.' neiþir bi Goddis creaturis / but aftir þe forme þat God
haþ tauȝt.' bi Ieremye þe prophet / Iere. iiii[o]. 'Iurabis viuit
dominus in veritate & in iudicio & in iusticia'[2] || Þat is to seie.
Þou schalt swere.' þe Lord lyueþ. in trouþe & in doome & in
riȝtwisenesse || Þe Lord lyueþ. is to mene bi God. or bi þin holidom.
20 or bi þi trowþe || Þis schalt þou not swere.' but wiþ þre con-
diciouns || Þe firste is trouþe in þe conscience of him þat I
sweriþ.' wiþouten ony gile || Þe secounde þat it be in dom.' II
to exclude al maner of idel & veyn sweryng || Þe þridde. þat III
it be in riȝtwisenes & in no maner disceyte.' ne hyndring
25 to oure neiȝbour. ne discording fro þe riȝtwisenes of God ||
But we mai in no case swere bi bookis.' as we han seide
aforne/ neiþir bi lyueli creaturis.' as bi seyntis or ony suche
oþir || For þe wise man seiþ. Ecclesi. xxiii[o]. 'Nominibus sanc-
torum non assuescas os tuum'[3] || Þat is to seie. Custum þou not
30 þi mouþ.' to sweryng bi names of seyntis / for Crisostom seiþ.

---

[1] Vulg. Ecclesiasticus xxiii. 12.
[2] Vulg. Jer. iv. 2.
[3] Vulg. Ecclesiasticus xxiii. 9, 10 'Iurationi non assuescas os tuum . . . nominatio vero Dei non sit assidua in ore tuo, et nominibus sanctorum non admiscearis.'

---

[a] Augustinus, *De Sermone Domini*, Lib. I, c. 30; Gratian, *Decreti* Pars Secunda, causa xxii, quaest. i, cap. v (Migne, tom. 187, col. 1123).

Fol. 84 b om. 12. 'Qui iurat per creaturam committit ydolatriam' ‖ | Iterum.
'qui iurat per creaturas. duppliciter peccat & si iurare liceret.
primo. quia iurat/ secundo quia deificat / quia quicquid est per
quod quis iurat deificat illud'ᵃ ‖ Þat is to seie. He þat sweriþ
bi a creature ./ doiþ ydolatrie / he þat sweriþ bi creatures ./ synneþ 5
duble foold / ȝhe þouȝ it were so ./ þat sweryng leeful / oones. for he
sweriþ / anoþir tyme. for he makiþ him a fals god / for what euer
it be þat a man sweriþ bi ./ þat þing he makiþ his god ‖ Lord hou
manye men & wymmen ./ maken hem fals goddis / siþen wel nyȝ
al þis world haþ in custum ./ to swere bi oo seynt or bi oþir / 10
Certis þise forseide enemyes ben cheef cause ./ of suche blasfemouse
sweryng / what wiþ her sclaundris ./ & sumtyme wiþ sore punysching / & freel peple kunnen not stonde ./ but ȝelden hem to þise
fendis tempting ‖

Þe .III. heest /

The Third Commandment.

Þe þridde comaundement of God is þis. Exodi. xx⁰. 'Memento
vt diem sabbati sanctifices. vi. dietus operaberis & facies opera
tua. septimo autem die sabbati domini dei tui est. Non facies
Fol. 85 a omne opus tu & filius tuus & filia tua & seruus tuus et | ancilla
tua iumentum tuum & aduena qui est intra portas tuas. vi. diebus 20
fecit deus celum & terram & mare & omnia que in eis sunt. &
requieuit in die septimo / Iccirco benedixit deus diei sabbati &
sanctificauit illud'¹/ Þat is to seie. Haue mynde þat þou halowe
þin halidai. In .vi. daies þou schalt worche ./ & do alle þin owne
werkis / forsoþe þe seuenþe dai. is þe sabot of þi Lord. þou schalt 25
not do ony seruyle werk / þise .vi. schal kepe þis holidai / þi sone
& þi douȝter / þi seruaunt & þin handmayde / þi beest & þi
straunger þat is wiþynne þi ȝatis ‖ In .vi. daies God mad heuene
& erþe & þe see. & alle þingis þat ben in hem ./ & he restid in þe
seuenþe dai / þerfore God blessid þe dai of þe saboth ./ & made it holi² / 30

---

¹ Vulg. Ex. xx. 8–11 'Memento . . . facies omnia opera tua . . . Non facies omne opus in eo, tu et filius tuus . . . Sex enim diebus,' etc.

² W. V. 'Haue mynde to halwe thin boly day; sixe daies thow shalt worche and doon alle thi werkis; the seuenthe forsothe dai is the haliday of the Lord thi God; thow shalt not doon al werk, thow, and thi sone, and thi dowȝter, and thi seruaunt, and thin handmayden thi beeste, and comlyng that is with ynne thi ȝatis; sixe forsothe daies God made heuene and erthe, the see, and alle thingis that ben in hem, and he restide the seuenthe day;

ᵃ S. Ioan. Chrysostomus, *Homilia XII* (*Opera*, ed. 1547, tom. ii, col. 819).

Capitulum .XII.

Aȝen þis comaundement: þe fende in hise membris / ȝyueþ leue *The devil leads men* to chapmen: to bie & to selle / ȝhe wiþynne þe sauntwary: on þe *to break the sabbath.* holi sundai / and vitileris of þe countre: holden comune market ‖ ȝet se more wlatsumnes: aȝens þis Goddis heest / greet feires of
5 þe ȝeere: for þe moost partie: ben sett on | þe saboth dai: bi þe *Fol. 85 b* fendis counceile / God tooke ful hidouse wreeche: vpon þe children of Isrel / whanne þei wrouȝt seruyle werke. vpon her saboth dai / as it is writen. Exº. xxxiº. 'Custodite sabbatum meum sanctum enim est vobis. qui polluerit illud. morte morietur / qui fecerit in
10 eo opus peribit anima illius de medio populi sui'[1] ‖ Þat is to seie. Halowe ȝe my saboth: forsoþe it is holi to ȝou / who þat haþ defoulid it: he schal be deed / & he þat doiþ ony seruyle werke þerynne: his lijf schal perische fro þe myddis of his peple[2] / & so for gedring of stikkis: on þe saboth dai / a man bi Goddis bidding
15 was stooned to þe deeþ ‖ þerfore Neemyas: a man þat dredde *nota* God / wolde suffre noon to bie ne selle: on þe sabot dai / wiþynne þe ȝatis of Ierusalem: neiþir aboute þe wallis / and chargid alle vitileris: þat þei schulde ceese / And if þei wolde not take heede: þei schulde fele his hondis / for he pouȝt to werre on hem: as on
20 Goddis enemyes / but þei wolde obeie to God: in halowing of his saboth / Þis processe is | writen in þe book of Neemyas: þe last *Fol. 86 a* chapitir[3] ‖ Loo hou streiȝtli þe Iewis: kepten Goddis bidding / & hou God smot hem wiþ bodili peyne: whanne þat þei dide forfet / But cristen men maken her boost: þat þei ben more
25 perfiȝt / in seruyse of her Lord God: þan euer were þe Iewis / who þat euer mekeli: proueþ his word in dede / þanne mai he

---

therfore the Lord blisside to the holiday and halwidė it.' 1388, ' Haue thou mynde, that thou halowe the dai of the sabat; in sixe daies thou schalt worche and schalt do alle thi werkis; forsothe in the seuenthe day is the sabat of thi Lord God; thou schalt not do ony werk, thou, and thi sone, and thi douȝtir, and thi seruaunt, and thin handmaide, thi werk beest, and the comelyng which is withynne thi ȝatis; for in sixe dayes God made heuene and erthe, the see, and alle thingis that ben in tho, and restide in the seuenthe dai; herfor the Lord blesside the dai of the sabat, and halewide it.'

[1] Vulg. Ex. xxxi. 14.
[2] W. V. ' Kepith myn holi day, holi forsothe it is to ȝow, who so poluteth it, with deth dye he; who so doth in it werk. shal perishe the lijf of hym fro the myddil of his puple.' 1388, ' Kepe ȝe my sabat, for it is hooli to ȝou; he that defoulith it, schal die bi deeth, the soule of hym, that doith werk in the sabat, schal perische fro the myddis of his puple.'
[3] Vulg. Neh. xiii. 15-22.

seie boldli ׃ þat þis tyme of *grace* ⫽ is of more *perfeccioun* ׃ *per vertu of* þe *sacramentis* ⫽ and fredom of þe gospel ׃ þan was Moises lawe ⫽ and þou a more *perfite* man ׃ *in* keping þis *perfeccioun* ‖ But & þou be apostataa ׃ *in* breking of Goddis heestis ⫽ þanne is þi peyne so miche þe more ׃ as Poul seide to þe Romayns ⫽ Ro. xi⁰. ⫽ 5 'Tu autem fide stas. noli altum sap*ere* s*ed* time ⫽ si *enim* d*eus* naturalib*us* ramis no*n* pep*er*cit. ne forte nec ti*bi* p*ar*cat'[1] ‖ Þat is to seie. Forsoþe þou stondist i*n* þe feiþ ׃ nyle þou be proude ⫽ ne bere þee neu*ere* þe hiȝer ׃ but abide þou mekeli ⫽ *in* þe holi drede of þe Lord ‖ Forsoþe siþen þat God sparid not. to þe 10 kyndli braunchis ⫽ þat is to þe Iewis ׃ þat ⸴ he chase to be hise kyndeli heiris ⫽ Bi war lest bi happe he spare not þee ׃ þat camest out of þe heeþen stokke ⫽ & arte plau*n*tid in bi *grace* ׃ of C*ri*st & hise gospel[2] ‖ Se now þyn apostasie ׃ þou vnkynde wrecche ⫽ & þe falsenes þat þou vsest ׃ aȝen C*ri*stis gospel ⫽ Mat. xxi⁰. 15 M*ar.* ix⁰. Luk. xix⁰. & Ion. ii⁰. ⫽ 'Int*r*auit Iesu *in* templu*m* dei. & eiciebat om*n*es vendentes & ementes *in* templo & me*n*sas nu*m*mulario*rum* & cathedras vendencium columbas eu*er*tit'[3] ‖ Þat is to seie. Ie*s*u entrid *in* to þe temple of God ׃ & he cast out alle sellars & biears i*n* þe temple ׃ & þe bordis of mony-makears ⫽ & he tu*r*ned 20 vp-so-dou*n* ׃ þe chaiers of hem þat soolde*n* dowues ⫽ and he seide vnto hem ׃ it is write*n* Isaye .lvi⁰.[4] my hous schal be clepid. an hous[5] of p*r*eiour ⫽ forsoþe ȝe han made it a den of þeeues[6] ‖ Criste forbediþ þe laite ׃ þe vsing of her marchau*n*dise ⫽ eiþ*ir in* toune or *in* chirche ׃ on her holy dai ⫽ & he dampneþ more streiȝtlier ׃ 25 among þise visiouse prestis ⫽ biyng of her beneficis ׃ & ⸴ selli*n*g of her *sacramentis* ⫽ as doct*our* Odo seiþ ׃ vpon þis same gospel ⫽ 'Columbas vendentês su*n*t q*ui* sp*iri*tualia vendu*n*t ⸴ & si no*n* clamant ore. tu*m* cu*m* iuda dicu*n*t ⫽ Quid uult*is* dare ׃ & ego

---

[1] Vulg. Rom. xi. 20, 21.

[2] W. V. 'Forsoth thou stondist by feith. Nyle thou sauere hiȝe thing, but drede thou, forsothe if God sparide not the kyndely braunchis, lest perauenture he spare not thee.'

[3] Vulg. Matt. xxi. 12; Luc. xix. 45; Joh. ii. 15.

[4] Vulg. Isaias lvi. 7.

[5] MS. hou.

[6] W. V. 'Jhesus entride in to the temple of God, and kest out of the temple alle sellynge and biynge; and he turnyde upsodoun the bordis of chaungeris, and the chaiers of men sellynge culveris. And he seith to hem It is writen, My hous shal be clepid an hous of priere; forsothe ȝe han made it a denne of thefes.'

Cap*itulu*m .XII.

vobis e*um*[1] trad*am* ? Sic clamant monachi ceteri*que* religiosi ./
h*abitum* & suffragia vendentes. *item* n*on* s*a*c*er*dotes diuina cele-
br*antes* & tales *in* ecclesia dei multiplicant*ur* ? vbi credis q*uo*d sit
5 dom*us* or*ationis*. ibi *in*venies speluncam latronu*m* / omnes qui
n*on* i*n*trant p*er* hostiu*m* id *est* chr*istu*m. sed p*er* pecuniam uel
seculi grat*ia*m fures sunt & latrones p*er* muru*m* fractum ingre-
dientes / quia mur*us* ecclesie rumpitur cu*m* prece uel pre*c*io aut
sanguine min*us* ydone*us* ad beneficium ecclesiasticum i*n*digne pro-
10 moueat*ur* ' ª / Hec ille ‖   Þat is to seie. þei be*n* sellers of dowues ./ Nota
þat spir*itu*el þingis selle*n* / & þouȝ þei crien not wiþ her mouþe ./ no*ta* bene
neþles [2] þei seyn wiþ Iudas / what wole ȝe ȝyue ./ & I schal bit*r*aie Sellers of
him to ȝou ? Þus crien mou*n*kis ./ & oþ*ir* bastard religiou*n* / þat break the
sellen as þei mai take þerfore ./ her habit & her suffragijs / & oþ*ir* ment.
15 pr*estis* don | als wick ./ þat treten diuine seruice / & suche ben Fol. 87 b
now multiplied ./ in þe chirche of God / þerfore where as þou
wenest ./ þat is þe hous of pr*eiour* / þere schalt þou redili fynde ./
a den of ma*n*i þeues / forsoþe alle þat e*n*tren not ./ bi þe door
þat is Crist / but bi money or seculere fauo*ur* ./ þei ben niȝt-
20 þeues & dai-þeues / þat entren *in* bi a broken wowe ./ vnwiting
Iesu Crist / for he proueþ not her dedis ./ & þat is his vnknowyng /
for þanne is þe chirche wowe ./ al to-broken dou*n* / whan*n*e þe
vnable is avau*n*sid ./ to þe chirches benefice / eiþir fo*r* pr*eiour* or
for pris ./ or for vndwe seruice ‖   no*ta* bene
25   Siþen oure Lord Iesu Crist ./ seide to his apostlis / þat oone of
hem was a deuel ./ & ment it bi Iudas / Be not þise apostataas ./ þat
don als yuel as he / worþi to be clepid deuel*is* ./ bi þe same resou*n* ?
Þei ben greet questione*rs* ./ & askars of þe lawe / but þei wole not
do so miche ./ as putt þerto her fynge*r* / & þei heepen charge on
30 oþ*ir* ./ more þan þei mai bere / Þei ben pr*e*isars of seint*is* ./ & no
þing her folowars / þei ben heerars | of þe lawe ./ but no þing þe Fol. 88 a
doars / þei ben alwey lernyng ./ & neu*ir* þei wole be p*er*fite / þus þei
boosten *in* þe lawe ./ wiþ worschip & wiþ wynnyng / but bi breking
of þe lawe ./ þei don dispise her God ‖

35 Þe .IIII. heeste ‖

Þe fourþe comaundement of God is þis Ex*o*. xx*o*. ' Honora p*at*rem The Fourth
tuu*m* & m*at*rem tuam vt sis longeu*us* sup*er* terram quam d*omi*n*us* Command-
                                                                  ment.

---

[1] MS. ēa.   [2] MS. neþels.

ª Odo of Cheriton, *Flores Sermonum*, fols. cvi, cvii.

deus tuus dabit tibi'¹ ‖ Þat is to seie. worschip þou þi fadir & þi modir þat þou be longlyuyng vpon erþe ⁊ þe whiche þi Lord God schal ȝyue to þee²⫽ And it swiþ of þis comaundement ⁊ þat þei þat worschipen not her parentis ⫽ schullen haue schort lijf here in erþe ⁊ & aftir þe lond of myschef ⫽ & þerfore Tobie tauȝt his sone ⁊ a litil 5 aforne his diyng⫽ Tobi. iiiiº. 'Corpus meum sepeli & honorem habebis matri tue omnibus diebus vite eius⫽ memor enim esse debes que & quanta pericula passa sit in vtero propter te'³ ‖ Sone birie þou my bodi ⁊ & þou schalt haue worschip to þi modir. alle þe daies of þi lijf⫽ þou owist for to haue in mynde ⁊ what perelles & how mani 10 sche haþ suffrid in hir wombe for þee⁴⫽

Fol. 88 b   Summe | counten it for no synne ⁊ to take fro her parentis ⫽ suche þing as þei haue ⁊ bi cause þei ben her children ⫽ but certis þis synne passeþ þeeft ⁊ & more it greueþ God ⫽ as þe wise man seiþ. Prouer. xxviiiº. 'Qui subtrahit aliquid a patre uel a matre 15 & dicit hoc non est peccatum particeps homicide est'⁵ ‖ Þat is to seie. who þat wiþdrawiþ ony þing from his fadir or his modir. & seiþ þat is no synne ⁊ he is partener of manslauȝtir⁶⫽ for worschip to oure parentes ⁊ stondiþ in worde & dede ⫽ boþe to teche hem & rule hem ⁊ if þei ben lewid or pore⫽ and it longiþ to þise parentes 20 to gouerne wel her children ⫽ & ordeyn oonli not for hem ⁊ þe goodis of þis world ⫽ but miche raþir dispose her lijf ⁊ toward þe blisse of heuene ⫽ as þe wise man seiþ. Prouer. xxiiiº. 'Noli sub-

¹ Vulg. Ex. xx. 12.

² W. V. 'Honour thi fader and thi moder, that thou be of long lijf upon erthe, that the Lord thi God shal ȝyue to thee.' 1388, 'Onoure thi fadir and thi modir, that thou be long lyuyng on the lond, which thi Lord God schal ȝyue to thee.'

³ Vulg. Tob. iv. 3, 4 'Corpus meum . . . passa sit propter te in utero suo.'

⁴ W. V. 'My bodi birie ; and wrshipe thou shalt han to thi moder alle the daȝes of thi lif; forsothe myndeful thou owist to be, what and how grete she suffride perilis for thee in hir wombe.' 1388, 'Byrie thou my bodi; and thou schal haue onour to thi moder in alle the daies of hir lijf; for thou owist to be myndeful, what perels and how grete sche suffride for thee in hir wombe.'

⁵ Vulg. Prov. xxviii. 24 'Qui subtrahit aliquid a patre suo et a matre et dicit hoc non esse peccatum,' etc.

⁶ W. V. 'Who withdrawith any thing fro his fader and moder, and seith that not to ben synne, parcener is of a man sleere.' 1388, 'He that withdrawith ony thing fro his fadir and fro his modir, and seith that this is no synne, is parcener of a manquellere.'

Capitulum .XII.

trahere a puero disciplinam. si enim percusseris eum virga non
morietur / tu virga percutis eum & animam eius de inferno
liberabis'¹/ þat is to seie. 'Nile þou wiþdrawe ./ teching from þi
childe / for þouȝ þou bete him wiþ a ȝeerde ./ he schal not die
5 þerou²/ | þou beetist him wiþ a baleys ./ & þou schalt delyuer his
soule from helle /³ he þat spariþ þis balys ./ hatiþ his childe /
forsoþe he þat loueþ him ./ wole teche him bisili / for a wise childe
gladiþ his fadir ./ forsoþe a foltid childe is þe sorow of his
modir ||

10 Aȝen þis comaundement ./ þe fende wiþ hise membris / what wiþ *The fiend*
ypocrisie ./ þat is feyned hoolines / what wiþ blynd pite ./ þat *encumbers Christ's*
regneþ in þe seculeris / he haþ encombrid Cristis chirche ./ wiþ *church with temporal*
miche worldli muk / & ouerladde oure modir ./ wiþ temporal posses- *possessions*
sioun / þat sche mai not rise ./ to heuenli contemplacioun / þerfore *so that her children*
15 hir owene children ./ waxen wilde & wantoune / & wole noþir take *neither fear nor obey her.*
awe ne lawe ./ alas þis is greet sorow / but oure fadir þat is in
heuene ./ to whom no þing is hid / seing hise sones frowardnes ./ is
sterid al to wraþþe / þouȝ þat he abide long ./ & differre his
veniaunce / suffring from dai to dai ./ if þat þei wolde amende / For
20 he forbadde to prestis ./ of þe oolde lawe / to take suche possessioun ./
among þe oþir tribis / but holde hem paied of | his part ./ for he
wolde be her eritage / for þei schulde prynte þis lore ./ & neuir go
þerfro / prise it is rehersid ./ þouȝ oones myȝt haue suffisid || Firste
in þe book of Numeri. xviiiº.⁴/ þe secounde in Deutº. xviiiº.⁵/ þe
25 þridde in Ezechiel. xliiiiº⁶/ And Crist in his gospel ./ twise for- *Temporal power for-*
bediþ hise prestis / to haue þis temporal lordschip ./ & regne as *bidden to priests in*
worldli kyngis || Oones in his worching ./ for he forsok it him silf / *the Gospel.*
Ion. viº.⁷/ and also in his teching ./ þat enemyes schulden not
seie / who mai lyue as Crist dide ? & neþles Gregor seiþ / Gregor.
30 om. xvii / 'Dominus Iesu Christus aliquando nos sermonibus
ammonet aliquando operibus ipsa etenim facta eius precepta sunt

---

¹ Vulg. Prov. xxiii. 13.   ² = ! þerof þouȝ.
³ W. V. 'Wile thou not withdrawe fro a childe discipline; if forsothe thou
smyte hym with ȝerde, he shal not die. Thou with a ȝerde smite hym, and
the soule of hym fro helle thou shalt deliveren.' 1388, 'Nile thou withdrawe
chastisyng fro a child; for thouȝ thou smyte hym with a ȝerde, he schal not
die. Thou schalt smyte hym with a ȝerde, and thou schalt delyuere his soule
fro helle.'
⁴ Vulg. Num. xviii. 20-4.   ⁵ Vulg. Deut. xviii. 1, 2.
⁶ Vulg. Ezech. xliv. 28.   ⁷ Vulg. Joh. vi. 15.

quia dum taciter aliquid facit quid agere debeamus innotescit'ᵃ ‖
þat is to seie. Oure Lord Iesu Crist sumtyme wiþ wordis sumtyme
wiþ dedis techiþ vs / forsoþe hise dedis ben comaundementis / for
whanne he doiþ ony þing stilli ./ in þat he makiþ knowen to vs.
what we schal do / and notwiþstanding. Crist forbediþ suche
possessioun ./ bi word to hise prestis / Mat. xx⁰ / Mar. x⁰ / Luk.
xxii⁰¹ ‖ | And if enemyes wollen not accept ./ God in hise boþe
lawes / neiþir obeie to her fadir ./ for his worde ne for his dede / to
whom heuene. helle. & erþe ./ kneelen on her knees / but stonden
stille obstinat ./ as yuel-willi traitours / to clense her modir holi
chirche ./ of þis foule corrupcioun / þanne schullen we leie forþe holi
seyntis ./ þat speken of þis mater / & saie for þei wole acorde ./ to
wordis þat þei han seide / and so rise vp to Goddis word ./ bi þise
seintis teching ‖ Seint Austin seiþ. 'Non debet ecclesia suscipere
que filio exheredato sibi offerunt. verum quicumque uult exheredato
filio. heredem facere ecclesiam querat alterum qui suscipiat. non
Augustinum . ymmo deo propicio ./ neminem inueniet'/ Hec
Augustinus in sermone de vita clericorum & xvii. q. iiii⁰. finali ᵇ ‖
þat is to seie. Þe chirche owiþ not ./ to take þoo þingis / þat ben
profrid to hir ./ of hem þat haþ no eire / þerfore who þat euer wile ./
make þe chirche his eire / seeke anoþir þat mai take it ./ but on
nowise Austin / but bi þe mercy of God ./ he schal fynde no man ‖
And Ierom seiþ / | 'Ex quo ecclesia creuit in possessionibus ./
decreuit in virtutibus' ‖ Fro þat tyme þat þe chirche ./ grew in
possessiouns. sche haþ lessid or dwyned in vertues ‖ Seint Bernard
forbediþ þise possessiouns ./ to be in prestis handis / & spekiþ to
Eugeny þe pope ./ in þise witti wordis / li⁰. ii⁰. 'Esto ut alia
ratione hec tibi vendices / sed non apostolico iure / Quomodo potuit
iste tibi dare quod non habuerit ./ quod habuit hoc dedit solicitu-
dinem super ecclesias . Numquid dominacionem ./ audi ipsum neque
dominantes inquit in clero / sed forma facti gregi / Et ne dicui sola
humilitate putes & non veritate. vox domini est in euangelio /
reges gencium dominantur eorum ./ vos autem non sic'ᶜ ‖ Þat is

---

[1] Vulg. Matt. xx. 25-7; Marc. x. 42-4; Luc. xxii. 25, 26.

[a] Gregorius Magnus, *Homilia XVII* 1 (Migne, tom. 76, col. 1139).
[b] St. Augustinus, *De Vita Clericorum*, Sermo II (Gratian, *Decreti Pars Secunda*, c. xvii, q. iv, cap. xliii (Migne, tom. 187, col. 1077-88).
[c] St. Bernard, *De Consideratione*, Liber II, p. 1528 (*D. Bernardi Opera Omnia*, ed. 1552).

Capitulum .XII.

to seie. Chalenge þou þise possessiouns ; bi anoþir resoun / but
þou maist not chalenge hem ; bi þe apostlis riȝt / Hou miȝt þe
apostle ȝyue ; þat he had not ? þat he hadde þat he ȝaue ; bisines
vpon chirchis / No wheþir seculere lordschip ? heere what he seiþ /
5 neiþir lording in þe clergie ; but mad in forme. to profite of þe
flok / & not oonli in mekenes ; trowe þou þis to be seid / | But also [Fol. 91 a]
in troupe of dede ; as Crist seiþ in his gospel / 'kyngis of erþe
lorden ouer hem ; forsoþe ȝe not so ' || It is pleyn to þe apostlis **Temporal**
þis lordschip is entirdiȝtid / hou darst þou þanne take þis lordschip **lordship forbidden**
10 vpon þee / eiþir lording apostilhed. eiþir apostilhed to lordschip ? **to the Apostles.**
pleynli þou art forboden þe tone / for if þou wilt haue boþe ; þou
schalt leese boþe / þat is to seie. þi presthod & þi lordschip / or
ellis þou schalt not be except of þis noumbre ; of þe whiche God
pleyneþ him || Þei han regned ; but not bi me / þey han ben
15 princis ; but I haue not knowen hem / Now if it availe to regne
wiþouten God ; þanne hast þou ioye ; but not anentis God || And
whane prestis holden þis entirdiȝting ; heere þei þanne þe Lordis
cry / ' He þat is more among ȝou ; be he made as þe ȝonger / and
he þat is made þe foregoer ; be he mad as þe mynystir'[1] / Þis is þe
20 forme of þe apostlis lyuyng / seculere lordschip is forboden ; but
mynystring & seruyng is boden || Wel | we witen of bileue ; þat [Fol. 91 b]
God & his lawe / ben euene acording togidir ; & þise seyntis wiþ
hem / þanne lie biside ȝoure poise ; & ȝoure heeþen talis / wiþ alle
oþir manglid lawis ; & conforme ȝou to God / to clense þe chirche
25 & bring it aȝen ; to þe former astate / and lyue ȝe on Cristis part ;
þat lordis myȝt haue her lordschip aȝen || But ȝit ȝe maken pursut ;
wiþ many greuouse chouris / & seyn þat seint Siluestir ; took þis **nota**
possessioun & seint Swithen & seint William ; wiþ manye oþir
seyntis || To þis we seyn þat Siluester ; wiþ suche oþir folowars /
30 weren seyntis in þis takyng ; of temperal possessiouns / as was
Petir forsakyng Crist & Poul purswyng þe chirche / Petir & Poul
dide verry penaunce ; & suffrid deeþ for Cristis sake / If þise men
diden þe same ; þus ben þei verry seyntis ||

Þe .V. heest. ||

35 Þe fifþe comaundement of God is þis. Exº. xxº / 'Non occides'[2] / **The Fifth Commandment.**

---

[1] W. V. Luc. xxii. 26, He that is the more in ȝou, be maad as the
ȝongere, and he that is bifore goer, as a seruaunt.' 1388, ' He that is grettist
among ȝou, be maad as ȝongere, and he that is bifor goere, as a seruaunt.'

[2] Vulg. Ex. xx. 13.

Persecucioun ?

Þou shalt not slee / neiþir in malice wiþ prisounyng / neiþir in worde wiþ bakbiting. neiþir wiþ dede. in vnlawful sched-|-yng out of blood /

Fol. 92 a

Three kinds of murder.

I   Of þe firste spekiþ seint Ion & seiþ. I. Ion. iii⁰. 'Qui odit fratrem suum homicida est'[1]/ He þat hatiþ his broþer ? is a manslear[2] || Summe haten synne in man ? & þis is a perfite hate / Ps. cxviii. 'Perfecto odio oderam illos &c'[3] || Summe haten vertu in man ? & þey ben mensleers / for who þat seiþ he loueþ his God ? & hatiþ þus his broþir / he is a lieer ? & þer is no trouþe in him ||

II   Of þe secounde spekiþ þe prophete & seiþ. Ps. xiii. 'Quorum os maledictione &c'[4] || Þe mouþe of bakbiters ? is ful of cursidnes & bittirnes / & her feet ben swift ? to scheed out blood[5] / for seint Bernard seiþ. Þe bakbiter & þe wilful heerer ? eiþir of hem[6] beriþ þe deuel in her tung / And þis bakbiter sleeþ þre at a strok. þat is to seie. his owene soule. his wilful heerar ? & him þat þei falsli sclaundren ||

III   Of þe þridde it is writen. Ge. iiii⁰.[7] Hou þat cursid Caym. slouȝ his innocent broþir Abel ? & hou his blood cried to God from þe erþe / for seint Ion seiþ. Apoc. vi⁰. 'Vidi subtus altare animas interfectorum | propter verbum dei & propter testimonium quod habebant. Et clamabant voce magna dicentes / vsquequo domine sanctus & verus non iudicas & vindicas sanguinem nostrum de hijs qui habitant in terra'[8] / Seynt Ion seiþ. I sawȝ vndir þe auter þe soules of hem þat weren slayn for þe word of God ? & witnesse þat þei hadden / & þei crieden wiþ a greet vois seiyng / holi Lord & trewe ? til whanne schalt þou abide / or þou wilt iugge and venge oure blod on hem þat dwellen in erþe / And it is seide vnto hem ? þat þei schulden be stille / ȝit a litil while ? til her felowis be comen / & her briþeren þat ben to be slayn ? as þei ben hem silf[9] || vndirstonde þat God forfendiþ ? al vnlawful

Fol. 92 b

---

[1] Vulg. 1 Joh. iii. 15.

[2] W. V. 'Ech man that haatith his brother is a manqueller.' 1388, 'Ech man that hatith his brother, is a man sleere.'

[3] Vulg. Ps. cxxxviii. 22.   [4] Vulg. Ps. xiii. 3.

[5] W. V. 'Whos mouth of cursing and bitterness is ful; swifte the feet of hem to sheden out blod.' 1388, 'Whos mouth is ful of cursyng and bittirnesse; her feet ben swift to schede out blood.'

[6] MS. of he.   [7] Vulg. Gen. iv. 8–12.

[8] Vulg. Apoc. vi. 9.

[9] W. V. 'I siȝe undir an auter the soules of men sleyn for the word of God,

Capitulum .XII.

sleeyng / as Crisostom declariþ. om. LI / 'Percutere est iniuste percutere / qui autem propter iustitie causam percutit ;' percutere non videtur. percutit enim non vt suum dolorem vindicet ;' sed vt illius animam saluet. sicut vero iusta ira non est ira sed diligencia ;'
5 sic iusta percussio non est percussio ;' sed correpcio ' ª / To smyt taken bi it silf ;' is vniustli to smyt / forsoþe he þat smytiþ ;' for þe cause of riȝt-|wisenes / he is not sen for to smyt ;' bi title of Goddis lawe / forsoþe he smytiþ not to venge ;' his owene wreechful herte / but to do þe wille of God ;' & saue his neibours soule / as
10 iust wraþþe is no wraþþe ;' but a feruent diligence / so riȝtwise smyting is no smyting ;' but a iust amending / for bi suche a feruent loue ;' Phines slowȝ to lecchours / & turned þe wraþþe of God ;' from þe children of Isrel / as it is writen. Numeri. xxvº.¹ / Also God sent his oostis ;' Titus and Vaspasian / two & fourty
15 wyntir ;' aftir þat Crist was slayn / for to venge Cristis deeþ ;' vpon þe cursid Iewis / as it is writen. Mat. xxiiº. 'Missis exercitibus suis perdidit homisidas illos & ciuitatem eorum succendit ' ² ||

Fyue þingis men must avoide ;' whanne þei schullen go to bataile / for þei ben aȝenst þis heest. & þus seiþ seint Austin /
20 'Nocendi cupiditas vlcisendi crudelitas implacabilis animus. feritas rebellandi libido dominandi. & sique sunt talia. hec sunt que in bello iure culpantur' / Hec Augustinus | contra Faustum ᵇ || þat is to seie. Coueitise of noiyng. cruelte of vengeyng. an vnpesible mynde. feersenes of fiȝtyng. lust of lordschiping. and what þat
25 ben lijke to þise / for þise ben þo þingis ;' þat of riȝt ben blamed in bataile /

nota bene

Righteous smiting admitted under five conditions.

Fol. 93 a

Fol. 93 b

nota

and for witnessing that thei hadden. And thei crieden with greet voys, seiynge, Hou longe, Lord, holy and trewe, demyst thou not, and vengist our blood of thes that dwellen in erthe? and it is seid to hem, that thei shulden reste ȝit a litil tyme, til the euen seruauntes of hem be fulfilled, and the britheren of hem, that ben to be slayn, as and thei.' 1388, 'Y say undur the auter the soulis of men slayn for the word of God, and for the witnessing that thei hadden. And thei crieden with a greet vois, and seiden, How long thou, Lord, that art hooli and trewe, demest not, and vengest not oure blood of these that dwellen in the erthe? and it was seide to hem, that thei schulden reste ȝit a litil tyme, til the noumbre of her felowis and of her britheren ben fulfillid, that ben to be slayn as also thei.'

[1] Num. xxv. 6–8.   [2] Vulg. Matt. xxii. 7.

[a] S. Ioan. Chrysostomus, *Homilia LI* (*Opera*, ed. 1547, tom. ii, col. 1112).
[b] S. Augustinus, *On the Manichaean Heresy* (reply to Faustus), xxii. 74 (Migne, tom. 42, col. 447).

The fiend incites men to persecution and spiritual starvation of Christ's followers, especially those who study God's law in English.

A3en þis comaundement ./ þe fende in his membris / settiþ wacche & bisie spie ./ where þat he may fynde / ony peple þat wole rede ./ priue or apert / Goddis lawe in englische ./ þat is oure modir tunge / ancon he schal be sumned ./ to come aforne hise iuggis / to answere what is seide to him ./ & bring his book wiþ him / and eiþir he must forsake his book ./ & reding of englische / & algatis he schal forswere ./ to speke of holi writ ‖ Þei sein lyue as þi fadir dide ./ & þat is ynow for þee / or ellis þou schalt to prisoun ./ as if þou were an heretike / & suffre peynes many & strong ./ & ful lickli þe deeþ / but þou wilt revoke þi worde ./ & make an open wondirment / at þi parische chirche at home ./ or in comune place ‖ 5

Fol. 94 a And wiþ þis þei prisoun ./ many an | houngry soule / wherof growiþ in þis rewme ./ a greuouse gocstli moreyn ‖ For who dar now in þise daies ./ talke of Crist or þe doom / & certis þe bodi may not lyue ./ wiþouten bodili food / no more may þe celi soule ./ 15

The soul may not live without God's word.

wiþouten Goddis worde / as seint Austin seiþ. 'Perit anima fame ./ si non pascitur celesti pane' / Þe soule dieþ for hungir ./ but if it be fedde wiþ heuenli breed / and þis breed is Goddis worde ./ as Crist seiþ in his gospel / Mat. iiiiº. Deutº. iiiiº. Mar. iº. Luk. iiiiº.[1] / 'Non in solo[2] pane viuit homo ./ sed de omni verbo 20 quod procedit de ore dei'[3] / A man lyueþ not oonli in bodili breed ./ but he lyueþ a betir lijf aftir þe soule / of iche worde þat passiþ ./ from þe mouþe of God[4] ‖ God tolde long aforn ./ þis houngir for to come / þat vntau3t men schulde aske þis breed ./ & no man schulde 3yue it hem / as he seiþ bi þe mouþe of þe 25 prophete Amos. viiiº. 'Ecce dies veniunt dicit dominus & mittam famem in terram. non famem panis. neque sitim aque ./ sed audiendi

Fol. 94 b verbum | domini'[5] ‖ Loo daies comen seiþ þe Lord ./ & I schal suffre hungir to be sent in to þe erþe / neiþir of breed ne of watir ./ but of heeryng þe word of þe Lord / Þanne men schullen be 30 meved ./ from þe ton[6] see to þe toþir / & fro þe norþe vnto þe eest ./ seeking þe worde of þe Lord / & þei schal not fynde it ./ seiþ

---

[1] Vulg. Matt. iv. 4, Deut. viii. 3, (Marc. i. 13), Luc. iv. 4.

[2] MS. sole.

[3] Vulg. Matt. iv. 4 'Non in solo pane vivit homo : sed in omni verbo,' etc.

[4] W. V. 'A man lyueth not in breed aloon, bot in euery word that cometh forth fro the mouthe of God.' 1388, 'Not oonli in breed lyueth man, but in ech word that cometh of Goddis mouth.'

[5] Vulg. Amos vii. 11.   [6] MS. to.

Capitulum .XII.

þe Lord God[1] ‖ for þouȝ þer be manye precheours ּ þer ben fewe
trewe prechours / and if ony preche þe trouþe ּ þe multitude schal
aȝenseie him / & þus men abiden stille ּ in her goostli hungir ‖
for þei wot neuer whom to folowe ּ her preching is so wondirful /
5 ioynyng in her coriouse wordis ּ þe trouþe to þe falsehede ‖ who
þat hauntriþ him to þis breed ּ for to slek his hungir / þouȝ he
were als hooli ּ as euere was seint Ion Baptist / he schulde not
faile to be sclaundrid ּ for a cursid Lollard / & pursued as an
heretik ּ of þise cruel enemyes ‖ But in þis þei ben miche werre ּ
10 þan þe heeþen folkis / þat trowen in her mawmetis ּ ∣ for wanting
of bileue / But þise han resceyued þe feiþ ּ & falsli gon þerfro /
and also dryuen beestli men ּ to peyne hem in her pinfold / wiþouten goostli mete or drinke ּ til þei sterue for hungir ‖ But we nota
reeden þe contrarie ּ of an heeþen kyng / for he dide miche betir ּ
15 to þe children of Isrel. IIII. Re. xvii⁰. 'Cumque filij Israel habitare cepissent in Samaria. non timebant dominum & immisit
dominus eis leones qui interficiebant eos'[2] / Þat is to seie. whanne
þe children of Isrel ּ bigunne to dwelle in Samarie / þei dreden
not þe Lord ּ & þe Lord sent among hem. liouns þat slowȝen hem /
20 & þanne was it tolde to þe kyng ּ of Assiry & seide / þe folkis þat
þou hast translatid ּ & mad hem to dwelle in þe cetees of Samarye /
þei knowe not þe laweful þingis ּ of þe God of erþe / & þe Lord
haþ sent ּ among hem lyouns / & lo þei slen hem ּ for as mich as
þei knowe not / þe riȝt or þe lawe ּ of þe Lord God of erþe ‖
25 Forsoþe þe kyng ∣ of Assarye ּ comaundid seiyng / lediþ þidir
oone of þe prestis ּ þat ȝe han brouȝt in to þis þraldom / þat he
may go & wiþ hem dwelle ּ to teche hem þe laweful þingis. of þe
God of erþe[3] ‖ God graunt oure cristen kyngis ּ to mark wel

---

[1] W. V. 'Loo! the days cummen, saith the Lord, and Y shall sende out hungre in to erthe; not hungre of breed nether thrist of water, bot of heeryng of the word of God. And thei shuln be moued to gydre fro see unto see, and fro the north unto the eest thei shuln cumpasse, seekynge the word of the Lord, and thei shuln not fynde.'

[2] Vulg. 4 Reg. xvii. 25 'Cumque ibi habitare coepissent, non timebant Dominum et immisit in eos Dominus leones, qui,' etc.

[3] W. V. 'And whanne there thei hadden begunne to dwellen, thei dreden not the Lord; and the Lord sent to hem lyouns, that slewen hem. And it is told to the kyng of Assiries, and seide, The folc that thou hast translatyde and maad to dwellen in the cytees of Samarye, knowen not the lawful thingis of the God of the lond; and the Lord sente in to hem lyouns, and loo! thei shuln slen hem; for thy that thei knowen not the custum of the God of the

þis story / þat þei mowe passe þis heeþen kyng ./ in þis forseide mater / þanne schulde lyouns þat ben synnes ./ soone be distried / if alle men hadden þe lawe ./ writen in her hertis / as þe Lord seiþ. Iere. xxxi⁰. 'Dabo legem meam in visceribus eorum ./ & in corde eorum scribam eam'¹ ‖ Þat is to seie. I schal ȝyue my lawe ./ in þe bowels of hem / & I schal write my lawe ./ in þe herte of hem² / O. ȝe prestis ben myche to blame ./ þat taken from þe peple / þe lawe þat God haþ writen him silf ./ in myddis of her herte / so þoruȝ ȝou þise forseide lyouns ./ now ben comen among vs / þat al to-teeren Cristis scheep ./ & murþeren hem to þe deeþ / certis ȝe lerned neuir þis loore ./ in dedis of þe apostlis / for þus it is writen. Actus. viii⁰. 'Et ecce vir ethiops. eunuchus &c.'³ / Loo | a clene chaast man ./ þe quenes tresourer of Ynde / þouȝ he were an heeþen man ./ and hadde not taken þe feiþ / ȝit he radde in Isaie ./ sitting in his chaare / Philip took not awey his booke ./ ne werned him to reede þeronne / But what þanne ? Philip declarid him prophecie ./ & tauȝt him for to vndirstonde it / til he bileued Iesu Crist ./ to be Goddis son of heuene / what bitidde þanne ? Philip bi stiring of þe spirit ./ whanne þis man bileued / confermed him in Cristis name ./ & ȝaue to him þe bapteme / How do ȝe prestis ./ performe þe apostlis lore / þat stoppen trewe cristen men ./ from werkis of her cristendom / Þe apostlis vsid not þat maner ./ whanne þei wenten aboute / to þe temple & mennes housis ./ preching & techyng / boþe to Iewis & heeþen men ./ þe lawis of Iesu Crist / Actus. v⁰. 'Omni autem die in templo & circa

The priests are to blame who rob men of God's law.

Fol. 96 a

lond. The kyng forsothe of Assiries comaundyde, seyinge, Bringith hidre oon of the prestis, the whiche in to caytyfte ȝe han brouȝt, that he goo, and dwelle with hem, and teche hem the lawful thingis of God of the lond.' 1388, 'And whanne thei bigunnen to dwelle there, thei dredden not the Lord; and the Lord sente to hem liouns, that killiden hem. And it was teld to the kyng of Assiriens, and was seid, The folkis whiche thou translatidist, and madist to dwelle in the cities of Samarie, kunnen not the lawful thingis of God of the lond; and the Lord sente liouns in to hem, and lo! liouns sleen hem; for thei kunnen not the custom of God of the lond. Sotheli the kyng of Assiriens comaundide, and seide, Lede ȝe thidur oon of the prestis, whiche ȝe brouȝten prisoneris fro thennus, that he go, and dwelle with hem, and teche hem the lawful thingis of God of the lond.'

[1] Vulg. Jer. xxxi. 33.

[2] W. V. 'Y shal ȝyue my lawe in the boweles of hem, and in the herte of hem Y shal write it.' 1388, 'Y schal ȝyue my lawe in the entrails of hem, and Y schal write it in the herte of hem.'

[3] Vulg. Act. viii. 27.

Capitulum .XII.

domos non cessabant ; docentes & euangelizantes christum Iesum ' [1] /
þat is to seie. Forsoþe iche dai in þe temple & aboute housis ;
þei ceessid not teching | and preching Crist Iesu [2] || Fol. 96 b
þe sixte heeste ||

5 The sixte comaundement of God is þis. Ex⁰. xx⁰. 'Non mecha- The Sixth
beris' [3] || þou schalt not do leccherie / Neiþir wiþ þin iȝe ; in Commandment.
leccherouse lookyng / Neiþir wiþ þin herte ; in lusti þenkyng / Three kinds
Neiþir wiþ þi bodi ; in þe dede doinge / and þus þis synne is of Lechery.
forbeden ; in sengle. in weddid. & in widowis ||

10 Of þe firste spekiþ seynt Austin & seiþ. 'Inpudicus oculus I
inpudici cordis est nuncius' [a] || An vnchaast iȝe ; is messagere of
an vnchaast herte ||

Of þe secounde spekiþ Crist in his gospel. Mat. v⁰. 'Qui viderit II
mulierem ad concupiscendum eam iam mechatus est eam in corde
15 suo' [4] / þat is to seie. who þat haþ seen a womman to do his lust
wiþ hir ; anoon he haþ done leccherie wiþ hir in his hert / [5] In
þis Crist techiþ. hou þe roote of synne springeþ from þe herte /

Of þe þridde spekiþ Poul. Ephe. v⁰. 'Hoc enim scitote intelli- III
gentes quod omnis fornicator aut immundus aut avarus quod est
20 ydolorum seruitus non habet hereditatem in regno dei & christi' [6] /
Forsoþe knowe | ȝe þis vndirstonding. þat neiþir fornicarer neiþir Fol. 97 a
vnclene filþe. neiþir avarouse wrecche. þat is seruage of ydols haþ
no heritage in þe rewme of Crist & God / [7] Hou euer þou lustily
treete ; þe membris of þi bodi / aȝens þe resoun of þi soule ; þanne
25 þou art a lecchour / and perfore schulde boþe man & womman ;
lerne to kepe her bodi / in clennes & in vertu ; to worschip of her

---

[1] Vulg. Act. v. 42.

[2] W. V. 'Forsoth ech day thei ceessiden not in the temple, and aboute housis, techinge and evangelisynge Jhesu Christ.'

[3] Vulg. Ex. xx. 14.   [4] Vulg. Matt. v. 28.

[5] W. V. 'Every man that seeth a womman for to coueite hire, now he hath do lecherie by hire in his herte.'

[6] Vulg. Eph. v. 5.

[7] W. V. 'Forsoth this thing wyte ȝe, undirstondinge that ech fornycatour, or unclene man, or coueytous, that is seruage of ydols, (or mawmetis), hath not heritage in the kingdom of Christ and God.' 1388, 'For wite ȝe this, and undurstonde, that ech letchour, or unclene man, or coueytouse, that serveth to mawmetis, hath not eritage in the kingdom of Christ and of God.'

---

[a] Augustinus, *Epistola CCXI* 10 (Migne, tom. 33, col. 961).

104   *Persecucioun :*

God / & not in foule brennyng desiris : as folkis þat knowiþ no
resun / as seint Austin seiþ. 'Dedit tibi deus potestatem per
spiritum sanctum. ut membra tua teneas / surgit libido : tene tu
membra / noli exhibere membra tua. arma iniquitatis peccato / noli
armare aduersarium tuum contra te / tene pedes. ne eant ad illi- 5
cita / libido surrexit : tene tu membra / tene manus ab omni
scelere / tene oculos. ne male attendant / tene aures : ne verba
libidinis libenter audiant / tene totum corpus tuum / tene latera.
_{nota} tene summa / tene yma / Quid facit libido ? surgere nouit. vincere
nota bene non nouit' / Hec Augustinus de verbis domini. sermone XLIII.[a] 10

Fol. 97 b   God haþ 3yuen to þee | powere : bi þe Holi Goost / þat þou holde
þi membris : from passing of resoun / luste risiþ : holde þou þi
membris / nile þou 3yue þi membris armour of wickidnes to synne /
arme not þin aduersarie a3ens þee : to þiu owene harme / Holde
þi feet : þat þei go not to vnleful þingis / Lust haþ risen : wiþ- 15
holde þou þi membris / holde þin handis. from alle felonye / wiþholde
þin i3en. þat þei tent not to yuel / wiþholde þyn eeris : þat þei
heere not þe talis of leccherie / wiþholde al þi bodi / holde þi
si3dis / holde hi3e / holde lowe / what can lust do ? rise it can :
ouercum can it not || 20

The devil   A3en þis comaundement : þe fende in hise membris / holdiþ
leads the
clerical   a court as he seiþ : of holi chirchis lawe / from oo weeke to
courts to
connive at a noþir : for to correct synnars / and þere þei clepen bi name : þe
this sin for
payment.   lecchour & his feere / þat lediþ þe lijf in hoordam : to ioyne hem
to her penaunce / þat is to walke þre market daies : aboute þe 25
comune market / bareheed in her schirt : wiþouten hosen or
Fol. 98 a schoon / & oþir þre sundaies : aboute her pa-|-rische chirche / wiþ
a tapir in her hond : of a pound of wax / & go biforn þe parische
prest : to bete hem wiþ a 3erde / Also stonding on her feet : til
þe messe be seide / & þanne offre vp her candils : to þe hi3e auter / 30
Þe sumnour is ful bisi : in al þis mene tyme / to rowne in her
eeris : & bidde hem aske grace / 'for 3e schal haue betir grace :
do bi my counseile / Paie doun money from 3oure purse : to my
lordis almes / & 3e schullen fynde him graciouse : to relese 3oure
penaunce' / Þanne þei take her leeue boþe : whanne þat þei ben 35
taxid / to contynue stille in hordam : as þei diden biforn / 3he
summe til her deeþ dai : so þat þis rent be paied / Certis þis is

---

[a] Augustinus, Sermo *CXXVIII*, cap. x (Migne, tom. 38, col. 719).

Capitulum .XII.

a cursid synne ŕ þat oure bischopis vsen / to maynten lecchours
in her owene hous ŕ & make hem her ordinarijs / þat laten synne
to greet hire ŕ for her lordis almes ǁ Heere ȝe what God seiþ to
ȝou. Eze. xliiii⁰. 'Sufficiant vobis omnia scelera uestra domus
5 Israel eo quod inducitis filios alienos incircumcisos corde & incir-
cumcisos | carne / ut sint in sanctuario meo. & polluant domum Fol. 98 b
meam & offertis panes meos adipem & sanguinem / Et dissoluistis
pactum meum in omnibus sceleribus uestris. & non seruastis precepta sanctuarij mei. & posuistis custodes obseruacionum mearum
10 in sanctuario meo vobismetipsis. hec dicit dominus'¹ ǁ Þat is to
seie. Suffice þei to ȝou ŕ hous of Isrel / alle ȝoure greet felonyes ŕ
þat ȝe vsen among ȝou / bicause þat ȝe bringen in ŕ alien sones /
vncircumcisid in her herte ŕ & in her fleische also / þat þei be in
my sauntwary ŕ & defoyle my hous / and ȝe offren my looues ŕ my
15 blood & my grece / but ȝe vndo my couenaunt ŕ in alle ȝoure foule
felonyes / & ȝe han not kept in dede ŕ þe biddingis of my sauntwary / but ȝe han sette þe wardeynes ŕ of myn obseruauncis / in
my sauntwarie ŕ to ȝoure owene avauntage / Þise þingis seiþ þe
Lord God ² ǁ Þis is þe moral witt ŕ of þis forseid sentence / hiȝe
20 prelatis of þe chirche ŕ schulde þenk ynowe / of her owene greet
synnes ŕ for to ȝyue a rekenyng | aforn God at domesdai ŕ & þei Fol. 99 a
wolde wel avise hem / þouȝ þei dide not sacre ŕ to þe ordir of
presthood / vnclene men in bodi & soule ŕ þat seken to be prestis /
neiþir in vertu ne in spirit ŕ but for to lyue in lustis / Þise
25 poluten Cristis chirche ŕ his fleische & his blood / & causen whi
þat Goddis lawe ŕ for her false court / Not cristen lawe. but cursid
lawe ŕ is holden among þe peple / Þis was not her couenaunt ŕ at
oo daies tyme / whanne þei hiȝten feiþ & trouþe ŕ to swe Cristis
steppis / & kepe hise biddingis in hem silf ŕ & teche hem oþir

---

¹ Vulg. Ezech. xliv. 6-9.
² W. V. 'ȝe hous of Yrael, alle ȝour grete trespassis suffice thei to ȝou,
for that that ȝe bryng yn alyen sonys, uncircumcided in hert, and uncircumcided in flesh, that thei be in my sayntuarie, and defoule myn hous. And
ȝe offren my louys, fatnesse and bloode, and ȝe undo my couenaunt in alle
ȝour grete trespassis. And ȝe kepte not the preceptis of my sayntuarie and ȝe
han putte keepers of myn obseruances, in my sayntuarie to ȝour self. These
thingus saith the Lord God.' 1388, 'ȝe hous of Israel, alle ȝoure grete
trespassis. . . And ȝe kepten not the comaundementis of my seyntuarie, and
ȝe settiden keperis of my kepyngis in my seyntuarije to ȝou silf. The Lord God
seith these thingis.'

men ‖ But now þei setten ordinarijs ; for her worldly profite /
þat heepen her purs wiþ money ; of many soold synnes / But
soulis þat God chargiþ hem wiþ ; to haue cure ouer hem / and
bring to þe blisse of heuene ; as scheep vnto þe foold / þei charge
not wheþir þei synk or swyme ; so þei moun regne as lordis / Þus 5
ben alle þre astaatis ; enfectid in leccherie / fro þe lewid man to
þe clerk ; and noon amenden oþir / and þerfore þe Lord seiþ. |

Fol. 99 b   Iere. v. 'Saturaui eos & mechati sunt & in domo meretricis
luxuriabantur / Equi amatores in feminas & emissarij facti sunt
vnusquisque ad vxorem proximi sui hinniebat[1] / Numquid super 10
hijs visitabo dicit dominus & in gente[2] tali vlciscetur anima

ncta   mea'[3] / I haue fedde hem ; & þei han don leccherie / þei han ben
horrels ; in þe comune bordel hous / þei ben as feers on wymmen ;
as hors ben on maris / & þei ben made stalowens ; þat seruen of
þat office / iche man waxiþ wood[4] ; aftir his neiȝbours wijf / vpon 15
þise þingis I schal visite ; seiþ þe Lord God / and vpon þis folk
I schal venge my wille ; seiþ þe Lord God[5] ‖

Þe .VII. heeste ‖

The Seventh Commandment.   Þe seuenþe comaundement of God is þis. Ex⁰. xx⁰. . 'Non
furtum facies'[6] ‖ Þou schalt not do þeeft / Neiþir knyȝtis ; by 20
tirauntrie / Neiþir prestis bi ypocrisie / Neiþir comvnes bi
stelþe & robry /

Three kinds of theft. I   Of þe firste it is writen. Isaie i⁰. 'Principes tui infideles
socij furum'[7] / Þi princis ben vnfeiþful ; & felowis of þeeues / alle
þei louen ȝiftis ; þei folowen rewardingis / þei deeme not riȝt 25
Fol. 100 a   doome ; | to þe modirles childe / þe cause of þe widowe ; entriþ
not to hem[8] /

[1] MS. inhiebat.   [2] MS. genti.

[3] Vulg. Jer. v. 7-9 'Saturavi eos . . . Equi amatores et emissarii . . .
Numquid super hiis non visitabo dicit dominus, et in gente tali non,' etc.

[4] MS. waxiþ waxiþ wood.

[5] W. V. 'I fulfilde them, and thei diden fornycacioun, and in the hous of
the strumpet thei diden leccherie. Horses loueres in to wymmen, and
courseres thei ben mad; eche to the wif of his neȝhebore neyȝede. Whether
upon these thingus Y shal not visite, seith the Lord, and in such a folc of
kynde shal not be vengid my soule?' 1388, 'Y fillide hem, and thei diden
awowtrie, and in the hous of an hoore thei diden letcherie. Then ben maad
horsis, and stalouns, louyeris to wymmen ; ech man neiȝede to the wijf of his
neiȝbore. Whether Y schal not visite on these thingis, seith the Lord, and
schal not my soule take veniaunce in siche a folc.'

[6] Vulg. Ex. xx. 15.   [7] Isaias i. 23.

W. V. 'Thi princes unfeithfull, felawes of theues ; alle thei loouen ȝiftus,

Capitulum .XII.

Of þe secounde spekiþ Crist in his gospel. Ion. x⁰. 'Qui non   II
intrat per hostium in ouile ouium. sed ascendit aliunde ./ ille fur
est & latro'¹ / He þat entriþ not bi þe dore ./ in to þe foold of
scheep / but comeþ in bi anoþir weye ./ he is a nyȝt-þeef & a day-
5 þeef² / þis is expouned in þe þridde comaundement ||
   Of þe þridde spekiþ Poul. Ephe. iiii⁰. / 'Qui furabatur iam   III
non furetur magis autem laboret vnusquisque manibus suis operando
quod bonum est. vt habeat vnde tribuat necessitatem pacienti'³ ||
He þat staale ./ steele he now no more / raþir traueile iche man ./
10 wirching wiþ hise hondis. þat þing þat is good / þat he mai
whereof haue ./ to dele to him þat suffriþ nede⁴ / Lord if þei
schullen be dampned ./ as þe gospel seiþ. Luk. xvi⁰.⁵ þat spenden
not þe trewe gotun goodis ./ aftir þe forme of Cristis teching /
Mat. xxv⁰. ⁶ / where schal þei be punyschid þat wasten her owene
15 or hiden her owene ./ & falseli steelen oþir mennes ? Seint Poul
seiþ. I. Cor. vi⁰. ' Fures regnum dei non possidebunt ' ⁷ || | Þeeues Fol. 100 b
schal not weelde ./ þe rewme of God⁸ / and in þis ben conteyned ./
þe þre forseid steelyngis / But siþen þat God alle þingis haþ
ordeyned ./ in noumbre. wheiȝt. & mesure. as þe wise man seiþ.
20 Sap. xi⁰. ' Omnia in mensura & numero & pondere disposuisti '⁹ ||
Who þat falsiþ ony of þise þre ./ or falseli vseþ hem / he is a þeef
& worþi peyne ./ as þe wise man seiþ. Prou. xi⁰. 'Statura dolosa
abhominacio est apud deum pondus equum voluntas eius' ¹⁰ ||

---

folewen ȝeldyngus; to the faderles child thei demen not; the cause of the
widewe goth not in to them.' 1388, 'Thi princes ben unfeithful, the felowis
of theuys; alle louen ȝiftis, suen meedis; thei demen not to a fadirles child,
and the cause of a widewe entrith not to hem.'

[1] Vulg. Joh. x. 1.

[2] W. V. 'He that cometh not in by the dore in to the fold of the sheep, but
stiȝeth up by another weye, is nyȝt thef and day thef.'

[3] Vulg. Eph. iv. 28 'Qui furabatur iam non furetur; magis autem laboret,
operando manibus suis,' etc.

[4] W. V. 'He that staal, now stele not; more forsoth traueile he in
worchinge with his hondis that that is good thing, that he haue wherof he
schal ȝyue to a man suffringe nede.' 1388, 'He that stal, now stele he not;
but more trauele he in worchinge with hise hondis that that is good, that he
haue wherof he schal ȝyue to nedi.'

[5] Vulg. Luc. xvi. 10–12. [6] Vulg. Matt. xxv. 29, 30.

[7] Vulg. 1 Cor. vi. 9 'Iniqui regnum dei,' etc.

[8] W. V. Wickide men schullen not welde the kingdom of God.'

[9] Vulg. Sap. xi. 21.

[10] Vulg. Prov. xi. 1.

A treccherous. þat is a fals balaunce ./ is abhominacioun anenst God / an euene whei3t ./ is þe Lordis wille¹ / as it is seide. Leuit. xix⁰. 'Nolite facere iniquum aliquid in iudicio in regula. in pondere. in mensura. statera iusta & equa sint pondera. iustus modius. equusque sextarius / Ego dominus deus uester'² ‖ Nile 5 3e do ony þing vnevenli ./ in ony of þise foure / In doome. in rule. in whei3t. in mesure / Loke þi balaunce be iust ./ & þi whei3tis euene / Loke þi buschel be iust ./ & þi mesure euene / I am 3oure Lord God³ ‖

A3en þis comaundement ./ þe fende wiþ his cautels / haþ whilid 10 in to | þe chirche ./ many strong þeeues / þat don steele boþe ny3t & dai ./ & 3it þei ben not hangid ‖ But God haþ ordeyned for hem ./ gallous in helle / & þei þat þere ben oones hangid ./ schal neuere be delyuered ‖ But þei þat hangen on mannes gallows ./ bi iugement of þis world / often bi þis schameful deeþ ./ & by verry 15 repentaunce / ben saued from þe endeles peyne ./ & so was þe þeef / þat hangid on Cristis ri3t si3de ./ in tyme of his passioun ‖ But þei þat fallen bakwarde ./ & may not se her fal / þei hang on Cristis left si3de ./ in perel of her soule / from whom Crist turneþ his graciouse face ./ as þe prophete seiþ / spekyng wiþ þe mouþe 20 of God ./ to þise forseide þeeues / Isaye. lix⁰. / 'Iniquitates vestre diuiserunt inter vos & dominum vestrum & peccata vestra absconderunt faciem eius a vobis. ne exaudiret. manus enim vestre plene sunt sanguine & digiti vestri iniquitate⁴. labia vestra locuta sunt mendacium. & lingua vestra iniquitatem fatur'⁵ ‖ 3oure wickidnes 25 haþ made a deuorse ./ bitwixe þe Lord & 3ou / & 3oure synnes han hidde | awey ./ his graciouse face from 3ou / þat he schulde not heere 3ou ./ whanne 3e crien vpon him / forsoþe 3oure handis ben ful of blood ./ & 3oure fyngers ful of synne / 3oure lippis han spoken lesing ./ & 3oure tung spekiþ wickidnes ‖⁶ Þe face of God is here 30

The fiend entices many strong thieves into the Church.

---

¹ W. V. 'A treccherous we3e abominacioun is anent God; and an euen wei3t the wil of hym.' 1388, 'A gileful balaunce is abhominacioun anentis God; and an euene wei3te is his wille.'

² Vulg. Lev. xix. 35, 36.

³ W. V. 'Nyle 3e do eny wickid thing in dome, in rewle, in wei3t, in mesure; ri3t balaunce, and even ben the wei3tis, ry3t bushel, and even sextarye; Y the Lord 3oure God.'

⁴ MS. iniquitatē.   ⁵ Vulg. Isaias lix. 2, 3.

⁶ W. V. '3oure wickidnesses deuydeden betwe 3ou and 3oure God, and 3oure synnes hidden his face fro 3ou, that he ful out here not. Fosothe 3oure hondis ben defoulid with blod, and 3oure fingris with wickidnesse; 3oure lippes

Capitulum .XII.

taken ʔ for his grace in mannes mynde / In anoþir place it is taken ʔ for Cristis incarnacioun ‖ and in anoþir place it is taken ʔ for þe glorie of God. in his euerlasting maieste / And þise þre ben turned awey ʔ from þise forseide spoylours / & cause whi þe
5 prophete seiþ. ben þise twoo þingis / Her handis & her fyngeris ʔ ben ful of blood and wickidnes ‖ vpon þis seiþ Parsiens / 'Qui aut furto aut vi aut fraude possidet vnde pauperes ali deberent ʔ pauperum sanguine manus habet pollutas' / Who þat haþ eiþir bi þeeft as robrie. eiþir bi strengþe. as tirauntrie. eiþir bi fraude
10 or gile as ypocrisie. þo þingis of þe whiche þe pore owid to be norischid. he haþ his handis pollutid. in þore mennes blood / and who þat cloþiþ him wiþ suche goodis. or fediþ him wiþ suche goodis. or reriþ vp bildyngis wiþ suche gooten goodis ʔ þanne is | he cladde in pore mennes blood. þanne is he fedde wiþ pore mennes Fol. 102 a
15 blood. þanne groundeþ he his bilding in pore mennes blood ‖

Summe men seyn it is no synne ʔ to take what þat men wole ȝyue hem / summe seyne þei wole spende her goodis ʔ þere þei haue moost deuocioun / summe morteisen hous. lond. watir. & wood ʔ in to deed mennes hondis ‖ To ȝou we asken þis questioun /
20 what profitiþ þe hand ʔ wiþouten fyngeris / or þe fyngers ʔ wiþouten hand ? If ȝe mowen seie þat eiþir of hem may worche his werke wiþouten oþir to mannes profite ʔ þanne mai ȝe seie þat deuocioun mai profite wiþouten discrecioun. & ellis not / for þus it is writen. Cant. v°. / 'Manus mee stillauerunt mirram. & digiti
25 mei mirram probatissimam'[1] ‖ Þise ben þe wordis of a trewe soule. myn hondis haþ droppid mirre ʔ & my fingeris moost proued mirre[2] / vpon þis seiþ seint Bernard. 'Deuocio sine discrecione. vacue iacet / discrecio sine deuocione precipitat ʔ felix est cui neutra[3] deest' [a] / | Deuocioun wiþouten discrecioun ʔ lieþ voide & doiþ no Fol. 102 b

Devotion without discretion profits not.

speeken lesing and ȝoure tunge wickenesse speketh.' 1388, 'Ȝoure wickidnesses han departid bitwixe ȝou and ȝoure God, and ȝoure synnes han hid his face fro ȝou, that he shulde not here. For whi ȝoure hondis ben defoulid with blood, and ȝoure fingris with wickidnesse; ȝoure lippis spaken leesyng, and ȝoure tunge spekith wickidnesse.'

[1] Vulg. Cant. v. 5 'Manus meae stillaverunt myrrham, et digiti mei pleni myrrha probatissima.'

[2] W. V. 'Myn hondis droppeden mirre, and my fingres ful of best proued myrre.' 1388, 'Myn hondis droppiden myrre, and my fyngris weren ful of myrre moost preued.'   [3] MS. veutra.

[a] Bernardus, *Super Cantica*, Sermo XXIII (*D. Bernardi Opera Omnia*, ed. 1552, p. 843).

110   Persecucioun ;

good / discrecioun wiþouten deuocioun ; þrowiþ doun heedlingis /
he is blessid ; þat wantiþ neiþir of þise / Loke what it profitiþ to
haue Crist in manhod ; wiþouten his godhood ? or to haue a bodi ;
wiþouten a soule ? or to haue feiþ in worde ; wiþouten dede ? or
to haue þe letter ; wiþouten vndirstonding ? or to haue a laump 5
wiþouten oyle ? So profitiþ deuocioun ; wiþouten discrecioun /

Such thieves do not serve God,
    Summen ȝit bisien hem ; to mayntene þis þeeft & seyn / Þise
men þat ȝe marken ; ben good prechours. þei ben deuoute preiars ;
& algatis amonge hem . God is faire serued ||

I   As to her preching ; Crist answeriþ & seiþ. Mat. vii°. Luk. 10
xii°[1] / 'Multi dicent mihi in illa die. Domine. Domine. nonne
in nomine tuo prophetauimus & in nomine tuo demonia eiecimus
& in nomine tuo virtutes multas fecimus ? & tunc confitebor illis
quia nunquam novi vos / discedite a me omnes qui operamini
iniquitatem ' || Manye schal come to Crist ; & seie to him in þe dai 15
Fol. 103 a of doome || Lord. Lord. han not we | prechid in þi name & casten
out deuelis in þi name. & wrouȝt many vertues in þi name / Seint
Austin seiþ. þe Lord schal not denaye þis / for who euer þe
prechour be ; a deuoute heerer may wynne him mede / but he schal
knoweleche to hem ; & seie / For I knew ȝou neuer. þat is to seie. 20
I approued neuere ȝoure werkis ; goo fro me alle ȝe þat wirken
wickidnesse [2] /

II   And as to her preiars. seint Austin seiþ in a book þat he
made ; of mounkis lijf / It profitiþ not to preie ; & late þe lond lie
leie /   25

III   And as to her faire seruice ; it is seide aforn / þat God is no
where faire serued ; but þere as his lawe is faire kept of þe peple ||

but deceive the people.
    But in þise þre ; þei disceyuen þe peple of her bileue / þei robben
hem of her vertu ; & þei spoylen hem of her goodis / as it is writen.
Miche. iii°. / 'Hec dicit Dominus super prophetas qui seducunt 30
populum meum qui mordent dentibus suis & predicant pacem & si
quis non dederit in ore ipsorum quippiam sanctificant super eum
Fol. 103 b prelium propterea nox [3] erit uobis pro visione | & tenebre vobis pro

---

[1] Vulg. Matt. vii. 22 ; Luc. xiii. 25-27.

[2] W. V. 'Many shul say to me in that day, Lord, Lord, whether we han not prophecied in thi name, and han cast out deuelis in thi name, and han don many vertues in thi name? And than Y shal knowliche to hem, For I knewe ȝou neuer : departe awey fro me, ȝe that worchen wickidnesse.'

[3] MS. vox.

Capitulum .XII.

diuinacione'[1] ‖ Þise þingis seiþ þe Lord vpon prechours ." þat
disceyuen my peple as wiþ her preching / þat biten wiþ her teeþ ."
as for her preiyng / & prechen pees ." as for her faire seruyng / and
who þat wole not ȝyue sumwhat ." in to þe mouþe of hem. þei
5 halowen bataile vpon him / þerfore þe Lord seiþ. Niȝt schal be to
ȝou ." for ȝoure visioun / & dercknes ." for ȝoure diuinacioun [2] /
Þise wole be meke ." wiþouten dispite / pore ." wiþouten defauȝt /
wel clad ." wiþouten bisines / diligatli fedde ." wiþouten traueile /
whili flatirars ." to hem þat þei bigilen / yuel-willi traitours ." to
10 hem þat þei haten / hasti pursuars ." of hem þat þei sclaundren /
soore bitars ." as doggis / descyuable ." as foxis / proude ." as lyouns /
enviouse ." as addris / wiþouten forþe ." as scheep / wiþynne forþe
as raueisching wolues / Þei wole be iugis ." wiþouten autorite / & at
þe laste ." false accusars & wanting al vertu / and þerfore þe wise
15 man seiþ. Prou. ‖ vi⁰.[3] þat þe Lord boþe hatiþ & wlatiþ him ." Fol. 104a
þat sowiþ discorde among neiȝbours / þise ypocritis wole suffre no
darte ." of correccioun to þrille hem / but in iche synne þat þei done ."
þei leien forþe þe bockelere of proude defence / and whanne ony of
hem ." is blamed for his wickidnes / he wil not þanne anoon ." þenk
20 hou he mai amende it / but he seekiþ bisili helpe ." hou he mai
defende it / Hec Gregorius. li⁰. xxx.

Þe .VIII. heeste ‖

Þe eiȝtiþ comaundement of God is þis. Ex⁰. xx⁰. 'Non loqueris   The Eighth
contra proximum tuum falsum testimonium'[4] ‖ Þou schalt not   Commandment.
25 speke fals witnes aȝens þi neiȝbour / Neiþir for ȝiftis taking /
Neiþir for mannes stering / Neiþir þi silf in synne excusing ‖
    Of þe firste it is writen . Isa. v⁰. 'Ve qui iustificatis impium   Three kinds
pro muneribus ." & iusticiam iusti aufertis ab eo'[5] ‖ woo to ȝou þat   of false
iustifien ." þe wickid man for ȝiftis / & take awey þe riȝtwisenes of   witness.
30 þe iust man ." for he mai not paye[6] ‖

---

[1] Vulg. Mich. iii. 5, 6.

[2] W. V. 'These thingus saith the Lord on the prophetis that disceyuen my
peple, & biten with her teeth, and prechen pees; and ȝif eny man shal not
ȝeve in the mouth of hem enything, thei halewyn bateyle on hym. Therefore
niȝt shal be to ȝou for visioun, (or prophecie), and derknessis to ȝou for
dyuynacioun.'

[3] Prov. vi. 19.   [4] Vulg. Ex. xx. 16.

[5] Vulg. Isaias v. 23.

[6] W. V. 'Wo that iustefien the unpitous for ȝiftes, and the riȝtwisnesse of
the riȝtwyse ȝee taken awey fro hym.' 1388, 'ȝe iustifien a wickid man for
ȝiftis, and ȝe taken awei the riȝtfulnesse of a iust man fro hym.

Fol. 104 b Of þe secounde spekiþ þe wise | man ⁙ Prou. xix⁰. 'Falsus testis non erit inpunitus ⁙ et qui mendacia loquitur peribit'[1] ‖ A false witnesberer ⁙ schal not be vnpunyschid ⁙ & he þat spekiþ liees ⁙ schal perische[2] ⁙ Ps. v⁰. 'Perdes omnes qui locuntur mendacium'[3] ⁙ Lord þou schalt leese alle þoo. þat speken lesing ⁙ for þe wise man 5 seiþ. Sap. i⁰.[4] þe mouþe þat lieþ ⁙ sleeþ þe soule ⁙ and þerfor seiþ Crist. Ion. viii⁰. 'vos ex patre diabolo estis &c'[5] ‖ Þat is to seie. ȝe liears ⁙ ben sones of ȝoure fadir þe deuel ⁙ & ȝe wil do þe desiris of ȝoure fadir ⁙ He was a mansleer fro þe bigynnyng ⁙ for he stood not in troupe. for troupe is not in him ⁙ whanne he spekiþ 10 lesing ⁙ he spekiþ of his owene autorite ⁙ for he is a lier ⁙ & þe fadir of lesing[6] ⁙

Of þe þridde spekiþ þe prophete Ps. cxl. 'Pone domine custodiam ori meo &c'[7] ‖ Lord putt þou warde to my mouþe ⁙ & a dore of circumstaunce to my lippis ⁙ bowe þou not my herte ⁙ in to þe 15 wordis of malice ⁙ to excusaciouns to be excusid in synne[8] ⁙ for þe wise man seiþ. Prou. ii. 'Qui letantur cum male fecerint & exul-
Fol. 105 a tent in rebus pessimis puniantur'[9] ⁙ Þat is to | seie. þei þat maken myry ⁙ whanne þei han done yuel ⁙ & ioyen in werst þingis ⁙ be þei punyschid wiþ eendles peyne[10] ‖ 20

The devil's snares are false witness and the corruption of juries,

Aȝen þis comaundement ⁙ þe fende wiþ hise cautels ⁙ haþ ȝouun leue to .XII. men ⁙ for twelue grootis ⁙ to passe forþe on a quest ⁙ aȝen a riȝtwise blood ⁙ & seie a false witnesse ⁙ þat þe man

---

[1] Vulg. Prov. xix. 5 'Testis falsus non erit impunitus, et qui mendacia loquitur non effugiet.'

[2] W. V. 'A fals witnesse shal not ben unpunshid; and he that lesing speketh, shal not ascapen.'   [3] Vulg. Ps. v. 6.

[4] Vulg. Sap. i. 11.   [5] Vulg. Joh. viii. 44.

[6] W. V. 'ȝe ben of the fadir, the deuel, and ȝe wolen do the desyris of ȝoure fadir. He was a mansleere fro the bigynnyng, and in treuthe he stood not; for treuthe is not in him. Whanne he spekith a lesinge he spekith of his owne thingis; for he is a lyiere, and fadir of it.'

[7] Vulg. Ps. cxl. 3 (A. V. Ps. cxli. 3).

[8] W. V. 'Put, Lord, warde to my mouth; and a dore of circumstaunce to my lippis. Bowe thou not doun my herte into the woordis of malice; to ben excusid excusaciouns in synnes.' 1388, 'Lord, sette thou a keping to my mouth; and a dore of stonding aboute to my lippis. Bowe thou not myn herte in to wordis of malice; to excuse excusing is in synne.'

[9] Vulg. Prov. ii. 14 'Qui laetantur cum malefecerint, et exultant in rebus pessimis.'

[10] W. V. 'Thei hat gladen, whan thei don euele, and ful out ioȝen in werst thingus.' 1388, 'Whiche ben glad, whanne thei han do yuel, and maken ful out ioye in worste things.'

Capitulum .XII.

is gilti / & anoon he schal be deed ./ þou3 it were Crist him silf ‖ In
þis þe fendis membris ./ grounden hem on Iesabel / III Re. xxi⁰.[1] for
sche sent lettris ./ in þe name of Acab / aseelid wiþ his synet ./ to
iourours of þe countre / & chargid hem þat þei schulde cheese ./
5 twoo men of Belial sones / þat my3t seie fals witnes ./ a3en þe
kny3t Naboth / þat he hadde waried ./ boþe God & þe kyng / and
by þis false witnesse ./ þei slowen þis giltles kny3t ‖ Certis so in
oure daies ./ who þat mediþ þise iullars / þat ben þe sones of Belial ./
& fals questmongars / he may slee & he may saue ./ þus fals were
10 neuer þe Iewis ‖ For whanne tweie oolde prestis ./ þat brenned in
leccherie / of þe womman Susan ./ as þe story telliþ / | Daniel. Fol. 105 b
xiii⁰.[2] / And sche wolde not consent ./ to do her foule lust / þanne
þei 3ouun a sentence ./ of her fals witnesse / wherbi sche was iugid ./
worþi to þe deed / As sche was ledde to þe fire ./ sche made hir
15 deuoute preiere / and þanne God rerid vp ./ þe herte of a 3ong
man / þat was clepid Daniel ./ & he reuokid her doom / and repreued
þise oolde prestis ./ of her false witnes / so þat Goddis aungel ./ wiþ
a scharp swerid / slow3e hem for her false doome ./ in si3t of alle þe
peple / and þei preised God almy3ti ./ of þis faire delyueraunce ‖
20 How schulde 3e iourours ./ scape þe fire of helle ./ þat for a litil
money ./ wole dampne 3e reck neuir whom / & diserite trewe eiris ./
of her iust eritage / For þoo þat wole not seie þe trouþe ./ but if
þei take mede / sellen Crist þat is trouþe ./ & ben werre þan Iewis ‖
Þei slou3en him whanne he cam to die ./ but now he regneþ vndeedli /
25 where schal þanne 3oure peyne be ./ þat wole seie false witnes /
for to cacche a vauntage ./ of sum worldli wynnyng ? 3e selle 3oure
silf boþe bodi | and soule ./ in to þe fendis seruyce ‖ Fol. 106 a

3it may we se more cumberaunce ./ of þe fendis worchynge / for nota
þer is noon officere ./ temperal ne spirituel / þan he is redi whanne and bribes
30 he may ./ for to take 3iftis / of þe pore comunes ./ & pille hem euer by all
anoon / & ellis þei schal no pees haue ./ from greuousear oppressyng ./ temporal
as is takyng of her beestis ./ wiþ corn & oþir vitails / and oþir spiritual.
payment gete þei noon ./ but a whit stik / til þei haue loost half on
half ./ wiþ myche more traueile ‖ Lord ! if þat 3e markid wel ./
35 what Ietro seide to Moyses / Ex⁰. xviii⁰.[3] soone 3e schulde amende
þis mys ./ or ellis 3e ben vncurable ‖ Ietro counseyled Moyses ./
þat he schulde wiseli ordeyne / mi3ti men þat dredden God ./ in

---

[1] Vulg. 3 Reg. xxi. 8–11.
[2] Vulg. Dan. xiii. 1–63.
[3] Vulg. Ex. xviii. 13–26.

whom was verry troupe / & þat hatid auarice ./ wiþ alle hir cursid
braunchis / & þei schulde haue office ./ in rulyng vndir Moises /
Moyses consentid ./ & wrou3t aftir his counseile / þerfore pees.
welþe. & grace regned in hise daies ‖ Rere vp 3oure wittis 3e
princis ./ & lordis in þis world / & se hou king Iosaphat ./ chargid 5
Fol. 106 b to hise officeris / II. Para. xix⁰. | 'Constituitque iudices terre in
cunctis ciuitatibus iuda precipiens eis. videte ait quid faciatis /
Non enim hominis exercetis iudicium sed domini. Et quodcumque
iudicaueritis in vos redundabit / Sit timor domini vobiscum ./ &
cum diligencia cuncta facite / Non est enim apud dominum nostrum 10
nota iniquitas. nec personarum accepcio. nec cupido munerum'[1] / Þat is

Upright
judges
ordained
among the
Jews.

to seie. Iosophat ordeyned iugis ./ in alle þe citees of Iurie / &
3aue hem þis bidding / Be war he seiþ what 3e do / forsoþe þis
doome þat 3e haunten. is not þe doome of man ./ but þe doom of
God / & what þat 3e demen ./ schal turne vpon 3oure silf / loke þe 15
drede of God be among 3ou ./ & doiþ alle þingis wiþ diligence /
forsoþe anenst þe Lord God ./ is no wickidnes / neiþir accepting of
persoones ./ neiþir coueitise of 3iftis / and he chargid prestis &
dekenes ./ þat þei schulde make knowen / alle þe dou3tis of þe
lawe ./ leste þe peple synned [2] ‖ If þis loore were wel lerned ./ of 20
oure cristen lordis / þe harde boondis of anticrist ./ schulde be
altobrosten / Cristen peple schulde haue leue ./ to do her office
Fol. 107 a treweli / & iche a man his freedam ./ to serue God in vertu / | Þanne
were þis good gouerneaunce ./ & sauyng of þe rewme / In pees. in

---

[1] Vulg. II. Para. xix. 5–7.

[2] W. V. 'And he sette domesmen of the lond in alle the strengthed citees
of Juda, by alle placis. And comaundyng to the iugis, Seeith, he seith, what
3e done; forsothe 3e enhaunten not dome of man, bot of the Lord; and what
euer 3e shul demyn in to 3ou it schal redoundyn; be the drede of the Lord
with 3ou, and with diligence alle thingus doith; forsothe ther is not anentis
the Lord oure God wickidnesse, ne acceptynge of persones, ne couetise of 3iftis.
And Josaphath in Jerusalem sette Leuytis, and prestis, and princes of the
meynees of Yrael, that dome and the cause of the Lord thei schulden deemyn
to the dwellers of it.' 1388, 'And he ordeynede iugis of the lond in alle the
strengthid citees of Judia, bi ech place. And he comaundide to the iugis, and
seide. Se 3e, what 3e doen; for 3e usen not the doom of man, but of the Lord;
and what euere thing 3e demen, schal turne in to 3ou; the drede of the Lord
be with you, and do 3e alle thingis with diligence : for anentis 3oure Lord God
is no wickidnesse, nether takynge of persoones nether coueitise of 3iftis. Also
in Jerusalem Josaphat ordeynede dekenes, preestis, and the princes of meynees
of Israel, that thei schulden deme the doom & cause of the Lord to the
dwellers of it.'

Capitulum .XII.

welþe. in euery astate ? as prestis. kny3tis & comunes / for þus seiþ
Crisostom. om. I. / 'Notandum quod quicumque regum placuerunt
deo diucius regnauerunt & prosperati sunt / & inimicos eorum
humiliauit deus sub eis / Quotquot autem maligne gesserunt velo-
citer & a regno & a uita cum amara morte percisi sunt & humiliauit
eos deus sub inimicis eorum' [a] || Þat is to seie. It is to noote þat
who of kyngis han plesid God ? þei han regned þe lenger / & þei
han ben welþi. & God haþ lowid her enemyes vndir hem / Forsoþe
als many as han don wickidli ? þei han ben kitt vp hastili / boþe
from her rewme & from her lijf ? wiþ a bittir deeþ / & God haþ
lowid hem ? vndir her enemyes þraldom ||

Þe nynþe heeste ||

The nynþe comaundement of God is þis. Ex⁰. xx⁰. Deut⁰. v⁰. **The Ninth Commandment.**
'Non concupisces domum proximi tui.'[1] / Þou schalt not coueite þe
hous of þi neibour || In þe seuenþe heest God forbediþ ? þe vnleful
takyng of oþir mennes goodis / & so in þat he refreyneþ ? þe vnskil-
fulnes of mannes dede / | But in þis heest God forbediþ ? þe Fol. 107 b
coueitise of vnleful taking / & in þat he refreyneþ ? þe vnordinat
appetite of mannes desire / namli in alle þo þingis ? þat ben
vnmoueable / þat is to seie. þat moun not move hem silf ? bi her
owene my3t from oo place to anoþir / as ben hous. lond. gold. &
suche oþir like to þise ||

And þis viciouse coueitise ? if it be conteyned / growiþ to deeþ **Three kinds of Covetousness.**
of þe soule ? from þe roote of mannes herte / for whanne þe wille
haþ consentid ? to do þat þing þat God forbediþ / þou3 þe dede   I
folowe not aftir ? in outward si3t of mannes doome / & no þing
lettiþ to do þe dede ? saue wille mai not as it wolde / þanne þe
soule is deed goostli ? wiþynne þe hous of þe bodi / And þis deeþ
is signified ? bi a persoones dou3tir / þat was deed wiþynne hir
fadris hous ? & Crist bi myracle 3aue hir lijf / Mat. ix⁰. / Mar. v⁰.
Luk. viii⁰.[2]

Summe norischen her coueitise ? til it spring vnto a dede / as a   II
careyn opunly deed ? þat lieþ bi þe weye enfecting þe peple / and
þis is tau3t in þe widouse sone ? þat was born deed on a beere /

---

[1] Vulg. Ex. xx. 17.
[2] Vulg. Matt. ix. 18-26 ; Marc. v. 22-43 ; Luc. viii. 41-56.

---

[a] S. Ioan. Chrysostomus, *Homilia I* (*Opera*, ed. 1547, tom. ii, col. 721).

Fol. 108 a wiþouten þe ȝatis of þe | citee ꞏ/ for to putt him in his graue /
Luk. vii⁰ ¹ / Crist rerid him bi his myracle ꞏ/ & ȝaue him aȝen to his
modir ||

Summe feeden her foule coueitise ꞏ/ wiþ lust & lykyng & delectacioun / in þouȝt. in worde. & in werke ꞏ/ & þis is moost abhomynable / for it was schewid in Lazarus / Ion. xi⁰.² þat lay deed foure
daies in his graue / & Crist bi miracle to turne þe Iewis ꞏ/ rerid vp
his bodi & ȝaue it þe spirit ||

Alle þise þre ben aȝenst þis heest of God / & ben worþi eendles
peyne ꞏ/ but if God þoruȝ his graciouse mercy / move hem to vertu
& to verry penaunce ꞏ/ þat ben deed in þise forseid foule coueitises /
þat is to seie. in coueitise of herte ꞏ/ of dede. & of custum / and
perfore þe wise man. Ecc. xviii⁰. 'Post concupiscencias tuas non
eas '³/ Go þou not awey fro þi God ꞏ/ aftir þin owene couetises⁴ ||
Lord hou schulde he kepe him from a viciouse dede ꞏ/ þat doiþ not
out of his herte. þe coueitise þerof? Certis it is as vnposible ꞏ/ as to
saue þat hous from brennyng / þat þou settist on fire ꞏ/ wiþ þin
Fol. 108 b owene handis || A weede may not be distried ꞏ/ but | if þat
delictable coueitise of synne. be pullid out of þe herte / for if þere
abide ony part of þis foule couetise ꞏ/ vndrawen vp in þe herte /
anoon aftir comeþ þerof. þeeft. false purchase ꞏ/ & suche oþir / and
þerfor seide Moyses ꞏ/ vnto þe children of Israel / Deut⁰. xix⁰. /
'Non assumes & transferes terminos proximi tui quos fixerunt
priores tui in possessione tua quam dominus deus tuus dabit tibi '⁵ ||
þat is to seie. þou schalt not take. ne þou schalt not passe þe termes
or þe boundes of þi neiȝbore ꞏ/ þe whiche þin elderis han sett / in þe
whiche possessioun ꞏ/ þat þe Lord þi God schal ȝyue to þee⁶ / For
who þat takiþ awey his neiȝboris grounde ꞏ/ þat is to seie. lond or
place. wood or watir. corn or grasse. in felde or in toune. þoruȝ ony
of þise forseide coueitises ꞏ/ he stondiþ in þat acursid of God & his

---

¹ Vulg. Luc. vii. 11–15.   ² Vulg. Joh. xi. 1–46.

³ Vulg. Ecclesiasticus xviii. 30.

⁴ W. V. 'After thi lustis go thou not.' 1388, 'Go thou not aftir thi
coueitises.'

⁵ Vulg. Deut. xix. 14.

⁶ W. V. 'Thou shalt not take, and ouerbere the teermes of thi neiȝbour,
the whiche han maad rather men in thi possessioun, that the Lord thi God
shal ȝyue to thee.' 1388, 'Thou schalt not take, and turne over the termes of
thi neiȝbore, which the formere men settiden in thi possessioun, which thi
Lord God schal ȝyue to thee.'

Capitulum .XII.

lawe/ for þus it is writen. Deut⁰. xxvii⁰./ 'Maledictus qui transfert terminos proximi sui'¹/ Cursid be þat man or womman. þat passiþ þe boundis of laweful mesure ꝰ bitwene her neiȝbours & hem ²/

5 Aȝen þis comaundement ꝰ þe fende wiþ hise cau-|-tels/ haþ largid þis couetise ꝰ to alle þre astatis/ þat vnneþ ony man. takiþ ony hede ꝰ hou þat he cum bi good. so þat he were riche ‖
Comunes han purchasid ꝰ at anticristis procatour/ to be fermours of þe chirche ꝰ for couetise of wynnyng/ and bi þis parischens ꝰ
10 ben brouȝt in many custumes/ þat stroyen pees & norischen baate ꝰ & quenchen Goddis lawe/ But who þat euere seiþ or biddiþ ꝰ biside Goddis wille/ þat is not proued in holy writ ꝰ & opunli declarid/ he is a false witnesar ꝰ & doiþ cursid sacrilege/ and so seiþ seint Austin/ 'Cum dominus dixit in euangelio. ego sum
15 veritas. & non dixit ego sum consuetudo. itaque veritate manifestata veritati cedat consuetudo/ Petrus qui circumsidebat cessit Paulo veritatem predicanti/ ergo cum christus veritas sit magis veritatem ｊuam consuetudinem sequi debemus quia consuetudinem racio & ⁻eritas semper excludunt'ᵃ/ whanne þe Lord God haþ seid in his
20 gospel. I am trouþe. & he seid not. I am custum ꝰ þanne whanne trouþe is schewid. custum mut nede ȝyue stede to trouþe/ Petir þat circumcidid. consentid to Poul. preching þe trouþe/ þerfor siþen ǀ Crist is troupe ꝰ we owen miche more to swe trouþe þan custum/ for euer-more resoun & troupe ꝰ schullen exclude custum/
25 and whanne resoun & troupe. excluden þise fermours. & alle her false custumes ꝰ he is a verry membre of þe deuel. þat mayntneþ þe contrarie/ & makiþ þe hous of Iesu Crist ꝰ þe comune schopp of marchaundise ‖

But lordis here ben more to blame ꝰ þat schulde chastise þis
30 synne/ for summe ben fermours hem silf ꝰ & fauouren for couetise/ þat þe persun schal haue ɉeue ꝰ to liee in grooti placis/ as an hogge in þe myre ꝰ & leeue his cure vnkept ‖ ȝhe lordis in þise daies ꝰ ben so smyten wiþ couetise/ þat þei holden false gooten

---

[1] Vulg. Deut. xxvii. 17.
[2] W. V. 'Cursid that overberith the teermes of his neiȝbore.'

---

[a] Augustinus, *De Baptismo contra Donatistas*, Lib. III, cap. vi-ix (Migne, tom. 43, cols. 143, 144); Gratian, *Decreti* Pars Prima, dist. viii, cap. vi (Migne, tom. 187, cols. 46, 47).

goodis ꞉ aȝens her owene conscience ⸝ and feele siþes reren strong
hand ꞉ armyd in wickidnes ⸝ to kille men boþe sleping & wakyng ꞉
to encrese her lordschipis ‖ Kyng Acab for couetise ꞉ of Nabathis
vynȝerde ⸝ þat he desirid for to haue had ꞉ aȝen þis knyȝtis wille ⸝
Fol. 110 a leide him gronyng on his bedde ꞉ & wolde taste | no mete ⸝ for 5
Nabath seide he wolde not chaunge ꞉ ne selle his kynde eritage ‖
But Iezabel þat wickid quene ꞉ ȝaue þe kyng suche counseile ⸝ þat
þei kesten þis manes deeþ ꞉ bi a fals sclaundir ⸝ & þus þei brouȝten
him to an eende ꞉ & reioyced his vynȝerde ‖ God sent worde to
Acab & to Iezabel ꞉ bi þe prophet Hely ⸝ þat for þei hadden do 10
þus coueitouseli ꞉ aȝens his comaundement ⸝ her blood schulde be
schadde on þe erþe ꞉ & houndis schulde lik it ⸝ And moreouere.
God took veniaunce ꞉ for þis greuouse synne ⸝ vpon þe seed þat
cam of hem ꞉ in to þe þridde & þe fourþe generacioun ⸝ And if
þat we tooke hede ꞉ hou lordis han slayn iche oþir ⸝ in scheding 15
her blood in þe felde ꞉ for coueitise of lording ⸝ we schulde not
woundir þouȝ Goddis hand ꞉ be strecchid ouere hise peple ⸝ to
smyt wiþ veniaunce as he doiþ ꞉ & no man may avoide it ⸝ and if
þou wilt wite ꞉ what is þis veniaunce ⸝ God seiþ bi þe prophete.
Fol. 110 b Ose. iiii⁰ ⸝ þat his veniaunce is ꞉ whanne he | wiþdrawiþ his 20
chastising. & þe ȝerde of amending ⸝ and suffriþ hise enemyes to
regne in her synne ꞉ to her deeþ day ⸝ & aftir to dampne hem bodi
& soule ꞉ euer wiþouten eende ⸝ And to þis acordiþ Gregory ꞉ in
hise morals vpon Iob ⸝ 'Deus quibusdam hec parcit ꞉ vt in eternum
feriat' ‖ Þat is to se. In þis lijf to summe God spariþ ꞉ þat he 25
may smyte hem wiþouten ende ⸝ and Iob seiþ. xxi⁰. 'Quare impij
viuunt subleuati sunt confortatique diuiciis ⸝ semen eorum permanet
coram eis propinquorum turba & nepotum in conspectu eorum domus
eorum secure sunt & pacate & non est virga dei super illos ⸝ Bos eorum
concepit & non abhortiuit ⸝ vacca peperit & non est priuata fetu 30
suo ‖ Egrediuntur quasi greges paruuli eorum & infantes eorum
exultant[1] lusibus ⸝ tenent timpanum & cytharam & gaudent ad
sonitum organi ⸝ Ducunt in bonis dies suos ꞉ & in puncto ad
nota inferna descendunt'[2] ‖ Þat is to seie. whi lyuen wickid men
avauncid & counfortid in richessis ? þe seed of hem dwelliþ biforn 35
Fol. 111a hem ꞉ & þe company of nyȝ | frendis & cosynes in her siȝt ⸝ her
housis ben siker. & þe ȝeerde of God. þat is clepid his chastising ꞉

[1] MS. exultauit.   [2] Vulg. Job xxi. 7-13.

Capitulum .XII.

is not vpon hem / Her heekfar consceyued ./ & kest not hir fruyt
or tyme / Hir cow bar hir fruyt ./ & was not braft þe profit of hir
wombe / Her striplyngis gon aforn hem ./ as flokis of beestis / and
her ȝonglingis ioyen ./ in pleyes & in games ‖ Þei holden þe tymber
5 & þe harp ./ & þei ioyen at þe sonde of þe organ / Þei leden her
daies in goodis. þat is to seie. in helþe & in welþe ./ & in worldli
worschip / and sodenli in a poynt ./ þei discenden or gon doun to
hellis [1] ‖ But aȝenwarde ./ Salamon in hise prouerbis. iii⁰.[2] / And
seint Poul to þe Hebre. xii⁰ [3] / And seint Ion in his apocalips. iii⁰.[4] /
10 seyn þat God repreueþ & chastisiþ ./ alle hem þat he loueþ. &
resceyueþ to blisse / And þerfore seiþ Iason. II. Macha. vi⁰. /
'Multo tempore non sinere peccatoribus ex sententia agere sed
statim vlciones adhibere magni beneficij est indicium'[5] ‖ Þat is to
seie. It is a greet token | of greet goodnes ./ not to suffre long   Fol. 111 b
15 tyme synners / of her wickid purpose ./ to swe her owene foly / but
soone put to hem ./ merciful chastisement / forsoþe þe Lord doþe
not so wiþ hise chosun ./ as he doiþ wiþ alien naciouns / þat is.
þoo þat he forsakiþ þoruȝ her diseruyng ./ & casteþ hem out of his
siȝt / whom he abidiþ pacientli ./ to punysche hem at þe fulle in
20 domesday / forsoþe he haþ not ordeyned so ./ to punysche hem þat
he loueþ / but he chastiseþ hem pacientli ./ & aftir resceyueþ hem
to his graciouse mercy ‖

But prestis in þis couetise ./ moost greuen her God / for þei ben   III. Among the clergy.

---

[1] W V. 'Whi thanne unpitous men liuen, and ben rered up, and coumfortid with richessis? The sed of hem abit stille beforn hem; and the cumpanye of neeȝh men, and of cosynes in the siȝte of hem. The housis of hem ben sikere, and pesible; and the ȝerde of God is not upon hem. The oxe of hem conceyued, and bar not abortif; the kow bar, and is not prived the frut. The little childer of hem gon out as flockis; and the fauntis of hem gladen out with pleies. They holden the timbre, and the harpe; and ioȝen at the soun of the orgne. Thei leden in goodis ther daȝis; and in a point to hellis thei go doun.' 1388, 'Whi therfor lyuen wickid men? Thei ben enhaunsid, and coumfortid with richessis. Her seed dwellith bifor hem; the cumpeny of kynesmen, and of sones of sones dwellith in her siȝt. Her housis ben sikur, and pesible; and the ȝerde of God is not on hem. The cow of hem conseyuede and calvede not a deed calf; the cow caluyde, and is not priued of hir calf. Her litle children goen out as flockis; and her ȝonge children maken fulli ioye with pleies. Thei holden tympan, and harpe; and ioien at the soun of orgun. Thei leden in goodis her daies: and in a point thei goen doun to hellis.'

[2] Vulg. Prov. iii. 12.
[3] Vulg. Heb. xii. 5, 6.
[4] Vulg. Apoc. iii. 19.
[5] Vulg. 2 Macc. vi. 13.

autours of þise synnes ./ þat we han seide aforn / Þei seyn þat þei
han a lawe ./ þat þei clepen hem silf / fredom of holi chirche ./ þouȝ
it be bondage of þe deuel / & bi þis þei may purchase ./ out of þe
seculere hand / ȝhe al her lijflood if þei myȝt wynne it ./ bi oo weie
or bi oþir / & what þei wynne in to her powere ./ þer may no man 5
reclem it / in to þe handis of seculers ./ for holy chirchis fredam /
Fol. 112 a & | who so do. schal be suspendid ./ for holi chirchis grippe / &
acursid bi her lawe ./ til he restore aȝen || Þus þei vndo seculere[1]
partie ./ wiþ her feyned holines / in cleping her sory chirche
holi chirche ./ & her þraldom fredom / & magnifien her serymoyns ./ 10
aboue þe lawe of God / so þat laymen ben oppressid ./ vndir þise
prestis daunger / as soore as þe Iewis weren ./ wiþ scribis &
farises ||

nota bene Þe deuel whanne he temptid Eve ./ made a faire semblaunt / for
to stire hir to coueitise ./ to breke Goddis biddyng || in eeting of þe 15
appil ./ wherbi deeþ schulde entre || Þis womman sauȝ þe appil ./ þat
it was good in biholding / & also faire in siȝt ./ & likerouse in
smelling / sche eet þerof ./ & ȝaue part to hir housbond / He boote
þerof. þanne boþe weren deedli. & losten þe ioye of paradise ||
Þe maistir of sentence seiþ þis appil ./ is synne þat God forbediþ / 20
þanne aftir þe wit of allegory ./ þis is þus to mene / whanne þat
seculere men ./ fermen spiritual office / and whanne þat prestis
Fol. 112 b bowiden doun ./ to take | temperel lordschip / bi tempting of þe
deuel ./ in her foule coueitise / Þanne þise twoo parties. as Adam
& Eve ./ & þei þat ben consentours / ben dryuen out of þe blisse 25
of heuen ./ wiþ þe scharpe swerde of Goddis word / Balaam was
cauȝt in þis coueitise ./ & his owene beest repreued him / & hirt his
foot aȝen a wal ./ for his iourney plesid not God / But þis man
wolde not be war ./ þerfore he was slayn among þe heeþen /
Numeri. xxii⁰. Þis couetise sterid Geizi ./ to take mede of Naaman / 30
for a spiritual benefice ./ þat God him silf hadde wrouȝt / bi his
seruaunt Helesie ./ in clensyng of his myselrie / & þerfore Geizi ./
wiþ his generacioun / were smyten for euer ./ wiþ þe leepre of
Naaman / IV. Re. v⁰. / Anany & Saphir his wijf ./ ouercomen wiþ
þis couetise / liȝed in her conscience ./ aforne seint Petris presence / 35
& þerfore þei died boþe ./ in þe synne of wanhope / Actus v⁰.[2] /
who þat rediþ þis blessid loore ./ þat is oure feiþ & Goddis lawe / but

---

[1] MS. secule.   [2] Vulg. Act. v. 1–11.

Capitulum .XII.

he leue þis couetise ./ he stondiþ in perel of his soule / as God seiþ
bi þe prophete. Isaie. v⁰. / 'Ve qui coniungitis domum ad domum
& agrum agro capulatis vsque ad | terminum loci / Numquid
habitabitis soli vos in medio terre ' ¹ ‖ Þat is to seie. Woo to ȝou
5 þat ioynen hous to hous. & couplen feelde to feelde ./ vnto þe terme
of a place / Nowheþir schul ȝe dwelle aloone in myddis of þe
erþe ? seiþ þe Lord God / In þis God forbediþ. þe vnleful coueitis ./
þat we han seid aforn / for if þis couetise cacche not roote in þe
herte ./ it schal neuer growe to þe deed. as it is seide aforn / and
10 þerfore seiþ seint Poul. I. Cor. x⁰. 'Non sumus concupiscentes
malorum. sicut quidam eorum concupierunt ' ² / Be we not coueiting of yuel ./ as summe of oure elders han coueited ³ / & we preien
ȝou for charite ./ looke in þise placis / & se what haþ fallen ./ for
þis synne of couetise Ge. iii⁰ / Numerj. xiiii⁰ / xvi⁰ / & xxii⁰ /
15 IIII Re. v⁰ / Actus. v⁰. ‖

Þe tenþe heest /

The tenþe comaundement of God is þis. Ex⁰. xx⁰. 'Non deside- *The Tenth Command-*
rabis vxorem proximi tui. non seruum. non ancillam. non bouem. *ment*
non azinum. nec omnia que illius sunt ' ⁴ ‖ Þou schalt not desire
20 þi neiȝbores wijf. ne his seruaunt. ne his handmayde. ne his oxe.
ne his asse. ne no þingis þat ben hise ./ oþirwise þan þou wilt he
coueite þin. aftir resoun & þe lawe | of Cristis gospel ‖ In þe *Fol. 113 b*
sixte comaundement ./ God forbediþ þe outwarde dede of leccherie /
& in þat he refreyneþ ./ þe vnleful treeting of þe bodi / but in þis
25 he forbediþ ./ þe inwarde consent of þe herte / & in þat he refrey- *lays stress upon a*
neþ ./ al vnleful desire or wille / nameli in þo þingis ./ þat ben *right will.*
moveable / Þat is to seie. þat han myȝt in hem silf ./ to remeve fro
oo place to anoþir / for desire & wille þat restiþ in þe inward man ./
makeþ merite or synne more or lesse. in þe presence of God / for
30 charitable werkis. þat ben in her owene kynde. myȝti & greet ./
ben don sumtyme wiþ a frowarde wille. & þanne þei wanten mede /
as Crist seiþ in his gospel. Mat. vii⁰ / 'Non omnis qui dicit mihi
domine domine intrabit in regnum celorum sed qui facit voluntatem
patris mei qui in celis est. ipse intrabit in regnum celorum ' ⁵ ‖
35 Þat is to seie. Not iche man þat seiþ to me. Lord Lord ./ schal

---

[1] Vulg. Isaias v. 8.
[2] Vulg. 1 Cor. x. 6 'Non simus concupiscentes malorum sicut et illi,' etc.
[3] W. V. 'Forsoth thes thingis ben don in figure of us, that we ben not coueyteris of yuelis, as and thei coueitiden.'
[4] Vulg. Ex. xx. 17.   [5] Vulg. Matt. vii. 21.

entre in to þe rewme of heuenes[1] / A man schal not be saued not
oonli for hise good wordis ne for his good dedes. wherfore þanne ?
But he þat doþ þe wille of my fadir þat is in heuenes ." he schal
Fol. 114 a entre in to þe rewme of heuenes[1] / Þat is to seie. aftir | þe desire
þat a man haþ in worde & dede. to do þe plesing wille of God ." 5
aftir þat he schal be rewardid in blisse / & bi þis greetnes of mannes
good wille. þouȝ þe werk be litile in kynde ." it askiþ greet rewarde
in blisse / and þerfore þe aungels soungen in Cristis birþe ." Luk. ii⁰.
'Pax hominibus bone voluntatis'[2] || Pees be in erþe ." to men of
good wille || for suche a good wille. traueileþ to plese God ." in 10

The will is counted for the deed. worde & in dede / and whanne it may no ferþir strecche ." þis wille
is countid for a dede / as þe maistir of sentence seiþ ." rehersyng
seynt Austin / þat þis modir ignoraunce. þat we clepen vnkunnyng-
nesse ." haþ þre douȝtren || Þe firste ben alle þoo ." þat myȝten
lerne & wole not || Þe secounde ben alle þoo ." þat wolden lerne 15
& moun not || Þe þridde ben alle þoo ." þat taken no hede || Þe
firste schullen algatis be dampned || Þe secounde schullen algatis
be saued ." bicause her wille answeriþ for þe dede || Þe þridde
acorden wiþ þe firste. but if it be so. þat þei schal haue lesse
peyne in helle / and þerfore yuel wille þat a man haþ ." to wynne | 20
Fol. 114 b him goostli strengþe / or to haue knowyng of verry bileue ." to do
þe plesing wille of God / is þe werst yuel þat comeþ to man. &
strangliþ him wiþ dispeire ." in our of his deeþ ||

The will of the godhead is threefold. But ȝit we schullen vndirstonde ." þat þe wille of þe Godheed /
stondiþ in þre þingis ." acording to þe Trinite / & we must do oure 25
I   vttirest ." to conforme oure wille to þis || Þe Fadir of his rial
II   wille ." comaundiþ þat riȝtwisenes were don || Þe Sone of his
witti wille suffriþ þe lesse yuel ." þe more to be fledde / & abidiþ
III synnars long ." bi vertu of his incarnacioun || Þe Holi Goost of
his charitable wille ." forbediþ al vnclennes || whanne þe strengþe 30
of oure wille ." is sette to do riȝtwisenes / þanne we be conformed ."
to do þe fadirs bidding / And whanne þe wisdam of oure wille ."
is turned to mercy / boþe to oure silf & to oþir ." þanne swe we
Cristis steppis || But whanne þe loue of oure wille ." splrediþ in
dwe ordir / boþe in heuene & in erþe ." as we han seide aforn / 35
Fol. 115 a þanne dwelliþ þe Holi Goost ." in oure inwarde | man || If þis
knot be treweli knitt ." in wille of oure soule / þer is non entre fro

---

[1] W. V. & 1388, 'kyngdam of heuenes.'   [2] Vulg. Luc. ii. 14.

Capitulum .XII.

þe deuel ׃ to trouble vs from vnite / as seint Ierom seiþ ‖ 'Dia- *If our will be conformed to it, the devil cannot trouble us.*
bolus non pugnat contra nos aperta facie ׃ sed fraude / nostra
contra nos vtitur voluntate / de nostro consensu vires accipit /
nostroque nos iugulat gladio / vincere non potest nisi nostra volun-
5 tate / procul ergo desperacio. remedium contra ipsum. est sacre
scripture studium ' Hec Ieromus. ep. 84 / Þat is to seie. þe deuel
fiȝtiþ not aȝens vs wiþ open face ׃ but wiþ gile / forsoþe he vsiþ
aȝens vs ׃ oure owene wille / he takiþ him strengþis ׃ of oure
owene consent / and he wirieþ vs ׃ wiþ oure owene swerde / He
10 may neuer ouerecome vs ׃ but þorȝ oure owene wille / þerfore.
feer be desperacioun ‖ Remedie aȝens þis deuel ׃ is studie in hooly
writ / And to þis entent spekiþ þe wisman. Prou. vi⁰. / 'Man-
datum¹ lucerna est. & lex lux. & via vite. & increpacio discipline vt
custodiat te a muliere mala & a blanda lingua extranie / non con-
15 cupiscat pulcritudinem eius cor tuum'² ‖ Þat is to seie. Goddis
comaundementis ben a lanterne ׃ & þat lawe | is liȝt / & þe weye *Fol. 115 b*
of lijf. & vndirnymyng of loore. þat it may kepe þee from an yuel
womman. & from þe smeþe tung of a straunge comlyng ‖ loke þin
herte coueite not ׃ þe fairenes of hir ‖ No wheþir may a man
20 hide fire in his shirte. & not brenne hise cloþis ? or walke on
brenning coolis ׃ & not brenne þe soolis of his feet ? So he þat
entriþ in to his neiȝboris wijf. schal not be clene ׃ whanne he
haþ leccherouseli touchid hir³ / for he þat is a voutrer. for þe foule
nedi desire of his herte ׃ schal lese his soule ، for he gadriþ to
25 him ׃ vilenye & schenschip / and his vpbreiding ׃ schal not be don
awey / for ȝeel & woodnes of þe man ׃ schal not spare in þe dai of
veniaunce / ne it schal not cese ׃ for preiours of ony man / ne he

---

¹ MS. mandata.   ² Vulg. Prov. vi. 23-5.

³ W. J. 'For the maundement is a lanterne, and the lawe liȝt, and the weie
of lif the snybbing of discipline; that thei kepe thee fro an evel woman, and
fro the flaterende tunge of the straunge womman. Coueite not thin herte the
fairnesse of hir: whether mai a man hide fir in his bosum, that his clothis
brenne not ; or gon upon colis, and his solis be not brent ? So he that goth
in to the womman of his neȝhebore ; schal not ben clene, whan he touchith
hir.' 1388, 'For the comaundement of God is a lanterne, and the lawe is
liȝt, and the blamyng of techyng is the weie of lijf; that the comaundementis
kepe thee fro an yuel wommàn, and fro a flaterynge tunge of a straunge
womman. Thin herte coueite not the fairnesse of hir. Whether a man mai
hide fier in his bosum, that hise clothis brenne not ; ethir go on colis, and
hise feet be not brent ? So he that entrith to the wijf of his neiȝbore schal not
be cleene, whanne he hath touchid hir.'

Persecucioun?

schal not take ony ȝiftis? for his redempcioun / for seint Ierom
seiþ / 'Cor habet gulosus in ventre lasciuus in libidine cupidus in
lucris auarus in pecunijs' ‖ Þat is to seie. A glotun haþ his hert
on his wombe / ∣ A wantoune man? on his leccherie / A coueitouse man on his wynnyng / An auarouse man on sore holdeyng / 5
and perfore seiþ Salamon. Prou. iiii°. / 'Omni custodia serua cor
tuum. quia ex ipso vita procedit'[1] ‖ wiþ al þi bisines kepe þin
herte? for lijf passiþ from it[2] / and Seynt Hewe seiþ. 'In omni
natura creatura que sub sole vanitatibus humanis occupantur?
nichil humano corde sullimius. nichil nobilius. nichil deo similius 10
reperitur / quapropter nichil aliud querit a te. nisi cor tuum' ‖ Þat
is to seie. In alle creaturis þat ben occupied vndir heuen in mannes
vanites? þer is no þing hiȝer þan mannes herte / þer is no þing
founden liker to God. wherfore God sekiþ no þing of þee? but þin
herte ‖ 15

nota Aȝen þis comaundement? þe fende wiþ hise cautels / moveþ
discorde in þe hertis? of hem þat ben weddid / til þei desire to be
departid? þe toone from þe toþir / Þanne þe man feyneþ a cause?
to go fro þis womman / & in þis þei ben acursid? as þe wise man
seiþ / Prou. xviii°. / 'Occasiones ∣ querit qui vult recedere ab 20
amico. omni tempore erit exprobrabilis'[3] ‖ Þat is to seie. He
sechiþ occasiouns? þat wole go awey from his frende / at alle tyme
he schal be cursid? & worþi vpbreiding[4] / Neþeles a foole wole
not resceyve? þe wordis of teching / but if þou seie to him suche
þingis? as his herte desiriþ / and perfore he renneþ forþe? in 25
woodnes of his herte / for to procur a devorse? bitwene his wijf
& him ‖ He cumeþ anoon to þe chirche? þat is clepid laweles /
Not for þe chirche. but for þe officeris? for þei be laweles hiȝnen /
He chesiþ him a notarie? & paieþ him his wagis / to make him
an instrument? of his forgid lesing / þanne goiþ he to þe maistris? 30
þat sitten on her seetis / wiþ furid hoodis & fonned heedis? &
ȝyueþ hem money greet plente / & preieþ hem to be his voketis?
þat þis deuorse were mad / for he wole be redi? at þe laweles dai /

---

[1] Vulg. Prov. iv. 23.

[2] W. V. 'With alle warde kep thou thin herte, for of it lif goth forth.'
1388, 'With al keping kepe thin herte, for lijf cometh forth of it.'

[3] Vulg. Prov. xviii. 1.

[4] W. V. 'Ocasioun secheth, that wil gon awei fro a frend; alle time
wariable he shal be.' 1388, 'He that wole go a wei fro a frend, sekith occasiouns; in al tyme he schal be dispisable.'

Capitulum .XII.

to bring forþe his twelueþ hand ." aforn þe iugge sir Symound ⁄ &
make good wiþ al þe court ." þat he haþ no riȝt ⁄ to þe | womman
þat he weddid ." for dedis don aforn ⁄ Þanne sir Symound ȝyueþ
his doom ." to dissolue trewe wedlock ⁄ & autoriseþ leccherie ." in
5 þise boþe partiees ⁄ for to lyue in hoordam ." fro þat dai forward ⁄
& sendiþ hem forþe at dyuerse doris ." departid iche from oþir ⁄
But lo what Crist seiþ. Mat. xix⁰. Mar. x⁰. Luk. xvi⁰.[1] ⁄ 'Propter
hoc dimittet homo patrem & matrem & adherebit vxori sue' ‖ Þat
is to seie. For matrimonye a man schal leeue his fadir & his modir ."
10 & he schal holde him to his wijf ⁄ & þei schal be tweyne in oo
fleische[2] ." þat is for her dwelling togidir ⁄ also þei ben not þanne
tweyne. but oo fleische ." þat is bi vertu of þe sacrament ‖ wherfore þat þing þat God haþ ioyned ." man may not departe ‖ I seie
forsoþe to ȝow ⁄ þat who euer haþ left his wijf ." except þe cause of
15 fornicacioun ⁄ & if he wedde anoþir ." þanne he is a lecchour ⁄ &
who þat weddiþ þis womman ." þat þis man haþ leeft ⁄ he lediþ his
lijf in leccherie ." als long tyme as he holdiþ hir ⁄ Siþen þat God
ioyneþ neuere ." | but in laweful maner ⁄ How dare ȝe purswe þis
deuorse ." in a laweles chirche ?
20 Seint Poul seiþ. Rom. ii⁰. 'Quicunque siue lege peccauerit ."
sine lege peribunt'[3] ‖ who euer þat synneþ wiþouten þe lawe ."
schal perische wiþouten þe lawe ⁄ For & þei weren blynde &
knewen not þe lawe ." þei myȝten happili þe hesiliar be excusid ⁄
but now þei seyn þei knowe þe lawe ." & don foole-hardili aȝen þe
25 lawe. þei haue non excusacioun ⁄ & þerfor þe wiseman seiþ an
holsum remedie ." aȝens þis synne of þe herte ⁄ Ecc¹. xviii⁰ ⁄ 'A
voluntate[4] tua auertere'[5] ⁄ Be þou turned from þyn owene wille ."[6]
& obeie þou to Goddis wille ⁄ and þanne seiþ seint Bernard ." þou
schalt neuere cum in helle ⁄ and þerfore while þou art hol & sounde ."
30 waveryng aboute in þouȝt ⁄ þoruȝ diuerse errours ." from God & from
vertu ⁄ brise doun not oonli suche vnleful coueitise ." but also alle
superflu & vnstable þouȝtis ⁄ & suffre hem not in ony wise ." to

[side-notes: Fol. 117a; Divorce contrary to Christ's law; Fol. 117b; Those who sin, knowing the law, have no excuse.]

---

[1] Vulg. Matt. xix. 5; Marc. x. 7 (Luc. xvi. 18).

[2] W. V. 'For this thing a man shal leeue fadir and modir, and he shal cleve, or drawe, to his wif; and thei shulen be two in oo flesh.'

[3] Vulg. Rom. ii. 12 'Quicunque sine lege peccaverunt,' etc.

[4] MS. volutate.   [5] Vulg. Ecclesiasticus xviii. 30.

[6] W. V. 'Fro thi wil turne thee awei.' 1388, 'He thou turned awei fro thi wille.'

growe to dede ne to custum / and | þis semeþ to be þe sentence of þe prophete ./ where he seiþ / Ps. cxxxvi. 'Beatus qui tenebit & allidet paruulos suos ad petram '[1] || Blessid be þat man. þat schal holde & hirte ./ hise ȝounglingis at þe stoon[2] / as þe werkis of man ben hise sones or hise douȝtren aftir goostli sens ./ so þoo 5 þouȝtis of þe inwarde man. ben hise ȝounglingis || Þanne he hirtiþ hise ȝounglingis ./ at þe stoon of riȝtwisenesse / whanne he distrieþ her sodeyn crepyngis ./ in þenkyng of þe lijf of oure Lord Iesu Crist / Forsoþe þis is a special remedie. to wiþholde wickid þouȝtis desiris & willis / þat þei flowe not to deepli wiþynneforþe ./ 10 neiþir þat þei fliȝe to fer wiþouten forþe || & in suche traueils ./ pryuen þoo þat God haþ chosun / for þei wil not in ony disese ./ neiþir be ouercomen. neiþir consent || to þise cautels of þe deuel ./ bi whiche he enprisouneþ / Goddis seruauntis for þei kepen ./ þise ten forseid heestis / But seint Hillary seiþ. 'Hoc habet proprium 15 ecclesia dum prosequitur floret / dum | opprimitur crescit / dum contempnitur proficit / dum leditur vincit / dum arguitur intelligit / tunc stat cum superari videtur ' || Hec Hillarius de trinitate. li⁰. VII⁰.[a] / Þat is to seie. þis propurte haþ Cristis chirche / whanne it is pursued ./ it florischiþ / whanne it is brissid doun ./ it growiþ / 20 whanne it is dispisid ./ it profitiþ / whanne it is hirte ./ it ouere-comeþ / whanne it is blamed ./ it vndirstondiþ / and þanne it stondiþ moost strongli. whanne it is seen in mannes iȝe ./ to be ouere-comen || Þis chirche is a trewe soule ./ as we han seid aforn / Summe þat ben tendir ./ & feble for to suffre / crien wiþ þe pro- 25 phete ./ seiyng þus to God / Abacuk. i⁰. ' vsquequo domine clamabo. & non exaudies ? vociferabor ad te vim paciens. & non saluabis ? Quare ostendisti mihi iniquitatem & laborem videre predam & iniusticiam contra me ? Quare respicis contemptores & taces con-culcantes impio iustiorem se '[3] || Þat is to seie. Lord hou long 30

---

[1] Vulg. Ps. cxxxvi. 9 'Beatus qui tenebit et allidet parvulos tuos ad petram.'

[2] W. V. 'Blisful that shal holden and hurtlen his little childer to the ston.' 1388, 'He is blessid, that schal holde and hurtle doun hise litle children at a stoon.'

[3] Vulg. Hab. i. 2, 3, 13; ver. 13 'Quare respicis super iniqua agentes, et taces devorante impio iustiorem se?'

---

[a] St Hilarius, *De Trinitate*, Lib. vii (Migne, tom. 10, col. 202).

schal I crie ."' & þou schalt not heere me ? Lord til whanne schal
I calle vpon þee ."' & þou schalt not make me saf ? whi hast þou
schewid me | wickidnes & traueile & to se þeeft ."' & vnriȝtwisenesse Fol. 119 a
aȝens me ? whi biholdest þou dispisears ."' & art stille ."' þe wickid
5 man defoiling. þe iustar þan he ? [1] Seint Ierom in his prolog seiþ ."'
þat þise ben wordis of mannes impacience / and settiþ an ensaumple ."'
of a sijke man swelling in fyuers / and askiþ coold watir ."' seiyng
to his leche || I suffre woo & am al to-turmentid ."' I am ful nyȝ
deed / how long schal I crye leche ."' & þou schalt not heere me ?
10 Þe witti & þe moost merciful leeche ."' answeriþ to him / I wot in
what tyme. me houeþ to ȝyue to þee ."' þat þou askist / I haue no
ruþe on þe now ."' for þis mercy were cruelte / & þin owene wille
askiþ aȝen þee || Also oure Lord God knowyng. þe weiȝt & þe
mesure of his mercy ."' sumtyme he heeriþ not þe crier anoon / þat
15 he may proue & more steere to preie ."' & as examyned bi þe fier /
þat he may make his seruaunt. boþe iuster & purer ."' to resceyue
grace & mede ||

What is þe fendis chirche ."' wiþ hir propurtees /
    Capitulum .XIIIᵐ. || |
20 To speke of þe þridde chirche ."' enproprid to þe deuel / þe Fol. 119 b
whiche is þe noumbre ."' of hem þat ben encombrid / to serue him The devil's church.
aftir his tising ."' aȝen Goddis heestis || Firste we schullen take
oure grounde ."' in wordis of þe prophete / Ps. xxv. 'Odiui ecclesiam
malingnancium' [2] || I haue haatid þe chirche of maliciouse lyuars [3] ||
25 Þise ben þoo þat straien awey ."' aftir hir owene desiris / walkyng
in þe large weye ."' þat lediþ hem to helle / neiþir þei wil be
gouerned ."' bi lawe ne bi grace / neiþir þei wole for drede ne loue ."'
cese & go fro synne / bi cause þis world is ful of lustis ."' & profriþ
hise louears. a ioye soone passing || But þei þat traueilen aftir
30 blisse ."' here þei suffren peyne / þerfore foolis wiþouten noumbre ."'
ioyen wiþ þis world / as Crist seiþ in his gospel. Mat. viiº. /

---

[1] W. V. 'Hou longe, Lord, shal Y crye, and thou shalt not heere graciously?
Y suffringe violence shal crie on heeȝ, and shalt thou not saue? Whi shewidist
thou to me wickidnesse aȝeinus me? Whi biholdist thou dispisers, and art
stille, the unpitouse man defoulyng a iuster than hym?'

[2] Vulg. Ps. xxv. 5.

[3] W. V. 'I hatide the chirche of wariende men.' 1388, 'I hatide the
chirche of yuele men.'

Of þe chirche ∴ of þe fende ∴

'Intrate per angustiam portam. quia lata porta & spaciosa est via que ducit ad perdicionem et multi sunt qui intrant per eam ‖ O quam angusta porta est & arta via que ducit ad vitam & pauci sunt qui inveniunt eam'[1] ‖ Þat is to seie. | Entre ȝe bi þe strayt ȝate. for large is þe ȝate & brood is þe weye þat lediþ to dampna- 5 cioun ∴ & manye þer ben þat entren bi it ‖ O, How peynful is þe ȝate & how streiȝt is þe weye þat lediþ to þe lijf ∴ & fewe þer ben þat fynden it[2], for seint Ion seiþ. v⁰. 'Mundus totus in maligno positus est'[3]/ Al þis world. þat is. alle þoo men & wymmen þat ben ouercomen wiþ þis world ∴ ben sett in malice.[4] þat is brennyng 10 in þe fire of foule couetise / For al þing þat is in þis world. eiþir it is þe couetise of iȝen. or ellis it is couetise of þe fleische. or ellis it is þe pride of þis lijf / and þerfor þis chirche is groundid vpon þe deuel ∴ in þe grauel of false couetise / as Poul seiþ. Thimo. vi⁰. ‖ 'Radix enim omnium malorum est cupiditas quam quidam appe- 15 tentes errauerunt a fide'[5] ‖ Forsoþe þe roote of alle yuelis is couetise / þe whiche summe desiryng ∴ haue errid from trewe bileue / & han ioyned hemsilf ∴ to many sorowis[6] ‖

The foundation of this church is in gluttony and lechery.

Þe rering vp of þis chirche ∴ is in glotenye & leccherie / as þe wisman seiþ. rehersing þe wordis | of hem þat schal be dampned / 20 Sap. ii⁰. 'vino precioso & vnguento nos impleamus / & non preteriat nos flos temporis. Coronemus nos rosis antequam marescant / Nullum pratum sit. quod non pertransiat luxuria nostra ‖ Nemo nostrum exsors sit luxurie nostre vbique relinquamus / signa leticie'[7] / Þat is to seie. Þise fendis lymes seyn. go we fille vs wiþ 25 preciouse wyn and an oyntment / & suffre we not þe flour of oure faire beaute ∴ to passe awey from vs / croune we vs wiþ roosis of iolite ∴ or þat þei welken awey / þer may be no medowe ∴ but if

---

[1] Vulg. Matt. vii. 13, 14.

[2] W. V. 'Entre ȝe bi the streyt ȝate; for the gate that ledith to perdicioun, or dampnacioun, is brode, and the weye large, and ther ben many that entren bi it. Hou streyt is the ȝate, and narewe the weye, that ledith to lijf, and ther fewe that fynden it.'

[3] Vulg. 1 Joh. v. 19.

[4] W. V. 'Al the world is put in wickid.' 1388, 'Al the world is set in yuel.'

[5] Vulg. 1 Tim. vi. 10.

[6] W. V. 'Sothly the roote of alle yuels is couetyse, the which sum men coueitynge, or desyringe, erreden fro the feith, and bisettiden hem with many sorwis.'

Vulg. Sap. ii. 7–9 'Vino pretioso et unguentis,' etc.

Capitulum .XIII.

oure leccherie passe þerbi / Noon of vs mai be lootles of his leccherie ." euery where leeue we. þe tookens of oure gladnes¹ / And þe hilling of þis chirche ." is pride & hiȝenes of lijf / as þe prophete seiþ. Ps. xxxvi⁰. 'vidi impium superexaltatum ." & eleua-
5 tum sicut cedros libani'²‖ þat is to seie. I haue sen þe vnpitiuouse & þe wickid enhaunsid & vplifted as þe cedre trees of Liban.³ & þei ben þe hiȝest trees of þis world / But as smoke riseþ sodenli. & soone vanischeþ to nouȝt ." so þe proude ben preisid for | a tyme ." & anoon þei fallen awey / & we witen not ." where þei bicomen ‖
10 Off þe bisines and occupacioun. þat dwellars of þis chirche vsen ." spekiþ þe prophete. Ps. liiii. 'Die ac nocte circumdabit eam super muros eius iniquitas & labor in medio eius & iniusticia'⁴/ þat is to seie. Niȝt & day. wickidnesse schal cumpasse aboute þis chirche vpon hir wallis ." & traueile in middis of it & vnriȝtwisnesse / &
15 okir-julling and treccherie ." haþ not stintid in þe weies of hir⁵ ‖ Of þis chirche wiþ þis maner of bilding spekiþ Crist in his gospel. Mat. vii⁰. Luk. vi⁰.⁶ 'Omnis qui audit verba mea & non facit ea similis est viro stulto qui edificauit domum suam super arenam / pro primo. & descendit pluuia / pro 2⁰. & flauerunt venti / pro 3⁰.
20 inruerunt in domum illam / pro. 4⁰. & fuit ruina eius ·magna'⁷/ Þat is to seie. who þat heeriþ my wordis & doiþ hem not. schal bilijke a foltid man þat haþ bildid his hous ." vpon þe grauel of coueitise & mysbileue / & reyne of glotenye & leccherie ." cam doun

The covering of this church is pride.

Fol. 121 a

The occupations of the members of this church.

---

¹ W. V. 'With precyous wiṅ and oynemens fille wee us; and passe not us the flour of tyme. Crowne wee us with roses, er thei welewen; no medwe be, that oure leccherie passe not thurȝ. Noon of us be withoute lot of oure leccherie; ouer al lefe wee signes of gladnesse.'

² Vulg. Ps. xxxvi. 35.

³ W. V. 'I saȝ the unpitouse aboue hauncid; and rerid up as cedris of Liban.' 1388, 'I siȝ a wickid man enhaunsid aboue; and reisid up as the cedris of Liban.'

⁴ Vulg. Ps. liv. 11, 12.

⁵ W. V. 'Dai and nyȝt wickidnesse shal enuyroune it upon the wallis of it; and travaile in the myddes of it, and unriȝtwisnesse. And ther failede not fro the stretis of it usure and treccherie.' 1388, 'Bi dai and nyȝt wickidnesse schal cumpasse it on the wallis therof, and trauel and unriȝfulnesse ben in the myddis therof. And usure and gile failide not fro the stretis therof.'

⁶ Vulg. Matt. vii. 26, 27; Luc. vi. 49.

⁷ Vulg. Matt. vii. 26, 27 'Omnis qui audit verba mea haec, et non facit ea, similis erit viro stulto, qui aedificavit domum suam super arenam; et descendit pluvia, et venerunt flumina, et flaverunt venti, et irruerunt in domum illam, et cecidit, et fuit ruina illius magna.'

Fol. 121 b on þis chirche / and þe wyndis of pride ./ blewen vpon | þis chirche / and feersli þise forseid synnes fellen in to þis chirche ./ & dryuen it doun / & þe fal of hir was greet / for sche fel from grace & glorie ./ to peyne & myschef wiþouten eend / as seint Austin seiþ || 'Non enim corpus domini est quod cum illo non erit in eternum quia 5 ypocrite non cum illo dicendi sunt quamuis in eius vidiantur esse ecclesia / Est enim diabolus caput impiorum qui sunt eius quodammodo corpus ituri cum illo in supplicium ignis eterni' [a] || Þat is to seie. Forsoþe þat is not þe bodi of þe Lord ./ þat schal not be wiþ him wiþouten eend / for ypocritis ben not seid to be wiþ 10 him ./ þou3 þei be seyn to be in his chirche / Certis þe deuel is heed of alle þe wickid ./ þe whiche ben on sum maner his bodi / to goo wiþ him ./ in to þe turment of euerlasting fier || For whanne þei tooken baptem ./ þei hi3ten feiþ & trouþe / to kepe Goddis heestis ./ as þe prophete seiþ / spekyng in þe persoone ./ of al þe 15 general chirche / Ps. cxviii || 'Iuraui & statui custodire iudicia iustitie tue'[1] / Lord I haue sworn & ordeyned ./ to kepe þy comaundementis[2] / and vpon þis couenaunt ./ Crist tooke hem to
Fol. 122 a his mariage / wiþ þe ryng | of stedfast feiþ ./ he sacrid þis holi spousaile / But now þei leeue þis chast loue ./ oure Lord Iesu 20 Crist / in breking of þis couenaunt ./ & han chosen an hoore maister / þe fend þat is a spouse-breker & ligiþ in avowtrie ./ wiþ her sijke soules / for seint Ion Crisostom seiþ . 'Omnis autem anima aut est sponsa Christi aut diaboli adultera est' / Hec nota Crisostomus om. xlix. Forsoþe euery soule. eiþir it is Cristis 25 spouse ./ or ellis it is avowtresse of þe deuel / for Crist & þe deuel may in no wise rest togidir ./ in þe bedde of mannes soule / for þei ben so contrarie. þat what euer þe toon biddiþ ./ þe toþir forbediþ || Crist sekiþ saluacioun ./ þe fende dampnacioun || Crist loueþ vertu ./ þe fende loueþ synne || Crist gadriþ togiddir ./ þe fende 30 scatiriþ abrood || as Poul seiþ. II. Cor. vi⁰. / 'Que enim participacio iustitie cum iniquitate ? aut[3] que societas lucis ad tenebras || Que autem comunicacio Christi ad Belial ? aut que pars fidelis cum

---

[1] Vulg. Ps. cxviii. 106.

[2] W. V. 'I swoor and sette to kepe the domes of thi ri3twisnesse.' 1388,
'I swoor, and purposide stidefastli ; to kepe the domes of thi ri3tfulnesse.'

[3] MS. ad.

---

[a] Augustinus, *De Doctrina Christiana*, Liber III, cap. xxxvii (Migne, tom. 34, cols. 82, 88).

Capitulum .XIII.

infideli ‖ Quis autem consensus templi dei cum ydolis'¹‖ þat is
to seie. what participacioun of riȝtwise-|-nesse wiþ wickidnesse?
what felaschip is of liȝt to dercknesse? what comunicacioun of
Crist to Belial? or what part is of a feiþful man. to an vnfeiþful
man? or what consent of þe temple of God to ydols?² certis noon ?
for iche of þise aȝenseyn oþir. aftir her owene worching ‖

Now schullen we telle what þei be ? þat dwellen wiþ þe fende / *The members of the devil's church.*
for to serue him in his chirche ? þat is þe temple of ydols ‖ warars.
cursars. schidars. sclaundirars & blasfemars / for Poul seiþ. I. Cor.
vi⁰. 'Neque malidici regnum dei possidebunt'³ / Þere ben vilen
spekars. liears. glosears. bacbitears. motrars. swerars. & forswerars.
as seint Ion seiþ. Ap. xxi⁰. 'Omnibus mendacibus pars illorum
erit in stagno⁴ ardenti igne & sulphure quod est mors secunda'⁵ /
þere ben michars. robbars. and extorcioneris. tyrauntis. & oppressours. for þe prophete seiþ. Zac. v⁰. 'Omnis fur sicut ibi scriptum
est iudicabitur'⁶ ‖ Þere ben vntrewe tilliars. vnfeiþful seruantis.
recheles hired men. & reble disciplis. & vnprofitable labureris | For
Crist seiþ. Mat. xxv⁰. 'Seruum inutilem pericite in tenebras
exteriores'⁷ ‖ Þere ben lecchours. fornicareris. avowtreris. incestours. þat is defoulears of her owene kyn. & alle vnclene men &
wymmen þat ben wiþynne ordir or professioun / for seint Ion seiþ.
Ap. vltimo. 'Foris canes & venifici & impudici & homicide & ydolis
seruientes. & omnis qui amat & facit mendacium'⁸ / Þere ben
ypocritis. sodomitis. sacrilegers, & sellars of sacramentis ‖ for
Crist seiþ. Mat. xxiiii⁰. & Luk. xii⁰.⁹ / 'Diuidet eum partemque
eius ponet cum ypocritis ibi erit fletus & stridor dencium' ‖ Þere
ben alle þat preien. seruen or ȝyuen ȝiftis for chirche or spiritual

---

¹ Vulg. 2 Cor. vi. 14–16 'Quae enim participatio ... quae autem conventio Christi ad Belial aut quae pars fideli cum infideli? Qui autem consensus templo Dei cum idolis?'

² W. V. 'Sothli what partynge, or comunynge, of riȝtwysnesse with wickidnesse? or what felowschip of liȝt to derknessis? sothli what acordinge of Crist to Belial? or what part of a feithful or cristen man, with unfeithful, or hethene? but what consent to the temple of God with ydols? 1388, '... and what consent to the temple of God with mawmetis?'

³ Vulg. 1 Cor. vi. 10. ⁴ MS. stang⁰.
⁵ Vulg. Apoc. xxi. 8. ⁶ Vulg. Zach. v. 3.
⁷ Vulg. Matt. xxv. 30 'Inutilem servum eiicite in tenebras exteriores.'
⁸ Apoc. xxii. 15.
⁹ Vulg. Matt. xxiv. 51; Luc. xii. 46.

benefice. alle false possessioneris. alle my3ti wilful mendineris. &
alle her sturdi maynteners / for seint Iude seiþ. i⁰. ca⁰. / 'Ve qui
in via caym abierunt. pro primo. et in errore Balaam mercede
effusi sunt. pro secundo. & in contradiccione chore perierunt.[1] pro
tertio'[1] / 'Ve' secundum magistrum historiarum notat eternam[2] 5
dampnacionem / Þere ben þoo men þat boosen her bristis. pinchin
her belies. parten her hosis. cracowen | her schoos. & alle disgisears
of garmentis / for God seiþ bi þe prophete Sopho. i⁰. ca⁰. / 'visi-
tabo super omnes qui induti sunt veste peregrina'[3] || Þere ben þoo.
þat steerchen or poppen her facis. þat bridilen her heedis wiþ 10
gigge haltiris. þat setten aboue honycombis. wiþ miche oþir
tatiryng. to make hemsilf salle-kene to synne & setten abrood her
pappis to cacche men wiþ her lym3erdes / for God seiþ bi þe
prophete. Ysa. iii⁰. 'Pro eo quod eleuate sunt filie syon et ambu-
lauerunt collo extento. &c. / decaluabit dominus verticem filiarum 15
syon'[4] || Þer ben false lawe makars. Goddis lawe haatars. fyndars
of custumes. distriears of vertues. autours of synnes || for Poul seiþ.
Rom. ii⁰. / 'In quo enim iudicas alterum te ipsum contempnas'[5] ||
In þis chirche ben mawmetrers. heretikis. ydolatreris. sortilogeris.
enchauntours. arioleris. charmours. & rerars of þe deuel. & alle þoo 20
þat trowen þat helþe may cum. of vsing Goddis word. þat we
clepen writtes oonli hangid or born on man. or þat þei | ben
medcinable to bodi or to soule ? so hangid or so born / for Gregor
seiþ. 26. q. 5 / 'Si quis ariolas aruspices incantatores obseruauerit
aut philaterijs vsus fuerit anathema sit'[a] / Idem Leuitici. 20. 25
'Anima que declinauerit &c.'[6] || Þere ben marchauntis. chappemen.
vitileris. vintineris. tauerneris. chaungeris. biggeris. sellers. þat
vsen disceit in whei3t. noumbre. or mesure / for Poul seiþ. I. Thess.
iiii⁰. / 'vindex est dominus de omnibus hijs'[7] || In þis chirche
ben vsureris. okureris. iourours. iullars. questmongars. & alle false 30
witnesse berars. for þe prophete seiþ. Ps. xiiii. / 'Qui peccuniam
suam non dedit ad vsuram et munera super innocentem non
accepit'[8] || In þis chirche ben pleetars. lawiars. sequestreris.

---

[1] Vulg. Jude i. 11. [2] MS. eterna.
[3] Vulg. Sophon. i. 8. [4] Vulg. Isaias iii. 16, 17.
[5] Vulg. Rom. ii. 1. [6] Vulg. Lev. xx. 6.
[7] Vulg. 1 Thess. iv. 6. [8] Vulg. Ps. xiv. 5.

---

[a] Gratian, Decreti Pars Secunda, causa xxvi, q. v (Migne, tom. 187, col. 1346).

Capitulum .XIII.

comissarijs. officials. denes. sumnouris. & allen þat sellen troupe or
synne to take money / for þe prophete seiþ. Ps. xxv. 'In quorum
manibus iniquitates sunt dextera eorum repleta est muneribus' [1]
In þis chirche ben auditours. resceyuours. tresoureris. procatours.
5 iuggis. & alle þat accepten persoones for | a cause inpertinent || Fol. 124 b
for seint Iames seiþ. ii⁰. / 'Si enim personas accipitis peccatum
operamini redarguti a lege quasi transgressores' [2] ||
 Þis chirche whanne it is beten. it wexiþ þe hardir / whanne it   Character-
is blamed / it wexiþ þe dullidar / whanne it is tauȝt / it is þe   istics of the
                                                                    devil's
10 lewidar / whanne it is done wel to / it is þe schrewidar / and   church.
                                                                    nota
þanne it falliþ doun & comeþ to noȝt. whanne it semeþ in mannes
iȝe / moost strongli to stonde || Seynt Austyn seiþ. Cristis chirche
pursweþ yuel lyuars in charite / bi weye of amendement || But
þe fendis chirche. pursueþ Cristis chirche in malice / bi weye of
15 sclaundir & sleeyng / and þus Caym. þat false enviouse cursid
man / slow his broþir Abel. þat blessid symple ynnocent man / as
þe fyue expositours seyn / in a prolog on þis spalme. 'Quid
gloriaris'.[3] þat Caym was þe bigynnyng of Babiloyn / and anticrist
schal be þe endar / And Abel was þe bigynner of Ierusalem / &
20 Crist þe endar || Forsoþe Ismael | pursued Ysac / but not so Fol. 125 a
Ysac Ismael / Esau pursued his broþir Iacob / but not so blessid
Iacob cursid Esau / for bi þe counseile of his modir / he fledde in
to Mesopatony / from þe wraþþe of his broþir / til þat it was
swagid || Þus oure modir holi chirche / counseiliþ hir children /
25 to flee þe malice of þe fendis chirche / til þat it be slakid / Mat. x⁰.
'Cum autem persequentur vos in ciuitate ista. fugite in aliam' [4] ||
Forsoþe whanne þe fendis chirche schal purswe ȝou in þis cite / flee
ȝe til anoþir / But þis must be don bi discrecioun / for hirting of
oure broþiris conscience || Crist pursued not þe Iewis / but þe Iewis
30 Iesu Crist || Heeþen men slowen þe apostlis / but not þe apostlis
heeþen men / Se now þe frowardnes of þis world / þat haþ ben
vsid fro þe bigynnyng / whanne Isaie þe holi prophete prophecied /
& prechid vnto þe peple / þei wolde not heere hise wordis / ne
suffre him on lyue / But peple þat risen aftir his deeþ / radden
35 hise bookis & seiden / 'If we hadde lyued in hise daies / he schulde
not haue be deed' / & | ȝit þei slowen Ieremye / þat wiþ þe spirit Fol. 125 b
of God / toold þingis þat were to come / & tauȝt hem verry trouþe /

---

[1] Vulg. Ps. xxv. 10.   [2] Vulg. Jac. ii. 9.
[3] Vulg. Ps. li (A. V. lii).   [4] Vulg. Matt. x. 23.

Of þe chirche ⸫ of þe fende ⸫

Hise successouris tooken hise bookis ⸫ & radde hem in her temple ⸪ & weiliden him for an holi man ⸫ þat he was so slayn amonges hem ⸪ But þei slowen Ezechiel ⸫ & many oþir moo ‖ Þanne þe Iewis maden faire ⸫ þe toumbis of þise prophetis ‖ as were scribis & pharisees ⸫ & seiden in ypocrisie ⸪ If þei hadden ben in her 5 daies ⸫ þey schulden not haue be slayn ⸪ but þei ȝyuen þe counseile ⸫ þat Crist schulde be dede ⸪ heed of alle seyntis ⸫ wiþ moost dispitouse deeþ ‖ Þe fendis chirche in þise daies ⸫ preesen aboue clowdis ⸪ Crist & hise hooli seyntis ⸫ wiþ wordis & wiþ signes ⸪ But þei pursuen to þe deeþ ⸫ þe louars of his lawe ⸪ and þus seiþ 10 Crist in his gospel. Luk. vi⁰. 'Secundum enim hec faciebant prophetis patres eorum'¹ ⸪ Þat is to seie. riȝt as ȝe don now ⸫ so dide ȝoure fadris to her prophetis in her daies ⸪ And þerfore woo to ȝow helle-houndis. for Crist seiþ. In þis world ȝe ben riche. faat

Fol. 126 a — fed. lauȝyng & preisid iche of oþir ⸫ weepe ȝe & make ȝe sorow ‖ for 15
Judgment shall come upon this church at the Day of Doom. — ȝoure peyne is myche in helle ‖ O. þise schal haue a dredeful dai ⸫ whanne þei ben reynd at þe barre of iugement ⸪ & Crist haþ rerid vp his croos ⸫ þe banere of his passioun ‖ Of þis dai spekiþ þe prophete Sopho. i⁰. 'Iuxta est dies domini magnus & velox nimis ⸪ vox diei domini amara tribulabitur ibi fortis ⸪ dies illa dies ire. dies 20 tribulacionis & angustie dies calamitatis & miserie. dies tenebrarum & caliginis. dies nebule & turbinis dies tube & clangoris'² ‖ Þe greet dai of þe Lord ⸫ is nyȝ & fast biside ⸪ & hiȝeþ toward wondir swiþe ⸫ it schal not long tarie ⸪ In þat dai schal be trublid ⸫ he þat is strong & myȝti ‖ for þe voice of þe Lord ⸫ is bittir to þe 25 dampned ⸪ þat dai is a dai of wraþþe ⸫ a dai of tribulacioun ⸪ þat is a dai of angir & tene ⸫ of schenschip & of wrecchidnes ⸪ þat is a dai of dercknes ⸫ & of þick smok ⸪ þat is a dai of cloude ⸫ & of þe wood whirlwynde ⸪ þat is þe dai of tromp ⸫ & of hidouse noise ⸪

Fol. 126 b — for þanne þei schal see ⸫ her ‖ iuge abouen hem. stirid to wraþþe ‖ 30 Þanne schal þei see ⸫ helle open bineþ hem ⸪ and aungelis on her riȝt siȝde ⸫ hasting hem to helle ⸪ fendis on her lift siȝde ⸫ drawyng hem to helle ⸪ Seyntis approuyng Goddis doome ⸫ & al þe world accusing ⸪ and her owene conscience ⸫ as open as a book ⸪ in þe whiche þei schal rede ⸫ her owene dampnacioun ‖ Þise wrecchis 35 biholding ⸫ þe greet glorie of hem ⸪ þat þei dispisid in þis world ⸫ þanne schal þei seie þise wordis. Sap. v⁰. 'Hij sunt quos aliquando habuimus in derisum & in similitudinem improperij. Nos insensati

---

¹ Vulg. Luc. vi. 23.   ² Vulg. Sophon. i. 14-16.

Capitulum .XIII.

vitam illorum estimabamus insaniam. & finem illorum sine honore ⫽ Quomodo ergo conputati sunt inter filios dei & inter sanctos sors illorum est ⫽ Ergo errauimus a via veritatis & iustitie lumen non luxit[1] nobis ⫽ Quid nobis profuit superbia aut diuiciarum iactancia
5 quid contulit nobis ⫽ transierunt omnia illa tanquam vmbra ' [2] ‖ Þise it ben þat we sumtyme hadde in scorne ⫽ & in to licknesse of vpbreydyng ‖ we witlesse dampned helle-brondis ⫽ trowiden her lijf hadde be woodnes & madnesse ⫽ & we gessiden þat her ǀ eende ⫽ had ben wiþouten worschip ⫽ how now for þei ben countid ⫽ among
10 þe sones of God ‖ & þei taken her loot ⫽ among hise seintis ⫽ Þerfore we han errid ⫽ from þe weie of trouþe ⫽ & þe liȝt of riȝtwisenesse ⫽ liȝtned not to vs ⫽ we ben wery of þe weye of wickidnesse & dampnacioun ⫽ what profite haþ oure pride don to vs? or greet avaunt. or boost of richessis ? what haþ it ȝyuen til us ? alle þo
15 þingis ben passid from vs ⫽ as þe schadowe[3] ⫽ Þanne schal þe iuge seie ⫽ to hem wiþ stirne cheere ⫽ Mat. xxvº. ⫽ 'Discedite a me maledicti in ignem eternum qui preparatus est diabolo & angelis eius ' [4] ‖ Go awey fro me ȝe cursid lymes ⫽ in to þe fire of helle euerlastyng ⫽ þat is ordeyned to þe deuel & hise aungels ⫽ [5] Þanne
20 may þe soule seie to þe bodi þise wordis ⫽ 'Cum on þou cursid careyn ⫽ cum & goo wiþ me ⫽ for I am compellid ⫽ to cum aȝen to

nota bene

Fol. 127 a

---

[1] MS. Luxiþ.   [2] Vulg. Sap. v. 3-6, 8, 9.

[3] W. V. 'Thes ben whom we hadden sum tyme in to scorn, and in to licnesse of repref. Wee unwise eymeden the lif of hem wodnesse, and the ende of them without wrshipe; hou thanne ben thei countid among the sonus of God, and among seyntis the lot of hem is ? Therfore wee erreden fro the weie of treuthe, and the liȝt of riȝtwisnesse liȝtede not to us, and the sunne off understanding is not sprungen to us. Weri wee ben in the weie of wickidnesse, and of perdicioun; and wee han gon harde weies. The wei forsothe of the Lord wee knewen not: what profitede to us pride, or bost of richessis, what ȝaf it to us ? Alle tho thingus passeden as shadewe.' 1388, 'We woode men gessiden her lijf woodnesse, and. the ende of hem with oute onour; hou therfor ben thei reckened among the sones of God, and her part is among seyntis ? Therfor we erriden fro the weie of treuthe, and the liȝt of riȝtfulnesse schynede not to us, and the sunne of undurstondyng roos not up to us. We weren maad weri in the wei of wickidnesse and of perdicioun; and we ȝeden hard weies. But we knewen not the weie of the Lord; what profitide pride to us, ether what brouȝte the boost of richessis to us ? All tho thingis passiden as schadewe.'

[4] Vulg. Matt. xxv. 41.

[5] W. V. 'Depart fro me, ȝee cursid in to everlastynge fijr, the whiche is maad redy to the deuyl and his angelis.'

Of þe chirche ṣ of þe fende ṣ

þee / þat we mowe go togidir ṣ eiþir to oþir schame / to take oure iewesse as we han disserued ṣ peyne for euermore / þat þing þat we loued ṣ now it is gon from vs / & al þat we haatid ṣ is turned vp-|-on vs. Now is oure ioye turned in to sorow ṣ and oure myrþe in to wepyng / Now is oure lawȝtir. turned in to mornyng ṣ & al oure game into weiling / No þing abidiþ to vs ṣ but fire hoot brennyng / watir coold chelling / wormes as addris / toodis & snakis euer gnawyng / euer diyng & neuer deed / dercknesse palpable. þat is so þick. þat it may be gropid / wanting þe siȝt of ony counfort / seyng al þat may discounforte / Feer intollerable. drede vntellable / quakyng of þe fendis felaschip / alwey discorde wiþouten frenschip / & ful dispeyre of ony eende' ||

Yet grace and mercy are offered to those who will leave the devil's church.

Neþeles assay in þis lijf ṣ if ȝe may leeue þe fendis chirche / & brynge ȝoure silf boþe bodi & soule ṣ in to þe chirch of Iesu Crist / while grace & mercy may be grauntid ṣ axe of him þat offrid him silf / vpon a cros wiþ wilful cheere ṣ to saue vs alle whanne we were loost / For þus it is writen of þe wordis of God ṣ þat he spekiþ to a synful soule / Cant. vi⁰. ' Reuertere reuertere. sunamitis '¹ / turne þee aȝen turne þee aȝen þou synful soule ṣ | turne þee aȝen. turne þee aȝen. þat we may biholde þee / for God knowiþ þi mys-gouernaunce ṣ & wil not forsake þee / if þou wilt turne aȝen ṣ as he seiþ bi þe prophete. Iere. iii⁰. ' Tu autem fornicata es cum amatoribus multis. tamen reuertere ad me dicit dominus & ego suscipiam te '² || Þat is to seie. Forsoþe þou hast don fornicacioun ṣ wiþ many louears / neþeles turne þee to me seiþ þe Lord ṣ & I schal resceyue þee / & take þee to grace / vpon þis seiþ seynt Gregory. ' Quantum nos diligit ostendit cum a nobis relinquitur ? nos non relinquit ' || In þis God schewiþ. how miche he loueþ vs / for whanne we forsaken him ṣ he forsakeþ not vs / as seiþ seynt Austin. ' O. homo. non diffidas de dei misericordia. quia maior est eius misericordia quam tua miseria ' ||. A. man mystrist þou not on þe merci of God ṣ for more is his mercy. þan þi wrecchidnes / And þus seid kyng Dauiþ to Abner / II. Re. iii⁰. ' Misit ergo Abner nuncios ad Dauiþ pro se dicentes / Cuius est terra. Et vt loquerentur / Fac mecum amicicias & erit manus mea tecum ¦ et reducam ad te vniuersum Israel / Qui ait / Optime ego faciam tecum amicicias ṣ sed³ vnam rem peto a te dicens / Non videbis

---

¹ Vulg. Cant. vi. 12.
MS. set.

² Vulg. Jer. iii. 1.

Capitulum .XIII.

faciem meam antequam adduxeris Michol et sic veniens videbis me'[1] ‖ Þis is þus schortli to seie. ȝe þat wil haue kyng Dauiþ ./ a merciful lord to ȝou / ȝe must bryng wiþ ȝou ./ þis womman Michol / if ȝe wole se ./ his gracious face / for Dauiþ loued myche
5 þis womman ./ as þis stoory telliþ here. Dauiþ þe kyng in þis place ./ beriþ þe figure of Iesu Crist / And Michol whanne it is declarid ./ is to seie þe watir of al ‖ Þanne is þis þus to mene / ȝe þat desiren in al ȝoure myȝt ./ to fynde & haue þe mercy of God / & se his graciouse face in blisse ./ ȝe must haue watir of verry
10 penaunce / from ȝoure herte wiþ ful contricioun ./ of wille neuere to turne to synne / and if þat ȝe wil be trewe ./ & no more breeke þis couenaunt / God wole not þat ȝe be deed ./ but þat ȝe haue euerelastyng lijf.

Amen. amen. so mot it be.

Eende ‖

[1] Vulg. 2 Reg. iii. 12, 13.

APPENDIX

SOURCES OF THE QUOTATIONS FROM THE BIBLE MADE IN THE TEXT

As is the case with most mediaeval theological writers, the author supports his argument by frequent references to Scripture and to the writings of the Fathers and famous mediaeval divines, although, in accordance with the views of the Lollards with regard to the relative value of these two authorities, he evidently looked upon the latter as of secondary importance. The quotations from patristic literature are as a rule adduced in support and interpretation of Biblical passages.[1]

In quoting from the Bible, the author's general practice is to give the text in Latin with an English translation. An investigation of the sources of both the Latin and the English texts follows.

A. *Latin Quotations.*

The Latin text of the Bible in use in the Middle Ages was the Vulgate. That there were many versions of this text current in England in the late fourteenth century is proved by contemporary evidence. The writer of the Prologue to the 1388 translation of the Bible bears witness to the corrupt state of the Latin Bibles of the time and speaks of the difficulty of making an accurate Latin text as not the least part of his task. 'First this symple creature hadde myche trauaile, with diuerse felowis and helperis, to gedere manie elde biblis, and othere doctouris and comune glosis . . . to make oo Latyn bible sumdel trewe. . . . If ony wijs man fynde ony defaute of the truthe of translacioun, let him sette in the trewe sentence and opin of holi writ, but loke that he examyne truli his Latyn Bible, for no doute he shal fynde ful manye biblis in Latyn ful false, if he loke manie, nameli newe; and the comune Latyn biblis han more nede to be correctid, as many as I have seen in my lif, than hath the English bible late translatid.'[2]

---

[1] The chief exception to this is on p. 37, where the author supports his attack on the costly decoration of churches mainly by an appeal to St. Jerome, St. Bernard, and William de St. Amour.

[2] *The Holy Bible . . . in the earliest English version by Wyclif*, ed. by J. Forshall and Sir F. Madden, 1850, vol. i, p. 57.

It is possible, to some extent, to reconstruct the standardized Latin text upon which the Wycliffite translation was based. The 1380 version, in particular, is a close literal rendering of the Latin original, and a comparison with it of the Biblical passages in the *Lanterne of Liȝt* shows that the author of the latter could not have used the same Latin text. As would naturally be expected, the original of the Wycliffite translation is nearer to the sixteenth-century standard Clementine edition of the Vulgate (C) than that used by the writer of the tract. Compare:

1 John ii. 18. L. of L. 'Nunc autem *sunt* multi antichristi.'
    W. V. 'Now many antecristes *ben made.*'
    C. 'Nunc Antichristi multi *facti sunt.*'
Rom. viii. 9. L. of L. '*Qui* non habet spiritum Christi nec est eius.'
    W. V. '*If ony* hath not the spirit of Crist, this is not his.'
    C. '*Si quis* autem spiritum Christi non habet, hic non est eius.'
Ecclesiasticus xiv. 20. L. of L. 'Omne opus corruptibile in fine deficiet et qui fecit illud *peribit* cum illo.'
    W. V. 'Eche corruptible werc in the ende shal faile; and he that wercheth it, *shal go* with it.'
    C. 'Omne opus corruptibile in fine deficiet et qui operatur illud, *ibit* cum illo.'
Ephesians i. 22. L. of L. 'Ipsum dedit caput *ecclesiae.*'
    W. V. '(God) ȝaf him heed *upon al the chirche.*'
    C. 'Ipsum dedit caput *supra omnem ecclesiam.*'

In the fourteenth and fifteenth centuries there were in existence a number of different versions of the Vulgate, which might conceivably have been known to the author. Of these, the best is the Codex Amiatinus (A), a version written in Northumbria in the seventh or eighth century at the command of Ceolfrid, Abbot of Wearmouth. The passages quoted in the text have been compared with A, and although they agree in many cases, the divergences of reading are too numerous to allow of the assumption that A was the text used by the author. Compare:

2 Pet. ii. 1. L. of L. 'Magistri mendaces qui *introducent* sectas perditionis.'
    A. 'Magistri mendaces qui *inducent* sectas perditionis.'
Matt. xxiii. 15. L. of L. 'Vae vobis scribe et pharisei quia circuitis *terram et mare.*'
    A. 'Vae vobis scribae et pharisaei hypocritae: quia circuitis *mare et aridam.*'
Jude ii. 16. L. of L. 'Mirantes personas *hominum* questus causa.'
    A. 'Mirantes personas questus causa.'

A comparison with other codices (e.g. Codex Armachanus,

Codex Cavensis, Codex Fuldensis) has been made where the Latin of the tract exhibits marked peculiarities. This has led to the same result as the comparison with A, namely, that the peculiarities of the text are not entirely shared by any of the more famous of the extant Vulgate versions.

It might be urged that when quoting from the Vulgate, the author relied entirely upon his own memory, and that the divergences from any other known Latin text are due to this fact. In a few cases the nature of the differences in reading lends colour to this theory, e. g.:

Matt. xiii. 25. L. of L. 'Inimicus *homo* superseminavit zizaunia.'
A. and W. V. 'Inimicus eius superseminavit zizania,' but
v. 28, 'Inimicus *homo* hoc fecit.'

and many places where the difference consists solely in the omission of such particles as 'enim', 'autem', 'vero', or in the inversion of two words; but such differences are equally likely to have arisen among the variant texts of the Vulgate in existence at the time, and it is more probable that the author of the *Lanterne of Liȝt* quoted from some actual current version. As has been shown, the particular text which he used differed from that upon which the Wycliffite translations of 1380 and 1388 were based, and also from that of the famous codices extant at the time, such as the Codex Amiatinus. In all probability it was one of the many 'Latyn biblis' current at that period, to the existence of which the Prologue to the 1388 Wycliffite Bible bears witness, but that it was not one of the more corrupt of these is proved by the fact that out of the two hundred and seventy-four passages quoted, one hundred and seventy agree with the readings of the standard Clementine version.

B. *The English Translation.*

By the beginning of the fifteenth century there were in existence a number of translations of different parts of the Bible in addition to the famous Wycliffite versions of 1380 and 1388. They are as follows:

I. The Psalter translated by Richard Rolle of Hampole.[1]
II. The West Midland Psalter.[2]
III. Commentaries upon the Gospels of St. Matthew, St. Mark, and St. Luke.[3]
IV. Translation of the Gospels for Sundays and Festivals, arranged to form a continuous narrative.[4]

---

[1] Bramley, *The Psalter . . . by R. Rolle of Hampole*, Oxford, 1884.
[2] Bülbring, *Earliest Complete English Prose Psalter*, E.E.T.S.
[3] Cf. *Wycl. Bible*, i, p. ix.
[4] MS. Pepys, 2498; cf. Paues, *English Bibl. Version*, 1902, Introduction.

V. The Pauline Epistles with a Commentary.[1]
VI. Apocalypse with a Commentary.[2]
VII. Part of St. Matthew, the Acts, Catholic Epistles, and Pauline Epistles.[3]
VIII. Wycliffite Translations of the Bible, 1380 and 1388.[4]

It might be expected that in a work of this kind, written during the early years of the fifteenth century and evidently directly inspired by the teaching of Wyclif, the English rendering of the quotations from the Vulgate would have been taken from either of the two Wycliffite translations of the Bible. This, however, is not the case, for on a comparison being made, it was found that in spite of occasional similarities of rendering, the divergences in translation are too many to allow of the theory that the author of the *Lanterne of Liȝt* used either the 1380 or the 1388 version.

The renderings in the text have also, where possible, been compared with those in the Biblical versions mentioned above. The comparison proved that none of these translations were used by the author, although with regard to the version edited by Miss Paues, there are three passages in the text which closely resemble its renderings:

James v. 16. *MS.* ' Þe bisi preier of þe riȝtwise is miche worþe.'
P. 'For muche worþ is a bysy preyere of a riȝtful man.'
James i. 18. *MS.* 'God haþ wilfulli & of his owene free wille gotun us þoruȝ þe worde of trouþe, þat we mai be summe bigynnyng of his creature.'
P. 'For wylfullyche he haþ bygeten ous þoruȝ þe word of trewþe, þat we ben sum bygynnynge of his creature.'
Acts v. 42. *MS.* ' Forsoþe iche dai in þe temple & aboute housis: þei ceessid not teching & preching Crist Jesu.'
P. ' Soþely euery day in þe temple & abowte howses þei cessed noghte of techinge ande prechinge of Jesu Criste.'

Elsewhere, however, the renderings are so different, that the resemblances in these three passages must be looked upon as accidental.

The natural inference is that the author of the *Lanterne of Liȝt* made his own translation from the Latin, a deduction which is borne out by the fact that Wyclif pursued a similar plan. Throughout his English works, the passages which Wyclif quotes from the Bible are not taken from the early Wycliffite version, but are translated from the Latin independently.[5]

---

[1] MS. Parker, 32, Corpus Christi College; cf. *Wycl. Bible,* i. p. xiii.'

[2] Formerly attributed to Wyclif; now proved to be a verbal rendering of twelfth-century Norman Apocalypse; cf. Paues, *Fourteenth-century English Bible Version,* p. xxvii.

[3] Paues, *Fourteenth-century English Bible Version.*

[4] *The Holy Bible . . . in the earliest English version by Wyclif,* ed. by J. Forshall and Sir F. Madden, 1850.

[5] *Cam. Hist. of Engl. Lit.,* vol. ii, pp. 52, 60.

Appendix

C. *The Value of the Translation.*

As an actual translation, the rendering in the *Lanterne of Liȝt* is of less value than the 1388 Wycliffite version. The translation is freer, and the author frequently adds words and phrases for which there is no justification in the Latin original. Sometimes these additions are merely explanatory; occasionally they are used to give a certain bias to the passage in order to make it more apposite to the argument. It was doubtless a tendency of this kind on the part of the Lollards which led to the constitution of 1409, which forbade unauthorized translations of the Bible or of any part of it, and which caused a popular writer against the Lollards to say:

> 'Ther the Bibelle is al myswent
> To jangle of Job or Jeremie,
> That construen hit after her entent
> For lewde lust of Lollardie.'[1]

Examples of such glossed passages will be found in the following:

p. 12. 1 John ii. 1. 'Filioli mei haec scribo vobis, ut non peccetis.'

'Mi litil sones, þise þingis I write unto ȝou, þat ȝe synne not *in þe synne of dispeire.*'

p. 23. Isaiah ix. 15. 'Longevus & venerabilis ipse est caput, propheta docens mendacium ipse est cauda.'

'A man of greet agee & worschipful holden to þe world, he is heed *and cheef anticrist*; a prophete or a prechour techyng lesing: he is þe taile *of þis anticrist.*'

p. 26. Jude i. 11. 'Vae qui in via Caym abierunt, & in errore Balaam mercede effuci sunt: & in contradictione Chore perierunt.'

'Woo to hem þat walken in þe weye of Caym: *þise ben fals possessioners.* And woo to hem þat ben schadde out for mede in þe errour of Balaam: *þise ben miȝti nedles mendiners.* And woo to hem þat han perischide in þe aȝenseiyng of Chore: *þise ben proude sturdi mayntenerɛ.*'

p. 63. Ecclesiasticus xiv. 20. 'Omne opus corruptibile in fine deficiet, & qui fecit illud peribit cum illo.'

'Iche corruptible werke *or iche werke þat is rotun in þe roote* schal faile in þe ende, & he þat is foundir of suche ungroundid werk schal faile & worþe to nouȝt þerwiþ *in þe last daies.*'

From the point of view of language, the renderings in the text compare very favourably with the 1388 version, and are greatly superior as regards idiomatic ease and clearness of expression to the 1380 translation.

---

[1] *Political Poems and Songs*, R. S., vol. ii, p. 243.

The following passages may exemplify this:

L. of L.	1380 W. V.	1388 W. V.
Rom. viii. 18. 'Þe passiouns of þis tyme … ben as noo passiouns in comparisoun to þe glorie þat is to come þat schal be schewid in us.'	'The passiouns of this tyme ben not euene worthi to the glorie to comynge, that schal be schewid in us.'	'The passiouns of this time ben not worthi to the glorie to comynge, that schal be shewid in us.'
Matt. xiii. 47. 'Þe rewme of heuenes is lijk to a nett þat is sent in to þe see & gadriþ togidre in to his cloos of alle þe kynde of diverse fisches & whanne þis nett was ful of fisches þe fischers drowen it to þe lond & þei sitting biside þe see brynk chosen þe good into her vessellis, þe yuel forsoþe þei sentten oute: & kesten hem aȝen in to þe see.'	'The kingdom of heuenes is lic to a nette sent in to the see, and of alle kynd of fishis gedrynge; the whiche whan it was fulfillid men ledynge out, and sittinge bysidis the brynke, cheesiden the good into her vessels, but thei senten out the yuel.'	'The kyngdom of heuenes is lijk to a nette cast into the see, and that gaderith togidere of al kynde of fisschis; which whanne it was ful, thei drowen up, and seten bi the brenke, and chesen the goode in to her vessels, but the yuel thei kesten out.'
Ps. xl. 1. 'Blessid be he þat takiþ hede on þe nedi & pore.'	'Blisful that understant up on the nedi and pore.'	'Blessid is he that undurstondith on a nedi man and pore.'
Ecclesiasticus xxix. 20. 'Forgete þou not þe kyndenes of þi borow; forsoþe he haþ ȝouun for þee his lijf.'	'The grace of the borȝ ne forgete thou; forsothe he ȝaf for thee his soule.'	'Forȝete thou not the grace of the borewe; for he ȝaf his lijf for thee.'

NOTES

p. 4, l. 6. seint Jon Crisostum seiþ. This passage, in common with many others attributed to Chrysostom in the text, is from a collection of sermons on St. Matthew's Gospel by an unknown writer (cf. *Opera D. Ioannis Chrysostomi*, vol. ii, p. 710, ed. by S. Gelenius, 1547).

p. 7, l. 5. þe philosophur: a designation specially applied to Aristotle.

p. 8, l. 25. Lincoln: Robert Grosseteste, Bishop of Lincoln from 1235 to 1253. He was born c. 1175, and studied at Oxford and Paris. On his appointment to the see of Lincoln, he set himself to reform the abuses existing in his diocese. He exercised considerable influence upon English thought and literature for two centuries. He is frequently quoted by Wyclif (cf. *English Works of Wyclif*, edited by F. D. Matthew, E.E.T.S., pp. 56, 92, 112, 385). Some of Grosseteste's 'Dicta' were printed by Brown in *Fasciculus Rerum Expetendarum et Fugiendarum*, 1690. None of those quoted in this text occur in Brown's collection (cf. *Dict. Nat. Biog.*, vol. xxiii, art. Grosseteste).

p. 11, l. 8. þei seien þis man haþ eten a fliȝe. Evidently a taunt brought against the Lollards by their enemies. They are looked upon as followers of Beelzebub, the god of flies, through whose agency they obtain their knowledge of God's law. To have 'eten a fliȝe' is probably equivalent to being possessed by a devil. 'Fly' is used later by B. Jonson for a 'familiar demon' (1610).

p. 11, l. 11. Lollardis. The name 'Lollard' is of uncertain origin; some derive it from 'lolium'—tares, citing Chaucer as their authority (*Shipman's Prologue*, ll. 15-17):

> 'This Loller here wol prechen us somwhat . . .
> He wolde sowen som difficulte,
> Or sprengen cokkel in our clene corn.'

But the more generally received explanation derives the word from M. Du. *lollen, lullen*, to sing softly, to mumble. The earliest official use of the name in England occurs in 1387 in a mandate of the Bishop of Worcester against five 'poor preachers', 'nomine seu ritu Lollardorum confoederatos'. Though the first example given in *N.E.D.* of the form 'Lollard' is in 1415—Lord Scrope in 43 Rep. Deputy Kpr. Rec. 591, 'Yif he drue to Loulardis thai wolde subuert thisl onde & the chirge'—the word is implied in 'Lollardy' (first used c. 1390). The form Loller, a variant of Lollard, occurs earlier in Chaucer, *Shipman's Prologue*, ll. 11, 15, 'I smelle a lollere in the wynde quod he'; and 'This lollere here wol prechen us somwhat'; and in *Piers Plowman*, C. vi. 2, 'Cloþed as a lollere . . . Among lollares of london and lewede heremytes.'

p. 12, l. 15. þe maister of sentence. 'Magister sententiarum' was the name given to Peter Lombard, Bishop of Paris in the twelfth century, from his book *Sententiarum libri quattuor*—a collection of comments from the Fathers on passages of Holy Scripture.

p. 13, l. 21. **for ȝe pullen as foxis to her hoolis children from fadris.** The charge of kidnapping or enticing children for their order, was one very frequently made against the friars; cf. *English Works of Wyclif*, E.E.T.S., p. 68, ' freris forsaken þe perfit pouert of Crist . . . to geten ȝonge childre to here feyned ordre by symonye, as aplis, purses, & oþere iapes & false bihestis, & bi false stelynge aȝenst here frendis wille, and aȝenst goddis comaundement.' The same charge is made in *Jacke Upland*:

> ' Why steal ye mens children
> for to make hem of your sect,
> sith that theft is against Gods hests
> and sith your sect is not perfect?'
> *Political Poems and Songs*, ii, p. 22 (R. S.).

p. 14, l. 21. **Lettir of lisence.** A copy of one of these letters of licence is preserved in Wilkins's *Concilia*, vol. iii, p. 389. It was granted to William Lyndewode, a bitter opponent of Lollardy, to whom the *Lanterne of Liȝt* was handed over for examination at the trial of John Claydon (see Introduction, p. viii). The text runs as follows : ' Licentia concessa Willelmo Lyndewode ab archiepiscopo Cant. ad praedicandum. Henricus, etc., dilecto in Christo filio magistro Willelmo Lyndewode utriusque iuris doctori . . . salutem. Ut in quibuscumque locis ad hoc convenientibus et honestis infra nostras civitatem, diocesim, et provinciam Cantuar. ubilibet constitutio verbum Dei clero et populo in lingua Latina seu vulgari licite proponere et praedicare valeatis, non obstante constitutione provinciali Oxon. nuper per bonae memoriae dominum Thomam Arundel Cant. archiepiscopum, praedecessorem nostrum, edita, et aliis constitutionibus nostris et praedecessorum nostrorum contra praedicantes huiuscemodi editis non obstantibus quibuscumque, vobis, quem literarum scientia, morumque laudabilis vitae meritis, aliisque virtutum praeconiis sufficienter (novimus) insignitum, liberam tenore praesentium concedimus facultatem.'

p. 16, l. 19. **þe weye of Caym.** To a Lollard, the word Caym (Cain) stood for the four orders of friars, because the four letters which make up the word were taken to designate respectively the Carmelites, the Augustinians, the Jacobites (or Dominicans), and the Minorites (Franciscans). This explains the term ' Caymes Castles ' used by Wyclif for the monasteries (cf. *S. E. W.*, iii, p. 348, l. 19 and note, p. 368, l. 27 ; *Wyclif*, E.E.T.S., p. 508, note).

p. 16, l. 19. **possessioners:** that is, such orders among the clergy as held possessions or endowments.

p. 17, l. 26. **þise newe constituciouns:** the constitutions of Arundel, Archbishop of Canterbury, issued in 1409 (see Introd., p. xii).

p. 18, l. 25. **sensuris:** a spiritual punishment inflicted by some ecclesiastical judge.

p. 22, l. 16. **Lire:** Nicholaus of Lyra, born at Lyra in Normandy, 1270, died at Paris, 1340. The tradition that he was of Jewish descent appears to have been an unfounded statement dating only from the fifteenth century. He took the Franciscan habit, studied theology, received the doctor's degree at Paris, and became a professor at the Sorbonne. He was the author of numerous theological works, the most famous of which is the *Postillae Perpetuae in Universam S. Scripturam.* It soon became the favourite manual of exegesis, and was the first Biblical commentary to be printed (cf. *Catholic Encyclopedia*, vol. xi, p. 63).

p. 23, l. 23. þe dedication of þe chirche. The service held at the dedication of a church according to the Use of Sarum contains the following words: 'Christus enim desponsat hodie matrem nostram norma iustitiae, quam de lacu traxit miseriae ecclesiam. In spiritus sancti clementia, sponsa sponsi laetatur gratia, reginis laudis cum gloria, felia dicta. . . . Sic typicis descripta sensibus, nuptiarum induta vestibus, coeli praestet hodie civibus, Christo iuncta.'

The service from which this passage is taken occurs in an early fifteenth-century pontifical in the Cambridge University Library (cf. Maskell, *Monumenta Ritualia Ecclesiae Anglicanae*, 2nd edit., vol. i, p. 237). Although the words as quoted in the text do not actually occur in this service, they must have been taken from one very similar.

p. 27, l. 8. To bigynne at Mary Cristis modir . . . A similar enumeration occurs in Don Michel's *Ayenbite of Inwyt* (E.E.T.S.), pp. 266, 267; and in 'Sawles Warde', Morris, *Specimens of Early English*, Pt. I, p. 91.

p. 28, l. 19. Mardoche = Mordecai (Vulg. Mardochaeus).

p. 35, l. 13. As Odo seiþ. Probably Odo of Cheriton or Sherston, an English Cistercian monk (d. 1247). His sermons on the Sunday Gospels were completed in 1219, and were printed at Paris by Matthew Macherel under the title 'Flores Sermonum ac Evangeliorum Dominicalium excellenties. Magistri Odonis Cancellarii Parrhisien.' The author in this edition is designated as 'Cancellarius Parisiensis' possibly from confusion with Odon de Châteauroux, Chancellor of Paris in 1238. This edition is extremely rare (cf. *Dict. Nat. Biog.*, vol. xli, p. 428, art. Odo of Cheriton).

p. 35, l. 14. anfest. No verb 'anfest' is recorded. 'Anfest' perhaps = 'Hanfest' for 'handfest', betroth, make a contract of marriage. The text shows several examples of irregularity in the use of the initial 'h'; cf. ailestorm, p. 46, l. 10; hesiliar, p. 125, l. 23; eire beside heire, p. 20, l. 25, p. 46, l. 9. The omission of medial *d* before *f* is not unknown in ME.; cf. Caxton, *Sonnes of Aymon*, iii. 107 (1489), 'Ye ben not worth an *hanfull* of strawe.'

p. 35, l. 17. haruest. Perhaps an error for 'hanuest' = handfest, marriage contract. No example of a noun 'handfest' is given in *N.E.D.* before 1611, Shaks. *Cymb.*, I. v. 78, 'The Remembrancer of her, to hold The handfast to her Lord.' For the form see note on 'anfest'.

p. 36, l. 19. as Jerom seiþ. The passage quoted does not seem to occur in the writings of Jerome. The exact words are to be found in one of the Homilies formerly attributed to St. John Chrysostom (see note on p. 4, l. 6).

p. 38, l. 3. William de Seint Amor. Born in 1202 of humble parents. He was educated at the University of Paris and became a stern opposer of the mendicant orders. His most famous work is 'Tractatus brevis de novissimorum temporum periculis ex scripturis excerptus et in certa capitula digestus' (cf. *Maitre Guillaume de Saint-Amour*, par Maurice Perrod, Paris, 1895).

p. 48, l. 10. louedaies: a day appointed for a meeting with a view to an amicable settlement of a dispute, and hence, an agreement entered into at such a meeting (*N.E.D.*); cf. Chaucer, *Prologue*, l. 258, 'In love-dayes ther coude he mochel helpe'; and *Piers Plowman*, iii. 157, 'She ledeth þe lawe as hire list & lovedayes maketh.'

p. 54, l. 18. **For it draweþ hem toward heuene as bocket in to welle.** Evidently a proverbial expression; cf. 'Complaint of the Ploughman', 'They follow Christ that shed his blood To heaven, as buckette into the well' (*Pol. Poems and Songs*, ii, p. 312, R. S.). For a somewhat different use of the same proverbial phrase, cf. Chaucer, *Knight's Tale*, l. 675, 'Now up, now down, as boket in a welle.'

p. 56, l. 23. **Ordinal**: a book setting forth the services of the Church, as they existed before the Reformation.

p. 59, l. 11. **Gregor in his decre.** 'In sancta Romana ecclesia dudum consuetudo est valde reprehensibilis exorta, ut quidam ad sacri altaris ministerium cantores eligantur, et in diaconatus ordine constituti modulationi vocis inserviant, quos ad praedicationis officium, et eleemosynarum studium vacare congruebat. Unde fit plerumque, ut ad sacrum ministerium, dum blanda vox quaeritur, quaeri congrua vita negligatur et cantor minister Deum moribus stimulet, quum populum vocibus delectat. Qua in re praesenti decreto constituo, ut in hac sede sacri altaris ministri cantare non debeant, solumque evangelicae lectionis officium missarum solennia exsolvant; psalmos vero ac reliquas lectiones censeo per subdiaconos vel, si necessitas exigit, per minores ordines exhiberi. Si quis autem contra hoc decretum meum venire tentaverit, anathema sit' (Migne, tom. 187, col. 430).

p. 60, l. 2. **Lucifer.** In Christian theology, Lucifer was regarded as the name of Satan before his fall, hence his association with 'the children of pride' (cf. the phrase, 'as proud as Lucifer').

p. 60, l. 4. **Belzebub.** From the New Testament designation of Beelzebub as the 'prince of demons', the word became, at an early period, one of the popular names of the devil. It is assumed that the Beelzebub of the New Testament is to be identified with the Philistine god of flies, one of whose special prerogatives it was to drive away the flies troubling the sacrifice, who were looked upon as evil spirits with no right to be there. The connexion of Beelzebub with 'the envious' is difficult. On p. 11, l. 1, there is a reference to Beelzebub as the 'god of flies, or ellis a god þat makiþ discorde', an idea which may have arisen from the passage in St. Matthew xii. 24–8, in which Christ refutes the charge of exorcizing devils by Beelzebub the prince of devils. The 'god þat makiþ discorde' might be looked upon as the spreader of calumny, and so as the lord of the envious.

p. 60, l. 5. **Abadon.** The name of the angel of the bottomless pit (Rev. ix. 11). 'Wanhope' or despair is one of the attributes of Sloth; hence the connexion between the lord of the bottomless pit and the slothful.

p. 60, l. 6. **Mammon.** The Aramaic word for 'riches' occurring in the Greek text of Matthew vi. 24 and Luke xvi. 9–13. Owing to the quasi-personification in these passages the word was taken by mediaeval writers as the proper name of the devil of covetousness. Cf. *Piers Plowman*, A. ix. 81, 'He ... with Mammonas moneye hath maked him frendes'; and *Ord. Crysten Men* (1502), II. xi. 117, 'A devyll named Mammona made unto the covetous man VI commaundementes.'

p. 60, l. 8. **Belphegor.** A form of Baal-Peor (cf. Deut. iv. 3, Num.

Notes 149

xxv. 5, Ps. cvi. 28). His connexion with gluttony may be accounted for by the fact that human sacrifices were offered to him.

p. 60, l. 9. Asmodeus (cf. Book of Tobit, iii. 8). In the Apocrypha occurs the story of the love of Asmodeus, an evil demon, for Sara, the daughter of Raguel, whose seven husbands were slain in succession by him on their respective bridal nights. From the part played by him in this story, he is regularly associated with the sin of lechery.

p. 60, l. 22. As Parisiens seiþ. Probably Peter Cantor Parisiensis, a native of Poitiers, died at Long Pont Abbey in 1197. In 1180 he was invested with the office of Precentor in the Cathedral of Paris. His *Verbum Abbreviatum* is quoted in the *Apology for Lollard Doctrines*, edited by J. H. Todd (1842), p. 53. Cf. Dr. Todd's note, p. 154.

p. 61, l. 3. Summe maken lettris ... to selle alle her suffragis. The reference is to the custom of granting letters of fraternity by the convents to their benefactors. These letters entitled those named in them to a share in the benefits of all prayers or merits of the convent or order. Cf. *Jacke Upland*:

'Freer, what charity is this,
. . . .
to such rich men give letters of fraternite,
confirmed by your generall seale,
and thereby to bear him in hand,
that he shal have part of all your masses,
mattens, preachings,
fastings, wakings,
and all other good deeds
done by your brethren of your order,
both whilest he liveth,
and after that he is dead.'

(*Pol. Poems and Songs*, R. S., ii, p. 33.)

p. 61, l. 6. þe decre saluator. A decree of Urban II against the practice of simony, beginning 'Salvator praedicit in evangelio'.

p. 67, l. 1. But pees-makars in þe fendis chirche confidren hem togidir in a fals pees. Cf. *S. E. W.*, i, p. 321, 'Here men seien soþeli þat þer ben two peesis, verri pees and fals pees, and þei ben ful dyvers. ... Fals pees is groundid in reste wiþ oure enemys, whanne we assente to hem wiþouten aʒenstonding,' &c.

p. 68, l. 2. Moneþ him. It is doubtful whether the verb 'moan' occurs before the sixteenth century. 'Mone' is often a misprint or a misreading for 'moue' = move, or for 'mene' = to lament. Two fifteenth-century instances are given in *N.E.D.*, but possibly the true readings may be 'mene' and 'mournyd' respectively. 1425, *Castle of Perseverance*, Macro Plays, 125, 'Mankynde! take kepe of chastite, & mone þee to maydyn Marye'. 1471, *Paston Letters*, iii. 4, 'Ther was kyllyd uppon the ffelde ... Sir Omffrey Bowghsher off our countre, whyche is a sore moonyd man her.'

p. 69, l. 10. þe comune gloose. *Glossa Ordinaria*, thus called from its common use in the Middle Ages. Its author, Walafrid Strabo (d. 849), had some knowledge of Greek, and made extracts chiefly from the Latin Fathers, and from the writings of his master, Rabanus Maurus, for the purpose of illustrating the various meanings of Scripture. Until the seventeenth century it remained the favourite commentary on the Bible. The second gloss, *Glossa Interlinearis*, was the work of Anselm of Laon (d. 1117). After the twelfth century, copies of the Vulgate were usually supplied with both these glosses, while later, from the fourteenth century onwards, the *Postilla* of Nicolaus of Lyra were added (cf. *Cath. Encyclop.*, vol. vi, p. 588).

p. 75, l. 26. þe maistir of sentence. See note on p. 12, l. 15.

p. 88, l. 29. Ordinarijs. An ordinary is an officer who has of his own right, and not by special deputation, immediate jurisdiction in ecclesiastical cases (*N.E.D.*).

p. 88, l. 30. Purgacioun. Canonical purgation is the affirmation on oath of his innocence by the accused in a spiritual court, confirmed by the oaths of several of his peers (*N.E.D.*).

p. 91, l. 4. Greet feires of þe ȝeere for þe moost partie ben sett on þe saboth dai. It seems to have been customary for fairs to have been held on Sunday and on High Feast Days, for in the middle of the fifteenth century a statute was enacted whereby fairs and markets were forbidden to be held on these days (Statutes of the Realm, 27 Hen. VI, c. 5). Cf. *Town Life in the Fifteenth Century*, Mrs. J. R. Green, vol. i, p. 156.

p. 92, l. 27. As doctour Odo seiþ. See note on p. 35, l. 13. The passage quoted here occurs also in an English translation in the *Apology for Lollard Doctrines*, p. 57. The editor, Mr. J. H. Todd, states that he discovered the original in the *Flores Sermonum* printed by Matthew Macherel in 1520. No copy of this work has been found in the British Museum or the Bodleian.

p. 97, l. 27. seint Siluestir took þis possession. For a similar passage cf. *English Works of Wyclif*, E.E.T.S., pp. 380-2, especially, 'And so musten oure clerkis argue whan þai aleggen for her lordeschip þe lyuynge of her patrons & sayntis, & sayen þus: Seynt thomas & seynt hwe & seynt Swiþune wer þus lordis, & in þis þai suyd cristis lyuynge & his lore; þerfore we may lefulli be þus lordis' (p. 382).

seint Siluestir. Silvester, Bishop of Rome, 314-35. The accounts of his papacy preserved in the *Liber pontificalis* are little else than a record of the gifts said to have been conferred on the Roman church by Constantine the Great.

p. 97, l. 28. seint Swiþun (d. 862): bishop of Winchester, and patron saint of Winchester Cathedral from the tenth to the sixteenth centuries. He was the tutor of Æthelwulf, King of Wessex, whom he persuaded to give a tenth of his royal lands to the Church.

p. 97, l. 28. seint William: perhaps William Fitzherbert, Archbishop of York. He was elected Archbishop in 1142 at the instance of the King, in opposition to the candidature of Henry Murdoc, a Cistercian monk. The validity of the election was disputed on the ground of alleged simony and royal influence. In 1143 the Pope decided that William should be consecrated if he could clear himself from the accusation of bribery. This he did conclusively, and the legate consecrated him Archbishop in the same year. He died in 1153, and was canonized in 1227.

p. 101, l. 6. hauntriþ: perhaps a frequentative of 'haunten', to frequent, resort to, although such a verb is not recorded. More probably hauntriþ = auntriþ, to venture to go, with an inorganic initial *h*, which is common in this text.

p. 104, l. 31. þe sumnour. For a somewhat similar description of the corrupt practices of the summoner, cf. Chaucer, *Canterbury Tales*, Prologue, ll. 649-58.

p. 107, l. 5. þis is expouned in þe þridde comaundement, cf. p. 93.

p. 112, l. 21. þe fende . . . haþ ȝouun leve to XII men for twelue grootis to passe forþe on a quest: a reference to the bribery and corruption of juries which prevailed at the time. Cf. *England in the Age of Wycliffe*, Trevelyan, pp. 216, 217 ; *Paston Letters*, i, nos. 155, 159.

p. 113, l. 33. oþir payment gete þei noon but a whit stik. Cf. *English Works of Wyclif*, E.E.T.S., p. 233, 'Also lordis many tymes don wrongis to pore men bi extorscions & unresonable mercymentis & unresonable taxis, & taken pore mennus goodis & paien not þerfore but white stickis . . .' The reference is to the custom of 'purveyance'—the right of the sovereign when travelling through the country to receive food and maintenance for himself and his retinue. The custom was liable to grave abuses. Not infrequently no payment was made; when it was, it often took the form of tallies—the 'whit stik' of the text—which gave the recipient the right to deduct the amount from any taxes he might have to pay in the future (cf. *Encyclop. Brit.*, art. 'Purveyance'; Stubbs, *Const. Hist.*, ii).

p. 120, l. 30. Geizi = Gehazi.

p. 120, l. 32. Helesie = Elisha.

p. 124, l. 8. Seynt Hewe seiþ. Perhaps Hugh of St. Victor (1078-1141), mystic philosopher, the author of many books. He, however, was not canonized. St. Hugh of Avalon (c. 1140-1200), Bishop of Lincoln, may be the 'seynt Hewe' of the text, but there is no evidence that he made any contribution to literature.

p. 132, l. 5. Magistrum historiarum: Peter Comestor (d. 1178), author of *Historia Scholastica*, a sacred history beginning at the Creation and continuing to the end of the incidents recorded in the Acts. It is from this work that he is known as ' Magister historiarum '.

p. 132, l. 6. þere ben þoo men þat boosen her bristis . . . For a similar passage, cf. *Select Works of J. Wyclif*, Arnold, vol. iii, p. 124, 'And so soche men þat boosen hor brestis, or pynchen hor belyes, to make hom smale wastes, or streynen hor hosis to schewe hor strong legges, semen to chalange God of giftes þat he hafs gyven hem . . .' For an interesting account of fashions in dress in the fourteenth and fifteenth centuries, cf. *English Life and Manners in the Later Middle Ages*, Abram, pp. 152-72.

p. 132, l. 7. parten her hosis = wear parti-coloured hose. For this use of ' part ' cf. *Wyclif* (E.E.T.S.), p. 471, ' Herfore biddiþ God in his lawe þat his men shulden not be cloþid in wollun & lynnun partid to-gidere,' and (1570) North, *Doni's Philos.*, 70, ' So goodly a beaste . . . with his parted hide (halfe blacke, halfe white).' *N.E.D.*

p. 132, l. 7. cracowen her schoos. This refers to the custom of wearing shoes with long pointed toes which projected far beyond the end of the foot; it is said to have been introduced into England by Anne of Bohemia, wife of Richard II, and the shoes were called 'cracowes', probably because they came from Cracow in Poland, at that time incorporated with Bohemia. Cf. Monk of Evesham, *Life of Richard II*, p. 126 : ' Cum ista Regina (i. e. Anne of Bohemia) venerunt de Boemia in Angliam abusiones illae execrabiles, sotulares cum longis rostis (Anglice Cracowys vel Pykys) dimidiam virgam largiter habentes ita ut oporteret eos ad tibiam ligari cum cathenis argenteis, antequam cum eis possent incedere.'

p. 132, l. 11. **gigge-haltiris**: probably a coined word used contemptuously for the chains or collars which were worn round the neck. *Gigge* = a flighty, giddy girl.

p. 132, l. 11. **Honycombis**: evidently the name given to some kind of head-dress fashionable at the time.

p. 135, l. 19. þanne may þe soule seie to þe bodi. The Dialogue between the Soul and the Body after Death was one of the most popular themes treated in mediaeval religious poetry, poems of the kind being found in nearly every Western European language.

GLOSSARY

ABBREVIATIONS USED

a.	adjective.	perh.	perhaps.
adv.	adverb.	*pl.*	plural.
aphet.	aphetic.	*pp.*	past participle.
coll.	collective.	*pref.*	prefix.
comp.	comparative.	*prep.*	preposition.
conj.	conjunction.	*pres.*	present.
f.	from.	*pron.*	pronoun.
fem.	feminine.	*pr. p.*	present participle.
fig,	figurative.	*refl.*	reflexive.
gen.	genitive.	*sb.*	substantive.
imp.	imperative.	*sing.*	singular.
impers.	impersonal.	*subj.*	subjunctive.
inf.	infinitive.	*super.*	superlative.
inter.	interjection.	*t.*	transitive.
i.	intransitive.	*v.*	vide.
L.	Latin.	*var.*	variant.
OE.	Old English.	*vb.*	verb.
OF.	Old French.	1	first person.
ON.	Old Norse.	2	second person.
p.	past tense.	3	third person.

A

Abak, *adv.* back, 22/23, 57/4.
Abasche, *vb. i. inf.* stand confounded, 47/14.
Abhominable, abhomynable, *a.* abominable, 45/7, 110/5.
Abhominacioun, *sb.* abomination, 68/9, 108/1.
Abide, *vb. i. inf.* remain, wait, abide, 4/15, 98/26; abidiþ, 3 *sing. pres.* 63/11; abiden, 3 *pl. pres.* 101/3; abiding, *pr. p.* 27/16; abidiþ, *vb. t.* 3 *sing. pres.* endures, suffers, 119/19.
Abiect, *a.* rejected, cast out, 41/9.
Abouen, *adv.* above, 46/11; *prep.* 9/28, 19/24, 19/28, &c.
Aboute, *prep.* about, 69/12.
Abreg(g)e, *vb. t, inf.* curtail, 18/28, 80/31.
Abrood, *adv.* abroad, 52/13, 130/31.
Abstinence, *sb.* abstinence, 79/10.
Abstynen, *vb. t.* 3 *pl. pres.* abstain, 48/14.

Accepten, *vb. t.* 3 *pl. pres.* accept, 133/5; accepting, *pr. p.* 88/30.
Accepting, *sb.* accepting, 114/17.
Accusars, *sb. pl.* accusers, 111/14.
Accusing, *pr. p.* accusing, 134/34.
Acordaunce, *sb.* agreement, 16/10.
Acorde, *sb.* accord, agreement, 2/14, 74/30.
Acorden, *vb. i.* 3 *pl. pres.* agree, 1/19, 12/18, 41/28, 42/15; acordiþ, 3 *sing. pres.* 23/13, 38/6; acording, *pr. p.* 58/16.
Acounte, *vb. t.* 1 *pl. subj.* count, 38/2.
Accioun, *sb.* action, 81/18.
Acumbrid, *pp.* encumbered, 80/14.
Acursid, *pp.* accursed, 116/30, 120/8.
Addre, *sb.* adder, 47/8; addris, *pl.* 43/6, 111/12, 136/7.
Aduersarie, *sb.* adversary, 104/14.
Aduersite, *sb.* adversity, 65/33.
Afe(e)rde, *pp.* afraid, 16/6, 57/3.
Affecciouns, affectiouns, *sb. pl.* passions, 29/17, 23, 65/30.

Affectuousli, *adv.* earnestly, 30/1.
Affermeþ, *vb. t.* 3 *sing. pres.* affirms, 6/1, 76/28.
Aforn(e), *adv.* before, 17/4, 28/6, 41/20, 61/22, 100/23, *prep.* 47/16.
Aftir, *adv.* afterwards, 7/27, 8/2, 43/14; *prep.* in accordance with, 2/19, 6/11, 9/2, &c.; *conj.* according as, 29/24.
Aftirward, *adv.* afterwards, 43/12.
Agee, *sb.* age, 14/3.
Aile-storm, *sb.* hail-storm, 46/10.
Al, *a. sing.* all, 2/14; al, alle, allen, *pl.* 2/16, 18, 3/16, 4/21, 133/1, &c.
Al, *adv.* entirely, 46/13, 30.
Albeit, *conj.* although, 11/27.
Algatis, *adv.* always, 40/28, 59/10; at any rate, 100/6.
Alien, *a.* alien, 73/11, 81/25.
Almes, *sb.* alms, 54/7, 54/17, 105/3.
Almes-dede, *sb.* almsgiving, 86/12.
Almisdoars, almysdoars, *sb. pl.* almsdoers, 48/7, 53/21, 54/14.
Almiʒti, *a.* almighty, 5/2, 31/4, 46/20, &c.
Aloone, *adv.* alone, 121/6.
Als, *adv.* as, 93/15, 93/27, 101/7.
Alwey, *adv.* always, 93/32.
Amende, *vb. t. inf.* amend, 38/24, 64/15; amendid, *pp.* 56/16.
Amendement, *sb.* amendment, 133/13.
Amending, *sb.* amending, 99/11, 118/21.
Amendis - making, *sb.* amends-making, 74/18.
Among(e), *prep.* among, 39/12, 62/28, 86/20.
Amys, *adv.* amiss, 53/17, 54/18.
Anagogy, *sb.* mystical interpretation, 24/24.
And, *conj.* if, 11/30, 54/26, &c.
Anentis, anenst, *prep.* with, 5/2, 5, 8/9; in the sight of, 97/16.
Anfest, *vb. t. inf.* = ? hanfest for handfest, betroth, make a contract of marriage, 35/14 (*see* note).
Angir, hanger, *sb.* anger, 44/24, 59/25.
Annon, anoon, *adv.* at once, 10/23, 50/23, 54/20, 66/13.
Anoyntyng, *sb.* anointing, 60/1.
Answere, *vb. t. inf.* answer, 100/5; answeren, 1 *pl. pres.* 72/10, 73/12.
Apaied, *a.* satisfied, contented, 86/25.
Apert, *adv.* openly, 100/3.
Apocalips, *sb.* Apocalypse, 119/9.

Apostasie, *sb.* apostasy, 41/2, 92/14.
Apostataa, *sb.* apostate, 92/4; *pl.* 22/23, 93/26.
Apostilhed, *sb.* apostlehood, 97/10.
Apostlis, *sb. pl.* apostles, 5/16, 60/17.
Appetite, *sb.* appetite, 115/19.
Appil, *sb.* apple, 120/16.
Ap(p)ropurid, *pp.* set apart, 35/11, 74/7.
Aproued, *vb. t.* 3 *sing. p.* approved, 39/3; approuyng, *pr. p.* 134/33; approued, *pp.* 32/17.
Araied, *pp.* arrayed, 31/17, 37/27.
Arioleris, *sb. pl.* soothsayers, diviners, 132/20 (OF. *ariole, hariole*); more usual form 'ariole', but cf. *Apol. Loll.* 92.
Arme, *vb. t. imp.* arm, 104/14; armyn, 3 *pl. pres.* 65/17; armed, armyd, *pp.* armed, 65/14, 118/2.
Armour, *sb.* armour, 52/11, 65/15, 20, 104/13; *pl.* 65/16.
Armyed, *a.* armed, 53/12.
Arow, *sb.* arrow, 72/1.
Article, *sb.* article, 75/14; articlis, *pl.* 47/11.
Aschamed, *pp.* ashamed, 68/10, 71/1.
Aseelid, *pp.* sealed, 113/3.
Aseeþ, *sb.* satisfaction, 78/33; made aseeþ, made atonement = OF. *fere aset*; L. *satis facere*.
Asigned, *vb. t.* 3 *sing. p.* appointed, 12/26.
Askars, *sb. pl.* questioners, 93/28.
Aske, *vb. t. inf.* ask, 69/30; axeþ, axiþ, 3 *sing. pres.* 27/11, 54/6, 65/32; asken, 3 *pl. pres.* 82/8; axe, *imp.* 13/13; axid, 3 *sing. p.* 38/5; *pp.* 52/6.
Asoyled, *pp.* assoiled, 76/5.
Aspiee, *vb. t. inf.* watch, 45/22.
Aspiseþ, for aspieþ, 3 *sing. pres.* spies upon, 19/4; perh. on analogy with 'despise'.
As(s)aile, *vb. t. inf.* assail, attack, 40/1, 65/18, 66/9; assailed, 3 *sing. p.* 66/12.
Assay, *vb. t. imp.* try, 136/13; assaiyng, *pr. p.* 53/20.
Asse, *sb.* ass, 121/21.
Astaat, astate, *sb.* state, estate, 33/19, 34/5, 10, 97/25; astaatis, *pl.* 106/6.
At, *prep.* from, 28/19.
Atwynne, *adv.* apart, 51/13.
Auarice, auarise, *sb.* avarice, 39/28, 58/27.
Auditours, *sb. pl.* auditors, 133/4.

Glossary 155

Aungel, *sb.* angel, 15/18, 18/1; aungelis, *pl.* 2/2, 15/3, 47/16.
Auter, *sb.* altar, 104/30; auters, *pl.* 37/26.
Autor, *sb.* author, 39/12; autours, *pl.* 120/1, 132/17.
Autorise, *vb. t. inf.* authorize, 42/9; autoriseþ, 3 *sing. pres.* 125/4.
Autorite, *sb.* authority, 32/15, 33/24, 111/13.
Autorysing, *sb.* sanctioning, 32/15.
Auȝt, *see* Owist.
Availe, *vb. t.* 3 *sing. subj.* avail, 97/15; availen, 3 *pl. pres.* 55/28.
Avarouse, auarouse, *a.* avaricious, 60/7, 103/22.
Avauncid, avaunsid, *pp.* advanced, 93/23, 118/35.
Avaunt, *sb.* boasting, 135/14.
Avauntage, *sb.* advantage, 105/18.
Avise, *vb. t. inf.* advise, 105/22.
Avoide, *vb. t. inf.* avoid, put away, 55/1, 99/18; avoiden, 3 *pl. pres.* 52/19.
Avoket, *sb.* advocate, 8/9.
Avowtreris, *sb. pl.* adulterers, 71/15, 131/19.
Avowtresse, *sb.* adulteress, 130/26.
Avowtrie, *sb.* adultery, 130/22.
Awake, *vb. t. imp.* awake, 35/3.
Awe, *sb.* fear, 95/16; power to inspire fear, 70/10.
Awey, *adv.* away, 4/15, 40/9, 52/14.
Axe, *see* Aske.
Axing, *sb.* asking, 5/5.
Aȝen, *adv.* again, 39/6, 59/2; *prep.* against, 6/16, 8/3, 11/5, &c.
Aȝen-biyng, *sb.* redemption, 32/12.
Aȝens, *prep.* against, 13/1, 5.
Aȝenseie, *vb. t. inf.* contradict, 101/3; aȝenseyn, 3 *pl. pres.* 131/6.
Aȝenseiyng, *sb.* contradiction, 26/26, 46/29.
Aȝenstonden, *vb. t.* 3 *pl. pres.* withstand, 13/11; aȝenstooden, 3 *pl. p.* 13/11; aȝenstonding, *pr. p.* 14/14.
Aȝenward(e), *adv.* on the other hand, 6/7, 7/31, 31/36.

B

Baate, *sb.* strife, 117/10.
Bak, *sb.* back, 58/25.
Bakbiter, *sb.* backbiter, 98/13; bakbiters, bacbitears, *pl.* 98/11, 131/11.
Bakbiting, *sb.* backbiting, 98/2.
Bakwarde, *adv.* backward, 108/18.

Balaunce, *sb.* balance, 108/1, 7.
Bal(e)ys, *sb.* rod, 94/5, 6; OF. *baleis* = besom, broom.
Banere, *sb.* banner, 134/18.
Baptem, baptyme, *sb.* baptism, 2/17, 28/14, 59/28.
Baptisid, *pp.* baptized, 35/17.
Bar, *see* Bere.
Bare, *a.* bare, naked, 46/3, 80/17.
Bareheed, *a.* bareheaded, 104/26.
Bargayn, *sb.* bargain, 61/5.
Barre, *sb.* bar, 134/17.
Bastard, *a.* bastard, 93/13.
Bataile, *sb.* battle, 71/6, 99/19; batailes, *pl.* 13/29.
Be, *vb. aux. inf.*, be, 3/20, 24; am, 1 *sing. pres.* 16/6; art, arte, 2 *sing. pres.* 6/20, 36/26, 75/22; is, 3 *sing. pres. passim*; arne, 3 *pl. pres.* 5/14; ben, 3 *pl. pres. passim*; was, 3 *sing. pres.* 21/8, &c.; weren, 3 *pl. p.* 5/16, &c.; be, 3 *sing. subj.* 7/7; be, *pp.* 2/5, 30/23.
Beaute, *sb.* beauty, 44/18, 49/21.
Bedde, *sb.* bed, 118/5, 130/27.
Bedemen, *sb. pl.* beadsmen, 45/27.
Beemes, *sb. pl.* beams, 37/26.
Beere, *sb.* bier, 115/34.
Beest, *sb.* beast, 3/26; beestis, *pl.* 2/20, 37/31, 45/10, 11.
Beest, *adv.* best, 41/15, 46/4, 58/9.
Beestli, *a.* resembling a beast in unintelligence; ignorant, foolish, 101/12.
Beforn, biforne, *prep.* before, 12/7, 47/18; biforn, *adv.* 43/14.
Beggers, *sb. pl.* beggars, 46/15.
Begry, *sb.* beggary, 43/17.
Behoueþ, bihoueþ, *vb. t.* 3 *sing. pres.* behoves, 3/20, 77/4, 84/10; behoued, 3 *sing. p.* 3/24.
Belchiþ, *vb. t.* 3 *sing. pres.* casts up, 45/6.
Beli, *sb.* belly, 50/1; belies, *pl.* 132/7.
Belle, *sb.* bell, 41/34.
Benefice, *sb.* benefit, 120/31; benefice, 93/23; beneficis, *pl.* 92/26.
Beneiþe, *see* Binep.
Bent, *a.* bent, 71/17.
Bere, *vb. t. inf.* bear, 93/30; 1 *pl. subj.* 38/2; beriþ, 3 *sing. pres.* 66/2, 87/5, 98/14; beren, 3 *pl. pres.* 24/25; bar, 3 *sing. p.* 119/2; born(e), *pp.* 2/11, 35/14, 76/13, 85/30.
Berne, *sb.* barn, 29/8.
Bestial, *a.* bestial, 45/11.
Bete, *vb. t. inf.* beat, 104/29; 2 *sing.*

subj. 95/4; beetist, 2 sing. pres. 95/5; beten, pp. 78/29, 30, 133/8.
Betingis, sb. pl. beatings, 8/18.
Betir, a. comp. better, 56/16, 82/24, 83/1, 100/22.
Bi, prep. according to, 104/33.
Bible, sb. Bible, 62/26.
Bicum, vb. i. inf. become, 79/21; bicomen, 3 pl. pres. come, 129/9.
Bidde, vb. t. inf. bid, 104/32; 3 sing. subj. 84/11; biddiþ, 3 sing. pres. 82/11; bad, 3 sing. p. 42/22; boden, pp. 79/19, 97/21.
Bidding, sb. command, 88/3; biddingis, pl. 8/15, 27/12, 105/16.
Bidene, adv. continuously, 81/9.
Bie, vb. t. inf. buy, 14/18, 60/31, 91/2; bouʒt, 3 sing. p. bought, 72/9.
Biears, bigger(i)s, sb. pl. buyers, 60/33, 92/20, 132/27.
Bigger(i)s, see Biears.
Bigile, vb. t. inf. beguile, 71/21; 3 sing. subj. 42/22; bigilen, 3 pl. pres. 14/9; bigilid, pp. 36/15; bigiling, pr. p. 25/26.
Bigunne, vb. i. 3 pl. p. began, 101/18.
Bigynnyng, sb. beginning, 112/9.
Bihap, adv. perchance, 78/2.
Bihiʒt, vb. t. 3 sing. p. promised, 64/21, 77/8.
Biholdest, vb. t. 2 sing. pres. beholdest, 127/4.
Biholding, sb. beholding, 120/17.
Bijlde, vb. t. inf. build, 3/14; bilden, pl. pres. 9/8, 19/14, 37/24; bildid, pp. 129/22.
Bilding, bildyng, sb. building, 40/3, 42/17, 109/15; bildingis, bildyngis, pl. 38/16, 109/13.
Bileuars, sb. pl. believers, 5/24.
Bileue, vb. t. inf. believe, 2/17.
Bileue, sb. belief, 32/17, 47/3, 55/29.
Bileue, vb. t. 1 sing. pres. leave, 64/23; bilefte, 3 sing. p. 64/24.
Bilijke, vb. t. inf. resemble, 129/22.
Bimene, vb. t. inf. mean, signify, 59/5.
Bineþ, beneiþe, adv. beneath, 76/13, 81/27; prep. 134/31.
Birie, vb. t. imp. bury, 94/8; biried, pp. 31/8.
Birþe, sb. birth, 122/8.
Bischopis, sb. pl. bishops, 43/11, 75/31.
Bisecheing, sb. besieging, 21/13.
Biside, adv. aside, 97/23; at hand, 134/23.

Biside, bisiʒde, prep. away from, 3/28; beside, 46/18, 65/3; contrary to, 117/12.
Bisi(e), bisy, a. earnest, importunate, 5/4, 35/4, 52/31, 63/7; busy, 100/2.
Bisi(e), vb. t. imp. busy, occupy, 62/29, 63/1; bisien, 3 pl. pres. 59/12, 110/7.
Bisili, adv. earnestly, 7/20; busily, diligently, 57/11, 95/7.
Bisines, sb. occupation, 40/4; care, solicitude, 97/3; industry, 111/8.
Bitars, sb. pl. biters, 111/11.
Biten, vb. i. 3 pl. pres. bite, 111/2; bitiþ, 3 sing. pres. 66/14; boote, 3 sing. p. 120/18.
Bitidde, vb. i. 3 sing. p. befell, 102/18.
Bitoken, vb. t. inf. betoken, 47/3.
Bitook, vb. t. 3 sing. p. gave, 28/11, 64/25.
Bitraie, vb. t. inf. betray, 93/12; bitraied, 3 sing. p. 60/19; bitraying, pr. p. 62/5.
Bittir, a. bitter, 44/20, 21.
Bittirnes(se), sb. bitterness, 47/27, 98/12.
Bitwixe, prep. between, 48/29, 108/26.
Biþenken, vb. t. 3 pl. pres. reflect, think, 59/15.
Blame, vb. t. inf. blame, 38/15, 18, 40/9; blameþ, 3 sing. pres. 42/8, 49/2, 49/21; blamed, 3 sing. p. 62/2.
Blasfem, vb. t. inf. blaspheme, 84/36; blasfemen, 3 pl. pres. 68/21; blasfemeden, 3 pl. p. 15/20.
Blasfemars, sb. pl. blasphemers, 131/9.
Blasfemouse, a. blasphemous, 90/11.
Blasfemye, sb. blasphemy, 11/20.
Blent, pp. blinded, 38/26.
Blesse, vb. t. inf. bless, 3/28; blessed, blessid, pp. 33/17, 19.
Blessing, sb. blessing, 58/11.
Blewen, vb. i. 3 pl. p. blew, 130/1.
Bleyne, sb. blain, blemish, 23/12, 17.
Blijndlingis, blyndlingis, adv. blindly, heedlessly, 3/30, 29/5.
Blindfelt, a. blindfold, 18/18.
Blis(se), sb. bliss, 7/27, 35/13, 43/28.
Blo(o)d, sb. blood, 4/23, 32/12, 98/27.
Blynde, a. blind, 69/7, 78/7.

Glossary

Blyndid, *pp.* blinded, 67/15.
Blyndnes, *sb.* blindness, 69/4.
Bockelere, *sb.* buckler, 111/18.
Bocket, *sb.* bucket, 54/19.
Boden, *see* Bidde.
Bodi, *sb.* body, 7/1, 21, 33/2, &c.
Bodili, *a.* bodily, 2/7, 49/20, 57/12.
Boldli, booldili, *adv.* boldly, 53/17, 92/1.
Bollen, *vb. i.* 3 *pl. pres.* are puffed up, 44/19.
Bolnyng, *sb.* swelling, 7/9.
Bondage, *sb.* bondage, 120/3.
Bookis, *sb. pl.* books, 85/21, 23, 88/2.
Boolden, *vb. t.* 3 *pl. pres.* encourage, enbolden, 71/5.
Boon, *sb.* bone, 46/3.
Boond, *a.* bound, 14/18.
Bo(o)ndis, *sb. pl.* bonds, 3/16, 25/34, 76/5.
Bo(o)rdis, *sb. pl.* tables, 37/28, 92/20.
Boosen, *vb. t.* 3 *pl. pres.* stuff out, 132/6; OF. *boce* (cf. Wyclif, 'On the Seven Deadly Sins,' *S. E. W.*, iii, p. 124, l. 1).
Boost, *sb.* boast, 19/11, 91/24, 135/14.
Boost, *vb. i. inf.* boast, 36/21; boostiþ, 3 *sing. pres.* 69/12; boosten, 3 *pl. pres.* 93/33.
Boot, *sb.* boat, 24/5, 8, 9.
Bordel-hous, *sb.* brothel, 106/13.
Borow, *sb.* surety, 78/35.
Borow, *vb. t. inf.* redeem, 79/3.
Boþe, *a.* both, 35/14.
Bounden, *see* Bynde.
Boundes, boundis, *sb. pl.* bounds, boundaries, 41/32, 116/26, 117/3.
Bowe, *sb.* bow, 71/17.
Bowe, *vb. i. inf.* bow, submit, 51/24; 3 *pl. pres.* 41/36; *v. t. imp.* 112/15; bowiþ, 3 *sing. pres.* stoops, 57/12; bowiden, 3 *pl. p.* 120/23.
Bowels, *sb. pl.* bowels, 102/6.
Braft, *pp.* bereft, 119/2. This form, without the vowel of prefix, apparently not recorded elsewhere.
Braied, *pp.* ground, 8/28.
Braunchis, *sb. pl.* branches, 92/11, 114/2.
Bre(e)d, *sb.* bread, 38/4, 5, 60/17, &c.
Breeke, *vb. t. inf.* break, 137/11; breken, 3 *pl. pres.* 58/13, 71/16; brooken, 3 *pl. p* 42/20.
Breest, *vb. t. inf.* burst, 66/6; brostun, *pp.* 74/12.
Breking, *sb.* breaking, 92/4.

Brenne, *vb. t. inf.* burn, 6/23, 7/3, 123/20; brennen, *pl. pres.* 43/8; brenned, 3 *pl. p.* 113/10; brennyng, *pr. p.* 104/1; brende, *a.* burnt, 82/23; brent, *pp.* 88/4.
Brennyng, *a.* burning, 58/12, 65/35; *sb.* 88/22, 23.
Bridal, *a.* bridal, 73/17.
Bridilen, *vb. t.* 3 *pl. pres.* bridle, 132/10.
Bring, *vb. t. imp.* bring, 86/15; bringeþ, 3 *sing. pres.* 40/6; brouȝt, *pp.* 5/24, 11/10, 17/24.
Brise, *vb. t. imp.* break, crush, 125/31; brisen, 3 *pl. pres.* 78/4; brissid, *pp.* 126/20.
Bristis, *sb. pl.* breasts, 132/6.
Broche, *sb.* boring, perforation; sette on broche, to tap and set running, fig. to start, 76/9.
Brood, *a.* broad, 69/17, 86/19, 128/5.
Broom, *sb.* broom, 63/19.
Broþer, broþir, *sb.* brother, 54/11, 98/5; briþeren, *pl.* 11/6, 11/16, 80/23.
Buschel, *sb.* bushel, 108/8.
But, *conj.* unless, 91/20, 120/37; *prep.* except, 3/20; but if, *conj.* unless, 7/7, 19, 11/23, &c.
Buxumnesse, *sb.* obedience, 23/7.
Bynde, *vb. t. inf.* bind, 3/28; bounden, *pp.* 73/18, 84/31.

C

Cacche, *vb. t. inf.* catch, 113/26, 132/13; caccheþ, cacchiþ, 3 *sing. pres.* 7/11, 18/25, 82/4; cac(c)hen, 3 *pl. pres.* 5/29, 52/14; cauȝt, *pp.* 45/5, 57/3.
Cage, *sb.* cage, 56/22.
Can, *see* Kunnen.
Candils, *sb. pl.* candles, 104/30.
Cannonisid, *pp.* sanctioned by the authority of the Church, 31/2 6
Canonysid, *a.* canonical, 21/10.
Capteyn, *sb.* captain, 66/21.
Careyn, *sb.* carrion, carcass, 9/31; corpse, 115/33, 135/21; body (contemptuously), 60/22; careynes, *pl.* 20/25.
Carful, *a.* sorrowful, 49/7.
Carles, *a.* careless, 26/34.
Castiþ, *see* Kast.
Catel, *sb.* goods, 19/30, 45/2, 53/22.
Cause, *sb.* cause, reason, 36/19, 43/15, 54/16; causis, *pl.* 52/2.
Causen, *vb. t.* 3 *pl. pres.* bring about, cause, 105/25.

Glossary

Cautel(l)s, *sb. pl.* plots, stratagems, 1/22, 45/2, 81/20.
Cedre-trees, *sb. pl.* cedar-trees, 24/14, 129/6.
Ce(e)se, *vb. t.* or *i. inf.* cease, 78/8, 80/29, 83/18, 91/18; cesiþ, *vb. i.* 3 *sing. pres.* 83/16, 18; cessen, *vb. t.* 3 *pl. pres.* 78/21; ceessid, *vb. t.* 3 *pl. p.* 103/3.
Celi, *a.* simple, 52/14, 100/15.
Certis, *adv.* certainly, 2/20, 11/13, &c.
Cesoun, *sb.* season, 46/10.
Chaare, *sb.* chariot, 102/15.
Cha(a)st, *a.* chaste, 23/8, 48/16, 102/13.
Chaff, *sb.* chaff, 6/22, 24, 7/5.
Chaffare, *vb. i. inf.* bargain, 14/8.
Chaier, *sb.* chair, 19/12; chaiers, *pl.* 92/21.
Chalenge, *vb. t. inf.* claim, 97/2; *imp.* 97/1; chalengeþ, 3 *sing. pres.* 82/6.
Chalise, *sb.* chalice, 41/34.
Chano(u)ns, *sb. pl.* canons, 16/14, 38/16, 39/7.
Chapman, *sb.* trader, dealer, 61/4; chap(pe)men, *pl.* 60/31, 91/2, 132/26.
Chapiter, *sb.* chapter, 91/22.
Chare, *vb. t. inf.* drive away (OE. *cierran* = to turn), 11/10.
Charge, *sb.* charge, burden, 54/31, 93/29; expense, 46/16.
Charg(e)ouse, *a.* burdensome, onerous, 5/5, 26/31.
Chargiþ, *vb. t.* 3 *sing. pres.* charges, 41/14, 106/3; cares, recks, 71/2; charge, 3 *pl. pres.* 106/4; chargid, 3 *sing. p.* 91/17; *pp.* 59/9.
Charite, *sb.* love, charity, 2/10, 43/19, 50/7.
Charitable, *a.* charitable, 121/30, 122/30.
Charmours, *sb. pl.* enchanters, 132/20.
Chasiþ, *vb. t.* 3 *sing. pres.* chases, 52/25.
Chastise, *vb. t. inf.* chastise, 117/29; chastisiþ, 3 *sing. pres.* 119/10.
Chastisement, *sb.* chastisement, 119/16.
Chastising, *sb.* chastising, 118/21, 118/37.
Chastite, *sb.* chastity, 45/29, 65/19, 21.
Chatiren, *vb. i.* 3 *pl. pres.* chatter, 56/22.
Chaumbre, *sb.* chamber, 62/22.
Chaunge, *vb. t. inf.* exchange, 118/6;

chaungyng, *pr. p.* changing, 53/18; chaungid, *pp.* changed, 85/10.
Chaungeris, *sb. pl.* money-changers, 132/27.
Chaungyng, *sb.* changing, 2/17.
Chaunting, *sb.* chanting, 59/4.
Cheef, *a.* chief, 90/11.
Che(e)re, *sb.* countenance, 42/20, 135/16, 136/16.
Che(e)se, *vb. t. inf.* choose, 6/7, 113/4; 1 *sing. pres.* 50/4; chesiþ, 3 *sing. pres.* 47/25; chase, 3 *sing. p.* 6/6, 54/33, 92/11; chosen, 3 *pl. p.* 44/10; *pp.* 32/11.
Chelling, *a.* chilling, 136/7.
Chere, *vb. t. inf.* cheer, 28/1.
Childe, *sb.* child, 2/25, 60/34, 106/26; children, *pl.* 33/11, 60/3, &c.
Chirche, *sb.* church, 1/11, &c.
Choise, *sb.* choice, 24/28, 37/28.
Chosen, *a.* chosen, 33/6, 71/8.
Chouris, *sb. pl.* = ? schouris, attacks, 97/27.
Chymney, *sb.* furnace, 47/27.
Circumcidid, *vb. t.* 3 *sing. p.* circumcised, 117/20.
Circumstaunce, *sb.* = L. *circumstantia*, 112/15.
Citee, *sb.* city, 40/32, 42/23; citees, cetees, *pl.* 101/21, 114/12.
Citizen, *sb.* citizen, 85/32.
Cleer(e), *a.* clear, 22/25, 81/17; *adv.* clearly, 41/13; completely, entirely, 63/12.
Cleerli, *adv.* clearly, 54/10.
Clene, *a.* clean, pure, 2/24, 23/8, &c.
Clennes, *sb.* purity, 11/19, 27/27, 103/26.
Clense, *vb. t. inf.* cleanse, 49/21, 50/28, 59/27; clensiþ, 3 *sing. pres.* 4/16, 35/31; clensen, 3 *pl. pres.* 43/1.
Clensing, *sb.* cleansing, 32/12.
Clepiþ, *vb. t.* 3 *sing. pres.* calls, 13/14, 49/2; clepen, *pl. pres.* 33/20, 54/17; clepid, *pp.* 1/2, 14/22, &c.
Clere, *a.* manifest (L. *praeclarus*), 49/26.
Clergie, *sb.* clergy, 83/20, 97/5; learning, 5/29.
Clerk, *sb.* clerk, 106/7; clerkis, *pl.* 84/23.
Clerte, *sb.* glory, 26/17.
Cley, *sb.* clay, 38/3.
Cloos, *sb.* enclosure, 44/8.
Clo(o)þ(e), *sb.* clothing, 9/15, 41/25, 73/17; cloþis, *pl.* clothes, 50/6.
Clo(o)þe, *vb. t. inf.* clothe, 9/28, 52/10; cloþiþ, 3 *sing. pres.* 109/12; cladde, *pp.* 45/28, 64/28, 109/14.

Glossary

Closiþ, *vb. t.* 3 *sing. pres.* closes, 3/9.
Cloþ, *sb.* cloth, 2/24.
Cloþing, *sb.* clothing, 64/28.
Cloude, *sb.* cloud, 81/21, 88/5; cloudis, clowdis, *pl.* 4/14, 46/13, 134/9.
Clowtiþ, *vb. t.* 3 *sing. pres.* patches, 2/24; clouten, 3 *pl. pres.* 55/28; cloutid, *pp.* 16/14.
Colour, *sb.* pretext. Under colour for, under pretext of, 55/20.
Colours, *sb. pl.* colours, 84/29.
Comaunde, *vb. t.* 3 *pl. pres.* command, 82/9; comaundid, 3 *sing. p.* 55/5, 56/12, 101/25.
Comaundementis, *sb. pl.* commandments, 33/14, 63/7.
Combriþ, *vb. t.* 3 *sing. pres.* overwhelms, destroys, 69/4; cumbrid, *pp.* cumbered, 51/1.
Com(e), cum, *vb. i. inf.* come, 8/23, 35/13, 50/14, 53/11; *imp.* 30/13; comeþ, 3 *sing. pres.* 3/21, 32/23; comen, 3 *pl. pres.* 43/31; cam, 3 *sing. p.* 54/31; camen, *pl. p.* 30/27; comen, *pp.* 4/4, 37/33.
Comendiþ, *vb. t.* 3 *sing. pres.* commends, 42/1.
Comissarijs, *sb. pl.* commissaries, 133/1.
Comlyng, *sb.* new-comer, stranger, 123/18.
Company, cumpany, *sb.* company, 71/15, 118/36.
Compelle, *vb. t. inf.* compel, 88/21, 28; compellid, *pp.* 4/9.
Comune, *a.* common, 6/15, 40/27, &c.
Comunes, *sb. pl.* commons, 19/29, 33/20, 46/14.
Comunicacioun, *sb.* communication, 131/3.
Comunyng, *sb.* communion, 31/13, 75/16.
Comyng, *sb.* assembling, 35/37.
Conclucioun, *sb.* conclusion, 31/28.
Condiciouns, *sb. pl.* conditions, 1/6, 48/13.
Confermed, *vb. t.* 3 *sing. p.* confirmed, 102/20.
Confermyng, *sb.* confirmation, 59/29.
Confidren, *vb. t.* 3 *pl. pres.* enter into alliance, 67/1; confedrid, *pp.* 20/9.
Conforme, *vb. t. imp.* conform, 97/24.
Confoundid, *pp.* confounded, 57/3, 68/10.

Confucioun, *sb.* confusion, 68/9.
Congelid, *pp.* frozen, 9/10.
Conpunccioun, *sb.* compunction, 8/17.
Consceyued, conseyued, *pp.* conceived, 31/6, 119/1.
Conscience, *sb.* conscience, 47/14, 54/10, &c.
Consent, *sb.* consent, 123/9, 131/5.
Consent, *vb. t. inf.* consent, 83/3, 113/12; consenten, 3 *pl. pres.* 53/14; consentid, *pp.* 115/25.
Consentours, *sb. pl.* consenters, 85/6.
Constreynen, *vb. t.* 3 *sing. subj.* constrain, 78/22; 3 *pl. pres.* 78/4; constreyned, *pp.* 4/9, 54/6, 88/14.
Contemplacioun, *sb.* contemplation, 95/14.
Conteyned, *pp.* contained, 107/17; retained, 115/23.
Continence, *sb.* continence, 65/23.
Contrarie, *sb.* contrary, 84/12, 101/14.
Contricioun, *sb.* contrition, 68/6, 137/10.
Contrit, *a.* contrite, 8/17.
Contynue, *vb. i. inf.* continue, 104/36.
Contynuaunce, *sb.* continuance, 50/14.
Conventiclis, *sb. pl.* assemblies, meetings, 60/29.
Coold, *sb.* cold, 47/28.
Coolde, *a.* cold, 2/10, 46/10.
Coolis, *sb. pl.* coals, 123/21.
Co(o)rde, *vb. i. inf.* agree, 44/22, 56/20.
Cootis, *sb. pl.* cots (= L. *habitacula*), 41/10.
Cootis, *sb. pl.* coats, 39/16.
Coragenes, *sb.* grossness, 48/15 (*Prompt. Parv.* coragenes = L. *crassitudo*).
Corde, *sb.* cord, 74/12; cordis, *pl.* 45/24.
Coriouse, *see* Curiouse.
Corn, *sb.* corn, 113/32, 116/29.
Correct, *vb. t. inf.* correct, 104/23.
Correcciouns, *sb. pl.* corrections, 84/5.
Corrupcioun, *sb.* corruption, 4/17, 35/32, 45/6.
Corrupt, *a.* corrupt, 39/27.
Corruptible, *a.* corruptible, 38/30.
Corrupting, *pr. p.* corrupting, 56/19.
Costious(e), *a.* costly, 30/23, 40/4.
Cosynes, *sb. pl.* relatives, 118/36.
Couchis, *sb. pl.* couches, 70/5.

Coueite, *vb. t. inf.* coveit, 115/14.
Coue(i)tise, coveitise, *sb.* covetousness, 14/14, 40/19, 60/8, &c.; coueitises, cove(i)tises, *sb. pl.* covetousness, 39/28, 116/11, 14.
Coueitouse, *a.* covetous, 54/5.
Coueitouseli, *adv.* covetously, 118/11.
Couenable, *a.* fit, suitable, 75/17.
Couena(u)nt, *sb.* covenant, 62/4, 105/15, 27.
Counceile, *sb.* council, 91/6.
Counfort, *sb.* comfort, 45/29.
Counfortid, *pp.* comforted, 118/35.
Counseile, *sb.* counsel, 52/4, 67/14.
Counseiliþ, *vb. t.* 3 *sing. pres.* counsels, 58/6, 62/25; counseyled, 3 *sing. p.* 113/36.
Counten, *vb. t.* 3 *pl. pres.* count, 67/7, 94/12; countid, *pp.* 122/12.
Countre, *sb.* country, 41/12, 67/8, 85/33.
Couplen, *vb. t. pl. pres.* couple, 121/5.
Court(e), *sb.* court, 59/12, 89/6, 104/22.
Cow, *sb.* cow, 119/2.
Coward, *a.* cowardly, 78/28.
Cracowen, *vb. t.* 3 *pl. pres.* make long points to, 132/7 (*see* note).
Craft(e), *sb.* craft, power, 36/11, 52/13.
Creature, *sb.* creature, 55/10; creation, 32/10; 48/30.
Crede, *sb.* creed, 31/3, 75/14.
Credence, *sb.* credence, 88/18.
Creping, *a.* creeping, 46/28.
Crepyngis, *sb. pl.* creepings, 126/8.
Crieþ, *vb. t.* 3 *sing. pres.* cries, 69/18; crien, *pl. pres.* 80/13, 108/28; crieden, 3 *pl. p.* 98/25.
Cristen, *a.* Christian, 72/9, 91/24, 101/28.
Cristendom, *sb.* Christianity, 74/1, 102/22.
Cristenyng, *sb.* christening, 60/34.
Crokid, *a.* crooked, 78/7, 86/16.
Croking, *pr. p.* croaking, 19/26.
Cronyclis, *sb. pl.* chronicles, 55/27.
Cro(o)s, *sb.* cross, 4/22, 35/33, 134/18, &c.
Croune, *sb.* crown, 28/5, 35/33, 81/10.
Cruciacioun, *sb.* torture, 71/3.
Crucified, *pp.* crucified, 79/28.
Cruel, *a.* cruel, 3/26, 35/20, 60/2; cruelar, *comp.* 38/5, 46/29.
Cruelte, *sb.* cruelty, 99/23, 127/12.
Cruet, *sb.* vial, 15/18.

Cumb(e)raunce, *sb.* trouble, distress, 8/1, 113/28.
Cumbrid, *see* Combriþ.
Cumpasse, *vb. t. inf.* encompass, 129/13; cumpassen, 3 *pl. pres.* 13/24.
Cuppis, *sb. pl.* cups, 37/29.
Cure, *sb.* cure, 117/32; care, 106/3; curis, *pl.* cures, 67/28.
Curiouse, coriouse, *a.* curious, elaborate, skilfully wrought, 37/8, 42/17, 58/13, 101/5.
Curse, *sb.* curse, 59/12.
Curse, *vb. t. inf.* curse, 3/28; cursiþ, 3 *sing. pres.* 62/3; cursid, *pp.* 57/6.
Cursid, *a.* cursed, 52/9, 61/8, 25.
Cursidnes, *sb.* wickedness, 98/11.
Custum, *vb. t. imp.* accustom, 89/29.
Custum, *sb.* custom, 90/10, 116/12, 117/24; custumes, *pl.* 117/10.

D

Dai, day, *sb.* day, 49/18, 62/12, 16; daies, *pl.* 2/4, 39/2.
Dalt, *see* Dele.
Dampnacioun, *sb.* damnation, 60/21, 61/19.
Dampned, *a.* damned, 50/21.
Dampneþ, *vb. t.* 3 *sing. pres.* condemns, 92/25; dampned, 3 *sing. p. pp.* 7/2, 61/7, 62/3.
Damysellis, *sb. pl.* damsels, 25/24.
Dar, *see* Dore.
Darte, *sb.* dart, 111/17; dartis, *pl.* 65/35.
Daunger, *sb.* jurisdiction, 52/3, 120/20.
Day-þeef, *sb.* thief by day, 107/4; dai-þeues, *pl.* 93/20 (cf. niȝtþeues).
Debate, *sb.* strife, conflict, 69/17; debatis, *pl.* 50/4.
Debitrice, *sb. fem.* debtor, 48/31 (L. *debitrix*).
Declarid, *vb. t.* 3 *sing. p.* explained, 102/17; *pp.* declared, 38/23, 56/25.
Decre, *sb.* decree, 34/2, 59/12, 61/6.
Dede, *sb.* deed, 2/21, 14/23, &c.; dedis, *pl.* 8/19, 15/21, &c.
Deed, *a.* dead, 31/8, 89/15, &c.; deathlike, 53/3, 11, &c.
Deedli, *a.* mortal, 5/18, 26/7, 41/27.
De(e)me, *vb. t. inf.* judge, 31/12; *pl. subj.* 65/2; deeme, demen, *pl. pres.* 106/25, 114/15; demed, 2 *pl. p.* 70/1.
Deepli, *adv.* deeply, 126/10.

Deere, *adv.* dearly, 72/9.
Deeþ, *sb.* death, 8/1, 13/17, &c.
Defauȝt, *sb.* lack, 30/7, 111/7.
Defence, *sb.* defence, 111/18.
Defend(e), *vb. t. inf.* defend, protect, 34/4, 41/2, &c.
Defoil, defoyle, defoule, *vb. t. inf.* defile, pollute, 10/16; defouleþ, 3 *sing. pres.* 45/8; defoyle, 3 *pl. pres.* 105/14; defoiling, *pr. p.* 127/5; defouled, defoulid, *pp.* 6/29, 9/19, 85/12.
Defoiling, defouling, *sb.* defilement, pollution, 2/18, 68/18.
Defoulears, *sb. pl.* defilers, 131/20.
Defouling, *see* Defoiling.
Defoyle, *see* Defoil.
Degre(e), *sb.* degree, rank, 46/1, 80/6, 7; degrees, *pl.* 65/22.
Deken, *sb.* deacon, 12/16; dekenes, *pl.* 114/19.
Dele, *vb. t. inf.* deal, distribute, 86/19; delen, *pl. pres.* 54/17, 86/12; dalt, 3 *sing. p.* 60/16.
Delectacioun, *sb.* delectation, 116/4.
Delictable, *a.* delectable, 116/19.
Delite, *sb.* delight, 40/23; delites, *pl.* 35/25.
Delitiþ, *vb. i.* 3 *sing. pres.* delights, 52/17; deliten, *vb. t.* 3 *pl. pres.* 15/24; delited, 3 *pl. p.* 78/2.
Delues, *see* Deuel.
Delyuer, *vb. t. inf.* deliver, 3/15, 77/8; delyuered, *pp.* 108/14.
Delyueraunce, *sb.* deliverance, 77/10, 113/19.
Den, *sb.* den, 92/23.
Denaye, deneye, *vb. t. inf.* deny, 27/26, 110/18.
Denes, *sb. pl.* deans, 133/1.
Departe, *vb. t. inf.* separate, 47/25, 66/16, 125/13; departiþ, 3 *sing. pres.* 66/14, 15; departen, 3 *pl. pres.* 64/5; depart, 3 *sing. subj.* 76/3; departid, *pp.* 124/18.
Der(c)knes, *sb.* darkness, 4/10, 14, 69/4.
Dere, *a.* dear, 5/2, 79/17.
Derke, *a.* dark, 15/19, 54/26.
Derworþier, *a. comp.* dearer, 79/18; derworþiest, 79/23.
Descyuable, *a.* deceitful, 111/11.
Desire, *sb.* desire, 5/5; desiris, *pl.* 39/27, 48/34.
Desiriþ, *vb. t.* 3 *sing. pres.* desires, 49/16, 53/15.
Desperacioun, *sb.* despair, 7/23, 66/4.
Destrie, *vb. t. inf.* destroy, 17/3; distrieþ, 3 *sing. pres.* 32/6, 69/13; destried, destroied, distried, distroied, *pp.* 3/13, 16/23, 39/13, &c.
Determynacioun, *sb.* decision, 31/28.
Deuel, *sb.* devil, 2/10, 43/21; delues, deuelis, *pl.* 45/9, 110/17.
Deuocioun, *sb.* devotion, 35/22, 56/5, &c.
Deuorse, devorse, *sb.* separation, divorce, 108/26, 124/26.
Deuoure, *vb. t. inf.* devour, 49/18; deuouren, 3 *pl. pres.* 46/3.
Deuoute, *a.* devout, 52/18, 110/8, 19.
Deuoutli, *adv.* devoutly, 35/4.
Dew, *sb.* dew, 32/23.
Dewe, *see* Due.
Deyntes, *sb. pl.* dainties, 35/24.
Die, *vb. i. inf.* die, 62/6; died, 3 *sing. p.* 78/30; diedist, 2 *sing. p.* 4/21.
Differre, *vb. t.* 3 *sing. subj.* defer, 95/18.
Diligatli, *adv.* delicately, 111/8.
Diligence, *sb.* diligence, 99/10, 114/16.
Diligentli, *adv.* diligently, 41/36, 56/17.
Dingeþ, *vb. t.* 3 *sing. pres.* knock, 3/10, 11.
Discenciouns, *sb. pl.* dissensions, 13/29.
Discenden, *vb. i.* 3 *pl. pres.* descend, 119/7.
Disceruen, *vb. t.* 3 *pl. pres.* deserve, 60/33; discerued, *pp.* 65/6, 85/22.
Disceyte, *sb.* deceit, 71/21, 89/24.
Disceyuabli, *adv.* deceitfully, 57/7.
Disceyuen, *vb. t.* 3 *pl. pres.* deceive, 68/20, 110/28.
Disciplis, *sb. pl.* disciples, 42/16, 44/3, 54/32.
Disclandris, *sb. pl.* slanders, 43/20.
Discorde, *sb.* discord, 111/16, 124/17.
Discorde, *vb. i. inf.* disagree, 65/10.
Discording, *sb.* disagreement, 89/25.
Discounforte, *vb. i. inf.* discomfort, 136/10.
Discrescioun, *sb.* discretion, 59/20, 109/23, 110/1, 6; discrimination, 1/17, 48/1.
Discret, *a.* discreet, 45/27.
Discryue, *vb. t. inf.* discriminate between, 48/3 (*N.E.D.* 1st ex. 1663).
Diserite, *vb. t.* 3 *pl. pres.* disinherit, 113/21.
Diseruyng, *sb.* deserving, 119/18.

M

Glossary

Disese, *sb.* discomfort, 126/12.
Disgisears, *sb. pl.* those who dress ostentatiously or fantastically, 132/7.
Dispeire, dispeyre, *sb.* despair, 8/8, 122/23, 136/12.
Dispendid, *pp.* spent, used, 9/33, 54/18.
Dispise, *vb. t. inf.* despise, 93/34; dispisen, 3 *pl. pres.* 80/1, 3; dispisid, 3 *sing. p.* 79/29; *pp.* 51/16, 126/21; dispisiden, 3 *pl. p.* 78/18.
Dispisears, *sb. pl.* despisers, 127/4.
Dispising, *sb.* despising, 30/3.
Dispit(e), *sb.* outrage, 11/20; contempt, scorn, 111/7.
Dispitouse, *a.* cruel, pitiless, 66/3, 134/7.
Dispose, *vb. t. inf.* order, arrange, 94/22; disposid, *pp.* 65/31, 74/16; prepared, 47/11.
Dissolue, *vb. t. inf.* dissolve, 125/4.
Distriears, *sb. pl.* destroyers, 132/17.
Distrieþ, *see* Destrie.
Disturbliþ, *vb. t.* 3 *sing. pres.* disturbs, 69/17; disturblen, 3 *pl. pres.* 12/29.
Disynes, *sb.* folly, 52/19 (OE. *dysigness*, folly).
Diuerse, *a.* divers, 2/12, 25/1, &c.
Diuersen, *vb. i.* 3 *pl. pres.* differ, 22/29.
Diuidid, *pp.* divided, 2/12, 51/3; diuided, *a.* 3/29.
Diuinacioun, *sb.* divination, 111/6.
Diuine, *a.* divine, 93/15.
Diyng, *sb.* dying, 94/6.
Doars, *sb. pl.* doers, 85/15, 93/32.
Docke, *vb. t. inf.* cut short, 12/5.
Doctour, *sb.* doctor, 41/19, 52/1; doctours, *pl.* 59/8, 60/27.
Doctrine, *sb.* teaching, 5/25.
Doggis, *sb. pl.* dogs, 111/11.
Domesdai, *sb.* Day of Judgment, 66/16, 125/21.
Do(o)me, *sb.* judgement, 17/5, 23/22, 89/18, &c.; doomes, *pl.* judgements, 8/20.
Don, *vb. t. inf.* do, 54/8; doiþ, doþe, 3 *sing. pres.* 45/19, 119/16; *imp.* 114/16; don, done, *pl. pres.* 27/28, 43/10; *pp.* 31/8, 37/9; diden, 3 *pl. p.* 60/17; doing, *pr. p.* 35/9.
Doombe, *see* Doumb.
Door, dore, *sb.* door, 93/18, 107/3, 112/14; doris, *pl.* 125/6.

Dore, *vb. i. inf.* dare, 11/3, 20/24; darst, 2 *sing. pres.* darest, 97/9; dar, 3 *sing. pres.* 70/10, 100/13; dar, 3 *pl. pres.* 84/36; dore, doren, dorne, 3 *pl. pres.* 12/4, 40/32, 52/4; durne, 3 *pl. pres.* 11/12; dursten, 3 *pl. p.* 11/2.
D(o)uble, *adv.* twice the extent, 13/25; *a.* double, 27/13, 41/4.
Doulful, *a.* sorrowful, 42/20.
Doumb, doombe, *a.* dumb, 10/22, 73/17.
Doun, *adv.* down, 3/10, 11, &c.
Doungun, *sb.* dungeon, 69/16.
Doute, *sb.* doubt, 55/25, 67/23; douȝtis, *pl.* 2/12, 114/19.
Douȝtir, *sb.* daughter, 33/6, 115/29; douȝtris, douȝtren, *pl.* 31/19, 122/14, 126/5.
Dowers, *sb. pl.* endowments, 26/9.
Dowery, dowerie, *sb.* dowry, 26/15, 26/22.
Dowid, *pp.* endowed, 9/26, 26/9, 22.
Dowues, *sb. pl.* doves, 92/21, 93/10.
Dragoun, *sb.* dragon, 19/19.
Drauȝt, *sb.* draught, 15/1.
Drawe, *vb. t.* or *i. inf.* draw, go, approach, 38/17, 45/23; draweþ, 3 *sing. pres.* 54/18; drawen, *pl. pres.* 43/8, 47/16; *pp.* 39/7, 74/14; drowen, 3 *pl. p.* 44/9.
Drede, *sb.* fear, 7/10, 8/30, &c.
Drede, *vb. t. inf.* dread, fear, 2/16, 82/13; *imp.* 81/6; drediþ, 3 *sing. pres.* 7/13, 17, 8/24; dreden, *pl. pres.* 33/13, &c.; dredde, 3 *sing. p.* 91/15; dred(d)en, 3 *pl. p.* 101/18, 113/37; dreding, dredyng, *pr. p.* 2/6, 10/20.
Dredeful, *a.* dreadful, 134/16.
Dredfulli, *adv.* dreadfully, 70/14.
Dreemes, *sb. pl.* dreams, 52/32.
Dremyngis, *sb. pl.* dreams, 55/27.
Drink, *sb.* drink, 45/18, 49/5; drynkis, *pl.* 45/19.
Drinkiþ, *vb. t.* 3 *sing. pres.* drinks, 50/5; drank, 3 *sing. p.* 60/17.
Drope, *sb.* drop, 21/9.
Droppid, *pp.* dropped, 109/26.
Drounklewnesse, *sb.* drunkenness, 30/20.
Droweneþ, *vb. t.* 3 *sing. pres.* drowns, 45/15, 16; drowenen, 3 *pl. pres.* 40/18; drowned, *pp.* immersed, overwhelmed, 6/1 (= L. *demergo*).
Drynes, *sb.* dryness, 63/21.
Dryue, *vb. t. inf.* drive, 52/31; driuen, 3 *pl. pres.* 46/9; dryuen,

Glossary 163

pp. 36/25; dryuen, 3 *pl. pres.* cause to fall, 130/2.
Duble, *a.* deceitful, 6/8.
Dublefoold, *adv.* twofold, 90/6.
Due, dwe, dewe, *a.* due, 21/31, 45/4, 53/21, 62/18.
Dullidar, *a. comp.* more foolish, 133/9.
Duriþ, *vb. i.* 3 *sing. pres.* lasts, endures, 21/5, 35/25; duren, 3 *pl. pres.* 41/27.
Dwellars, *sb. pl.* dwellers, 42/19.
Dwelle, *vb. i. inf.* dwell, 41/10, 57/23, 63/21; dwellen, 3 *pl. pres.* 98/27.
Dwelling, *a.* remaining (=L. *manentem*), 40/31.
Dwynen, *vb. i.* 3 *pl. pres.* wither, 45/12; dwyned, *pp.* languished, 96/25.
Dyn, *sb.* din, noise, 58/15.
Dynt, *sb.* blow, 65/36.
Dyuerse, diuerse, *a.* different, 35/37, 43/31, 45/19.
Dyuersli, *adv.* diversely, 37/26.

E

Ebbiþ, *vb. i.* 3 *sing. pres.* ebbs, 44/14.
Eddris, *see* Addre.
Edifie, *vb. t. inf.* edify, 55/5.
Edifiyng, *sb.* edification, 5/12.
Eeke, *vb. t. inf.* increase, 74/13, 20; eekid, *pp.* 74/16.
Eendles, endeles, *a.* endless, 60/33, 75/19, 112/20.
Eere, *sb.* ear, 36/5; eeris, *pl.* 36/9, 58/15, 60/26.
Eest, *sb.* east, 100/32.
Eete, *vb. t. inf.* eat, 49/17; eetiþ, 3 *sing. pres.* 50/5; eeten, 3 *pl. pres.* 46/2, 51/19; eet, 3 *sing. p.* 120/18; eeting, *pr. p.* 46/4.
Eft(e), *adv.* again, afterwards, 12/26, 40/18, &c.
Egle, *sb.* eagle, 24/22.
Eire, heire, *sb.* air, 20/25, 46/9.
Eire, *sb.* heir, 96/20; eiris, heirirs, *pl.* 60/30, 61/23, 92/12, 113/21.
Eiȝtiþ, *a.* eight, 111/23.
Elder(i)s, *sb. pl.* forefathers, 116/26, 121/12.
Ellis, *adv.* else, 11/1, &c.
Elliswhere, *adv.* elsewhere, 74/10.
Eloquence, eloquens, *sb.* eloquence, 5/12, 75/5.
Emparise, *sb.* empress, 27/9.
Enchauntours, *sb. pl.* enchanters, 132/20.

Encombrid, *pp.* encumbered, 95/12.
Encrese, *vb. t. inf.* increase, 118/3; encresing, *pr. p.* 57/24.
Endar, *sb.* ender, 133/19.
E(e)nde, *sb.* end, 42/28, 74/21; endis, *pl.* 37/33.
Endurid, *a.* hardened, 8/32.
Enemy, *sb.* enemy, 2/22; enemy(e)s, *pl.* 35/33, 42/28, 65/1.
Enemyte, *sb.* enmity, 70/7.
Enfectid, *pp.* infected, 106/6; enfecting, *pr. p.* 115/33.
Englische, *sb.* English, 100/3, 6.
Enhaunsid, *pp.* exalted, 129/6.
Enprisouneþ, *vb. t.* 3 *sing. pres.* imprisons, 126/14.
Enproprid, *a.* appropriated, belonging, 127/20.
Ensaumple, *sb.* example, 25/26, 41/15, 127/6.
Enspirid, *vb. t.* 3 *sing. p.* inspired, 5/17.
Entent, *sb.* intention, purpose, 11/7, 54/27, 28, 29.
Enterditiþ, *vb. t.* 3 *sing. pres.* interdicts, 17/26; entirdiȝtid, *pp.* forbidden, 97/9.
Enterdiȝting, *sb.* prohibition, 97/17.
Entirmetenen, *vb. t.* 3 *pl. pres.* meddle, 46/15.
Entridist, *vb. i.* 2 *sing. p.* didst enter, 73/16; entr(i)en, *pl. pres.* 7/26, 8/1; entrid, 3 *sing. p.* 60/18; *pp.* 40/17.
Envie, *sb.* envy, 44/21, 50/1.
Envious, *a.* envious, 60/4.
Epistile, *sb.* epistle, 39/19.
Eritage, *sb.* heritage, 95/22, 113/22, 118/6.
Erre, *vb. i. inf.* err, 85/22; errid, *pp.* 128/17, 135/11; erring, *pr. p.* 25/25.
Errours, *sb. pl.* errors, 125/30.
Erþe, *sb.* earth, 9/7, 20/26, &c.
Erþeli, *a.* earthly, 40/19.
Eschewe, *vb. t. inf.* eschew, 41/37.
Essees, *sb. pl.* Essenes, 39/5.
Esy, *a.* easy, 84/2; hesiliar, *adv. comp.* 125/23.
Euaungelist, *sb.* evangelist, 12/1.
Euene, *a.* even, 108/8; *adv.* exactly, 97/22.
Euenecristen, *sb.* fellow Christian, 23/7, 52/24.
Euer(e), *adv.* ever, 2/4, 7/3, &c.
Eueremore, *adv.* evermore, 3/30, 84/28.

M 2

Euerlasting, *a.* everlasting, 35/25, 55/26.
Evidence, *sb.* evidence, 50/7.
Examyned, *pp.* examined, 127/15.
Except, *pp.* excepted, 97/13.
Excesse, *sb.* excess, 45/18.
Exclude, *vb. t. inf.* exclude, 89/23, 117/24; excluden, 3 *pl. pres.* 117/25.
Excusaciouns, *sb. pl.* excuses, 112/16.
Excusid, *pp.* excused, 112/16; excusing, *pr. p.* 111/26.
Execucioun, *sb.* execution, 20/11.
Expositours, *sb. pl.* expositors, 133/17.
Expouned, *pp.* expounded, explained, 107/5.
Extorcioneris, *sb. pl.* extortioners, 131/14.
Extorcioun, *sb.* extortion, 70/9.
Extremytees, *sb. pl.* extremes, 43/16.

F

Face, *sb.* face, 47/18.
Fadir, *sb.* father, 4/5, 5/15, &c.; fadris, *gen. pl.* 43/4.
Faging, *a.* flattering, 58/18.
Faile, *vb. i. inf.* fail, 38/31; 3 *sing. subj.* 54/12; failiþ, 3 *sing. pres.* 49/16; failing, *pr. p.* 80/26; failiþ, *vb. t.* 3 *sing. pres.* lacks, comes short of, 29/4.
Faire, *a.* fair, beauteous, 2/2, 32/20, &c.
Faire, *adv.* fairly, well, 37/2, 3.
Fairenes, *sb.* fairness, beauty, 123/19.
Fal, *sb.* fall, 108/18, 130/3.
Falle, *vb. i. inf.* fall, 62/18; falliþ, 3 *sing. pres.* 44/14; falle(n), 3 *pl. pres.* 2/6, 46/11, 46/17, &c.; fel, 3 *sing. p.* 36/23, 130/3; fellen, 3 *pl. p.* 130/2.
Fallen, *pp.* befallen, 121/13.
Fals(e), *a.* false, 38/22, 57/1, 62/8.
Falsehed(e), falshede, falsheed, *sb.* falsehood, 6/9, 55/28, 65/28, &c.
Fals(e)li, *adv.* falsely, 57/7, 65/2.
Falsiþ, *vb. t.* 3 *sing. pres.* falsifies, 107/21.
Fantasies, *sb. pl.* fancies, 51/1.
Farises, *sb. pl.* Pharisees, 120/13.
Fast, *adv.* highly, 50/30; quickly, 86/19.
Fastars, *sb. pl.* fasters, 48/6, 14, 50/8, &c.

Fasten, *vb. i.* 3 *pl. pres.* fast, 48/37, 49/1, &c.
Fasting, *sb.* fasting, 49/6, 7, 21, &c.
Fattnes, *sb.* fatness, 83/1.
Fauȝt, *sb.* fault, 38/24.
Fauour, *sb.* favour, 57/14, 93/19.
Fauouren, *vb. t.* 3 *pl. pres.* approve, 117/30.
Feble, *a.* feeble, 86/16, 126/25.
Feding, *sb.* feeding, food, 46/7.
Feed, *vb. t. inf.* feed, 7/2; fediþ, 3 *sing. pres.* 109/12; feeden, 3 *pl. pres.* 54/14; feeding, *pr. p.* 56/1; fedde, *pp.* 54/23, 67/23.
Fe(e)lde, *sb.* field, 78/29, 116/29.
Feelde-asse, *sb.* wild-ass, 46/7.
Feel(e), *a.* many, 21/18, 44/15.
Feer, *sb.* fear, 136/10.
Fe(e)r, *adv.* far, 4/13, 40/29, 50/33, &c.
Feere, *sb.* companion, 60/7, 104/24.
Fe(e)rful, *a.* fearful, dreadful, 14/24; afraid, 8/20.
Feer(i)s, *a.* fierce, 8/19, 35/30, 106/13.
Feersenes, *sb.* fierceness, 99/24.
Feersli, *adv.* fiercely, 130/2.
Feestyng, *pr. p.* feasting, 56/1.
Feet, *see* Foot.
Feire, *sb.* fair, 60/31; feires, *pl.* 91/4.
Feiþ, *sb.* faith, 2/16, 5/7, &c.
Feiþful, *a.* faithful, 47/14, 60/27.
Feiþfulli, *adv.* faithfully, 52/20.
Felaschip, *sb.* fellowship, 74/32, 76/4, 131/3.
Fele, *vb. t. inf.* feel, 91/19.
Fellen, *see* Falle.
Felonye, *sb.* wickedness, crime, 83/3, 104/16; felonyes, *pl.* 105/11.
Felowis, *sb. pl.* fellows, companions, 98/29, 106/24.
Fende, *sb.* fiend, devil, 35/18, &c.; fendis, *gen. sing.* 1/22, 4/14.
Ferforþe, so ferforþe, *adv.* to such a degree, extent, 4/1, 14/14, 63/10.
Ferful, *see* Feerful.
Ferfulli, *adv.* fearfully, 70/21.
Fermen, *vb. t.* 3 *pres.* farm out, 120/22.
Fermours, *sb. pl.* farmers, 117/8, 25, 30.
Ferþir, *adv.* further, 122/11.
Feruent, *a.* fervent, 58/1, 99/10, 12.
Fewe, *a.* few, 59/7.
Feyned, *a.* false, 9/7, 14/8, &c.
Feyneþ, *vb. t.* 3 *sing. pres.* fashions,

Glossary 165

81/18; feynen, 3 *pl. pres.* feign, 46/17, 84/4.
Feynyng, *sb.* deceit, 54/12.
Fier, fire, *sb.* fire, 6/23, 47/27, 127/15, &c.
Figure, *sb.* image, 137/6; in figure, as a type, 37/32.
Fillid, *pp.* filled, 89/2.
Filþe, *sb.* filth, 45/6, 103/22.
Firmament, *sb.* firmament, 32/21, 24.
Firste, *a.* first, 60/2, &c.; *adv.* 36/19, &c.
Fische, *sb.* fish, 47/7, 9; fisches, *pl.* 44/8, 9, 46/2, &c.
Fischers, *sb. pl.* fishers, 44/9, 47/16.
Fiȝt, *vb. i. inf.* fight, 83/2; fiȝtiþ, 3 *sing. pres.* 35/29; fiȝten, 3 *pl. pres.* 45/11.
Fiȝting, *a.* fighting, 60/1; fiȝting chirche = church militant.
Fiȝtyng(e), *sb.* fighting, 70/6, 99/24.
Flatirars, *sb. pl.* flatterers, 111/9.
Flatiryng, *a.* flattering, 52/7.
Flee, *vb. t. inf.* escape, shun, avoid, 39/17, 43/6, 45/22; fled, *pp.* 7/6, 41/31; fleeþ, *vb. i.* 3 *sing. pres.* flees, 52/25, 78/28.
Fleische, *sb.* flesh, 9/3, 32/6, &c.
Fleischeli, *a.* fleshly, 39/28, 53/1, 55/31.
Fliȝe, *sb.* fly, 11/9; fliȝes, *pl.* 11/1, 10.
Fliȝe, *vb. i.* 3 *pl. subj.* fly, 126/11.
Flok, *sb.* flock, 97/6; flokis, *pl.* 119/3.
Flom, *sb.* river, 35/18.
Floodis, *sb. pl.* rivers, 24/19.
Florischiþ, *vb. i.* 3 *sing. pres.* flourishes, 126/20.
Flour, *sb.* flower, 128/26; flouris, *pl.* 62/21, 24.
Flowe, *vb. i. inf.* flow, 44/26; 3 *pl. subj.* 126/10; flowiþ, 3 *sing. pres.* 44/14.
Foli, *sb.* folly, 41/38.
Foli, *a.* foolish, 57/14.
Folkis, *sb. pl.* people, nations, 3/24, 47/22, &c.
Folowar, *sb.* follower, 69/4; folowars, *pl.* 42/28, 61/24, 84/25.
Folowe, *vb. t. inf.* follow, 48/32; folowyng, *pr. p.* 3/29, 50/8.
Foltid, *see* **Foultid.**
Fonned, *a.* foolish, 56/18, 124/31.
Food, *sb.* food, 59/25.
Foold, *sb.* fold, 106/4, 107/3.

Foole-hardili, *adv.* foolhardily, 125/24.
Fo(o)lis, *sb. pl.* fools, 36/22, 60/29, 83/8, &c.
Foot, *sb.* foot, 56/26, 73/18; feet, *pl.* 4/13, 87/23.
For, *conj.* because, 12/14, 27/23, &c.; so that, 36/14.
Forbeede, *vb. t. inf.* forbid, 12/4; for(e)bediþ, 3 *sing. pres.* 37/9, 41/19; forbeden, 3 *pl. pres.* 60/27; forbadde, 3 *sing. p.* 95/20; forbede, *imp.* 11/23; forboden, *pp.* 12/3, 97/11.
Foregoer, *sb.* leader, 97/19.
Forfendiþ, *vb. t.* 3 *sing. pres.* forbids, 98/30.
Forfet, *vb. i. inf.* sin, transgress, 91/24.
Forgid, *pp.* fashioned, 84/29; *a.* false, 124/30.
Forhe(e)d, *sb.* forehead, 13/5, 7, 14/19.
Foriuggid, *vb. t.* 3 *pl. p.* condemned, 43/12.
Forknowyng, *sb.* foreknowledge, 52/32.
Forme, *sb.* form, manner, 36/6, 40/6, &c.
Formed, *a.* formed, 52/21.
Former, *a.* former, 69/8, 97/25.
Fornicacioun, *sb.* fornication, 39/26.
Fornicarer, *sb.* fornicator, 103/21; fornicareris, *pl.* 131/19.
Forsake, *vb. t. inf.* forsake, 40/17; forsakiþ, 3 *sing. pres.* 38/13; forsake(n), *pl. pres.* 40/1, 52/9; forso(o)k, 3 *sing. p.* refused, 62/2, 95/27; forsoke, 3 *pl. p.* forsook, denied, 80/19, 85/2; forsake, 3 *sing. subj.* 43/21; forsakyng, *pr. p.* 97/31; forsaken, *pp.* 58/18.
Forseid(e), *pp.* aforesaid, 15/1, 48/13, 102/9.
Forsoþe, *adv.* truly, 5/14, 6/17, &c.
Forswerars, *sb. pl.* perjurers, 131/11.
Forswere, *vb. t. inf.* forswear, 100/7; forsweren, 3 *pl. pres.* 88/25.
Forswering, *sb.* forswearing, 88/25.
Forþe, *adv.* forth, 46/32, 50/24, &c.
Forþeren, *vb. t.* 3 *pl. pres.* further, 18/1.
Fortune, *sb.* fortune, 44/18.
Forȝete, *vb. t. inf.* forget, 78/3; forȝeten, *pp.* 79/7.
Forȝetil, *a.* forgetful, 8/21.
Forȝyuenes, *sb.* forgiveness, 50/12.

166   Glossary

For3uep, vb. t. 3 sing. pres. forgives, 34/20.
Foule, a. foul, 39/27, 41/2, &c.
Foulis, sb. pl. birds, 20/25.
Fo(u)ltid, a. foolish, 3/26, 13/4, 15/8, &c.
Foundir, sb. founder, 39/1.
Fourþe, a. fourth, 33/2.
Foxis, sb. pl. foxes, 111/11.
Fraude, sb. fraud, 57/11, 109/9.
Fraudilentli, adv. fraudulently, 57/7.
Frecheli, adv. freshly, 50/15.
Fre(e)dam, fredom, sb. freedom, 92/2, 114/23, 120/2.
Freel, a. frail, 90/13.
Freeli, adv. freely, 35/8, 54/30, 32.
Frende, sb. friend, 71/22, 124/22; frendis, pl. 5/2.
Frenschip, sb. friendship, 136/12.
Freris, sb. pl. friars, 11/4, 16/14, &c.
Fro, prep. from, 3/4, 30/14, &c.
Froost, sb. frost, 9/11.
Froward, a. froward, 64/5.
Frowardnes, sb. frowardness, 95/17.
Fruycioun, sb. enjoyment, pleasurable possession, 26/24.
Fruyt(e), sb. fruit, 44/27, 62/17; fruytis, pl. 32/25, 62/24.
Ful, a. full, complete, 33/7, 43/20; adv. very, fully, 5/5, 42/23; at fulle, at þe fulle, adv. fully, 57/16, 119/19.
Fulfille, vb. t. inf. fulfil, 56/14; 3 sing. subj. supply, 53/24; imp. perform, carry out, 35/7; fulfillid, pp. fulfilled, 38/29.
Fulli, adv. completely, perfectly, 34/24, 69/30.
Furid, a. furred, 124/31.
Furneise, sb. furnace, 18/30, 58/12.
Fylle, vb. t. inf. fill, 58/15; fillid, pp. 89/2.
Fynali, adv. finally, 9/1.
Fynde, vb. t. inf. find, 36/27, 43/22, &c.; finden, fynden, pl. pres. 50/23, 26, 60/29; founden, pp. 20/5, 63/11, 80/18.
Fynding, sb. finding, 39/11.
Fynger, sb. finger, 93/29; fynger(i)s, pl. 109/20, 26.
Fyue, a. five, 99/18.
Fyuers, sb. pl. fevers, 127/7.

G

Gaddir, vb. t. inf. gather, 47/21; gadriþ, 3 sing. pres. 30/17, 44/7; gedre, 2 pl. pres. 85/3.

Gadiryng, sb. collection of money, 55/24; gedering, gedring, gathering, 25/3, 39/29, 91/14.
Galatheis, sb. pl. Galatians, 79/24.
Gallous, gallows, sb. gallows, 108/13, 14.
Game, sb. joy, mirth, 136/6; games, pl. games, 119/4.
Garmentis, sb. pl. garments, 132/8.
Gedering, gedring, see Gadiryng.
Gendring, pr. p. engendering, 16/3.
Generacioun, sb. generation, 82/1, 118/14, 120/33.
General, a. general, universal, 51/7, 130/16.
Gessiden, vb. t. pl. p. supposed, conjectured, 135/8.
Gete, vb. t. inf. get, 49/20; getist, 3 sing. pres. 54/29; gooten, gotun, pp. 54/10, 107/13, 109/13; begotten, 32/9, 14.
Gigge-haltiris, sb. pl. 132/11; see note.
Gile, sb. guile, 64/12, 72/2.
Gilti, a. guilty, 67/21, 88/22, 113/1.
Giltid, pp. gilded, 40/22.
Giltid, vb. i. 3 sing. p. sinned, 78/32.
Giltles, a. guiltless, 113/7.
Girdil(e), sb. girdle, 65/19, 24.
Girdip, vb. t. 3 sing. pres. girds, 65/21.
Gladip, vb. t. 3 sing. pres. makes glad, 95/8.
Gladnes, sb. gladness, 129/2.
Glasse, sb. glass, 41/33.
Glistiren, vb. i. 3 pl. pres. glisten, 37/26.
Gloosars, glosears, sb. pl. flatterers, 52/7, 131/11.
Glorie, sb. glory, 54/20, 23, 64/2.
Glori(e)fie, vb. t. inf. glorify, 41/37, 55/18.
Glose, sb. gloss, 85/30.
Glosears, see Gloosars.
Glosing, a. flattering, 58/18.
Glotenye, glotenie, sb. gluttony, 6/29, 19/26, 45/16.
Glotun, sb. glutton, 124/3.
Gnasting, sb. gnashing, 47/28.
Gnawyng, pr. p. gnawing, 136/8.
Gneching, sb. gnashing, 73/20; ? var. of gnaching, cf. Prompt. Parv. 200/2, Gnastynge (K. gnachynge, fremitus).
Godhe(e)d, godhood, sb. godhead, divine nature, 33/22, 34/15, 110/3.
Godli, a. godly, divine, 85/18.
Gold, sb. gold, 37/26, 38/12.
Gon, goon, vb. i. 3 pl. pres. go,

Glossary

18/9, 43/13, &c.; goyng, *pr. p.* 55/9; goo, *pp.* gone, 9/31.
Good, *a.* good, 2/2.
Good, *sb.* good, 1/15, 48/29, &c.; property, wealth, 52/6, 54/10, 16; goodis, *pl.* goods, 44/18, 52/14; good things, 119/6.
Goostli, *a.* spiritual, 4/17, 10/17, &c.; *adv.* spiritually, 19/6, 58/1, &c.
Gospel, *sb.* gospel, 30/7, 34/1, &c.
Gospeleris, *sb. pl.* evangelists, 24/19 (error for gospels = L. *evangelia*).
Gotun, *see* **Gete.**
Gouerne, *vb. t. inf.* govern, 94/21; gouerned, *pp.* 33/2, 127/27.
Gouerneaunce, *sb.* governance, guidance, 50/13, 87/3, 114/24.
Grace, *sb.* grace, 2/4, 7/27, &c.; good fortune, 10/12, 44/18.
Graciouse, *a.* gracious, 36/4, 54/11, &c.
Graciouseli, *adv.* graciously, 51/11.
Graduat, *a.* graduate, 5/16.
Grasse, *sb.* grass, 44/26, 116/29.
Graue, *sb.* grave, 87/6, 116/1, 7; graues, *pl.* 43/4.
Grauel, *sb.* gravel, 128/14, 129/22.
Grauen, *a.* graven, 81/26.
Graunt, *vb. t. inf.* grant, 61/23, 63/7; *imp.* 60/37; graunten, 1 *pl. pres.* 32/17; grauntid, 3 *sing. p.* 35/16, 36/6; *pp.* 45/30; grauntiþ, *vb. i.* 3 *sing. pres.* agrees, 39/8.
Grece, *sb.* fat, 105/15.
Gredi, *a.* greedy, 39/29.
Greedili, *adv.* greedily, 45/20.
Greet(e), *a.* great, 2/5, 14/3, 37/9, &c.; gretter, *comp.* 79/10; greetest, *super.* 42/27, 79/13.
Greete, *vb. i. inf.* weep, mourn, 77/15.
Greetli, *adv.* greatly, 4/1.
Greetnes(se), *sb.* greatness, 71/1, 88/29.
Greue, *vb. t. inf.* grieve, 65/28; greueþ, 3 *sing. pres.* 94/14; greuen, 3 *pl. pres.* 44/23, 119/23.
Greuous, grevouse, *a.* grievous, 7/3, 44/23; greuousear, *comp.* 113/31.
Grippe, *sb.* grasping power, 120/7.
Grisely, *a.* grisly, grim, 45/9.
Gronars, *sb. pl.* groaners, 54/15.
Gronyng, *pr. p.* groaning, 118/5; groonyngis, *sb. pl.* groanings, 26/1.
Grooti, *a.* muddy, 117/31 (N.E.D. 1st ex. 1848).
Grootis, *sb. pl.* groats, 112/22.

Gropid, *pp.* felt, 136/9.
Grounde, *sb.* ground, basis, 44/2, 44/27, 46/11.
Grounde, *vb. t. inf.* base, 59/8; groundeþ, 3 *sing. pres.* founds, 109/15; grounde, 1 *pl. pres.* fix firmly, 65/11.
Growe, *vb. i. inf.* grow, 44/26; 3 *sing. subj.* 39/13; growiþ, 3 *sing. pres.* 35/12, 63/20, &c.; grewe, 3 *pl. p.* 39/6.
Grucchiþ, *vb. i.* 3 *sing. pres.* grumbles, grudges, 76/19; grucchiden, 3 *sing. p.* 11/28.
Grucchyng, *sb.* grumbling, 79/20.
Gynnes, *sb. pl.* engines, 21/3, 66/3.

H

Haasten, *vb. t.* 3 *pl. pres.* hasten, 60/29.
Haatars, *sb. pl.* haters, 132/16.
Ha(a)te, *sb.* hate, 43/21, 98/6.
Ha(a)ten, *vb. t.* 3 *pl. pres.* hate, 56/26, 66/28, 82/1; hatyng, *pr. p.* hating, 65/7; ha(a)tid, *pp.* hated, 65/8, 127/24.
Habit, *sb.* habit, 93/14; dress, clothing, 15/12.
Habundaunce, *sb.* abundance, 2/9, 10/14, 53/24.
Habunding, *pr. p.* abounding, 19/13.
Haburioune, *sb.* habergeon, coat of mail, 65/27 (F. *haubergeon*).
Half, *sb.* side, 31/11; half on half, half the total amount, 113/33.
Halidai, holidai, *sb.* day set apart for religious observance, 90/24, 26.
Halowe, *vb. t. inf.* hallow, consecrate, 36/18, 37/1; 3 *sing. pres.* 90/23; halowiþ, 3 *sing. pres.* 36/18, 20; halowen, 3 *pl. pres.* 111/5; halowyng, *pr. p.* 82/13; halowid, *pp.* 35/38, 38/1, 63/23.
Hand, hond, *sb.* hand, 3/4, 43/24; handis, hondis, *pl.* 33/18, 53/10, &c.
Handiwerk, *sb.* handwork, 41/25.
Handmayde, *sb.* handmaid, 90/27, 121/20.
Hang, hangen, *vb. t.* or *i. pl. pres.* hang, 43/8, 108/14, 18; hangid, 3 *sing. p.* 108/17; 3 *pl. p.* 43/13; hanging, *pr. p.* 65/37; hangid, *pp.* 108/12, 13.
Hanger, *see* **Angir.**
Happe, *sb.* chance, 92/12.
Happeli, happili, *adv.* perchance, 72/8, 125/23.

Hard(e), *a.* hard, difficult, 48/12, &c.; hardir, *comp.* 133/8.
Hardenes, *sb.* hardness, 66/4.
Hardid, *pp.* hardened, grown hard, 18/31.
Harm(e), *sb.* harm, 45/15, 104/14.
Harp(e), *sb.* harp, 59/5, 119/5.
Haruest, *sb.* ? for hanuest = handfest, marriage contract, 35/17; *see* note.
Hasti, *a.* hasty, 111/10.
Hasting, *pr. p.* drawing on, 134/32.
Hast(i)li, *adv.* hastily, 13/28, 115/9.
Hastite, *sb.* anger, 50/1 (OF. *hastiveté*).
Haue, *vb. aux.* 1 *sing. pres.* have, 4/4, &c.; haþ, 3 *sing. pres. passim*; have, han, haþ, *pl. pres.* 4/5, 13/25, 109/26, &c.; hadde, 3 *sing. p. passim*; *pp.* 61/20; hadden, 3 *pl. p.* 98/25; hauyng, *pr. p.* 33/22.
Hauen, *sb.* haven, 45/24.
Haunt, *vb. t. inf.* practise, frequent, 17/17; hauntiþ, 3 *sing. pres.* 78/6; haunten, *pl. pres.* 52/8, 114/14.
Hauntriþ, *vb. refl.* 3 *sing. pres.* = ? auntriþ, dares to go, 101/6; *see* note.
Hede, *sb.* heed, 2/26, 53/27, &c.
Heed, *sb.* head, 11/2, 19/19, &c.; heedis, *pl.* 132/10.
Heedlingis, *adv.* headlong, 17/9, 110/1.
Heekfar, *sb.* heifer, 119/1; cf. dial. heifker.
Heele, *sb.* health, 45/20, 49/20.
He(e)le, *vb. t. inf.* heal, 3/3, 15/10, 67/14; heeliþ, 3 *sing. pres.* 4/17, 21; heliden, 3 *pl. p.* 68/6; helid, *pp.* 4/20.
Heepen, *vb. t.* 3 *pl. pres.* heap, 93/29, 106/2.
Heer, *sb.* hair, 87/24.
He(e)re, *vb. t. inf.* hear, 14/21, 38/17, &c.; 3 *sing. subj.* 81/10; heeriþ, 3 *sing. pres.* 36/4; heeren, *pl. pres.* 5/28, 58/24, 28; hard, herde, *pp.* 27/4, 51/6; hard, 3 *sing. p.* 11/19.
Heerer, *sb.* hearer, 98/13, 110/19; heerars, *pl.* 93/31.
Heeryng, heering, *sb.* hearing, 81/10, 100/30.
Heest(e), *sb.* command, 81/23; heestis, *pl.* 1/23, 27/29, &c.
Heete, *sb.* heat, 29/6.
He(e)þen, *a.* heathen, 22/4, 92/13, 133/30.
Heire, *sb.*, *see* Eire.

Heiris, *sb. pl.*, *see* Eiris.
Helle, *sb.* hell, 3/30, 52/12.
Hellebroond, *sb.* brand of hell, 13/25; hellebrondis, *pl.* 135/7.
Helle-houndis, *sb. pl.* hounds of hell, 134/14.
Helme, *sb.* helmet, 66/1, 5.
Helpe, *sb.* help, 50/12, 111/20.
Helpe, *vb. t. inf.* help, 64/26, 74/21; *imp.* 5/2; helpen, 3 *pl. pres.* 34/21, 60/1; holpen, *pp.* 30/28.
Helples, *a.* unavailing, 55/27.
Helpe, *sb.* health, 119/6, 132/21; safety, salvation, 45/24, 66/1.
Hem, *pron.* them, *passim*.
Her, *pron.* their, *passim*.
Herbe, *sb.* herb, 4/20.
Herborowid, *pp.* sheltered, 30/21.
Here, *adv.* here, 1/1, &c.
Heresie, *sb.* heresy, 31/31.
Heretik(e), *sb.* heretic, 100/9, 101/9; heretikis, *pl.* 132/19.
Heritage, *sb.* heritage, 47/24, 103/23.
Herkneþ, *vb. i.* 3 *sing. pres.* listens, 18/22.
Herowdis, *sb.* Herod's, 43/14.
Hert(e), *sb.* heart, 4/16, 8/16, &c.; hertis, *pl.* 14/9, 34/18.
Hesiliar, *adv. comp.*, *see* Esy.
Heuene, *sb.* heaven, 3/5, 19, 5/29, &c.
Heuenli, *a.* heavenly, 5/18, 48/5, 57/15, &c.
Heuy, heui, *a.* heavy, sad, 8/29, 77/16.
Heuynes, *sb.* heaviness, sorrow, 77/16, 79/22.
Hide, *vb. t. inf.* hide, 52/10; hideþ, hidiþ, hiȝdeþ, 3 *sing. pres.* 30/16, 46/19, 78/28; hiden, 3 *pl. pres.* 107/15; bid, hidde, *pp.* 39/25, 95/17; hidde, *a.* secret, hidden, 38/19.
Hidir, *adv.* hither, 73/16.
Hidouse, *a.* hideous, 4/10, 17/17, &c.
Hillen, *vb. t.* 3 *pl. pres.* cover, 25/6.
Hilling, *sb.* covering, 129/3.
Himsilf, *pron.* himself, 2/2.
Hindir, *vb. t. inf.* hinder, 74/36; hyndriþ, 3 *sing. pres.* 10/16; hindren, 3 *pl. pres.* 11/16.
Hir, *pron.* her, 1/11, &c.
Hire, *sb.* hire, 105/3.
Hired, *a.* hired, 131/17.
Hirsilf, *pron.* herself, 35/31.
Hirte(n), *vb. t. inf.* hurt, 18/26, 126/4; hirtiþ, 3 *sing. pres.* 126/6;

Glossary 169

hirten, 3 *pl. pres.* 68/1; hirt(e), *pp.* 81/12, 126/21.
Hirting, *sb.* hurting, 133/28.
Hise, *pron.* his, 2/2, 3/15, &c.
Hiȝe, *a.* high, 7/9, 10/20, &c.; *adv.* 47/2; hiȝer, *comp.* 24/14; hiȝest, *super.* 20/18, 69/29.
Hiȝeli, *adv.* highly, 75/8.
Hiȝenes, *sb.* arrogance, 44/19,129/3.
Hiȝeþ, *vb. i.* 3 *sing. pres.* hastens, 134/23; hiȝen, 3 *pl. pres.* 86/19.
Hiȝnen, *sb. pl.* servants, followers, 19/32, 124/28.
Hiȝten, *vb. t.* 3 *pl. p.* promised, 105/28, 130/14.
Hoge, *a.* huge, 43/18.
Hogge, *sb.* hog, 117/32.
Hol, see Ho(o)l.
Holde, *vb. t. inf.* hold, contain, observe, 2/4, 36/24, &c.; 2 *sing. subj.* 7/20; holdiþ, 3 *sing. pres.* 35/32; holden, *pl. pres.* 43/9, 52/20; *pp.* 14/3, 15, 24.
Holidom, *sb.* halidom, 89/19.
Holsum, *a.* wholesome, 52/30, 125/26.
Honest, *a.* honest, 41/30.
Honeste, *sb.* honesty, 52/30, 62/25.
Honouren, *vb. t. pl. pres.* honour, 43/3; honourid, *pp.* 40/24.
Honourmentis, hournementis, *see* **Ournmentis.**
Honycombe, *sb.* honeycomb, 63/3.
Honycombis, *sb. pl.* ? some kind of head-dress, 132/11; *see note.*
Hoodis, *sb. pl.* hoods, 124/31.
Ho(o)li, *a.* whole, 68/1, 80/26, 125/29.
Ho(o)li, *a.* holy, 2/6, 31/18, &c.
Hoolid, *pp.* pierced, 8/29.
Hoolis, *sb. pl.* holes, 13/21, 19/23.
Hoolynes, *sb.* holiness, 52/23.
Ho(o)pe, *sb.* hope, 66/2, 5, 74/7.
Ho(o)rdam, *sb.* whoredom, 104/24, 36.
Hooris, *sb. pl.* whores, 41/39, 53/19.
Hoot, *a.* hot, 136/6.
Hope, *vb. t. inf.* expect, 24/25; *imp.* 80/23; hopid, *pp.* 5/24.
Horrels, *sb. pl.* adulterers, 106/13; var. of holour, assimilated to hore.
Hors, *sb. pl.* horses, 106/14.
Hosen, hosis, *sb. pl.* hose, 104/26, 132/7.
Hou, *adv.* how, 1/18.
Houeþ, *vb. t.* 3 *sing. pres.* behoves, 127/11.
Houeuer, *adv.* however, 103/23.

Houndis, *sb. pl.* hounds, 11/14, 118/12.
Hounger, hungir, *sb.* hunger, 13/29, 49/27, 101/3, 6.
Houngry, *a.* hungry, 100/12.
Hounting, *sb.* hunting, 46/6.
Hournementis, *see* **Ournmentis.**
Hous, *sb.* house, 7/20, 38/1, &c.; housis, *pl.* 41/9, 23, &c.
Housbond, *sb.* husband, 52/5, 120/18.
Housles, *a.* homeless, 30/21.
Hous-meyne, *sb.* retainers, 11/4.
Hyndring, *sb.* hindrance, 89/27.
Hyndriþ, *see* **Hindir.**

I

Iaies, *sb. pl.* jays, 56/21.
Ianglen, *vb. t.* 3 *pl. pres.* chatter, 56/21.
Iangling, *sb.* jangling, 51/2.
Iapars, *sb. pl.* jesters, 54/17.
Iape, *vb. t. inf.* trick, 37/7.
Iche, *a.* each, 1/13, 10/11, 22/30; *pron.* 48/4.
Idel, *a.* idle, 89/24.
Iewesse, *sb.* judgement, punishment, 136/2.
Ignoraunce, *sb.* ignorance, 122/13.
Impacience, *sb.* impatience, 127/6.
Impassibilite, *sb.* state of exemption from suffering, 26/22.
In, *prep.* in the person of, 1/22; on, 27/19, 35/25.
Incarnacioun, *sb.* incarnation, 35/12, 109/2, 122/29.
Incarnat, *a.* incarnate, 6/6.
Incestours, *sb. pl.* those guilty of incest, 131/19.
Indulgence, *sb.* indulgence, 76/11.
Infirmite, infirmyte, *sb.* infirmity, 52/33, 88/11, 13.
Innocent, *a.* innocent, 98/18.
Inpertinent, *a.* irrelevant, 133/5.
Irepentaunt, *sb.* non-repentance, 9/1, var. of irrepentance; cf. inreguler.
Instrument, *sb.* instrument, 124/30.
Intermyssioun, *sb.* omission, 56/18 (*N.E.D.* 1st ex. 1635).
Interrupcioun, *a.* interruption, 56/18.
Intollerable, *a.* intolerable, 136/10.
Inward, *sb.* secretness, inner nature, 69/30.
Iogullers, *sb. pl.* jesters, buffoons, 54/16.
Ioie, *sb.* joy, 1/21, &c.
Iolite, *sb.* revelry, 128/28.

Glossary

Iourney, *sb.* journey (= L. *iter*), 78/2.
Iourours, *sb. pl.* jurors, 113/4, 20, 132/30.
Ioye, *vb. i. inf.* rejoice, 77/15; *imp.* 76/25; ioyen, 3 *pl. pres.* 112/19, 119/4, 5; ioyed, 3 *pl. p.* 80/19; ioieyng, *pr. p.* 47/13.
Ioyne, *vb. t. inf.* enjoin, impose, 104/24.
Ioyneþ, *vb. t.* 3 *sing. pres.* joins, 125/18; ioynen, 2 *pl. pres.* 121/5; ioyne, 1 *pl. subj.* 80/17; ioynyng, *pr. p.* 101/5; ioyned, *pp.* 125/13.
Iudiciarij, *a.* judiciary, 76/1.
Iugge, *vb. t. inf.* judge. 27/20; iuggid, iugid, *pp.* 69/15, 113/13.
Iugge, *sb.* judge, 89/13; iug(g)is, *pl.* 100/4, 111/13.
Iug(g)ement, judgement, 10/10, 11/21, &c.
Iullars, *sb. pl.* ? deceivers, 113/8, 132/30; perh. variant of 'gyler', f. OF. *gileor*.
Iurie, *sb.* Jewry, 37/28.
Iust, *a.* just, 43/24, 99/11; iustar, *comp.* 127/5.
Iustifie, *vb. t. inf.* condemn to punishment, 34/4; iustifien, 2 *pl. pres.* 111/29.
Iustli, *adv.* justly, 36/10.
Iȝe, *sb.* eye, 27/3, 52/20, 54/26; iȝen, *pl.* eyes, 36/8.

K

Kast, *vb. t. inf.* cast, 73/9; castiþ, 3 *sing. pres.* 45/6; casten, 3 *pl. pres.* 47/26, 60/10; kest, 3 *sing. p.* 10/21, 119/1; kesten, 3 *pl. p.* 44/11; plotted, devised, 118/8.
Keie, *sb.* key, 3/9; keies, keyes, *pl.* 3/4, 75/23.
Kele, *vb. t. inf.* cool, 2/9.
Kepe, *vb. t. inf.* keep, preserve, observe, 2/18, 8/15, 48/15; kepiþ, 3 *sing. pres.* 65/22; kepen, 1 *pl. pres.* 43/22; kepten, 3 *pl. p.* 91/22; kept, *pp.* 47/14.
Kepers, *sb. pl.* keepers, 1/23.
Kirnel, *sb.* kernel, 78/26.
Kisse, *vb. t. inf.* kiss, 85/26.
Kitt, *vb. t.* 3 *sing. p.* cut, 66/10; kutting, *pr. p.* 12/13; kitt(e), *pp.* 88/12, 115/9.
Knees, *sb. pl.* knees, 96/9.
Knele, *vb. i. inf.* kneel, 85/25; kneelen, 3 *pl. pres.* 96/9.
Knittiþ, see **Knytt**.

Kniȝt, *sb.* knight, 24/22; knyȝtis, *pl.* 34/16, 43/12, 14.
Kniȝtting, *sb.* knitting, uniting, 32/2.
Knocking, *pr. p.* knocking, 50/11.
Knot(t), *sb.* knot, 74/9, 122/37.
Knowe, *vb. t. inf.* know, 1/17, 42/5; &c.; knowiþ, 3 *pl. pres.* 104/1; knowen, *pp.* 7/7, 41/15.
Knoweleche, *vb. t. inf.* acknowledge, 110/20.
Knowing, knowyng, *sb.* knowledge, 22/24, 26/25, 69/12.
Knytt, *vb. t. inf.* join, knit, 53/10; knittiþ, 3 *sing. pres.* 83/11; knytten, 3 *pl. pres.* 74/8; knitt, *pp.* 74/9.
Knyȝthod, *sb.* knighthood, 34/3, 14, 40/17.
Kunnen, *vb. aux.* 3 *pl. pres.* can, 45/17, 90/13; can, *v. t.* 3 *sing. pres.* knows, 13/5.
Kunnyng, *sb.* wisdom, 75/24.
Kutting, see **Kitt**.
Kyn, *sb.* kin, 131/20.
Kynde, *sb.* kind, nature, 35/15, 59/20, 121/30; alle þe kynde of, all kinds of, 44/8.
Kynde, *a.* natural, 118/6.
Kynd(e)li, *a.* natural, 9/26.
Kyndenes(s), *sb.* kindness, grace, 50/15; hence, love, 79/9, 10, 14.
Kyng, *sb.* king, 58/5; kyngis, *pl.* 69/28.
Kyngdom, *sb.* kingdom, 23/2.

L

Labur, *sb.* labour, 33/18.
Laburer(i)s, *sb. pl.* labourers, 33/11, 17, 48/6, 131/17.
Lackiþ, *vb. i.* 3 *sing. pres.* is lacking, 50/7.
Ladi, *sb.* lady, 29/1.
Laite, *sb.* laity, 20/18, 92/24.
Lake, *sb.* blame, 44/15 (M.Du. *lac*).
Lake, *sb.* pit (= L. *forea*), 69/8 (after Vulg. *lacus*).
Lame, *a.* lame, 78/7.
Lanterne, *sb.* lantern, 1/2, 4/11, &c.
Large, *vb. t. inf.* increase, enlarge, 27/23, 74/17; largen, 3 *pl. pres.* 52/12, 80/11; larging, *pr. p.* 45/26; largid, *pp.* 117/5.
Large, *a.* broad, 127/26, 128/5; large(a)r, *comp.* 51/21, 83/19.
Largeli, *adv.* generously, 54/17, 61/5.
Largenes, *sb.* generosity, 25/37.

Glossary

Last, *a.* last, 39/2.
Last(e), *vb. i. inf.* last, endure, 40/25, 62/2, 80/16.
Lastingli, *adv.* continually, 25/3, 35/10.
Late, *vb. t. inf.* let, 110/24; laten, 3 *pl. pres.* 105/2.
Laump, *sb.* lamp, 41/34, 110/5.
Lauȝyng, *pr. p.* laughing, 134/15.
Lawe, *sb.* law, 34/4, 45/11, &c.; lawis, *pl.* 2/24, &c.
Laweful, *a.* lawful, 101/27, 117/3.
Laweles, *a.* lawless, 124/33.
Lawiars, *sb. pl.* lawyers, 132/33.
Lawȝtir, *sb.* laughter, 136/5.
Laymen, *sb. pl.* laymen, 120/11.
Lecoherie, *sb.* lechery, 6/29, 45/8.
Leccherouse, *a.* lecherous, 60/9, 103/7.
Lecchours, *sb. pl.* adulterers, 105/1.
Leche, *sb.* physician, 8/15, 127/8; lechis, *pl.* 67/13.
Leed, *sb.* lead, 41/33.
Le(e)de, *vb. t. inf.* lead, 6/10, 18/24, 59/11; le(e)diþ, 3 *sing. pres.* 9/2, 60/9; leden, 3 *pl. p.* 119/5; lediþ, *imp.* 101/25; leeding, *pr. p.* 45/27; ledde, *pp.* 58/19, 113/14.
Le(e)der, *sb.* leader, 46/28, 69/4.
Leef, *a.* dear, 79/17 (OE. *leof*).
Leef, *sb.* leaf, 62/18.
Leeftenaunt, *sb.* lieutenant, 2/11; leeftenauntis, *pl.* 82/7.
Leeful, *a.* permissible, 90/6, var. leveful.
Leepre, *sb.* leprosy, 120/23.
Le(e)se, *vb. t. inf.* lose, destroy, 49/8, 97/12, &c.; leesiþ, 3 *sing. pres.* 45/15; leese(n), 3 *pl. pres.* 41/39, 54/13; losten, 3 *pl. p.* 120/19; loost, *pp.* 43/27, &c.
Leest, *a.* least, 21/20, 38/16, 64/10.
Leest, *conj.* lest, 43/21.
Leeue, leeve, *vb. t. inf.* leave, 41/11, 45/28, 53/20; 3 *pl. subj.* 88/3; le(e)uest, 2 *sing. pres.* 37/1, 48/33; le(e)ueþ, 3 *sing. pres.* 9/4, 65/20; leeft, lefte, *pp.* 57/4, 64/27, &c.
Left, lift, *a.* left, 108/19, 134/32.
Lefte, *pp.* liftid, 36/9.
Leggeharnes, *sb.* leg-armour, 65/30.
Leie, *vb. t. inf.* lay, bring forward, allege, 79/16, 88/2; 3 *sing. subj.* 37/28; leieþ, 3 *sing. pres.* 72/3; leie(n), leyn, *pl. pres.* 12/10, 96/11, 111/18; leide, 3 *sing. p.* 79/5, 118/5; leied, leide, *pp.* 82/3, 87/6.
Leie, *a.* fallow, 110/25.
Lendis, *sb. pl.* loins, 65/21.

Lenger, *adv. comp.* longer, 115/7.
Lerid, *a.* learned, 27/28.
Lerne, *vb. t. inf.* learn, teach, 35/18, 69/22; lernyng, *pr. p.* 93/32.
Lerned, *a.* learned, 7/12, 60/15.
Lernyng, *sb.* instruction, 7/8.
Les(s)e, *a.* less, 62/9, 74/34; *adv.* 37/5.
Lesing, lesyng, *sb.* lying, 14/5, 71/24, &c.
Lessid, *pp.* decreased, 96/25.
Lessouns, *sb. pl.* 35/5, 48/8, &c.
Lettir, *sb.* letter, 56/19; lettris, *pl.* 61/3, 113/3; lettirs, learning, 5/18.
Lettiþ, *vb. t.* 3 *sing. pres.* hinders, 115/27; lettid, *pp.* 11/24.
Lettrure, *sb.* learning, 69/9.
Leue, *sb.* leave, 62/1, 91/1.
Lewid, *a.* ignorant, 7/12, 18/4, &c.; lewidar, *comp.* 133/10.
Lickli, *adv.* likely, 100/10.
Lickned, *vb. t.* 3 *sing. p.* likened, 25/28; *pp.* 24/2, 12.
Lickness(se), *sb.* likeness, 9/29, 24/21; licknesses, *sb. pl.* 1/12, 22/12, &c.
Lie, *vb. i. inf.* lie, speak falsely, 51/16; lieþ, 3 *sing. pres.* 112/6; liȝed, 3 *pl. p.* 120/35.
Liee, *vb. i. inf.* lie, 117/31; lieþ, ligiþ, 3 *sing. pres.* 109/29, 115/33, 130/22; lien, liggen, *pl. pres.* 9/10, 70/4; liȝed, 3 *pl. p.* 120/35.
Lie(e)r, *sb.* liar, 98/9, 112/11; liears, *pl.* 112/8.
Liees, *sb. pl.* lies, 112/3.
Lift, *see* Left.
Lijf, *sb.* life, 4/22, 9/2, &c.
Lijflo(o)d, *sb.* livelihood, means of sustenance, 49/28, 120/4.
Li(j)k(e), *a.* like, 44/7, 13, 99/25; &c.; liker, *comp.* 124/14.
Lik, *vb. t. inf.* lick, 118/12.
Likerouse, *a.* pleasant, 14/9, 58/15, 120/7.
Likeþ, *vb. t.* 3 *sing. pres.* pleases, 46/4.
Likyngis, *see* Lyking.
Lioun, *sb.* lion, 24/21, 46/6; liouns, lyouns, *pl.* 101/19, 23, &c.
Lippis, *sb. pl.* lips, 50/30, 108/29, &c.
Lisensid, *pp.* licensed, 11/27.
Litil, *a.* little, 7/8, 8/6, &c.
Liuere, lyuerey, *sb.* livery, 28/9, 29/9.
Liȝt, *sb.* light, 1/2, 4/11, &c.
Liȝten, *vb. i.* 3 *pl. pres.* light, 66/5;

Liȝtneþ, 3 *sing. pres.* shines, 4/16; liȝtned, *pp.* 32/19.
Liȝtli, *adv.* easily, 22/7, 51/23, 78/5.
Logge, *sb.* lodge, dwelling-place, 45/9.
Loke, *vb. i. inf.* look, 45/7; looke, *imp.* 53/24, 55/17.
Lombe, *sb.* lamb, 15/3.
Lond, *sb.* land, 13/24, 15/9, &c.
Long, *a.* long, 51/20; longe, *adv.* 70/4.
Longabiding, *sb.* long suffering, 10/7, 25/36, 45/25.
Longiþ, *vb. i.* 3 *sing. pres.* belongs, 15/13, 39/29, 94/20; longen, 3 *pl. pres.* 36/12, 41/35, 47/11.
Longlyuyng, *a.* of long life, 94/2.
Loones, *sb. pl.* loans, 46/16.
Lo(o)re, *sb.* lore, teaching, doctrine, 5/18, 8/3, &c.
Loot, lott, *sb.* lot, 61/21, 135/10.
Lootles, *a.* without a part, free from, 129/1 (= L. *exsors*).
Looþe, *adv.* with difficulty, 74/12 (= L. *difficile*).
Looues, *sb. pl.* loaves, 105/14.
Lord, *sb.* lord, *passim*; lordis, *pl.* 83/19, 84/2.
Lordiþ, *vb. i.* 3 *sing. pres.* rules, 60/4; lorden, 3 *pl. pres.* 70/22, 97/8; lording, *pr. p.* 97/10.
Lordschip(e), *sb.* lordship, 7/15, 60/5, &c.
Lordschiping, *sb.* ruling, 99/24.
Lose, loosen, *vb. t. inf.* loose, 3/28, 19/25.
Losse, *sb.* loss, 2/6.
Loþles, *a.* innocent, 26/33 (OE. *lāplēas*).
Loue, *vb. t. inf.* love, 2/16; loueþ, louen, 3 *pl. pres.* 50/17, 106/25; louyng, *pr. p.* 65/7.
Loue, *sb.* love, 34/19, &c.
Louedaies, *sb. pl.* love-days, 48/10; *see* note.
Loue-gelous, *a.* jealous, 81/29.
Louer, *sb.* lover, 60/25; louears, *pl.* 35/34, 77/19.
Loute, *vb. t. inf.* bow to, 81/29, 85/16, 28.
Lowe, *a.* lowly, 70/24; low, 82/10; lowest, *super.* 33/19.
Loweli, *a.* lowly, 41/23.
Loweþ, *vb. i.* 3 *sing. pres.* descends, comes down, 84/34; lowid, *pp.* subdued, brought low, 115/8, 11.
Lowid, *adv.* loudly, aloud, 82/10.
Lowid, *see* Loweþ.

Lurken, *vb. i.* 3 *pl. pres.* lurk, hide, 38/20.
Luschborue, *sb.* a base coin made in imitation of a silver penny and imported from Luxemburg in the reign of Edward III, 69/19.
Lust, *sb.* lust, desire, 63/8; lustis, *pl.* 2/19, 39/28, &c.
Lusti, *a.* merry, cheerful, 58/28; lustful, 67/19, 103/7.
Lustily, *adv.* lustfully, 103/23.
Lyking, lykyng, *sb.* liking, 39/27; sensuality, 116/4; likyngis, *pl.* pleasures, 75/8.
Lyme, *sb.* lime, 36/11, 41/33.
Lymes, *sb. pl.* limbs, 61/6, 84/4, 135/18.
Lymitid, *pp.* limited, 38/18.
Lymȝerdes, *sb. pl.* snares, limed twigs, 132/13 (OE. *lim + gierd*).
Lynkis, *sb. pl.* links, 74/13.
Lyuars, *sb. pl.* livers, 34/4, 51/8.
Lyue, *vb. i. inf.* live, 33/18, 64/1; 2 *sing. subj.* 6/20; lyueþ, 3 *sing. pres.* 6/19, 48/26; lyuen, 3 *pl. pres.* 45/34; lyueden, 3 *pl. p.* 85/2.
Lyue, *sb.* on lyue, *adv.* alive, 133/34.
Lyuelood, *sb.* manner of life, 86/25.
Lyueli, *a.* living, 84/29, 89/27; *adv.* ardently, greatly, 47/8.
Lyuerey, *sb.* livery, 29/9.
Lyuyng, *sb.* life, living, 39/4, 48/27, 51/14.

M.

Maddid, *a.* mad, 63/9, 18.
Magnifien, *vb. t.* 3 *pl. pres.* magnify, 46/18, 120/10.
Maidens, *sb. gen. sing.* maiden's, 60/25; maidens, *pl.* 65/22.
Maieste, *sb.* majesty, 109/3.
Mailed, *pp.* mailed, 65/28.
Maist, *see* Mow.
Maistir, *sb.* master, 42/18, 62/5; maistris, *pl.* 84/23.
Maistirliears, *sb. pl.* 13/16 (= L. *magistri mendaces*, false teachers).
Make, *vb. t. inf.* make, give, 39/14; maken, 3 *pl. pres.* 90/9; mad(e), 3 *sing. p.* 5/17, 11/29, 90/30; mekid, 3 *pl. p.* 5/18; mad(e), *pp.* 7/14, 32/21, &c.
Malice, malise, *sb.* malice, 11/10, 43/5, 60/3.
Maliciouse, *a.* malicious, 127/24.
Man, *sb.* man, *passim*.
Maner(e), *sb.* form, fashion, custom,

19/22, 35/16, 52/9, &c.; maner(i)s, *pl.* 11/6, 32/18, 39/24.
Manglid, *a.* mangled, 97/24.
Manhed, manho(o)d, *sb.* manhood, 6/6, 34/8, 16, &c.
Mani, manye, *a.* many, *passim.*
Mankynde, *sb.* mankind, 7/12, 8/12, 46/32.
Manslauȝtir, *sb.* manslaughter, 88/24, 94/18.
Manslear, mansleer, *sb.* manslayer, 98/6, 112/9; mensleers, *pl.* 98/8.
Manyfold, *a.* manifold, 40/4.
Marbel, *a.* marble, 37/25.
Marchaundise, *sb.* merchandise, 60/32, 61/7.
Marchauntis, *sb. pl.* merchants, 14/8, 60/32, 132/26.
Mariage, *sb.* marriage, 35/24, 60/38, 130/19.
Maried, *pp.* married, 23/20, 25.
Maris, *sb. pl.* mares, 106/14.
Mark(e), *vb. t. inf.* mark, 48/12, 101/28; markiþ, 3 *sing. pres.* 52/1; marked, markid, *pp.* 41/36, 61/22.
Market, *sb.* market, 91/3, 104/26.
Marriþ, *vb. t.* 3 *sing. pres.* spoils, 81/21; marrid, *pp.* perplexed, 2/11, 22/30.
Martirdam, *sb.* martyrdom, 85/21.
Martris, *sb. pl.* martyrs, 25/22, 27/22, 80/11.
Mater, *sb.* matter, 55/29, 96/12, 102/2.
Material, *a.* material, 33/21, 35/35, &c.
Matrimonye, *sb.* matrimony, 59/29, 65/23.
Mawmentrie, *sb.* idolatry, 18/8.
Mawmetis, *sb. pl.* idols, 101/10 (OF. *mahumet,* idol, from Mahomet).
Mawmetrers, *sb. pl.* idolaters, 132/19.
Maynten, *vb. t. inf.* maintain, uphold, 12/27, 32/14, 34/4; maynten, mayntynen, 3 *pl. pres.* 14/22, 43/20, 53/17.
Maynteners, *sb. pl.* maintainers, 16/22.
Medcinable, *a.* medicinal, 132/23.
Mede, *sb.* reward, 16/20, 49/8, &c.; merit, worth, 26/21; medis, *pl.* rewards, 57/12.
Medeful, *a.* meritorious, 16/4, 37/7.
Medicyn, *sb.* medicine, 8/12, 49/19, 59/18.
Mediþ, *vb. t.* 3 *sing. pres.* rewards, 113/8.

Medlyng, *sb.* interference, 63/12.
Medowe, *sb.* meadow, 128/28.
Me(e)dfulli, *adv.* worthily, 31/24, 54/8.
Meenes, *sb. pl.* means, 41/30, 42/8.
Meke, *a.* meek, 19/4, 111/7.
Mekeli, *adv.* meekly, 35/19.
Mekenes(se), *sb.* meekness, 45/24, 97/6.
Meking, *sb.* humbling, 42/2.
Mele, *sb.* meal, 45/20.
Melodie, *sb.* melody, 57/16.
Melte, *vb. i. inf.* melt, 52/31.
Membris, *sb. pl.* members, 1/23, 11/17, &c.
Mende, *vb. t. inf.* mend, 43/24; mendid, *pp.* 43/19.
Mendiner(i)s, *sb. pl.* beggars, 16/21, 132/1; var. mendinant, OF. *mendinant.* Form not recorded elsewhere.
Mending, *sb.* amending, 30/29.
Mene, *vb. t. inf.* mean, 15/21, 17/22, &c.; meneþ, 3 *sing. pres.* 12/13, 52/24; meneþ, menen, 3 *pl. pres.* 38/19, 56/22; ment, 3 *sing. p.* 93/26.
Mene, *a.* intervening, 104/31.
Merci, mercy, *sb.* mercy, 2/3, 7/30, &c.
Merciful, *a.* merciful, 2/3, &c.
Mercy-asker, *sb.* mercy-asker (=L. *propitiatio*), 8/10.
Merit(e), *sb.* merit, 60/32, 79/23, 121/29.
Mervaile, *vb. i. inf.* marvel, 41/24; *v. t.* wonder at, 41/26.
Merveilouse, *a.* marvellous, 2/2.
Message, *sb.* message, 47/17.
Messe, *sb.* mass, 60/36, 104/30.
Mesure, *sb.* measure, 74/20, 108/7; moderation, 29/28, 45/28.
Mete, *sb.* food, meat, 7/1, 41/19, &c.; metis, *pl.* 45/19.
Meved, see **Moven.**
Meyne, *sb.* retinue, 18/31.
Mi, *pron.* my, *passim.*
Michars, *sb. pl.* petty thieves, 131/14; cf. *Lay Folks Catech.* 825, 'Who brekys þe seuynt comaundement, Mechers, Robbers and extorcioners'.
Miche, *a.* much, great, 9/6, 19/28, &c.; *adv.* much, 5/4, 10/17, &c.
Militaunt, *a.* militant, 35/26.
Minstralsie, *sb.* minstrelsy, 51/2.
Miraclis, *sb.* miracles, 84/34.
Miriest, see **Myry.**
Mirour, *sb.* mirror, 56/15.

Mirre, *sb.* myrrh, 109/26, 27.
Mirpe, *sb.* mirth, 26/32.
Mische(e)f, *sb.* mischief, evil, 42/26, 53/3, &c.
Miȝt, *adv.* mightily, 18/7 (*a.* miȝt = mighty, used as an adverb).
Miȝt, myȝt, *sb.* might, power, 22/15, 34/14, &c.
Miȝti, *a.* mighty, 4/21, 16/21, &c.; miȝtiar, *comp.* 46/30.
Modir, *sb.* mother, 94/2, 96/10, &c.
Modiratli, *adv.* moderately, 29/26.
Modirles, *a.* motherless, 106/26.
Monestip, *vb. t.* 3 *sing. pres.* admonishes, exhorts, 34/23; monesting, *pr. p.* 57/24.
Monep, *vb. t.* 3 *sing. pres.* laments, 68/2; *see* note.
Money(e), *sb.* money, 61/16, 62/1, &c.
Money-makears, *sb. pl.* moneymakers, 92/20.
Moo, *a.* more, 45/19, 50/17.
Moone, *sb.* moon, 32/18, 20.
Moone, *sb.* moan, 46/26.
Mo(o)rnyng, *sb.* mourning, 4/2, 39/16, 46/26.
Moost, *adv.* most, mostly, 6/15, 31/33, 63/7.
Moral, *a.* moral, 105/19.
More, *a. comp.* greater, 122/28.
Moreyn, *sb.* murrain, 100/13.
Morne, *sb.* morning, 60/25.
Morowe, *a.* morning, 64/19.
Mortars, *sb. pl.* morters, 37/29.
Morteisen, *vb. t.* 3 *pl. pres.* amortise, alienate in mortmain, 109/18.
Mortifie, *vb. t. imp.* mortify, 39/25; mortified, *pp.* 48/33, 34.
Moselles, *sb. pl.* morsels, 46/4; var. morselle (OF. *morsel*).
Mot, mut, *vb. i.* 3 *sing. pres.* must, 48/33, 63/17; mut, musten, *pl. pres.* 76/28, 82/5.
Motrars, *sb. pl.* mutterers, grumblers, 131/11.
Moun, *see* Mow.
Mounk, *sb.* monk, 40/7; mounkis, *pl.* 38/16, 39/6, &c.
Mount, *sb.* mount, 78/31.
Moup(e), *sb.* mouth, 3/1, 50/11, &c.
Moven, *vb. t.* 3 *pl. pres.* influence, 64/20; meved, mevid, *pp.* moved, 8/18, 100/31.
Mow, mowen, *vb. i. inf.* be able, 22/15; maist, 2 *sing. pres.* 87/24; mowen, moun, 3 *pl. pres.* 4/15, 11/3, 41/16, &c.

Muk, *sb.* muck; *fig.* money (contemptuous term), 95/13.
Multiplied, *pp.* multiplied, 51/10, 93/16.
Mumling, *pr. p.* mumbling, 50/29.
Murperen, *vb. t.* 3 *pl. pres.* murder, 102/10.
Musik, *sb.* music, 58/28.
Mut, *see* Mot.
Myddis, *sb.* midst, 91/13; in myddis, in the midst of, 121/6.
Mylde, *a.* mild, 46/8.
Myn, *pron.* my, 36/8.
Mynde, *sb.* mind, 49/26, 50/15, &c.
Myndeful, *a.* mindful, 56/5.
Mynstrals, *sb. pl.* minstrals, 54/16.
Mynysterie, *sb.* ministry, 35/8.
Mynystir, *sb.* minister, administrator, 97/19; mynystrars, minastrars, mynystris, *pl.* 48/9, 60/13, 75/31, &c.
Mynystren, *vb. t.* 3 *pl. pres.* administer, 60/14; mynystring, *pr. p.* 35/8.
Myracle, *sb.* miracle, 115/30, 116/2.
Myre, *sb.* mire, 117/32.
Myrili, *adv.* merrily, 58/28.
Myry, *a.* merry, 59/25, 112/19; miriest, *super.* 36/25.
Mys, *sb.* wrongdoing, 43/24, 113/36.
Mysbileue, *sb.* unbelief, 39/30, 76/15, 129/23.
Mysdispendid, *pp.* ill-spent, 9/33, 50/13.
Mysdoars, *sb. pl.* wrongdoers, 34/5.
Myselrie, *sb.* leprosy, 120/32 (OF. *mesel(l)erie*, f. *mesel*, leprous).
Mysgouernaunce, *sb.* misbehaviour, 136/21.
Mystrist, *vb. i. imp.* distrust, 136/31.
Myȝtili, *adv.* mightily, greatly, 70/24.

N

Naciouns, *sb. pl.* nations, 119/17.
Nakid, *a.* naked, bare, 38/13, 44/27.
Name, *vb. t. inf.* name, 7/7.
Name, *sb.* name, 3/19, 21, &c.
Namli, *adv.* especially, 86/24.
Nappe, *vb. i. inf.* nap, 53/9; nappen, 3 *pl. pres.* 53/14.
Napping, *sb.* napping, 53/13.
Naye, *inter.* nay, 47/8, 70/10.
Ne, *conj.* nor, 14/18.
Necessarijs, *sb. pl.* necessaries, 36/12.
Neoligence, *sb.* negligence, 40/6.

Glossary

Necligent, a. negligent, 40/20, 52/19.
Nede, sb. need, necessity, 38/16, 42/7, &c.; nedis, pl. 40/19, 51/3.
Nede, nedis, adv. of necessity, 43/18, 48/33.
Neden, vb. t. 3 pl. pres. need, 54/16.
Nedful, a. necessary, 5/11.
Nedi, a. needy, 9/9, 38/13, &c.
Nediþ, vb. i. 3 sing. pres. is in need, 38/12.
Nedles, a. having no want, 16/21.
Neische, a. tender, yielding, 52/1 (OE. hnesce).
Neiȝ, vb. i. inf. draw near, 74/22; neiȝe, imp. 8/32; neiȝed, 3 pl. p. 42/16.
Neiȝbo(u)r, neiȝbore, sb. neighbour, 2/13, 5/12, 41/14, &c.; neibours, gen. sing. 99/9.
Nett, sb. net, 44/7, 13, &c.; nettis, pl. 52/13.
Neþ(e)les, adv. nevertheless, 37/32, 48/12, &c.
Neuere, adv. never, passim.
Newe, a. new, 38/15, 52/21, 59/7.
Nile = ne wile, 12/3, 23/1, &c. (= L. nolite).
Noiouse, a. harmful, 44/17.
Noise, noyse, sb. noise, 50/29, 58/8.
Noiyng, sb. injuring, 99/23.
Noo(n), a. no, 7/15, 50/16.
No(o)n(e), pron. no-one, none, 3/5, 44/22, 59/7.
Noote, vb. i. inf. be noted, 115/6.
Nootis, sb. pl. notes, 58/13.
Norische, vb. t. inf. nourish, 7/2; norischeþ, 3 sing. pres. 59/24; norischen, nurischen, 3 pl. pres. 19/32, 115/32; norischid, pp. 109/11.
Norþe, sb. north, 100/31.
Notarie, sb. notary, 124/29.
Noþir ... ne, neither ... nor, 80/4, 87/1.
Noumbre, sb. number, 3/29, 14/20, &c.
No(u)ȝt, sb. nothing, 8/18, 55/28, 56/23.
Novise, sb. novice, proselyte, 13/24.
Noye, sb. harm, 52/26.
Noyse, see Noise.
Nutt, sb. nut, 78/25.
Nyȝ, adv. nigh, closely, 46/9, 85/19, 90/9.
Nyȝt, sb. night, 24/30, 53/18, &c.
Nyȝt-þeef, sb. thief by night, 107/4; niȝt-þeues, pl. 93/19 (cf. day-þeef).

O

Obedience, sb. obedience, 82/6, 8.
Obeied, pp. obeyed, 82/23.
Observauncis, sb. pl. observances, 105/17.
Obstinacioun, sb. obstinacy, 8/16, 66/3.
Obstinat, a. obstinate, 34/17, 89/5.
Occasiouns, sb. pl. occasions, 124/22.
Occupacioun, sb. occupation, 35/38, 40/5, &c.
Occupied, pp. occupied, 58/7.
Of, prep. from, 7/10, 19/29, &c.; by, 10/20, 12/14, 33/2; concerning, 1/15, 17, &c.; for, 15/21.
Of, adv. off; beriþ of, turns away, wards off, 66/2.
Office, sb. office, 34/19, 48/35, &c.
Officeris, sb. pl. officers, 53/13, 82/8, 14.
Officials, sb. pl. officials, 133/1.
Offre, vb. t. inf. offer, 83/1; imp. 84/35; offriden, 3 pl. p. 37/31; offrid, pp. 1/2, 59/23.
Offryng, sb. offering, 85/17; offryngis, pl. 82/23.
Often, adv. often, 59/9.
Okir-iulling, sb. ? defrauding by usury, 129/15, see Iullars (W. V. and 1388 usure).
Okureris, sb. pl. usurers, 132/30 (= Swed. ockrare, f. ON. okr).
On, prep. in, 60/24; on alwise, adv. in every respect, 41/14, 30.
Oolde, a. old, 9/11, 95/20.
Oones, adv. once, 95/23.
Oonhed, sb. unity, 2/19, 74/9.
Oonli, adv. only, solely, 1/11, 3/21, &c.
O(o)ny, a. any, 2/26, 9/33, &c.
Oostis, sb. pl. sacrifices, OF. oiste, f. L. hostia, 37/31; hosts, armies, OF. ost, f. L. hostem (hostis), 71/26, 99/14.
Ooþ, sb. oath, 88/27; ooþis, pl. 88/31.
Open, a. open, manifest, 32/13, 57/2, &c.
Open, opyn, vb. t. inf. open, reveal, 3/5, 34/9; opineþ, opyneþ, 3 sing. pres. 3/6, 9, 10; opened, 3 pl. p. 27/25.
Oppressioun, sb. oppression, 70/9.
Oppressours, sb. pl. oppressors, 131/14.
Oppressyng, sb. oppression, 113/31.
Opunli, opunly, adv. openly, manifestly, 11/25, 53/15, &c.

Opyniouns, *sb.* opinions, 2/13.
Or, *conj.* before, 45/15, 98/26; *prep.* 119/2.
Ordeyn(e), *vb. t. inf.* order, appoint, 94/21, 113/37; ordeyned, *pp.* 41/29, 50/22, 107/19.
Ordinal, *sb.* ordinal, 56/23; *see* note.
Ordinarijs, *sb. pl.* ordinaries, 88/29, 105/2.
Ordinaunce, *sb.* ordinance, 43/23, 63/18.
Ordir, ordre, *sb.* order, 9/35, 34/3, 56/20, &c.; ordination, 59/29.
Organ, *sb.* organ, 5/12, 119/5.
Oþir, *pron.* 3/5, 6, &c.
Ouercum, ouer(e)come, *vb. t. inf.* overcome, 46/31, 64/28, 104/20; ouercomen, *pp.* 53/3.
Ouere, *prep.* over, 54/15.
Ouere-hipping, *pr. p.* passing over, omitting, 56/19.
Ouereleden, *vb. t.* 3 *pl. pres.* rule, govern, 67/8; ouerladde, 3 *sing. p.* overwhelmed, 95/13; ouerledde, *pp.* 28/17.
Ouerlepiþ, *vb. t.* 3 *sing. pres.* springs upon, 19/5.
Ouerrenniþ, *vb. t.* 3 *sing. pres.* overpowers, crushes, 19/5.
Oueresett, *pp.* overcome, 51/2.
Our(e), *sb.* hour, 43/12, 13, 122/23.
Oure, *pron.* our, *passim.*
Ournmentis, honourmentis, hournementis, *sb. pl.* adornments, 1/13, 9/8, 35/35, 41/35.
Outaken, *pp.* excepted, 89/10; outake, *prep.* except, 21/19.
Outcry, *sb.* auction, 76/9 (*N.E.D.* 1st ex. 1600).
Oute, *adv.* out, 73/9.
Outecaste, *a.* outcast, 41/9.
Outrage, *sb.* excess, exaggeration, 18/17, 84/27; outtrage, excessive luxury, 41/32.
Outstraies, *sb. pl.* acts of straying from the right, 43/20 (*N.E.D.* 1st ex. 1643).
Outward, *adv.* outside, 43/1; outwarde, *a.* outward, 43/10.
Ouȝt, *sb.* aught, 19/33.
Owene, *a.* own, *passim.*
Owist, *vb. t.* 3 *sing. pres.* oughtest, 94/10; owiþ, 3 *sing. pres.* 96/19; owen, *pl. pres.* 41/24, 42/5, 82/12; owid, auȝt, 3 *sing. p.* 25/11, 109/10.
Oxe, *sb.* ox, 121/20.
Oyle, *sb.* oil, 110/6.
Oyntment, *sb.* ointment, 128/26.

P

Paast, *sb.* paste, 59/26.
Pacience, *sb.* patience, 45/25.
Paie, *vb. t. inf.* pay, 46/14, 61/5; *imp.* 104/33; paied, *pp.* 95/21, 104/37; contented, 44/32.
Palet, *sb.* armour, head-piece, 66/6 (OF. *palet*).
Palpable, *a.* palpable, 136/8.
Pannes, *sb. pl.* pans, 37/29.
Pappis, *sb.* breasts, 132/13.
Parable, *sb.* parable, 44/2, 12.
Paradise, *sb.* paradise, 36/24, 37/4, &c.
Pardon, *sb.* pardon, 60/37.
Parentis, *sb. pl.* parents, 84/22, 94/4.
Parischens, parischynes, *sb. pl.* parishioners, 41/29, 117/9.
Part(e), *sb.* part, lot, share, 44/29, 49/17, 80/18; side, 97/25.
Parte, *vb. t. inf.* separate, 76/15; parten, 3 *pl. pres.* 40/27, 51/12; parten, 3 *pl. pres.* share, 33/12; parten her hosis, 132/7; *see* note.
Partener(e), *sb.* partner, 75/12, 94/18.
Parteyneþ, perteyneþ, *vb. i.* 3 *sing. pres.* pertains, belongs, 12/17, 34/3.
Participacioun, *sb.* share, participation, 131/2.
Parti(e), *sb.* part, 91/5; parties, partijs, partise, *pl.* 13/32, 43/31, 62/3, &c.; in parti, in part, 85/5; partie, *adv.* partly, 22/3.
Pask, *sb.* passover, 59/24.
Passe, *vb. t. inf.* surpass, 102/1; passiþ, 3 *sing. pres.* 9/32, 81/17; passing, *pr. p.* 24/27; passiþ, 3 *sing. pres.* passes, 46/32, 50/20; passe, 1 *pl. subj.* 84/24; passid, *pp.* 87/6.
Passing, *sb.* passing away, 104/12.
Passing, *a.* surpassing, 32/10; passinge, *a:* transient, 30/3; passingli, *adv.* surpassingly, 13/34, 20/5, 41/32.
Passioun, *sb.* passion, 47/15, 59/17; passiouns, *pl.* sufferings, 26/6.
Payment, *sb.* payment, 46/17, 63/14.
Pees, *sb.* peace, 21/27, 43/22, &c.
Peesibly, *adv.* peaceably, 66/7.
Peesis, *sb. pl.* pieces of armour; at alle peesis, at all points, completely, 65/14.
Peesmakars, *sb. pl.* peacemakers, 65/13, 66/23.

Peirement, *sb.* damage, hurt, 9/30 (aphet. f. OF. *ampeirement*).
Penaunce, *sb.* penance, 3/24, 34/21, 59/29.
Peny, *sb.* penny, 69/19.
Peple, *sb.* people, 3/28, 34/9, &c.
Per, *prep.* by, 92/1.
Perdicioun, *sb.* perdition, 3/26.
Perel, peril, *sb.* peril, 47/13, 108/19; perelles, perellis, *sb. pl.* 45/22, 94/10.
Perfeccioun, *sb.* perfection, 88/13.
Perfite, perfijt, perfiȝte, *a.* perfect, 6/9, 46/31, 58/18, &c.
Perfiȝtli, *adv.* perfectly, 58/3, 65/32; perfiȝtlier, *comp.* 32/5.
Performe, *vb. t. inf.* perform, 102/21.
Perilouse, *a.* perilous, 44/16.
Perische, *vb. i. inf.* perish, 91/13, 112/4.
Persecucioun, *sb.* persecution, 77/1, &c.
Persoone, *sb.* person, 34/10, 75/12; persoones, *gen. sing.* 115/29; persones, *pl.* 56/2.
Persun, *sb.* parson, 117/31.
Pestelence, *sb.* pestilence, 13/30.
Peticioun, *sb.* petition, 1/5, 5/1.
Peyne, *vb. t. inf.* pain, afflict, 49/7, 88/5, 101/12.
Peyne, *sb.* pain, 2/7, 4/9, &c.; peynes, *pl.* 24/1, 100/9.
Peynful, *a.* painful, difficult, 40/18, 128/6.
Peyntid, *a.* painted, 52/10, 85/19, &c.
Peynting, *sb.* painting, 41/35.
Peyntour, *sb.* painter, 84/28.
Peyren, *vb. i.* 3 *pl. pres.* decay, deteriorate, 40/5 (aphetic).
Philosophur, *sb.* philosopher, 7/5, 83/17; philosophurs, *pl.* 13/26.
Pilage, *sb.* pillage, 41/1.
Pilars, *sb. pl.* pillars, 37/25.
Pilgrimage, *sb.* pilgrimage, 40/29, 41/8, &c.
Pilgrimes, *sb. pl.* pilgrims, 40/29, 85/30.
Pille, *vb. t. inf.* pillage, rob, 113/30.
Pinchin, *vb. t.* 3 *pl. pres.* compress, 132/6.
Pinfold, *sb.* pinfold, 101/12.
Pirwittis, *sb. pl.* ? storms, tempests, 44/23 (cf. dial. *pirr, pirry*, a sudden storm of wind).
Pistil, *sb.* epistle, 57/17.
Pite, *sb.* pity, 52/5, 75/6.
Pitousli, *adv.* piteously, 52/6.

Pitt, *sb.* pit, 84/20.
Place, *sb.* place, 36/10, 53/19; placis, *pl.* 38/19, 59/7.
Plaistir, *sb.* plaster, 4/20, 41/33.
Platis, *sb. pl.* pieces of silver money, 62/4 (OF. *plate*, thin plate of metal).
Plaunt, *sb.* plant, 39/9.
Plauntid, *vb. t.* 3 *sing. p.* planted, 39/2; *pp.* 39/10, 92/13.
Pleetars, *sb. pl.* advocates, 132/33.
Plege, *sb.* pledge, 79/5.
Plener, *a.* plenary, 76/11 (OF. *plenier*).
Plente, *sb.* plenty, 2/9, 8/12, &c.
Plenteuous, *a.* plenteous, 5/17, 32/21, 25.
Plentiuousli, *adv.* plenteously, 57/23.
Plesaunce, *sb.* pleasure, 6/11.
Plese, *vb. t. inf.* please, 34/22, 42/18, 58/14; plesiþ, 3 *sing. pres.* 47/12; plesen, 3 *pl. pres.* 57/16; plesid, *pp.* 7/29, 115/7.
Plesing, *a.* pleasant, giving pleasure, 27/11.
Pleyes, *sb. pl.* sports, games, 119/4.
Pleyn, *a.* plain, 97/8.
Pleyneþ, *vb. t.* 3 *sing. pres.* complains, 97/14.
Pleynli, pleynly, *adv.* plainly, 35/29, 47/8.
Pleynt, *sb.* complaint, 11/29.
Poise, *sb.* poesy, 97/23; poyses, *pl.* 55/27.
Poluten, *vb. t.* 3 *pl. pres.* pollute, 105/25; pollutid, *pp.* 109/11.
Polutid, *a.* polluted, 60/21.
Poppen, *vb. t.* 3 *pl. pres.* paint the face with cosmetics, 132/10.
P(o)ore, *a.* poor, 6/6, 38/1, 54/5, &c.
Poreli, *adv.* humbly, 54/7.
Possessioneris, *sb. pl.* possessioners, 16/19, 132/1.
Possessioun, *sb.* possession, 43/16.
Poudir, *sb.* powder, 38/26.
Pouert(e), *sb.* poverty, 38/2, 41/32, 53/12.
Pound, *sb.* pound, 104/28.
Power(e), *sb.* power, 4/23, 33/22, &c.
Poynt, *sb.* instant, moment, 119/7; in poynt to, on the point of, 86/20.
Poyntel, *sb.* writing instrument (=L. *stilus*), 57/2.
Poysen, *vb. t. inf.* poison, 76/14.
Poyses, *see* Poise.

178 Glossary

Pray, *sb.* prey, 46/6.
Preche, *vb. t. inf.* preach, 12/12, 16; prechen, 3 *pl. pres.* 55/4, 20; prechiden, 3 *pl. p.* 24/22; precheing, *pr. p.* 35/7; prechid, *pp.* 3/24, 36/2.
Preching, *sb.* preaching, 55/11, 59/7, 14.
Prechour, *sb.* preacher, 19/21; prechours, prechars, *pl.* 5/22, 48/8, 54/30, &c.
Precious(e), *a.* precious, 4/23, 37/27, 50/6, &c.
Preesen, *see* Preise.
Preiars, preiers, *sb. pl.* men who pray, 48/7, 50/10, 29.
Preie, *vb. i. inf.* pray, 47/9; priien, 3 *pl. pres.* 50/10; preiyng, *pr. p.* 35/4; preid, *pp.* 36/10.
Preier(e), preiour, *sb.* prayer, 5/2, 4, 6/10, &c.; preiars, preiers, preiours, *pl.* 8/18, 36/5, 51/10, &c.
Preisars, *sb.* praisers, 93/30.
Preise, *sb.* praise, 44/15.
Preise, preesen, *vb. t.* 3 *pl. pres.* praise, 50/30, 134/8; preisid, *pp.* 10/13 (OF. *preisier*).
Preising, preisyng, *sb.* praising, praise, 33/23, 49/4, 65/5, &c.
Prelat, *sb.* prelate, 84/11; prelatis, *pl.* 84/23, 105/20.
Presence, *sb.* presence, 120/35, 121/29.
Present, *a.* present, 50/14, 86/1.
Prest, *sb.* priest, 9/7, 12/18; pre(e)stis, *pl.* 9/9, 12/22, &c.
Prestho(o)d, *sb.* priesthood, 34/15, 61/1, 75/24.
Presumpcioun, *sb.* presumption, 7/11, 15, 31.
Presumptuouse, *a.* presumptuous, 67/28.
Pretendist, *vb. t.* 2 *sing. pres.* pretendest, 3/27.
Pride, *sb.* pride, 41/18, 49/28, &c.
Pri(j)s, *sb.* value, price, 29/9, 30/25, 62/9, &c.; money, 93/24.
Princis, *sb. pl.* princes, 97/15, 106/24.
Pris, *see* Prijs.
Prisoun, *sb.* prison, 3/15, 81/8.
Prisoun, *vb. t. inf.* imprison, 76/20; 3 *pl. pres.* 161/15.
Prisounyng, *sb.* imprisoning, 98/1.
Priue, *vb. t. inf.* deprive, 12/6; priueþ, 3 *sing. pres.* 17/27; priuen, pryuen, 3 *pl. pres.* 55/25, 126/12.
Priue, *adv.* privately, 100/3.
Priueli, *adv.* secretly, 72/3.

Priuetees, *sb. pl.* secrets, 65/4.
Procatour, *sb.* procurator, 117/8; procatours, *pl.* 133/4.
Processe, *sb.* narrative, story, 91/21.
Procur, *vb. t. inf.* procure, 124/26.
Professioun, *sb.* profession, 131/21.
Profit(e), *sb.* profit, 36/13, 56/13, 62/10.
Profi(ȝ)te, *vb. t. inf.* profit, 41/16, 74/33; profiteþ, profitiþ, 3 *sing. pres.* 49/27, 52/24.
Profre, *vb. t. inf.* offer, 67/28; profrid, 3 *sing. p.* 61/16; *pp.* 96/20.
Prolog, *sb.* prologue, 1/4, 2/1, 62/25.
Promissioun, *sb.* promise, 25/27 (= L. *promissum*).
Proof, *sb.* proof, 71/7.
Prophecie, *sb.* prophecy, 102/17.
Prophecied, *vb. i.* 3 *sing. p.* prophesied, 133/32.
Prophet(e), *sb.* prophet, 7/27, 46/20, 24; prophetis, *pl.* 43/3.
Proprid, *pp.* appropriated, 1/11, 22/11.
Propurte, *sb.* property, characteristic, 126/19; propurte(e)s, *pl.* 1/25, 28/15.
Proud(e), *a.* proud, 6/27, 54/5.
Proue, *vb. t. inf.* prove, 71/27; proueþ, 3 *sing. pres.* approves, 93/21; proued, *pp.* 37/30.
Prouyng, *sb.* proving, 80/24.
Prynte, *vb. t. inf.* fix in the mind, 95/22.
Pryue, *a.* secret, 46/19.
Psalmis, *sb. pl.* psalms, 57/24.
Puff, *sb.* puff, 58/14.
Pullid, *vb. t.* 3 *sing. p.* pulled, 39/4.
Punysche, *vb. t. inf.* punish, 34/5, 119/19; punyscheþ, 34/17; punyschid, *pp.* 107/14.
Punysching, *sb.* punishing, punishment, 78/23, 90/12.
Puplische, *vb. t. inf.* publish, 10/24.
Purchase, *sb.* taking by violence, 116/21.
Purchase, *vb. t. inf.* gain, acquire, 120/3; purchasiþ, 3 *sing. pres.* 44/31; purchas(s)en, 3 *pl. pres.* 19/23, 45/1; purchasid, *pp.* 117/8.
Pure, *a.* pure, 59/26.
Purgacioun, *sb.* purgation, 88/30.
Purgatori, purgatory, *sb.* purgatory, 35/26, 31.
Purge, *vb. t. inf.* purge, cleanse, 80/

12; purgeþ, 3 *sing. pres.* purifies, 4/16.
Purpose, *sb.* purpose, 2/6, 119/15.
Purs(e), *sb.* purse, 49/6, 104/33, 106/2.
Pursuars, purswars, *sb. pl.* pursuers, 66/28, 111/10.
Pursut(e), purswet, *sb.* pursuit, 24/11, 43/15, 97/26.
Purswe, *vb. t. inf.* pursue, 80/30; *imp.* 63/2; pursueþ, 3 *sing. pres.* 1/22; purswen, 3 *pl. pres.* 89/3; purswyng, *pr. p.* 97/31.
Purswyng, *sb.* pursuing, 43/4.
Purueiyng, *pr. p.* providing, 8/22.
Purviaunce, *sb.* foresight, 26/34.
Putt, *vb. t. inf.* put, 74/19; putt, putten, 3 *pl. pres.* 46/11, &c.; puttidist, 2 *sing. p.* 4/22; putten abak, reject, repel, 16/1.

Q

Quake, *vb. i.* 1 *sing. pres.* tremble, quake, 16/6.
Quaking, quakyng, *sb.* quaking, trembling, 47/28, 136/11.
Quart, *sb.* health, 65/38 (f. ON. *kverr, kwert,* quiet, still; Icel. *kyrr*).
Quenche, *vb. t. inf.* be extinguished, 6/24; quench, 65/34; quenchen, 3 *pl. pres.* 117/11; quenchid, *pp.* 6/23.
Quene, *sb.* queen, 118/7; quenes, *gen. sing.* 102/13.
Quere, *sb.* choir, 27/6.
Quest, *sb.* inquest, official inquiry, 112/23.
Questioners, *sb. pl.* questioners, 93/28.
Questioun, *sb.* question, 88/22; questiouns, *pl.* 56/24.
Questmongers, *sb. pl.* those who make a business of conducting judicial inquiries or inquests, 113/9, 132/30.
Quick(e)nyng, *sb.* quickening, 4/23, 63/24.
Quickneþ, *vb. i.* 3 *sing. pres.* quickens, 33/1; quickned, *pp.* 32/27.
Quik, *a.* quick, active, 47/1.
Quite, *vb. t. inf.* release, free, 3/15.
Quiver, *a.* nimble, 47/1 (OE. *cwifer*).

R

Raggis, *sb. pl.* rags, 2/24.
Rames, *sb. pl.* rams, 83/2.

Ransake, *vb. t. inf.* examine thoroughly, investigate, 67/26.
Raþer, rapir, *adv.* rather, 55/1, &c.; raþest, *super.* especially, 52/7.
Raunsun, *sb.* ransom, 78/31.
Raueisching, *a.* ravishing, 38/21, 111/13.
Raveyn, *sb.* robbery, 43/2.
Reble, *a.* rebel, rebellious, 48/15, 131/17.
Reche, reck, *vb. t.* ɟ *l. pres.* care, 50/30, 113/21.
Recheles, *a.* reckless, careless, 50/8, 19, 131/17.
Reck, *see* **Reche.**
Reckenyng, *sb.* reckoning, 47/23, 83/15.
Reclem, *vb. t. inf.* reclaim, win back, 120/6.
Recounseile, *vb. t. inf.* reconcile, 67/13.
Redempcioun, *sb.* redemption, 62/7, 78/33.
Redi, *a.* ready, 5/12, 43/15, 60/31.
Redili, *adv.* readily, 93/17.
Reding, *sb.* reading, 56/5, 100/6.
Re(e)dars, *sb. pl.* readers, 48/8, 56/4, 21.
Re(e)de, *vb. t. inf.* read, 9/9, 100/3, 102/16; redist, 2 *sing. pres.* 56/11; rediþ, 3 *sing. pres.* 18/23; re(e)den, *pl. pres.* 28/26, 56/4, 17; radde, 3 *sing. p.* 102/14; radden, 3 *pl. p.* 133/34; re(e)de, *imp.* 21/12, 56/10; rad(d)e, *pp.* 11/26, 36/2, 56/12.
Re(e)st, *sb.* rest, 35/27, 64/20, 73/11.
Refreyne, *vb. t. inf.* restrain, 18/28; refreyneþ, 3 *sing. pres.* 115/16, 121/24; refreynen, 3 *pl. pres.* 41/23.
Refute, *sb.* refuge, 20/4.
Regne, *vb. i. inf.* reign, 65/1, 95/26; regneþ, 3 *sing. pres.* 7/11, 15/23; regned, *pp.* 97/14.
Rehersiþ, *vb. t.* 3 *sing. pres.* rehearses, repeats, 60/22, 64/14; rehersid, 1 *pl. p.* 68/7; *pp.* 41/20, 65/11.
Reioyced, *vb. t.* 3 *pl. p.* enjoyed as possessor, had full possession and use of, 118/9.
Relaps, *a.* relapsed, 88/4.
Relese, *vb. t. inf.* remit, 104/34.
Releuen, *vb. t.* 3 *pl. pres.* relieve, 9/9, 53/21, 75/6.
Religioun, *sb.* religion, 51/24, 52/10; *coll.* religious orders, 93/13.

Remedi(e), *sb.* remedy, 123/11, 125/26.
Remeve, *vb. i. inf.* remove, 121/27.
Remewen, *vb. t. inf.* change, alter, 27/6.
Remyssioun, *sb.* remission, 3/21, 25, 37/31.
Renagatis, *sb. pl.* renegades, 79/21.
Rendels, *sb. pl.* streams, runnels, 50/26, 62/17 (=Sc. *rindell*).
Rendid, *pp.* torn, 65/8.
Renneþ, *vb. i.* 3 *sing. pres.* runs, 50/24, 124/25.
Rent, *sb.* rent, 104/37.
Rent, *pp.* rent, torn, 39/10.
Reparailen, *vb. t. inf.* repair, 40/5.
Repentaunce, *sb.* repentance, 108/16.
Repid, *pp.* reaped, 29/7.
Replete, *a.* replete, full, 43/2.
Representiþ, *vb. t.* 3 *sing. pres.* represents, 34/10; representen, 3 *pl. pres.* 33/12; representing, *pr. p.* 34/14, 15.
Repreueþ, reproueþ, *vb. t.* 3 *sing. pres.* reproves, 55/21, 119/10; reproue, 1 *pl. pres.* 76/19; repreued, 3 *sing. p.* 113/16.
Rerars, *sb. pl.* raisers, 132/20.
Rere, *vb. t. inf.* raise, 63/25; *imp.* 114/4; reriþ, 3 *sing. pres.* 3/11, 109/13; reren, 3 *pl. pres.* 40/20, 118/1; rerid, 3 *sing. p.* 113/15, 116/2, 7; *pp.* 15/9; rering, *pr. p.* 21/3.
Rering, *sb.* building, founding, 128/19.
Resceyue, *vb. t. inf.* receive, 4/9, 10, 53/25; resceyue(n), 3 *pl. pres.* 60/11, 20; resceyued, *pp.* 49/4.
Resceyuours, *sb. pl.* receivers, 133/4.
Res(o)un, *sb.* reason, 32/13, 39/14, 40/3, &c.; resouns, *pl.* 38/23.
Rest, *vb. i. inf.* rest, 75/8; restiþ, 3 *sing. pres.* 35/23; restid, 3 *sing. p.* 90/29.
Resting-place, *sb.* resting-place, 62/22.
Restore, *vb. t. inf.* restore, 120/8.
Retenwe, *sb.* retinue, 43/21, 60/6.
Reuel, *vb. i. inf.* revel, 53/19.
Reuersen, *vb. t.* 3 *pl. pres.* reverse, 41/17.
Revoke, *vb. t. inf.* revoke, 100/10; renokid, 3 *sing. p.* 113/16.
Rewarde, *sb.* reward, 43/25, 55/26.
Rewardid, *pp.* rewarded, 122/6

Rewardingis, *sb. pl.* rewards, 106/25.
Rewme, *sb.* realm, kingdom, 15/18, 30/14, 44/6.
Reynd, *pp.* arraigned, 134/17 (aphetic form).
Reyn(e), *sb.* rain, 21/8, 129/23.
Rial, *a.* royal, 122/26.
Riche, *a.* rich, 42/6, 46/3; richest, *super.* 41/18.
Richesse, *sb.* riches, wealth, 38/2, 46/19, 49/15; richesses, -is, *pl.* 46/13, 85/3.
Rijf, *a.* rife, 49/14.
Ripeþ, *vb. i.* 3 *sing. pres.* becomes ripe, 29/7.
Rise, *vb. i. inf.* rise, 53/8, 95/14; riseþ, 3 *sing. pres.* 44/24; risen, 3 *pl. pres.* 5/29, 44/15, 46/13; 3 *pl. p.* 133/34; roos, 3 *sing. p.* 31/9.
Riȝt, *sb.* right, 97/2.
Riȝt, *a.* right, 14/19, 31/10; *adv.* just, right, 12/20, 47/1.
Riȝtwise, *a.* righteous, 5/4, 7/14, 10/10, &c.
Robbars, *sb. pl.* robbers, 131/14.
Robben, *vb. t.* 3 *pl. pres.* rob, 110/28.
Robrie, robry, *sb.* robbery, 106/22, 109/9.
Roosis, *sb. pl.* roses, 128/27.
Roote, *sb.* root, 7/11, 38/31, 103/17; rootis, *pl.* 39/4, 11, 65/9.
Rore, *sb.* confusion, tumult, 71/6, esp. in ' to set in rore '.
Roten, rotun, *a.* rotten, 2/24, 38/31.
Rouȝt, *vb. i. inf.* to be riotous, 53/20.
Rowne, *vb. i. inf.* whisper, 104/31.
Ruful, *a.* rueful, sorrowful, 49/1.
Rule, *sb.* rule, 41/17, 62/2; rulis, *pl.* 56/23.
Rule, *vb. t. inf.* rule, govern, 54/27, 94/20; rulid, *pp.* 50/16, 54/29.
Rust, *sb.* rust, 35/32.
Ruþe, *sb.* pity, 127/12.
Ruyn, *sb.* ruin, 69/1.
Rwiþ, *vb. t.* 3 *sing. pres.* grieves, 50/20.
Ryng, *sb.* ring, 71/5, 130/19.

S

Sa(a)f, *a.* safe, 3/20, 8/13, 21/7, 127/2, &c.
Saale-keene, salle-kene, *a.* ? for sale to the highest bidder, 76/9, 132/12; cf. G. *verkaufslustig*.

Glossary

Sabot(h), *sb.* sabbath, 90/25, 30.
Sachel, *sb.* wallet, 49/6.
Sacramentis, *sb. pl.* sacraments, 34/21, 35/8, &c.
Sacrar, *sb.* consecrator, 60/25.
Sacre, *vb. t. inf.* consecrate, 105/22; *imp.* 61/1; sacren, 3 *pl. pres.* 12/8; sacrid, 3 *sing. p.* 130/19; *pp.* 35/24.
Sacrifice, *sb.* sacrifice, 85/17; sacrificis, *pl.* 82/23, 24.
Sacrilege, *sb.* sacrilege, 117/13.
Sacrilegers, *sb. pl.* committers of sacrilege, 131/24.
Sadli, *adv.* seriously, 16/11, 63/13.
Sale, *sb.* sale, 61/20, 62/10.
Saluacioun, *sb.* salvation, 3/17, 52/24.
Salue, *sb.* salve, 59/18.
Saruauntis, *see* Seruauntis.
Saue, *vb. t. inf.* save, 8/12, 43/19; saueþ, 3 *sing. pres.* 50/17, 65/21; saued, *pp.* 75/9.
Sauiour, *sb.* saviour, 8/11.
Sauntwary, *sb.* sanctuary, 91/2, 105/16.
Sauour, *vb. i. inf.* taste, 77/18; *sb.* smell, taste, 69/3.
Sauȝt, *sb.* assault, 17/19, 19/1, &c.; sauȝtis, *pl.* 17/17, 35/30 (aphetic).
Scape, skape, *vb. i. inf.* escape, 3/4, 45/1, 82/4, 113/20 (aphetic).
Scatiriþ, *vb. t.* 3 *sing. pres.* scatters, 130/31; scatrid, *pp.* 15/10.
Schadde, *pp.* separated, 16/20; shed, 118/12.
Schadowe, *sb.* shadow, 135/15.
Schal, *vb. aux.* 1 *sing. pres.* shall, 3/3; 3 *sing. pres.* 6/10; schalt, 2 *sing. pres.* 53/9; schul, schullen, *pl. pres.* 14/15, 52/15, &c.; schulde, 3 *sing. p.* 5/24; schulde(n), 3 *pl. p.* 12/14.
Schame, *sb.* shame, 54/7, 88/3.
Schameful, *a.* shameful, 108/15.
Schameþ, *vb. t.* 3 *sing. pres.* makes ashamed, feels shame with regard to, 8/24, 11/14.
Scharp(e), *a.* sharp, 66/14, 67/5, 113/18.
Scharpli, *adv.* sharply, 64/6.
Scharpnes, *sb.* sharpness, 78/1.
Sche, *pron.* she, *passim*.
Schedyng, *sb.* shedding, 98/2.
Scheed, *vb. t. inf.* shed, 33/14, 98/12; schedden, 3 *pl. p.* 27/22; schadde, *pp.* 118/12.
Scheep, schepe, *sb. pl.* sheep, 12/25, 102/10, 106/4, &c.

Schelde, schilde, *sb.* shield, 65/34, 36.
Schenship, *sb.* shame, 68/6, 123/25.
Schepard, *sb.* shepherd, 3/26, 15/8.
Schete, *vb. t. inf.* shoot, 71/17.
Schewe, *vb. t.* and *i. inf.* appear, show, 42/17, 59/19, 70/21; 3 *sing. subj.* 41/31, 43/10; schewen, 3 *pl. pres.* 41/18, 49/1; schewid, 3 *sing. p.* 80/10; schewid, *pp.* 39/14, 117/21.
Schewing, *sb.* appearing, 10/10.
Schidars, *sb. pl.* shrews, scolds, 131/9 (*Prompt. Parv.* 'Cukstoke for flyterys, or schyderys').
Schirt, shirte, *sb.* shirt, 104/26, 123/20.
Schoon, schoos, *sb. pl.* shoes, 104/27, 132/7.
Schopp, *sb.* shop, 117/27.
Schort, *a.* short, 63/2, 94/4.
Schortli, *adv.* shortly, 137/2.
Schoyng, *sb.* shoeing, 65/30.
Schrewidar, *a. comp.* more wicked, 133/10.
Schrewidnes, *sb.* wic edness, 34/18, 68/23, 73/8.
Schrifte, *sb.* confession, 9/7, 74/17.
Schrynes, *sb. pl.* shrines, 43/8.
Schyne, *vb. i. inf.* shine, 69/2; 3 *sing. subj.* 55/17; schineþ, schynneþ, 3 *sing. pres.* 4/14, 38/11, 46/8; schynnen, 3 *pl. pres.* 31/2.
Schynful, *a.* shining, bright, 88/5.
Schyn(n)yng, *sb.* shining, illumination, 17/3, 28/16, 81/17.
Schynyng, *a.* shining, 37/25.
Sclaunderars, sclaundirars, *sb. pl.* slanderers, 66/28, 131/9.
Sclaundir, *sb.* slander, 11/12, 64/3; sclaundris, *pl.* 11/16, 25/35.
Sclaundir, *vb. t. inf.* slander, 11/11; sclaundriþ, 3 *sing. pres.* 10/15; sclaundren, 3 *pl. pres.* 11/5, 63/22; sclaundrid, 3 *pl. p.* 10/25; *pp.* 43/23, 101/8.
Scolis, *sb. pl.* schools, 5/16.
Scorne, *sb.* scorn, 135/6.
Scorne, *vb. t. inf.* scorn, 71/22.
Scribis, *sb. pl.* scribes, 42/26, 43/1, &c.
Scripture, *sb.* scripture, 56/18.
Se, *vb. t. inf.* see, 1/2, 55/17; seeþ, *vb. t.* 3 *sing. pres.* 52/20; sen, 3 *pl. pres.* 46/12; sauȝ, sawe, 1, 3 *sing. p.* 24/3, 27/32, 49/13, 98/23; siȝen, 3 *pl. p.* 27/14; seing, *pr. p.*

46/25; sen, seen, seyn, *pp.* 12/2, 27/3, 40/16, 103/15.
Sechiþ, *see* Seeke.
Secounde, *a.* second, 1/19, 7/23.
Sectis, *sb. pl.* sects, 38/15, 39/3, &c.
Seculare, *a.* secular, 51/3, 88/30.
Seculeris, *sb. pl.* seculars, 95/12.
See, *sb.* sea, 2/12, 13/24, &c.
See-brynk, *sb.* edge of the sea, 44/10.
Seed, *sb.* seed, offspring, 2/23, 118/13, 35.
Se(e)ke, *vb. t. inf.* seek, 63/1, 85/24; sechiþ, sekiþ, 3 *sing. pres.* 18/22, 57/13, 124/22; se(e)ken, 3 *pl. pres.* 4/11, 54/9, 85/22, &c.; souȝt, *pp.* 58/18.
Seeme, *vb. i.* 3 *sing. subj.* 47/13; semeþ, 3 *sing. pres.* 81/19; semen, 3 *pl. pres.* 38/3; semeden, 3 *pl. p.* 2/5.
Seet(e), *sb.* seat, 25/11, 40/15, 38/20; seetis, *pl.* 41/35.
Seie, *vb. t. inf.* say, 2/9, 3/3, 49/25; seist, 2 *sing. pres.* 4/24; seiþ, 3 *sing. pres.* 2/7; sei(e)n, seyn, 3 *pl. pres.* 31/26, 61/1, 2; seid(e), 3 *sing. p.* 5/7, 39/6, 61/8; 1 *pl. p.* 13/31; *pp.* 40/3, 68/22; seiyng, *pr. p.* 85/9.
Seiling, *pr. p.* sailing, 45/25.
Seintis, seyntes, *sb. pl.* saints, 2/3, 21/16, 43/8.
Seiyng, *sb.* speech, 55/13.
Selle, *vb. t. inf.* sell, 61/3, 91/16; sellen, 3 *pl. pres.* 60/30; soold, 3 *sing. p.* 62/5; soolden, 3 *pl. p.* 92/21; soold, *pp.* 106/2.
Sellers, *sb.* sellers, 60/33.
Selling, *sb.* selling, 62/8.
Sellis, *sb. pl.* seats, 27/10 (F. *selle*, L. *sella*).
Semblaunt, *sb.* appearance, 120/14.
Semeþ, *see* Seeme.
Sende, *vb. t. inf.* send, 81/19; sent, *pp.* 44/7.
Sengle, *a.* single, 103/9.
Sens, *sb.* sense, 126/5.
Sensers, *sb. pl.* censers, 37/29.
Sensuris, *sb. pl.* censures, 18/25, *see* note.
Sentence, *sb.* sentence, meaning, 6/2, 12/13, 63/5; maister of sentence, 12/15, *see* note.
Sequestreris, *sb. pl.* sequesters, 132/33.
Serche, *vb. t. inf.* search, 67/27.
Sermon, *sb.* word (L. *sermo*), 61/21; sermouns, *pl.* 59/1.

Seruage, *sb.* bondage, slavery, 103/22.
Seruauntis, saruauntis, *sb. pl.* servants, 6/12, 48/10, 60/11.
Serue, *vb. t. inf.* serve, 41/10; seruen, *pl. pres.* 41/11; *vb. i.* 106/14.
Seruice, seruise, seruyse, *sb.* service, 7/22, 38/14, 39/29, &c.
Seruyle, *a.* servile, 90/26, 91/7, 12.
Serymoyns, *sb. pl.* ceremonies, 120/10.
Settiþ, *vb. t.* 3 *sing. pres.* sets, 8/18; setten, 3 *pl. pres.* 106/1; sett, 3 *sing. p.* 2/14; *imp.* 63/1; *pp.* 44/32, 84/30.
Seuene, *a.* seven, 35/8, 60/1.
Shirte, *see* Schirt.
Sidis, *see* Siȝde.
Signes, *sb. pl.* signs, 38/22, 41/39, 134/9.
Signified, *pp.* signified, 115/29.
Sijk(e), *a.* sick, 30/25, 59/19, 127/7.
Sijknes, *sb.* sickness, 45/20, 65/38.
Siker, *a.* sure, 25/5, 37/1, 65/1.
Sikerli, *adv.* surely, 74/9.
Sillable, *sb.* syllable, 56/19.
Singars, syngars, *sb. pl.* singers, 48/8, 57/15, 58/13.
Sitten, *vb. i.* 3 *pl. pres.* sit, 58/24.
Siþen, *conj.* since, 11/2, 12/8, 85/1.
Siþes, siþis, *sb. pl.* times, 21/18, 44/15, 45/14.
Sixt(e), *a.* sixth, 13/1, 43/13.
Siȝde, *sb.* side, 19/24, 84/4; sidis, siȝdis, *pl.* 66/14, 104/19.
Siȝde, *a.* full, wide, flowing, 30/24.
Siȝen, *see* Se.
Siȝt, *sb.* sight, 13/11, 15/3, &c.; siȝtis, *pl.* 37/8.
Skape, *see* Scape.
Slakid, *see* Sleke.
Slawȝtir, *sb.* slaughter, 43/11.
Slee, *vb. t. inf.* slay, 17/1, 76/20, 113/9; sleeþ, 3 *sing. pres.* 8/15. 45/18, 98/14, 112/6; slen, 3 *pl. pres.* 84/18, 101/23; slouȝ, slow(ȝ), 3 *sing. p.* 98/18, 99/12, 133/16; slouȝen, slow(ȝ)en, 3 *pl. p.* 101/19, 113/24; slayn, *pp.* 98/26, 29.
Sleep, *sb.* sleep, 53/3, 9, &c.
Sleep(e), *vb. i. inf.* sleep, 51/7, 53/8; slepiþ, 3 *sing. pres.* 2/25, 35/26.
Sleeyng, *sb.* slaying, 99/1, 133/15.
Sleiȝtis, *sb. pl.* tricks, 51/23.
Slek(e), *vb. t. inf.* slake, 35/30, 101/6; slakid, *pp.* 133/25.
Slepand, *a.* sleeping, 35/27.
Sliden, *pp.* fallen, 80/23.
Sliȝ, *a.* sly, 45/2.

Sloumbre, *vb. i. inf.* slumber, 53/9; sloumbriŋ, *pr. p.* 53/2.
Sloumbring, *sb.* slumbering, 53/13, 16.
Slouþe, *sb.* sloth, 44/28.
Slouȝ, slowȝ, *a.* slothful, sluggish, 53/8, 60/6 (= L. *piger*).
Smak, *vb. t. inf.* savour of, 31/28; smacchiþ, 3 *sing. pres.* 63/13.
Smale, *a.* small, 7/8, 46/2, 10.
Smelling, *sb.* smelling, 120/18.
Smeþ(e), *a.* smooth, 25/22, 123/18.
Smok(e), smook, *sb.* smoke, 47/28, 129/7, 134/28.
Smyt(e), *vb. t. inf.* smite, 43/14, 67/5, 99/5, &c.; smytiþ, smyteþ, 3 *sing. pres.* 18/25, 59/12, 99/6; smot, 3 *sing. p.* 66/10, 91/23; smyten, *pp.* 117/33.
Smyting, *sb.* smiting, 99/11.
Snakis, *sb. pl.* snakes, 136/8.
Snare, *sb.* snare, 45/5, 57/3; snaris, *pl.* 82/3.
Sobre, sobur, *a.* sober, 35/9, 52/33, 59/11.
Socour, *sb.* help, 47/14.
Socour, *vb. t. inf.* help, 74/36.
Sodenli, *adv.* suddenly, 5/17, 45/14, &c.
Sodeyn, *a.* sudden, 126/8.
Sodomitis, *sb. pl.* practisers of sodomy, 131/24.
Softe, *a.* soft, 8/17.
Soilmentis, *sb. pl.* absolutions, 76/10 (aphetic for assoilment).
Solace, *vb. t. inf.* solace, comfort, 64/27.
Solempne, *a.* solemn, 84/30.
Somme, *see* Summe.
Sonde, *sb.* sound, 119/5.
Son(e), *sb.* son, 33/4, 34/16; sones, *pl.* 38/13, 39/30.
Songis, *sb. pl.* songs, 57/15, 58/1, 59/5.
Soolis, *sb. pl.* soles, 123/21.
Soone, *adv.* soon, 7/20, 51/24, 70/21.
Sooper, *sb.* supper, 60/16.
So(o)re, *adv.* sorely, grievously, 34/5, 44/24, 71/25, &c.; with trouble, 63/13; sorer, *comp.* 68/1.
So(o)ris, *sb. pl.* sores, 4/17, 59/19.
Soot, *sb.* soot, 44/22 (cf. *Roman de la Rose*, 10670, 'amer plus que n'est suie', Littré).
Sore, *a.* painful, grievous, 124/5.
Sorow, *sb.* sorrow, 40/16.
Sorow, *vb. i. inf.* to be grieved for, 4/1; sorowiþ, 3 *sing. pres.* sorrows, 67/9.

Sorowful, *a.* sorrowful, 49/2, 18.
Sortilogeris, *sb. pl.* diviners by lot, 132/19.
Sory, *a.* sorry, wretched, 120/9.
Sotil, *a.* subtle, 13/4, 27; sotiler, *comp.* 61/3.
Sotilte, *sb.* subtlety, 26/20.
Sottiþ, *vb. i.* 3 *sing. pres.* grow besotted, 19/3.
Soþe, *sb.* truth, 27/30, 39/16, 88/26.
Souereyn, *sb.* sovereign, 82/11; souereyns, *pl.* 82/12, 83/14.
Souereyn, *a.* sovereign, chief, 48/29, 30.
Soule, *sb.* soul, 6/24, &c.; soulis, *pl.* 3/1, &c.
Soumneþ, *vb. t.* 3 *sing. pres.* summoneth, 17/27; sumned, *pp.* 100/4.
Sounde, *sb.* sound, 58/28.
Sounde, *a.* sound, 125/29.
Souȝt, *see* Se(e)ke.
Sowel, *sb.* dirt, mire, 42/25.
Sowiþ, *vb. t.* 3 *sing. pres.* sows, 111/16; sowen, *pp.* 2/22.
Sowrische, *a.* sour, 44/20.
Soyle, *vb. t. imp.* assoil, 60/35.
Spalme, *sb.* psalm, 133/17; var. psalme.
Spare, *vb. t.* or *i. inf.* spare, 49/6; spare (to), 79/6; spariþ, 3 *sing. pres.* 95/6; sparid (to), 3 *sing. p.* 92/10.
Speche, *sb.* speech, 14/9.
Special, *a.* in special, in particular, 13/32, 35/16.
Speciali, *adv.* specially, 76/2.
Spede, *sb.* speed, success, 45/26, 83/18.
Spediness, *sb.* ? quickness or prosperity, 25/37.
Spedy, *a.* profitable, 81/19.
Speke, *vb. t. inf.* speak, 22/13, 43/31; 1 *sing. pres.* 4/25; spekiþ, 3 *sing. pres.* 2/20, 4/11, &c.; speken, *pl. pres.* 5/15, 25/1; spak, 3 *sing. p.* 25/7.
Spende, *vb. t. inf.* spend, 45/4, 109/17; spenden, 3 *pl. pres.* 107/12.
Spensis, *sb. pl.* expenses, 38/13.
Spie, *sb.* spying, 100/2; spies, *pl.* spies, 72/3.
Spille, *vb. i. inf.* perish, 86/21.
Spirit, *sb.* spirit, 4/22, 7/10, 46/25, &c.
Spiritual, spirituel, *a.* spiritual, 46/2, 78/16.
Spoile, *vb. t. inf.* rob, 17/25; spoilen, spoylen, 3 *pl. pres.* 38/21.
Spoiling, *sb.* robbing, 85/4.

Spottis, *sb. pl.* spots, 56/1.
Spousaile, *sb.* espousal, 130/20.
Spouse, *sb.* spouse, 35/21, 24, &c.
Spousebreche, *sb.* adultery, 70/5.
Spousebreker, *sb.* adulterer, 130/22.
Spoylours, *sb. pl.* robbers, 109/4.
Sprediþ, *vb. i.* 3 *sing. pres.* spreads, 122/34; spradde, *pp.* 52/13.
Springeþ, springiþ, *vb. i.* 3 *sing. pres.* 40/26, 50/23, 103/17.
Staale, *see* Steele.
Staate, *sb.* state, 46/1.
Stable, *vb. t. inf.* establish, 47/10; stablen, 3 *pl. pres.* 60/11.
Stable, *a.* stable, firm, 2/6.
Staff-beggers, *sb. pl.* beggars (with a staff), 54/15 (cf. ON. *staf-karl*).
Stalowens, *sb. pl.* stallions, 106/14.
Staring, *a.* staring, glittering, 37/8, 39/18.
Stede, *sb.* place, 117/21.
Stedfast, *a.* steadfast, 76/4, 130/19.
Steele, *vb. i. inf.* steal, come secretly, 53/12, 65/36; *v. t. inf.* steal, 108/11; 3 *sing. subj.* 107/9; steelen, 3 *pl. pres.* 107/15; staale, 3 *sing. p.* 107/9.
Steelyngis, *sb. pl.* stealings, 107/18.
Steerchen, *vb. t.* 3 *pl. pres.* powder with starch, 132/10.
Ste(e)re, *vb. t. inf.* guide, incite, 5/11, 127/15; steriþ, 3 *sing. pres.* 70/4; sterid, *pp.* stirred, 95/18.
Stelþ3, *sb.* stealth, 106/22.
Stepile, *sb.* steeple, 41/35.
Steppis, *sb. pl.* steps, 40/8, 43/4, 51/15.
Stering, stiring, *sb.* prompting, inciting, 53/14, 102/19, 111/26; steryngis, *pl.* 65/26.
Sterres, sterris, *sb. pl.* stars, 13/18, 28/5.
Sterue, *vb. i.* 3 *pl. pres.* die, perish, 101/13.
Stik, *sb.* stick, 113/33; stikkis, *pl.* 91/14.
Stille, *a.* quiet, still, 58/8, 98/32; *adv.* 96/10.
Stilled, *pp.* become silent, 16/8.
Stilli, *adv.* silently, 96/4.
Stink, *sb.* stink, 69/3.
Stinking, *a.* stinking, 42/25, 60/21.
Stintid, *see* Stynt.
Stire, *v. t. inf.* incite, 120/15; stiriþ, 3 *sing. pres.* 47/4.
Stirne, *a.* stern, 135/16.
Stiʒe, *v. i. inf.* rise, ascend, 15/4;

stiʒe(n), 3 *pl. pres.* 34/7, 75/8, 79/9; stiʒed, 3 *sing. p.* 27/4, 31/10.
Stiʒyng, *sb.* ascension, 55/6.
Stokke, *sb.* stock, 92/13.
Stonde, *v. i. inf.* stand, 90/13; stondiþ, standiþ, 3 *sing. pres.* stands, consists, 3/16, 22/24, 34/25; stonden, 3 *pl. pres.* 65/14, 66/21; stonding, *pr. p.* 104/29.
Stonyen, *v. i.* 3 *pl. pres.* are amazed, 11/13.
Stool, *sb.* stool, 87/22.
Stoon, *sb.* stone, 36/11, 41/33; stoones, *pl.* 37/26, 27, 38/12, &c.
Stooned, *pp.* stoned, 91/15.
Sto(o)ry, *sb.* story, 102/1, 137/5.
Stoppen, *vb. t.* 3 *pl. pres.* stop, hinder, 102/21.
Stormes, *sb. pl.* storms, 44/23.
Stounde, *sb.* moment, instant, 47/18.
Straien, *vb. i.* 3 *pl. pres.* stray, 127/25; straied, 2 *pl. p.* 70/2.
Strangliþ, *vb. t.* 3 *sing. pres.* strangles, 122/23.
Straunge, *a.* strange, 41/12, 48/11, 73/4.
Straunger(e), *sb.* stranger, 49/18, 90/28; straungers, *pl.* 40/28.
Strayt, streiʒt, *a.* strait, narrow, 128/4, 6.
Strecche, *vb. i. inf.* stretch, reach, 122/11; 3 *pl. pres.* 9/34; 3 *sing. subj.* 44/30; strecchiþ, 3 *sing. pres.* 11/20; strecchid, *pp.* 71/16.
Streemes, *sb. pl.* streams, 50/24.
Streiʒt, *see* Strayt.
Streiʒtli, *adv.* strictly, 27/12, 60/27, &c.; streiʒtlier, *comp.* 92/25.
Strenger, *a. comp.* stronger, 12/17, 71/3.
Strengþe, *sb.* strength, 50/11, 63/2, 18; strengþis, *pl.* 9/27.
Strengþe, *vb. t. inf.* strengthen, 55/12.
Stressiþ, *vb. t.* 3 *sing. pres.* distresses, 3/14.
Stretis, *sb. pl.* streets, 86/15.
Strijf, *sb.* strife, 50/3.
Strikars, *sb. pl.* ? walkers, 54/15 (OE. *strican*, to go); or ? beggars, cf. G. *Landstreicher.*
Striplyngis, *sb. pl.* striplings, 119/3.
Striueyng, *pr. p.* striving, 56/22.
Stroi(e)þ, *vb. t.* 3 *sing. pres.* destroys, 44/28, 46/33; stroyen, 3 *pl. pres.* 117/10.
Strong, *a.* strong, 54/15.

Glossary

Stro(o)k, *sb.* stroke, 66/14, 98/14; strookis, *pl.* 66/2, 5.
Stroumpetis, *sb. gen. sing.* strumpet's, 13/7.
Stryuyng, *sb.* strife, 70/6.
Studiars, *sb. pl.* students, 48/9, 62/12, 63/9.
Studie, *sb.* study, 57/12, 62/28, 63/1; studies, *pl.* 64/19.
Studie, *vb. t. inf.* study, 62/20; studien, 3 *pl. pres.* 61/6, 62/12, &c.; studiyng, *pr. p.* 35/5.
Sturble, *vb. t. inf.* disturb, 65/29.
Sturdi, *a.* sturdy, 132/2. 19/32 16/22
Stynt, *vb. i. imp.* stop, cease, 43/23; stintid, *pp.* 129/15.
Successouris, *sb. pl.* successors, 134/1.
Suche, *a.* such, 38/3, &c.
Suffice, *vb. i.* 3 *pl. subj.* be sufficient, 105/11; suffisid, *pp.* 95/23.
Suffragis, *sb. pl.* spiritual powers or indulgence, 61/4, 76/8, 10, &c.
Suffre, *vb. t. inf.* suffer, 6/24, 35/19, &c.; suffreþ, suffriþ, 3 *sing. pres.* 51/6, 54/12; suffren, *pl. pres.* 5/28; suffring, *pr. p.* 35/9.
Suffurable, *a.* tolerable, 12/28.
Suget, *a.* subject, 31/37, 48/16, 84/1.
Summe(n), somme, *a.* some, 33/21, 34/7, &c.
Sumnour, *sb.* summoner, 104/31; sumnouris, *pl.* 133/1.
Sumtyme, *adv.* sometimes, 70/5.
Sundai, *sb.* Sunday, 91/3.
Sunne, *sb.* sun, 32/19, 46/8, 49/14.
Superflu, *a.* superfluous, 125/32.
Supersticiouse, *a.* superstitious, 88/12.
Superstitioun, *sb.* superstition, 88/14.
Suppose, *vb. t.* 3 *pl. pres.* suppose, 88/27; 3 *sing. subj.* 51/5.
Suspendid, *pp.* suspended.
Swagip, *vb. t.* 3 *sing. pres.* assuages, 4/17, 79/22; swagid, *pp.* 133/24.
Swe, *vb. t. inf.* follow, 30/19, 51/14, 105/28; sueþ, swiþ, sweþ, 3 *sing. pres.* 12/2, 16/11, 94/3; swen, *pl. pres.* 43/4, 79/8; swed, 3 *sing. p.* 40/8.
Sweilid, *pp.* stifled, 78/24 (OE. *swǣlan*, burn).
Swelling, *sb.* arrogance, 6/28.
Swelliþ, *vb. i.* 3 *sing. pres.* swells, 49/28; swelling, *pr. p.* burning, 127/7.
Swerars, *sb. pl.* swearers, 131/11.

Swerde, swerid, *sb.* sword, 33/21, 45/19, 120/26, &c.
Swere, *vb. i. inf.* swear, 85/25; *imp.* 87/21; swore, 3 *sing. p.* 89/4; sworn, *pp.* 130/17.
Swerte, *sb.* surety, careless confidence, 26/32.
Sweryng, *sb.* swearing, 88/31.
Swet, *a.* sweet, 57/16; swetter, *comp.* 63/3, 77/11.
Sweyling, *sb.* burning (= L. *combustio*), 6/29.
Swift, *a.* swift, 98/12.
Swipe, *adv.* quickly, 134/24.
Swyme, *vb. i. inf.* swim, 106/5; swymmen, 3 *pl. pres.* 30/24, 45/34. &c.
Symonye, *sb.* simony, 62/1, 68/7.
Symonyentis, *sb.* practisers of simony, 62/4.
Symple, *a.* simple, 5/19, 46/14, 82/9, &c.
Synagogis, *sb. pl.* synagogues, 38/20.
Synet, *sb.* signet, 113/3 (OF. *sinet*, var. *signet*).
Synful, *a.* sinful, 43/17, 52/9, &c.
Syngen, *vb. t.* 3 *pl. pres.* sing, 57/15; soungen, 3 *pl. p.* 58/11; *pp.* 58/28; singyng, *pr. p.* 58/1.
Synk, *vb. i. inf.* sink, 66/6; 3 *pl. pres.* 106/5.
Synnars, synners, *sb. pl.* sinners, 2/3, 34/18.
Syn(n)e, *sb.* sin, 7/11, 52/33; synnes, *pl.* 3/25, 50/18.
Synne, *vb. i.* 2 *pl. pres.* sin, 8/7; synned, *pp.* 8/8.
Syouns, *sb. pl.* branches, shoots, 70/3.

T

Taaris, *sb. pl.* tares, 2/22.
Taast, taste, *vb. t. inf.* taste, 44/21, 118/5.
Takars, *sb. pl.* receivers, 61/25, 62/3.
Take, *vb. t. inf.* take, receive, 4/6, 51/5; takiþ, 3 *sing. pres.* 2/25, 53/27; taken, *pl. pres.* 33/21, 44/1; *pp.* 4/5, 55/2; took(e), 3 *sing. p.* 35/13, 60/15; tooken, 3 *pl. p.* 130/14.
Talis, *sb. pl.* tales, 55/27, 97/23, 104/18.
Tapir, *sb.* taper, 104/28.
Tarie, *vb. i. inf.* tarry, delay, 134/24; taried, *pp.* 59/14.
Tasting, *sb.* tasting, 44/20.

Tatiryng, *sb.* slashing of garments, 132/12.
Tauerneris, *sb. pl.* tavern-keepers, 132/27.
Taxid, *pp.* taxed, 104/36.
Taxis, *sb. pl.* taxes, 46/16.
Teche, *vb. t. inf.* teach, 38/23, 71/8, 94/19; techiþ, 3 *sing. pres.* 8/2, 39/18, 48/17; techen, 3 *pl. pres.* 34/16, 19; tauȝt, 3 *sing. p.* 17/5, 21/14, 42/20; *pp.* 11/25, 59/11; teching, *pr. p.* 57/24.
Teching, *sb.* teaching, 43/21, 55/14.
Teep, *sb. pl.* teeth, 47/28, 73/20.
Telle, *vb. t. inf.* tell, 39/16; tolde, 3 *sing. p.* 100/23; *pp.* 101/20.
Temperal, *a.* temporal, 43/16, 46/2, 84/2.
Temperalte, *sb.* temporal affairs, 82/14.
Tempestis, *sb. pl.* tempests, 44/16, 45/14.
Tempir, *vb. t. inf.* moderate, 48/15.
Temple, *sb.* temple, 37/28, 42/18, 21, 45/9; templis, *pl.* 40/21, 24.
Temptacioun, *sb.* temptation, 35/19; temptaciouns, *pl.* 4/15.
Temptid, *vb. t.* 3 *sing. p.* tempted, 120/14; *pp.* 35/18.
Tempting, *sb.* tempting. 76/13.
Tendir, *a.* tender, 126/25.
Tene, *sb.* anger, vexation, sorrow, 44/25, 59/25, 134/27.
Tent, *sb.* heed, 34/24.
Tent, tenten, *vb. i.* 3 *pl. pres.* attend, pay heed, 41/39, 56/4, &c.
Tere, *vb. t. inf.* tear, 49/27.
Terme, *sb.* boundary, 121/5; termes, *pl.* 44/32, 116/25.
Terren, *vb. t.* 3 *pl. pres.* make angry, provoke, 51/15 (OE. *tergan*).
Testament, *sb.* testament, 59/7.
Til, *prep.* to, 34/17; *conj.* until, 45/17.
Tilliars, *sb. pl.* farm-labourers, 131/16.
Tirauntrie, *sb.* tyranny, 70/9, 106/21, 109/9.
Tising, *sb.* enticing, 127/22 (aphetic).
Title, *sb.* title, 99/7.
Tixt(e), *sb.* text, 9/12, 22/16, 47/8.
To, *prep.* for, 6/6, 12/28, 30/14; *adv.* too, 52/9, 126/10, 11; *a.* two, 99/12.
To-broken, *pp.* broken in pieces, 93/22.
Tobrosten, *pp.* broken in pieces, 114/22.

Togider, togiddir, *adv.* together, 12/18, 25/3, 35/37, &c.
Token, *sb.* token, 119/14; tooken(e)s, *pl.* 15/16, 53/20, 129/2.
To-laken, *vb. t.* 3 *pl. pres.* blame, 46/14.
Toodis, *sb. pl.* toads, 136/7.
Toour, *see* Toure.
To-teeren, *vb. t.* 3 *pl. pres.* tear in pieces, 102/10.
To-turmentid, *pp.* tormented, 127/8.
Toþir, *pron.* other, 69/13.
Touchid, *pp.* touched, 123/23.
Touching, *sb.* touching, 61/15.
Toumbes, toumbis, *sb. pl.* tombs, 43/3, 134/4.
Toune, *sb.* town, 86/27, 92/24.
T(o)ung, *sb.* tongue, 5/11, 8/12; *pl.* t(o)ungis, 15/19, 24.
Toure, toour, *sb.* tower, fortress, 35/33, 54/31.
Toward, *adv.* frowards, onward, 134/23; *prep.* 54/19.
Traitours, *sb. pl.* traitors, 96/10, 111/9.
Translatid, *pp.* removed, 101/21.
Trappe, *sb.* trap, 84/26.
Traueile, *sb.* toil, 33/12, 35/28; traueils, *pl.* troubles, 126/11.
Traueilen, *vb. i. pl. pres.* work, toil, 41/12, 48/8; traueile, *imp.* 35/5; traueilid, traueiled, *pp.* 5/18, 71/25.
Traueiling, *pr. p.* travelling, 53/19.
Trayne, *sb.* stratagem, 62/8.
Treccherie, *sb.* treachery, 71/25.
Treccherous, *a.* treacherous, 108/1.
Treden, *vb. t.* 3 *pl. pres.* tread, 56/26.
Tree, *sb.* tree, 62/16.
Tre(e)ten, *vb. t.* 3 *pl. pres.* treat, handle, 12/8, 60/14, 93/15; treete, 2 *sing. subj.* 103/24; tretid, *pp.* 36/1.
Tre(e)ting, *sb.* treatment, 121/24; handling, consecrating, 21/27.
Tresour, *sb.* treasure, 17/24, 59/18, &c.
Tresourer, *sb.* treasurer, 102/13; tresoureris, *pl.* 133/4.
Tresourist, *vb. t.* 2 *sing. pres.* treasurest, 10/9.
Tretable, *a.* ? able to be treated, or ? palpable, tangible, 56/17.
Tretise, *sb.* treatise, 1/1, 7/8.
Trewe, *a.* true, 3/8, 5/11, &c.; *adv.* truly, 54/10.
Treweli, trueli, *adv.* truly, 35/7, 55/5, 59/11.

Glossary

Tribis, *sb. pl.* tribes, 95/21.|
Tribulacioun, *sb.* tribulation, 1/21, 47/12.
Trinite, *sb.* Trinity, 34/10, 74/15.
Triste, *sb.* trust, 7/24, 19/7, 63/17.
Tristen, *vb. t.* 3 *pl. pres.* trust, 7/30.
Tristi, *a.* trusty, 64/28, 66/2.
Triumphant, *a.* triumphant, 35/28.
Tromp, *sb.* trunp, 134/29.
Trone, *sb.* throne, 87/22; troones, *pl.* 27/20.
Trouble, *vb. t. inf.* trouble, 81/18, 123/1.
Tr(o)uþe, *sb.* truth, 6/5, &c.
Trouppliȝt, *a.* trothplight, 35/20.
Trowe, *vb. t. inf.* believe, 89/14; *imp.* 97/6; trowist, 2 *sing. pres.* 61/20; trowen, 3 *pl. pres.* 101/10, 132/21; trowiden, 1 *pl. p.* 135/7; trowid, *pp.* 52/11.
Trowing, *sb.* belief, 19/7.
Trublid, *pp.* troubled, 134/24.
Tuicioun, *sb.* intuition (aphetic), 26/23.
Turment, *sb.* torment, 130/13; turmentis, *pl.* 20/13.
Turmentid, *pp.* tormented, 15/2, 78/19.
Turmentrie, *sb.* torment, 15/4, 21/3, &c.
Turne, *vb. t. inf.* turn, 38/4; turneþ, 3 *sing. pres.* 45/8; *vb. i.* 32/24; turnen, 3 *pl. pres.* 7/4, 58/26; turnyng, *pr. p.* 34/18; turned, *pp.* 58/25.
Tweie, *a.* two, 113/10.
Tweluer, *a.* twelfth, 125/1.
Tweyne, *sb.* two, 9/28.
Twise, *adv.* twice, 95/25.
Twoo, *a.* two, 43/20, 31, 59/27.
Tymber, tymbre, *sb.* timber, 36/11, 41/33.
Tymber, *sb.* timbral, 119/4.
Tyme, *sb.* time, 4/10, 32/11, 35/16, &c.; tymes, *pl.* 50/12.
Tyrauntis, *sb.* tyrants, 84/3, 131/14.

Þ

Þan, þanne, *conj.* than, 83/8, &c.
Þank, *vb. t. inf.* thank, 45/4.
Þankingis, *sb. pl.* thanks, 54/7, 58/4.
Þankis, *sb. pl.* thanks; her þankis = willingly, 19/25.
Þanne, *adv.* then, 3/10, &c.
Þee, *pron.* thee, 3/29, 30, &c.
Þeeft, *sb.* theft, 78/7, 94/14.

Þe(e)ues, *sb. pl.* thieves, 53/19, 92/23.
Þei, þey, *pron.* they, *passim.*
Þenk, þink, *vb. t.* or *i.* think, meditate, 62/15; *imp.* 43/24; þenken, 3 *pl. pres.* 50/17, 20.
Þenkyng, *sb.* thinking, thought, 103/7.
Þen(n)s, *adv.* thence, 13/18, 31/11.
Þer, *pron.* their, 12/6, 27, &c.
Þer(e), *adv.* there, 3/19, &c.; where, 38/16, &c.
Þerbi, *adv.* thereby, 65/19.
Þerfro, *adv.* therefrom, 9/31.
Þeronne, *adv.* thereon, 102/16.
Þerynne, *adv.* therein, 42/19, 64/28.
Þewis, *sb. pl.* customs, 40/7, 21.
Þi, *pron.* thy, 3/29.
Þick, *a.* thick, 134/28, 136/9.
Þicli, *adv.* thickly, 65/28.
Þider, þidir, *adv.* thither, 32/24, 101/25.
Þingis, *sb. pl.* things, 1/2, &c.
Þink, *sb.* thing, 84/11.
Þink, *see* þenk.
Þise, *a.* these, *passim.*
Þo(o), *pron.* those, 30/21, 43/20; *a.* 14/21, &c.
Þoruȝ, *prep.* through, 19/34, 42/7, &c.
Þos, *pron.* those, 30/24.
Þou, *pron.* thou, 2/26.
Þousandis, *sb. pl.* thousands, 82/1.
Þouȝ, *conj.* although, 37/32, &c.
Þouȝt, *sb.* thought, 63/6; þouȝtis, *pl.* 51/1.
Þraldom, *sb.* bondage, 81/25, 101/26.
Þre, *a.* three, 1/8, 98/14.
Þrefolde, *a.* threefold, 74/11.
Þretingis, *sb. pl.* threats, 8/18.
Þridde, *a.* third, 18/20, 32/26.
Þrille, *vb. t. inf.* pierce, 111/17.
Þrise, *adv.* thrice, 35/18, 95/23.
Þrist, *sb.* thirst, 25/34.
Þristid, *pp.* thirsted, 30/17.
Þritti, *a.* thirty, 62/4.
Þrowen, *vb. t.* 3 *pl. pres.* throw, 67/6; *pp.* 13/19, 17/9; þrowiþ (at), 3 *sing. pres.* aims, 66/2.

V (U)

Vgli, *a.* frightful, 45/7; *adv.* terribly, 16/6.
Vnable, *a.* incapable, 93/23.
Vnbuxum, *a.* disobedient, 84/25.
Vncerteyne, *a.* uncertain, 65/3.
Vnchaast, *a.* unchaste, 108/11, 12.

Vncircumcisid, *pp.* uncircumcised, 105/13.
Vnclene, *a.* impure, 51/1.
Vnclennes, *sb.* uncleanness, 39/27.
Vncurable, *a.* incurable, 113/36.
Vndeedli, *a.* immortal, 62/9, 113/24.
Vndeedlines, *sb.* immortality, 26/16.
Vndefoulid, *pp.* undefiled, 23/13.
Vndir, *prep.* under, 3/19, 56/26.
Vndirloute, *a.* submissive, subject to, 31/37.
Vndirloute, *vb. i. inf.* be subject, 32/4; *vb. t. imp.* subject, 83/14; vndirlouted, *pp.* 32/17.
Vndirneþe, *adv.* underneath, 81/28.
Vndirnymyng, *sb.* blaming, rebuking (= L. *increpatio*), 123/17.
Vndirputten, *vb. t.* 3 *pl. pres.* set beneath, 37/25.
Vndirstondars, *sb. pl.* men of understanding, 7/8.
Undirstonde, *vb. t. inf.* understand, 52/15; vndirstandid, *pp.* 64/10.
Undirstonding, *sb.* undirstanding, 69/9.
Vndirtake, *vb. t. inf.* undertake, 67/28.
Vndo, *vb. t. pl. pres.* break, undo, 105/15, 120/8.
Vndrawen, *pp.* undrawn, unrooted, 116/20.
Vndwe, *a.* undue, 93/24.
Vnevenli, *adv.* unevenly, 108/6.
Vnfeiþful, *a.* unfaithful, 8/19, 106/24.
Vngroundid, *a.* ungrounded, 39/1, 48/37.
Vnite, *sb.* unity, 2/19, 76/4.
Vniustli, *adv.* unjustly, 99/6.
Vnkept, *pp.* untended, 117/32.
Vnknowen, *a.* unknown, 73/10.
Vnknowyng, *sb.* ignorance, 93/21.
Vnkunnyngenes(se), *sb.* ignorance, 13/26, 122/13.
Vnkynde, *a.* unnatural, 8/19, 92/14.
Vnlawful, *a.* unlawful, 98/2, 30.
Vnle(e)ful, *a.* unlawful, 52/32, 115/15.
Vnlettrid, *a.* unlettered, ignorant, 5/23.
Vnmoveable, *a.* immovable, 115/20.
Vnneþ, *adv.* scarcely, 44/22, 117/6.
Vnordinat, *a.* inordinate, 115/18.
Vnpesible, *a.* implacable, 99/23.
Vnpitiuouse, *a.* unmerciful, 129/5.
Vnpos(s)ible, *a.* impossible, 5/6, 116/16.

Vnprofitable, *a.* unprofitable, 64/19, 131/17.
Vnpunyschid, *pp.* unpunished, 112/3.
Vnresonable, *a.* without reason, 45/17.
Vnriʒtwisenesse, *sb.* unrighteousness, 127/3, 129/14.
Unrulid, *a.* without rule or guidance, 2/19.
Vnschamefast, *a.* unashamed, 8/20.
Vnskilfulness, *sb.* unreasonableness, 115/16.
Vnstable, *a.* unstable, 125/32.
Vnstablenes, *sb.* weakness, 26/18.
Vntauʒt, *a.* ignorant, uneducated, 5/29, 100/24.
Vntellable, *a.* untrue, 136/11.
Vntrewe, *a.* untrue, 131/16.
Vnwiting, *pr. p.* ignorant of, 93/20.
Vnworþier, *a. comp.* more unworthy, 37/5.
Vnworþili, *adv.* unworthily, 60/14, 20.
Vp, *adv.* up; born up = advanced, exalted, 10/13.
Vpbreiding, upbreyding, *sb.* upbraiding, 123/25, 124/23.
Vpbreidiþ, *vb. t.* 3 *sing. pres.* upbraids, 10/15.
Vphaunsid, *pp.* lifted up (= L. *exaltatus*), 28/22.
Vplifted, *pp.* uplifted, 129/6.
Vppon, *prep.* upon, 54/1, 4, 65/10.
Vprising, *sb.* resurrection, 31/15.
Vpsodoun, *adv.* upside-down, 7/21, 92/21.
Vpsprongen, *pp.* sprung up, 28/21, 24.
Vse, *vb. t. inf.* use, practise, 59/20, 62/1; vsiþ, 3 *sing. pres.* 65/20; vsen, 3 *pl. pres.* 48/4, 53/1.
Vsing, *sb.* using, 92/24.
Vsureris, *sb. pl.* usurers, 132/13.
Vtterli, vttirli, *adv.* completely, 37/9, 39/11; outwardly, 19/15.
Vttirar, *a.* outer, 73/19; uttirest, *super.* uttermost, 27/29, 122/26.

V (consonantal)

Vale, *sb.* vale, 47/18, 22.
Vanischeþ, *vb. i.* 3 *sing. pres.* vanishes, 129/8; vanischen, 3 *pl. pres.* 4/15.
Vanite, *sb.* vanity, 38/10, 49/19; vanites, *pl.* 38/10, 39/18.
Vary, *vb. i. inf.* vary, differ, 40/8; varien, 3 *pl. pres.* 48/13.

Vauntage, *sb.* advantage, 46/12, 113/26.
Vaunting, *sb.* boasting, 46/13.
Venge, *vb. t. inf.* avenge, 98/27, 99/8; vengid, *pp.* 72/5, 6, 7.
Vengeyng, *sb.* avenging, 99/23.
Veniaunce, vengeance, 13/30, 33/23, &c.
Venȳm(o)us, *a.* poisonous, 16/14, 43/6.
Verr(e)y, verri, *a.* true, 9/2, 4, &c.
Verrili, *adv.* truly, 48/3.
Vertu, *sb.* virtue, power, 3/16, 5/24, &c.; vertues, *pl.* 32/12, 44/28.
Vertuouse, *a.* virtuous, 41/30, 42/7, 45/23.
Vertuousli, *adv.* virtuously, 55/11.
Vessel, *sb.* vessel, 47/26; vessell(i)s, *pl.* 44/10, 45/15.
Vestment, *sb.* vestment, 41/34.
Veyn, *a.* vain, 37/8, 38/13, 41/37, &c.
Veynli, *adv.* vainly, 88/14.
Viciouse, *a.* vicious, evil, 36/22, 42/8, 43/16, &c.
Vicis, *sb.* vices, 49/26.
Victorie, *sb.* victory, 35/33.
Viker, *sb.* vicar, 34/15, 16.
Vilen, *a.* vile, 131/10 (? OF. *vilains*).
Vileny(e), *sb.* villany, 27/25, 68/11.
Vintineris, *sb. pl.* vintners, 132/27.
Vintre, *sb.* vine, 48/6 (OE. *wintrēōw* = vine).
Virginite, *sb.* virginity, 65/22.
Virgyn, *sb.* virgin, 79/3.
Vise, *see* **Wijse**.
Visioun, *sb.* vision, 68/20, 111/6.
Visitacioun, *sb.* visitation, 64/13, 78/8.
Visite, *vb. t. inf.* visit, 72/4; visiten, 1 *pl. pres.* 86/11; visitid, *pp.* 61/2.
Vitails, *sb. pl.* victuals, 113/32.
Vitileris, *sb. pl.* victuallers, 91/3, 18.
Voice, vois, *sb.* voice, 46/26, 58/15, &c.
Voide, *a.* empty, 109/29.
Voketis, *sb. pl.* advocates, 124/32.
Voutrer, wowtrere, *sb.* adulterer, 23/21, 123/23.
Vowe, *vb. i. inf.* make a vow, 85/24.
Vynȝerde, *sb.* vineyard, 118/4, 9.

W

Wa(a)st, *vb. t. inf.* waste, 10/16; wastiþ, 3 *sing. pres.* 44/27; wasten, 3 *pl. pres.* 107/14; rob, spoil, 46/25.

Wa(a)st, *a.* vast, 30/22, 38/19.
Wacche, wecche, *sb.* watch, 52/25, 30, 53/1.
Wade, *vb. i. inf.* go, depart, 63/19.
Wagis, *sb. pl.* wages, 124/29.
Wake, *sb.* watch, 79/9.
Wak(e)ars, *sb. pl.* watchers, 52/18, 53/1.
Waken, *a.* watchful, 52/20.
Waker, *a.* watchful, 25/11 (OE. *wacor*).
Wakiþ, *vb. i.* 3 *sing. pres.* keeps watch, 2/25, 57/11; waken, 3 *pl. pres.* 52/18, 53/18.
Wakyng, *sb.* watching, 52/23; wakingis, *pl.* 25/32.
Wal, *sb.* wall, 120/28; wallis, *pl.* 91/17.
Walken, *vb. i.* 3 *pl. pres.* walk, 33/13, 17, 83/15.
Wandriþ, *vb. i.* 3 *sing. pres.* wanders, 25/31; wandren, 3 *pl. pres.* 43/9; wandiryng, *pr. p.* 48/4.
Wanen, *vb. i.* 3 *pl. pres.* vacillate, 52/1.
Wanhope, *sb.* despair, 7/23, 66/4.
Wanten, *vb. t.* 3 *pl. pres.* want, lack, 52/15, 74/2, 121/31; wantiþ, *vb. imp.* 3 *sing. pres.* is lacking, 40/22, 49/17.
Wanting, *sb.* lack, 101/10.
Wantoune, *a.* wanton, 35/31, 95/15.
War, *a.* wary, 62/11.
Warars, *sb. pl.* cursers, 131/8.
Warde, *sb.* guard, 112/14.
Wardeynes, *sb. pl.* guardians, 105/17.
Wardiþ, *vb. t.* 3 *sing. pres.* assigns, 74/3.
Waried, *vb. t.* 3 *sing. p.* cursed, 42/27; *pp.* 16/15, 18/9, 113/6.
Wariyng, *sb.* cursing, 17/11.
Warme, *adv.* warmly, 46/8; *a.* warm, 50/24.
Warneþ, *vb. t.* 3 *sing. pres.* warns, 52/8.
Warre, *see* **Werre**.
Wasche, *vb. t. inf.* wash, 50/27.
Waschinge, *a.* washing, 50/23.
Watir, *sb.* water, 32/12, 35/18, &c.; watris, *pl.* 19/16, 50/26, &c.
Watriþ, *vb. t.* 3 *sing. pres.* waters, 32/24; watrid, *pp.* 32/21.
Waveren, *vb. i.* 3 *pl. pres.* waver, 55/30; waveryng, *pr. p.* 125/30.
Wawis, *sb. pl.* waves, 2/12, 35/30, &c.

Wawiþ, *vb. i.* 3 *sing. pres.* waves, fluctuates, 44/17 (OE. *wafian*).
Wax, *sb.* wax, 104/28.
Waxiþ, wexiþ, *vb. i.* 3 *sing. pres.* grows, 106/15, 133/9; waxen, 3 *pl. pres.* 95/15; wex, 3 *sing. p.* 73/17.
Wecche, *see* **Wacche.**
Weddid, *a.* wedded, 65/23, 103/9.
Weddiþ, *vb. t.* 3 *sing. subj.* weds, 125/16; wedde, 3 *sing. subj.* 125/15; weddid, *pp.* 124/17.
Wedir, *sb.* weather, 46/9.
Wedlock, *sb.* wedlock, 125/4.
Weede, *sb.* weed, 116/18.
Weeke, *sb.* week, 104/22.
Weelde, *vb. i. inf.* possess, 107/17.
We(e)pe, *vb. i. inf.* weep, 77/15; wepen, 1 *pl. pres.* 50/27; wept, 3 *sing. p.* 42/22.
We(e)ping, *sb.* weeping, 47/27, 73/19.
Weie, *see* **Weye.**
Weiliden, *vb. t.* 3 *pl. p.* mourned, lamented, 134/2.
Weiling, weilyng, *sb.* wailing, 17/10, 136/6.
Weiward, weywarde, *a.* perverse, wayward, 18/17, 46/32, &c.
Wei3t, whei3t, *sb.* weight, 74/20, 107/19, 108/2, 7; whei3tis, *pl.* 108/7.
Wel, *adv.* well, 33/19, 24, &c.
Wel(e), *sb.* weal, 11/15, 25/7, 45/32.
Welken, *vb. i.* 3 *pl. pres.* fade, wither, 45/12, 128/28.
Welle, *sb.* well, source, 16/9, 50/23, 54/19.
Welle, *vb. t. inf.* melt, weld, 71/27 (= Vulg. *conflo*).
Welpis, *sb. pl.* whelps, 43/6.
Welþe, *sb.* wealth, 85/2, 114/4, 119/6.
Welpi, *a.* prosperous, wealthy, 62/19, 115/8.
Wene, *vb. t. inf.* think, expect, 18/9; wenest, 2 *sing. pres.* 36/27, 93/17; weneþ, 3 *sing. pres.* 21/2; wenen, 3 *pl. pres.* 60/32, 61/23; wenyng, *pr. p.* thinking, 42/18.
Went, *vb. i.* 3 *sing. p.* went, 42/16; wenten, 3 *pl. p.* 37/32, 102/23.
Weren, *vb. t.* 3 *pl. pres.* wear, 30/24.
Werk(e), *sb.* work, 6/10, 37/7, &c.; werkis, *pl.* 5/9, 10/11, &c.
Werne, *vb. t. inf.* refuse, 11/30, 12/3, 52/6; werned, 3 *sing. p.* 102/16.

Werre, warre, *adv. comp.* worse, 11/3, 62/8, 85/5; *a. comp.* 101/9, 113/23; werst, *super.* 112/19.
Werre, *sb.* war, 71/6.
Werre, *vb. i. inf.* war, 91/19.
Wery, *a.* weary, 135/12.
Weye, weie, *sb.* way, 10/21, 16/19, &c.; weies, *pl.* 33/18.
Weyefering, *a.* wayfaring, 53/11.
Weywarde, *a.* wayward, 18/17.
Whan(n)e, *adv.* when, 4/21, 10/12, 20/12, &c.
Whei3t, *see* **Wei3t.**
Whennes, *adv.* whence, 76/8.
Wherof, *adv.* why, 46/14.
Wherto, *adv.* why, for what purpose, 43/7, 88/27.
Wherþoru3, *adv.* whereby, 59/13.
Whepir, *pron.* whichever, 87/7.
While, *sb.* while, time, 53/9, 10, 63/3.
Whili, *a.* wily, 111/9.
Whilid, *see* **Whi3len.**
Whilis, *sb. pl.* wiles, 51/23.
Whilis, *conj.* whilst, 2/25, 35/25.
Whirlwynde, *sb.* whirlwind, 134/29.
Whischeþ, *see* **Wischiþ.**
Whit, whi3t, *a.* white, 87/24, 113/33.
Whi3len, *vb. t.* 3 *pl. pres.* obtain by wiles, 19/29; whilid, *pp.* wiled, 108/10.
Whi3tli, *adv.* quickly, boldly, 47/17.
Wichcrafte, *sb.* witchcraft, 83/2.
Wick, *adv.* wickedly, 93/15.
Wickid, *a.* wicked, 51/8.
Wickidnes(se), *sb.* wickedness, 2/9, 7/11, &c.
Widowe, *sb.* widow, 66/10; widouse, *gen. sing.* 115/34; widowis, *pl.* 51/20, 52/2, 14.
Wijf, *sb.* wife, 106/15, 121/20.
Wijs(e), *vise,* wise, *a.* wise, 4/17, 62/23, &c.
Wijs(e)li, wiseli, *adv.* wisely, 45/3, 58/7, &c.
Wil, wole, *vb. aux.* 3 *sing. pres.* will, 4/8, 8/15, &c.; *pl. pres.* 13/19, 45/3; wol, wollen, *pl. pres.* 52/19, 89/14, 93/12; wolden, 3 *pl. p.* 122/15; wolde, 3 *pl. subj.* 8/13.
Wilde, *a.* wild, 70/3, 95/15.
Wildirnes, *sb.* wilderness, 46/7, 63/20, 24.
Wilful, *a.* willing, 98/13, 15, 136/16.
Wilfulli, *adv.* willingly, 32/8, 40/18, 80/19; wilfully, 50/18.

Glossary 191

Wille, sb. will, 43/11, 50/19.
Wirchen, wirken, see Worche.
Wiriep, vb. t. 3 sing. pres. destroys (= L. iugulat), 123/9 (OE. wyrgan = strangle).
Wischip, whischep, vb. t. 3 sing. pres. wishes, 52/8, 64/16.
Wis(e)dam, sb. wisdom, 5/10, 6/8, &c.
Wite, vb. t. inf. know, 118/19; imp. 51/13, 70/10; witen, pl. pres. 129/9; witing, pr. p. 80/24.
Witingli, adv. knowingly, 50/18.
Witles(se), a. foolish, witless, 86/20, 135/7.
Witnes, sb. witness, 87/5, 111/25.
Witnesar, sb. witness, 117/13.
Witnesberer, sb. witness-bearer, 112/3.
Witnessip, vb. t. 3 sing. pres. witnesses, 63/26; witnessing, pr. p. 56/27.
Wit(t), sb. knowledge, 30/8, 34/9, &c.; mind, 52/33, 81/16; meaning, sense, 105/19; to þis witt, to this intent, 47/4; wittis, pl. wits, 44/29, 45/17, 81/22, &c.
Witti, a. wise, 96/27, 122/28.
Wittirli, adv. wisely, 59/16.
Wiþ, prep. against, 2/13; by, 9/3.
Wiþdrawe, vb. t. inf. withdraw, 49/28, 70/25; wiþdrawiþ, 3 sing. pres. 94/17; wiþdrawen, 3 pl. pres. 49/5.
Wiþholde, vb. t. imp. withhold, 104/15.
Wiþouten, prep. without, passim; wiþouten, forþe, adv. without, 111/12.
Wiþynne, adv. within, 6/19; prep. 37/5; wiþynne forþe, adv. within, 111/12.
Wlank, a. rich, flourishing, 19/13.
Wlappiþ, vb. t. 3 sing. pres. wraps, 38/12; wlappid, pp. 50/6.
Wlatful, a. disgusting, 9/31.
Wlatiþ, vb. t. 3 sing. pres. despises, feels disgust at, 18/19, 111/15.
Wlatsumli, adv. disgustingly, 45/12.
Wlatsumnes, sb. abomination, 91/4.
Woden-drem, sb. madness, 38/11 (OE. wōden drēam = furor animi).
Wolues, sb. pl. wolves, 38/21, 111/13.
Wom(m)an, sb. woman, 33/11, 34/7, &c.; womanes, gen. sing. 33/21; wommen, wymmen, pl. 52/3, 15, 90/9, &c.

Wondir, sb. wonder, 69/2; adv. wondrously, 134/23.⁵
Wondirfulli, adv. wonderfully, 43/3.
Wondirment, sb. spectacle, 100/11.
Wonnen, see Wynne.
Wonneþ, vb. i. 3 sing. pres. dwells, 46/18; wonnen, 3 pl. pres. 86/27.
Woo, sb. woe, 45/32, 52/8.
Wood, sb. wood, 109/19.
Wood, a. mad, fierce, 8/20, 106/15, &c.
Woodnes, woodnis, sb. madness, 21/29, 36/21, 80/31.
Worche, vb. t. or i. inf. work, make, 11/12, 74/25, 90/24; worchiþ, 3 sing. pres. 5/9, 74/31; wirchen, wirken, worchen, pl. pres. 53/15, 64/12, 110/21; worche, imp. 9/33; wrouʒt, 3 sing. p. 10/26; 3 pl. p. 73/7; pp. 57/2; wirching, pr. p. 107/10.
Worching, worchyng, sb. working, act, 79/4, 84/33.
Word(e), sb. word, 4/21, 32/14, &c.; wordis, pl. 4/25, 52/25.
World, sb. world, 35/31, 50/20; worldis, gen. sing. 42/28; pl. 37/33.
Worldli, a. worldly, 35/38, 40/4, 41/18, &c.
Wormes, sb. pl. worms, 136/7.
Worschip, vb. t. inf. honour, 14/11; worschipiþ, 3 sing. pres. 14/26, 50/33; worschiping, pr. p. 56/2.
Worschip(e), sb. honour, 9/6, 49/16, &c.
Worschipful, a. honourable, 14/3.
Worþe, a. worth, 5/4.
Worþe, vb. i. inf. become, come, 39/1.
Worþi, a. worthy, 11/14, 14/24, &c.
Worþili, adv. worthily, 62/7.
Worþines, sb. worth, worthiness, 35/22, 59/16.
Wot, vb. t. 1 sing. pres. know, 127/10; 3 pl. pres. 56/22, 83/9.
Wounde, sb. wound, 67/27.
Wounding, pr. p. wounding, 72/1.
Woundir, vb. t. inf. wonder, 118/17.
Wo(u)ndirful, a. wonderful, 24/3, 28/28.
Wowis, sb. pl. walls, 37/25, 38/11, &c.
Wowtrere, see Voutrer.
Wraþþe, sb. wrath, 10/10, 33/23, &c.
Wrec(c)he, sb. wretch, 8/32, 46/31; wrecchis, pl. 54/14.

Wrecchid, a. wretched, 7/5, 86/27, 45/10.
Wrecchidnes, sb. wretchedness, misery, 49/19.
Wrechidli, sb. wretchedly, 2/12, 51/3.
Wreeche, sb. vengeance, 91/6.
Wreechful, a. revengeful, 99/8.
Writ, sb. writ, scripture, 35/5, 56/15, &c.; writtes, pl. 132/22.
Write, vb. t. 1 sing. pres. write, 8/7; writen, 3 pl. p. 27/17; pp. 3/17, 37/33, 91/21.
Wrong, sb. wrong, 45/2, 45/18.
Wrongfulli, adv. wrongfully, 43/17.
Wyn, sb. wine, 15/2, 60/17, 128/26.
Wynde, sb. wind, 52/1, 58/14; wyndis, pl. 130/1.
Wynne, vb. t. inf. gain, 9/30, 34, &c.; wynneþ, 3 sing. pres. 44/31; wynnyn, 3 pl. pres. 45/3; wonnen, pp. 19/31, 35/33.
Wyn(n)yng, sb. gain, 14/12, 56/3, &c.
Wynnyng, a. mercenary, 17/23.
Wyntir, sb. pl. winters, 99/15.

Y

Ydiotis, sb. pl. uneducated people, 5/19.
Ydolatreris, sb. pl. idolaters, 85/6, 132/19.
Ydolatrie, sb. idolatry, 83/3.
Ydole, sb. idol, 15/12; ydols, pl. 39/29, 103/22.
Yeuel, see Yuel.
Ymage, sb. image, 84/28, 34; ymages, ymagis, pl. 85/4, 24.
Ymplied, pp. filled, 40/19.
Ympnys, sb. pl. hymns, 58/1.
Yne, prep. in, 5/11.
Ynne, adv. in, 41/10, 11.

Ynnocent, a. innocent, 133/16.
Ynow(e), a. enough, 100/8; adv. 105/20.
Ynward, a. inward, 42/19, 52/20.
Ypocrisie, sb. hypocrisy, 41/3, 52/11, &c.
Ypocritis, sb. pl. 38/19, &c.
Yuel, sb. evil, 7/6, 33/23, &c.
Yuel, yeuel, a. evil, 11/6, 56/16.
Yuel-willi, a. evilly-disposed, 96/10, 111/9; cf. Sc. ill-willy.

ʒ

ʒate, sb. gate, 128/5; ʒatis, pl. 3/5, 7/26, &c.
ʒe, pron. ye, passim.
ʒeel, sb. zeal, 123/26.
ʒeere, sb. year, 91/5; ʒeer(e), ʒeeris, pl. 21/15, 24, 76/11, &c.
ʒe(e)rde, sb. rod, 95/4, 104/29, 118/37.
ʒelde, vb. t. inf. yield, give, requite, 10/11, 83/15; ʒelden, 3 pl. pres. 90/13; ʒelding, pr. p. 58/4.
ʒhe, inter. yea, 18/1, 59/9.
ʒhis, inter. yes, 69/8.
ʒift, sb. gift, 61/20; ʒiftis, pl. 60/12, 61/24, &c.
ʒit, adv. yet, still, 85/5, 97/26.
ʒong, a. young, 25/24, 113/15; ʒonger, comp. 97/18.
ʒonglingis, sb. pl. younglings, 119/4, 126/4, 6.
ʒou, ʒow, pron. you, 4/25, 8/7, &c.; ʒoure, your, 5/2, 51/11, &c.
ʒyuars, sb. pl. givers, 62/3.
ʒyue, vb. t. inf. give, 5/10, 52/4; ʒyueþ, 3 sing. pres. 9/21; ʒyuen, 3 pl. pres. 59/6; ʒauest, 2 sing. p. 4/22; ʒaue, 3 sing. p. 35/17, 62/2; ʒouun, 3 pl. p. 113/13; ʒyven, ʒouun, pp. 3/19, 9/24, &c.

The manufacturer's authorised representative in the EU for product
safety is Oxford University Press España S.A. of El Parque Empresarial
San Fernando de Henares, Avenida de Castilla, 2 - 28830 Madrid
(www.oup.es/en or product.safety@oup.com). OUP España S.A. also acts
as importer into Spain of products made by the manufacturer.
Printed and bound by CPI Group (UK) Ltd, Croydon, CR0 4YY

22/04/2026

02094916-0002